DARK CONCRETE

DARK CONCRETE

Black Power Urbanism and the
American Metropolis

Kimberley Johnson

CORNELL UNIVERSITY PRESS   ITHACA AND LONDON

First published 2025 by Cornell University Press

Library of Congress Cataloging-in-Publication Data

Names: Johnson, Kimberley S., 1966– author
Title: Dark concrete : Black Power Urbanism and the American metropolis /
    Kimberley Johnson.
Description: Ithaca [New York] : Cornell University Press, 2025. | Includes
    bibliographical references and index.
Identifiers: LCCN 2025009505 (print) | LCCN 2025009506 (ebook) |
    ISBN 9781501781827 hardcover | ISBN 9781501781834 paperback |
    ISBN 9781501781841 epub | ISBN 9781501781858 pdf
Subjects: LCSH: Black power—United States | Urban policy—United States |
    African Americans—Political activity—United States | United States—
    Race relations—Political aspects
Classification: LCC E185.615 J623 2025 (print) | LCC E185.615 (ebook) |
    DDC 323.1196/073—dc23/eng/20250709
LC record available at https://lccn.loc.gov/2025009505
LC ebook record available at https://lccn.loc.gov/2025009506

Contents

MAKING BLACK POWER URBANISM

We want freedom. We want power to determine the destiny of our Black Community.

—The Black Panther Party for Self-Defense Ten-Point Platform and Program

Black Power seeks—to create for Black Americans leverages for the kind of coalescence which will change the current patterns of Black defeat in employment, education and civic life into new patterns of power and fulfillment.

—"Black Power Manifesto and Resolutions," National Conference on Black Power, Newark, NJ, 1967

"People move. Humans move. Power to the people, whether they're black, white, blue, whatever," was Bobby Seale's philosophical comment about the 2013 sale of 809 Fifty-Seventh Street, his parent's North Oakland house, to real estate investors. The house, which Seale's parents bought in 1960 for $13,000, was sold for $200,000. Renovated and listed for $400,000, the property was described as a "light-filled house with maple, stainless steel and quartz features . . . a trendy showpiece worthy of Better Homes and Gardens."[1] In a strange irony, Bobby Seale and Huey Newton had created the Oakland branch of the Black Panther Party in 1966 in the house's dining room, where they crafted the party's Ten-Point Program, which offered a blueprint for a radical new construction of urban life based on the broad pillars of "Land, Bread, Housing, Education, Clothing, Justice and Peace."[2] Seale also demonstrated a less philosophical tone about the sale, stating that he was "dismayed by the 100 percent markup" as it was "the same crap that got this [2008] financial debacle started in the first place." The "debacle"—actually a human-made disaster—that Seale referred to was the 2008 subprime mortgage collapse, which decimated Black and Brown mortgage holders and neighborhoods across the United States. In the decade before the collapse, financial institutions like Wells Fargo Bank targeted Black and Brown neighborhoods, and particularly elderly Black women, with subprime mortgages and other kinds of predatory loans.[3] Indeed, one study found that "between 2007 and 2011, 1 in 7 Oakland mortgages entered default, with 1 in 14 eventually lost to foreclosures," and these foreclosures were almost all located in the city's Black and Brown neighborhoods, especially in West and East Oakland.[4] More disturbingly, researchers would later find that the location of these foreclosed homes mapped almost perfectly onto Oakland's HOLC (Home Owners' Loan Corporation) "redlining" map (see figure P. 1). By the 1950s, this 1930s-era HOLC map had become the guide to the "blighted" spaces that the city would deem in need of "urban renewal."[5] In 2016, three years after the sale of 809 Fifty-Seventh Street, a report released by the Greenlining Institute (a local racial justice and economic opportunity think tank) documented profound disparities in mortgage lending, finding that in 2013, "the top-12 lenders helped African American borrowers purchase a mere four homes in Oakland."[6]

This racialized risk and exclusion carried over into the streets. For longtime neighborhood residents, daily life was fraught with uncertainty and dread. One neighbor reflected that "when I moved here in '94, the whole block was black . . . Now, there are probably three black owners. Some people call it gentrification."[7] Indeed, the few remaining Black residents of Seale's neighborhood described feeling increasingly under surveillance, reporting that "the new people have a very negative perception of [the neighborhood's] young Black males."[8] This sense of disquiet and alienation was rooted in reality. The city's Black population had

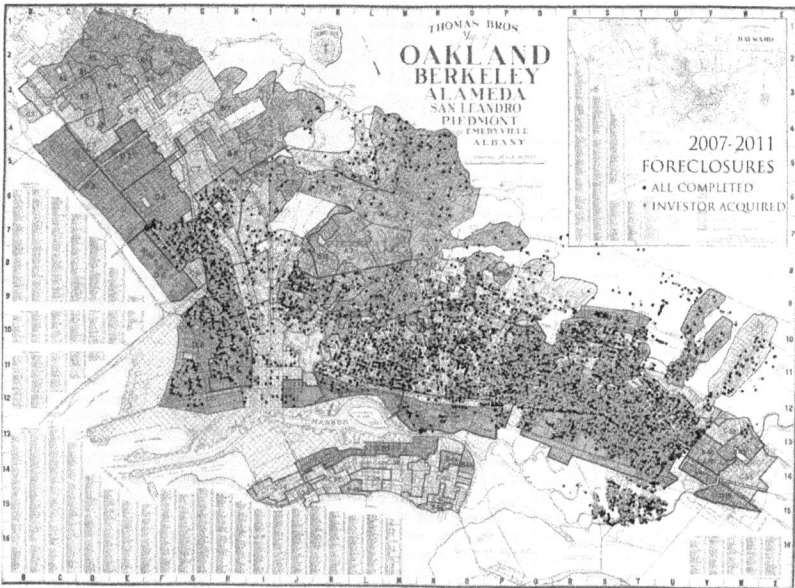

FIGURE P.1.   Risk, foreclosure, and the long shadow of the HOLC

Source: Steve King, "Who Owns Your Neighborhood? The Role of Investors in Post-Foreclosure Oakland," Urban Strategies Council, June 2012, https://www.neighborhoodindicators.org/sites/default/files/publications/whoown syourneighborhood_report.pdf.

dropped by over half, from 47 percent in 1980 to 22 percent in 2020.[9] As Oakland went, so too did the rest of the Bay Area. San Francisco's Black population (13 percent at its highest), was at a low of 5.7 percent. East Palo Alto, 60 percent Black in 1970, was now about 10 percent Black.[10]

By 1966, at the time of the Black Panther Party's (BPP) founding, Oakland's HOLC redlining map was more than merely lines drawn on paper: it was geography that shaped, embedded, and reproduced the sharp and unequal distribution of powers, resources, and space between the mostly White elites ensconced in the hills above Oakland and the mostly Black, Brown, and Asian working class in the sprawling flatlands below. By the mid-1960s Black Oakland was embedded in its own distinctive socio-spatial geography shaped by almost a decade's worth of urban renewal policy; a long history of municipal disinvestment, brutal policing, and political powerlessness; and an equally long history of Black placemaking and congregation in West Oakland. In the face of these forces, members of the city's Black and Brown communities, as well as those of other marginalized groups within the city, would organize not only for the right to stay in the face of urban renewal and planned displacement, but also for the right to build a city that reflected their social, political, and spatial needs and aspirations. As the Panthers' Ten-Point Program boldly stated: "We want freedom. We want power to determine the destiny of our Black Community."[11]

But the Black Panther Party was not the sole actor in this struggle to remake Oakland. The Black citizens of Oakland—divided as they were by migrant status, age, education, class, and gender—emerged as collective actors fighting for a new kind of city. Black Oakland's neighborhoods would become sites of resistance to an urban regime that dispossessed their residents, miseducated their children, overpoliced their communities, and unleashed the urban renewal machine that tore down their neighborhoods. Black Oakland, as well as other Black spaces across America's segregated and unjust cities, would become the collective birthplace of Black Power Urbanism (BPU). They would become sites of creativity and innovation, contestation and resistance, as Black urban citizens attempted to envision new ways of creating a city.[12] Black Power Urbanism would emerge both as an assertion of a distinctively *Black* "right to the city" and as the formulation of a political program that would transform these claims into reality.[13]

Dark Concrete traces the rise and fall of Black Power Urbanism—a newly formulated claim to remake the American city and reorder the basis of urban politics and metropolitan spaces. It was a demand that the city both could and should be the site of a new urban order that saw African Americans as the major actors in shaping the late twentieth-century city, rather than junior partners or victims in the postwar urban renewal order. Black Power Urbanism claimed the right of Black people to shape urban spaces as "just cities"—places to survive and thrive—rather than accepting that they were simply objects to be controlled and contained in urban space.[14] In these new "just cities," Black Power Urbanism reenvisioned and attempted to put into place ideas about the centrality of space and race (both real and imagined) and the ways in which Black life could or ought to be lived in the city. These visions, which George Lipsitz calls the Black spatial imaginary, were based on a view of communal life that "privileg[ed] use value over exchange value, sociality over selfishness, and inclusion over exclusion" in the face of ongoing forces of displacement, dispossession, and exclusion.[15] Black Power urbanists served as examples for this new expansive imaginary by showing that homes were places to live and thrive, not vehicles for investment; that schools should nurture children rather than expel them; and that cities were places where living, drinking, or socializing while Black was not automatically considered the basis for heavy-handed, if not brutal, policing. Black Power urbanist cities were imagined places where living a good life rested on communal support and solidarity rather than self-interest. This was a vision of urban life where everyone is brought together rather than sorted into winners and losers.

Black Power Urbanism, which existed roughly from 1963 to 1980, was a distinctive political order—meaning that it was a collection of ideas and understandings, interests, and organizations that spatially and temporally cohered around a vision of Black urban life that centered race and space, both past as well as present, and shaped urban governance over a period of time.[16] The Black Power Manifesto issued at the 1967 National Conference on Black Power was one instance where this belief was fully articulated: "Black Power seeks—to create for Black Americans leverages for the kind of coalescence which will change the current patterns of Black defeat in employment, education and civic life into new patterns of power and fulfillment."[17] This ideational coherence in turn would help to build and sustain political as well as governing coalitions that could not only exert power on, but also reconstitute, existing institutions and structural arrangements.[18] These new ideas and socio-spatial reconstitutions of who and what a city was for created what Charles Hamilton and Stokely Carmichael would call "new forms" for the city.[19]

This book explores the different conditions under which Black Power Urbanism emerged and developed and the ways in which it subsequently declined and then disappeared as a distinctive political order. Chapter 1 lay outs the contours of the complex story of its rise and fall through the lens of race, space, and political development. The chapter situates this analysis within a comparative urban political developmental framework that reveals how Black Power Urbanism was shaped across place and time by local, state, and national concatenations of political and institutional structures and Black urban political development. Space, understood as actual sites of placemaking and contestation, of processes of inclusion and community-building, and of predation and dispossession, linked these two political spheres. The chapter outlines the logic of the case study approach and introduces the cases themselves. I sketch Black Power Urbanism's path across four different Black metropolitan spaces: Newark and East Orange, New Jersey, and Oakland and East Palo Alto, California; as well as across three policy areas central to urban governance: housing, education, and policing. Through these multiple strands, I explore the different formations under which Black Power Urbanism emerged and developed and the factors that shaped both the order's fragility and death (in the case of Oakland and East Palo Alto), and its durability and evolution (in the case of Newark and East Orange).

Chapter 2 traces the political and socio-spatial lineages of the Black Power movement and more specifically Black Power Urbanism. I investigate its complicated relationship with older modes of Black politics, as well as the division and contestations within the Black Power movement itself. I then turn to developing a more precise definition of Black Power Urbanism that draws explicitly from the Black Power archive: the conventions and meetings, manifestos and posters, plays and songs, the activists and interest groups that together presented a radical world of alternative possibilities. From this archive, I lay out the broad contours of Black Power Urbanism, seeing it as the result of imaginings, ideas, insurgencies, and instantiations.

The next four chapters turn to specifics. Chapter 3 looks at the case of Newark, New Jersey and chapter 4 at the case of East Orange, Newark's suburban neighbor. In these chapters, I follow the development of Black urban citizenship and the ways in which Black spaces existed in the institutional and political context of the State of New Jersey, which had hundreds of independent political jurisdictions, a long legacy of strong local and state "machine" party organizations, and a robust capacity in local service delivery. Newark and East Orange also had a long history of Black urban political development stretching back to the nineteenth century. These political structural arrangements and legacies would provide spatial as well as institutional toeholds from which local actors could instantiate Black Power Urbanism. Black Power Urbanism, coupled with a degree of control within local institutions, would allow these Black Power urbanist localities to co-opt, deflect, and/or mitigate state intervention in areas such as housing, education, and police reform. BPU's long-term prospects, however, were contested. The Black Power Urbanism of post-rebellion Newark would eventually be crowded out by the Black urban regime established by Newark's second Black mayor, Sharpe James, and later by the neoliberal administration of Cory Booker. Ras Baraka's election would ultimately turn Newark back toward its Black Power urbanist past as Baraka regained local control over schools, established a civilian review board for the police, and recentered low-income and affordable housing as centerpieces of the city's neighborhood development strategy.

In East Orange, Black Power Urbanism would be refracted through the lens of the politics of Black suburban respectability due to an influential Black middle class that had been in place since the early twentieth century. In the decades since the first Black mayor was elected in 1969 and the city became more than 80 percent Black in 1980, the city's Black and mostly middle-class leadership would cling to a vision of the city as a successful case of liberal integrationism—especially in terms of community development policies—with the city seen as a place graced with "interracial harmony and no ghettoes."[20]

Chapters 5 and 6 turn to examining the specifics of Oakland and East Palo Alto. Black Power Urbanism emerged in cities that had adopted various reform political structures: nonpartisan, at-large elections; weak mayors/city manager–style governments; and fragmented local bureaucratic capacity and policy delivery. These truncated democratic structures, coupled with the small size of each city's Black population (prior to the Second Great Migration), would lead to a path of Black urban political development marked by a historical legacy of elite-brokerage politics. The postwar focus of Oakland's white political elites on relentlessly containing and/or pushing out Black Oaklanders would result in the mass displacement event of urban renewal. Black resistance to this displacement would take many forms, from middle-class elite brokers to the explosive emergence of the youthful Black Panther movement. Each would shape Oakland's path toward Black Power Urbanism.[21] While these political and institutional structural arrangements are important, the scale of state surveillance of the Black Panthers and the Black people of Oakland (and across the Bay Area) only constricted the limited spaces in which Black Power Urbanism could flourish.

East Palo Alto's development as a "new" postwar blue-collar suburb was shaped by its adjacency to Palo Alto as well as by its extreme spatial marginalization on the edges of an emerging Silicon Valley. By the early 1960s, rapid out-migration of whites and in-migration of Blacks made the city a node within the Bay Area's Black Power networks. This spatialization of race and class led to an intense moment of community activism oriented around building a new Black city called "Nairobi." Contestations over schooling, housing, and policing led to innovative attempts to link community concerns to just and equitable policy outcomes. However, for both East Palo Alto and Oakland, the possibilities of Black Power Urbanism were periodically reshaped by what Daniel HoSang calls California's "racial propositions."[22] These propositions included limiting the construction of public housing; the (temporary) repeal of fair housing laws; and most critically, the passage of Proposition 13, which put California's local governments under near-permanent austerity budgets and constrained attempts to bring Black Power Urbanism to life in places like Oakland and East Palo Alto. While Proposition 13 would undercut the fiscal future of the city, by the 1980s the War on Drugs and several rounds of "predatory inclusion" of subprime mortgages targeting Black and Brown residents had led to the massive displacement and dispossession of a generation of Black East Palo Altoans and Oaklanders. As the neoliberal metropolis took shape, the broad-based moment of Black Power urbanist reimagining was a touchstone that local activists would invoke as they sought to fight for what remained of their communities.

In the conclusion I explore the complex unwinding and ending of this "search for new forms" and its afterlives. The varied successes of the political and policy coalitions created both before and during the era of Black Power Urbanism intersected with the waning days of the Keynesian urban renewal order, a federal policy regime that encompassed targeted spending on social welfare programs and infrastructure investment in cities coupled with a large-scale program of demolition and reconstruction of urban spaces in line with modernist planning principles, and its last iteration via Lyndon B. Johnson's Great Society. These efforts to reassemble a more just city would be challenged and slowly crushed as Nixon's New Federalism and his Southern (suburban) strategy laid the groundwork for the neoliberal metropolis that the Reagan administration would begin to usher in by the early 1980s.

While the story of these cities and the rise of urban neoliberalism could be read as an "archaeology of failure"—of multiple, overlapping urban crises— I believe otherwise. This book uses the pillars of Black Power Urbanism's order (housing, education, and policing) to trace its history and to understand how the struggle to realize Black Power Urbanism can help us reimagine future possibilities for attaining just cities for all.

Abbreviations

AATA	Afro-American Teachers Association
AAVE	African American Vernacular English
APD	American political development
ARCH	Architects' Renewal Committee in Harlem
BART	Bay Area Rapid Transit
BPI	Black Power insurgencies
BPP	Black Panther Party
BPU	Black Power Urbanism
BUPD	Black urban political development and placemaking
CAP	Community Action Program
CAP	Congress of African People
CFUN	Committee for a Unified Newark
CIO	Congress of Industrial Organizations
COINTELPRO	Counterintelligence Program
CORE	Congress of Racial Equality
CPB	Central Planning Board
CTA	California Teachers Association
CURE	Community United for Relevant Education
DOL	Department of Labor
ECP	Eastside College Preparatory
EFL	Education Facilities Laboratories
EOMS	East Orange Middle School
EOPD	East Orange Police Department
EOSDC	East Orange School Design Center
EPA	East Palo Alto
EPAMC	East Palo Alto Municipal Council
ERAP	Economic Research and Action Program
ESEA	Elementary and Secondary Education Act
FHA	Federal Housing Administration
GM	General Motors
GNRP	General Neighborhood Renewal Plan
GSCA	General and Specialty Contractors Association
HI	historical institutionalism
HOLC	Home Owners' Loan Corporation

LAFCO	Local Agency Formation Commission
LEAA	Law Enforcement Assistance Administration
MESBIC	Minority Enterprise Small Business Investment Company
MORE	More Oakland Residential Housing Inc.
NABSE	National Association of Black School Educators
NCBM	National Conference of Black Mayors
NCUP	Newark Community Union Project
NDCC	Newark Day Care Council
NFCCWC	Northern Federation of California Colored Women's Clubs
NHA	Newark Housing Authority
NJPAC	New Jersey Center for Performing Arts
NPD	Newark Police Department
NPS	Newark Public Schools
NTA	Newark Teachers Association
NTU	Newark Teachers Union
OCCUR	Oakland Citizens' Committee for Urban Renewal
OCR	Office of Civil Rights
OEDC	Oakland Economic Development Council
OHAPD	Oakland Housing Authority Police Department
OICW	Opportunities Industrial Center West
ONE	Organization of Negro Educators
OPD	Oakland Police Department
ORA	Oakland Redevelopment Agency
OSPD	Oakland School Police Department
OUSD	Oakland Unified School District
OVL	Oakland Voters League
PAC	Project Area Committee
PCAPBR	People's Committee Against Policy Brutality and Repression
PFMC	People's Free Medical Clinics
PHA	public housing authorities
PHI	political historical institutionalism
PREP	Project Rehabilitation Employment Project
RAM	Revolutionary Action Movement
RED	Regional Enforcement Detail
SAFE	Seniors Against a Fearful Environment
SCBM	Southern Conference of Black Mayors
SDS	Students for a Democratic Society
SDS-ERAP	Students for a Democratic Society-Economic Research and Action Project
SLA	Symbionese Liberation Army

SMCBAC	San Mateo County Black Action Conference
SNCC	Student Nonviolent Coordinating Committee
SSSD	Security and Safety Services Department
SWP	Socialist Workers Party
TMC	tenant management council
UCC	United Community Council
UNIA	Universal Negro Improvement Association
VISTA	Volunteers in Service to America
WOAC	West Oakland Advisory Committee
WOPC	West Oakland Planning Council
WRO	Welfare Rights Organization

DARK CONCRETE

BLACK CITIES

Race, Space, and Urban Political Development

> **There's a lot of chocolate cities, around**
> **We've got Newark, we've got Gary**
>
> —Parliament, "Chocolate Cities"

As Bobby Seale's Oakland house hit the market in 2013, Newark's mayor-elect Ras Baraka was confronting Newark's own subprime mortgage crisis. Like Oakland, Newark had been aggressively targeted by banks who saw the city's working- and middle-class homeowners of color (and especially the elderly Black women homeowners) as a prime source for generating explosive profits.[1] The scale of harm was immense, with thousands of homes in foreclosure, millions of dollars lost due to deflated home values and unpaid property taxes, and neighborhoods destabilized by vacant and neglected homes. In January 2014, Baraka, embracing a more capacious stewardship role than had been usual, argued that unless the city took "decisive action," the situation "would only get worse."[2] To keep Newark's homeowners in their homes (and to stabilize the city's neighborhoods), Baraka proposed using the city's eminent domain clause to purchase loans that were "underwater" from the companies that owned or serviced the loans and then sell those mortgages back to the original owners at current value. For the first time in recent Newark history, a city leader asserted the city's right to restrain the depredations of the private residential market. The banking and mortgage industry immediately pushed back, threatening Newark's bond rating and that of any other municipality that attempted to protect their residents from the man-made disaster they had released upon the most economically fragile citizens and neighborhoods.[3] Newark, however, had no choice: the city had to at least try such a radical step, as Newark and its neighboring minority-majority suburbs, including East Orange, had some of the highest subprime mortgage foreclosure rates in the United States. A report on the crisis highlighted the city council testimony of Grace Alexander, a longtime resident of Newark, who stated: "I am here today because I'm fighting to save my home. And I'm not alone. The impacts of foreclosure in my West Ward community are painfully evident, with boarded-up homes that create huge safety hazards due to higher crime and the risk of fire. I don't want my home to become one of them."[4]

Baraka would later start off his second term in office (January 2017) with the signing of two local ordinances into law. The first, the Inclusionary Zoning for Affordable Housing ordinance, would require developers of projects with more than thirty units to set aside 20 percent of their residential units for affordable housing. Baraka argued that the city could not wait until economic prosperity arrived and then "create affordability." By waiting, Newark would make the mistake that other cities (like Hoboken, Jersey City, or New York City) were making, "now deciding they want to have inclusionary zoning in their community, but there's nowhere [to] build anything." The second ordinance required that all developers who received long-term abatements would have to "partner with a Newark-based minority contractor, provide jobs to Newark residents, and make a contribution to Newark's Community School Trust Fund to help improve the quality of the city's schools." The attempt to provide a municipal shield for the city's victimized homeowners, to ensure housing affordability, and to couple real estate development with community development hearkened back to an earlier era of community empowerment in the 1960s, during which Amiri Baraka (Ras Baraka's father) held a singularly visible role as the leader of the Committee for a Unified Newark (CFUN). At the time, Amiri Baraka had proclaimed:

> We want to set an example in Newark because the cities will be black and whites will have to come to the mature understanding that no matter what they'd like to see happen, blacks will determine the way it will happen. . . . We want to get control of the space where 300,000 black people live, not only for us to live in, but for our ideas and the development of concepts that are of benefit to us as a people with a peculiar ethos.[5]

Decades later, the elder Baraka's proclamation would be echoed by the younger mayor Baraka, who after signing the two 2017 ordinances into effect, stated that "there are hundreds of developers who are in this city who are black and brown who in this community would not have the access without this, and if you want something from us you have to grab our people and pull them up with you, and think that that is a very important part of this legislation, and that we take a piece of it and turn it over to our school system."[6]

"You have to pull them up with you" was a new articulation of the reparative and emancipatory elements of the Black Power Urbanism that had animated Newark politics during the 1960s and 1970s. Emancipation was echoed in the words of the funk music group Parliament, with their anthem "Chocolate City" proclaiming that though African Americans "did not get forty acres and mule, they got chocolate city," a "piece of the [Plymouth] rock."[7] The lyrics echoed the formulation by activists and labor intellectuals Grace Lee Boggs and James Boggs of the city as the "Black Man's Land," where "you don't need the bullet when you got the ballot."[8] The lyrics proclaimed that the Black city (or "Chocolate City") was not only a political project, it was also a cultural and social project and the embodiment of Black urban America, which would be presided over by an all-star administration of James Brown, Muhammed Ali, Reverend Ike ("Secretary of the Treasure"), Richard Pryor ("Minister of Education"), Stevie Wonder ("Secretary of FINE Arts"), and "Miss Aretha Franklin, the First Lady."[9] More concretely, the chocolate city would be the site of an emancipatory Black polity powered by an expansive reenvisioning and development of what the authors of *Black Power*, Charles Hamilton and Stokely Carmichael (now Kwame Ture), called "new forms" of self-governance; in short, Black Power Urbanism.

While Parliament's celebration of Chocolate City rested on the idea of majority-Black cities achieving a form of emancipatory and reparative status, the appearance of Black Power Urbanism was not simply an acceptance of demography as destiny. Rather, Black Power Urbanism was political as much as it was cultural and spatial; it was a deliberative and collective act of repair and rebuilding on the part of Black residents and other allies in the face of the forces of racial containment, dispossession, and predation. By the early twenty-first century, fifty years or so after their explosive emergence, the tenets of Black Power Urbanism appeared to be newly reinvigorated and flourishing in Newark; yet, as the sale of Bobby Seale's house suggests, Black residents and Black Power Urbanism seemed to be on the verge of disappearance from Oakland.[10] What happened? Why did these two centers of Black Power end up in different places? And why does it matter?

Political Development and Black Power Urbanism

The analytical framework used here to explain the rise and fall of Black Power Urbanism—the act of collective repair and envisioning in the wake of urban (Negro) removal—draws from theories of American political development (APD) and historical institutionalism (HI).[11] According to this framework, Black Power Urbanism was shaped by three factors (see figure 1.1): first, the processes

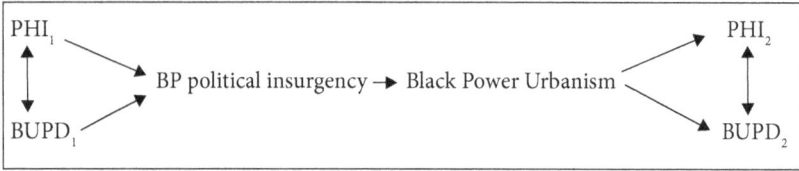

FIGURE 1.1. Theorizing Black Power Urbanism

of political historical institutionalism (PHI); second, Black urban political development and placemaking (BUPD); and third, Black Power–infused political insurgencies. These factors are sketched out as processes that occur across time and space.

Political historical institutionalism (PHI) is a way of identifying the long-term ideational, political, and institutional frameworks from which Black Power Urbanism emerged. An APD approach to political development is defined here as the constitutive process by which multilayered, "interconnected" combinations of "orders"—ideational, political, organizational, and institutional configurations and arrangements that are "internally coherent and mutually reinforcing"—come together to exercise "durable governing authority" over a policy domain, regime, or political order.[12] A durable shift in governing authority is explained as "change in the locus or direction of control, resulting in a new distribution of authority among persons or organizations within the polity at large or between them and their counterparts outside."[13] A political developmental approach thus emphasizes both the pattern of institutional configurations and understandings and the centrality of time as a critical variable.[14]

Complementing this APD understanding of political development is the historical institutional (HI) approach, which "examines how the context within which policy development takes place affects policy choices and their subsequent continuity or transformation. It examines, in particular, the impact of prevailing institutional rules and temporal factors, like the timing, sequence and/or conjuncture of events, on the behaviour of political actors, and hence, as well, on political and policy developments."[15] Political orders do not stand alone. Rather, as Karen Orren and Stephen Skowronek argue, a political order reflects and encompasses the "multiple and disjointed orderings that overlay one another, with the interplay among them breaking down the period-bound distinction between order and change."[16] At the same time, institutions or political orders rarely disappear; instead, in a process of intercurrence (or the "simultaneous operation of different sets of rules"), they can leave a variety of traces as governing authority shifts via processes of change, whether gradual, such as path dependency and policy feedback, or sudden, such as punctuated equilibrium or critical junctures.[17] Following this theoretical approach, urban political orders are defined as time-bound assemblages of local, state, and federal actors, institutions, structures, and processes that have developed over time and under different social, economic, and political conditions and that exert "durable governing authority" over political spaces—both real and imagined.[18] Varied types of local political, institutional, and ideational formations have characterized local US polities over time.[19] These regime types range across time and space: from the political machines of older northeastern cities to the "morning glory" reform governments of the West from the Progressive Era onward and to the biracial growth machine regimes of the post–Civil Rights South. These local configurations are layered within state as well as federal structures, such as the Keynesian urban renewal order of targeted federal spending on social welfare and infrastructure investment in cities coupled with demolition and reconstruction of urban spaces in line with modernist planning principles of the post–World War II era.[20] Transnational orderings, too, interleave state and federal structures, including the transatlantic urban renewal order of the postwar era or the urban neoliberal order of the late twentieth century.[21]

Black urban political development (BUPD) is defined as the long-standing processes of political and social mobilization of African Americans within urban areas in the United States. It encompasses the historical and contemporary efforts of Black communities to secure political power, advocate for their rights, and address systemic issues affecting their communities.[22] This political and social mobilization occurred in racialized spaces within cities and suburbs where Black residents created a sense of community, from the physical manifestations of schools, churches, small businesses, saloons, and the street corner, to the affective and at times solidaristic ties created by the sharing of these racialized spaces.[23] A more recent formulation of this concept of Black sense of place is what Marcus Hunter and others have called "Black placemaking"; that is, the ways in which "urban black Americans create sites of endurance, belonging, and resistance through social interaction."[24] Newark, East Orange, Oakland, and East Palo Alto each had its own unique lineage of Black urban political development that reflected both Black placemaking and the influence of the larger political and institutional configurations in which BUPD took place.

Black urban political development does not exist within an empty space. The process of claiming Black urban citizenship had its own effect in shaping American urban and metropolitan space and place. If for African Americans the primary struggle of the modern American city was the struggle to define and claim urban citizenship and urban places, for much of white urban America urban politics and urban placemaking were struggles to control the limits of those Black citizenship claims through the state's ability to order space, as well as its ability to shape the boundaries of political, social, and economic exclusion/inclusion. Indeed, as W. E. B. Du Bois presciently pointed out in his metaphor of the color line, attempts by white citizens and institutions to control claims of Black urban citizenship fundamentally shaped urban/metropolitan policy, politics, and space for much of the twentieth century.

While broad in aspirations, Black urban politics exhibited its own ideational, political, organizational, and institutional configurations and arrangements. These political configurations varied across institutional space and political time (see figure 1.2). On one end of this developmental spectrum are two types of political modes: the personalized politics of patron-client relations and elite-brokerage politics. These types of politics reflect a nearly complete lack of formal political power (voting) and absence of any kind of formal political incorporation (decision-making).

On the other end of the spectrum, a variety of Black urban political formations demonstrate attainment of formal political power and political incorporation. Among these are a politics of inclusion via biracial or multiracial regimes, a politics of ethnic political machine succession, and a politics of replacement in which a Black urban regime takes over a city's political structure and redefines its civic identity. For the better part of the mid-twentieth century, Black community politics lay somewhere between suburban respectability and liberal integrationism. The success of the "Double-V" campaign—for democracy abroad

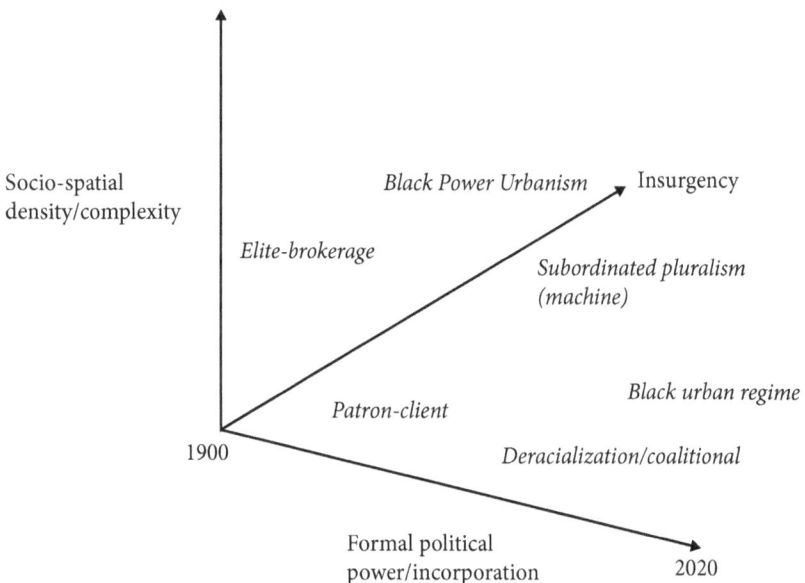

FIGURE 1.2. Black urban political development: Power, insurgency, and space

and at home—raised new expectations about attaining the full fruits of urban citizenship, the stakes of which were heightened with the programmatic expansion of the postwar welfare state.[25] The end result and new levers of political participation and action weakened older patterns of elite-brokerage politics and strengthened the efforts of Black activists to move from junior partners to equal participants in polities where machine politics prevailed. By the mid-1960s, older forms of Black political development had begun to be discarded or transformed as new ideas and understandings arose about what a city should and could do in order to be a just and emancipatory place for its most marginalized citizens.

Political and institutional development and lineages of local Black urban political development were necessary though insufficient components in creating the context in which Black Power Urbanism unfolded. Black Power insurgencies—the linkage between ideas/imaginings about what a city could be and direct actions to bring about the realization of those imaginings—were also needed. Black Power insurgencies (BPI) are defined as local political and cultural mobilizations infused by both the "Black Consciousness" touted by Black Power advocates and by the aspirational "search for new forms." The insurgencies were made up of a coalition of actors ranging from everyday citizens, community activists, intellectuals, and new middle-class professionals (along with the new professional associations created by them), to some (not all) elected and appointed government officials. While many of these actors felt themselves to be formally within the "Black Power" movement, others saw themselves as simply adjacent to it. These actors attempted to put their ideas into action, particularly at the level of local government, but also at the state and national level. While these Black Power insurgencies often drew upon preexisting organizational structures and commitments, they were equally likely to develop new organizational forms and modes of action that reflected the need to find new ways of creating better neighborhoods and cities. Black Power insurgencies embraced multiple modes of action, from rent strikes and sit-ins, marches and urban rebellions, to independent forays into local electoral politics. The end result of Black Power insurgencies would be new formations and pathways of political and historical development (PHI_2) and Black urban political development $(BUPD_2)$.

New Forms: Instantiating Black Power Urbanism

The focus of these new insurgencies was the instantiation of Black Power Urbanism as the adoption of a policy and/or process that centered "new forms" of self-government and communal care. Amiri Baraka's formulation of Black Power Urbanism is notable for its spatial, temporal, and political specificity in regard to the urban renewal order: "If the black community was to become the master of its own house, then it had to have control over urban renewal in terms of the funding and the redesign of urban spaces."[26] Though speaking about Newark, Baraka's thoughts on the how and why of controlling urban space, and particularly the importance of community control, applied to Black cities across the nation. Why were there no parks for their children in Newark's Central Ward? Why had the city built nothing but overcrowded and rapidly deteriorating high-rise projects with public housing funds? Why, in the face of peaceful civil rights protests in the early 1960s and the police brutality that met the protestors, did Newark's white mayor say to George Richardson, a Black member of his administration who lobbied for a civilian review board: "I am the police, the police is me"?[27]

Many of the "new forms" of both control and care that Black activists were seeking would be articulated as part of the Black Power conventions movement (both national and local) occurring throughout the height of the Black Power movement (1967–72). The "Black Power archives" demonstrate the programmatic content of Black Power Urbanism through manifestos, publications, and speeches of the day, from Hamilton and Ture's book *Black Power* to the Black Panthers' survival programs, the resolutions of Newark's 1967 Black and Puerto Rican Political Convention, and onward to the 1972 Gary Convention.[28] While many historical accounts of these Black Power conventions focus on the attempts to create a national Black political party and to provide solidarity and support to African liberation movements and other kinds of internationalism, the specificities of Black Power Urbanism also took shape at these conventions. Thus, alongside calls for reparations, the creation of national health insurance, or an increase in the minimum wage were numerous platform items that directly addressed the daily conditions of Black urban life. Among them were demands for community control of schools rather than busing; Black-controlled drug education and treatment programs; tenant protections; protection of the elderly poor; Black control of local media; community control over policing, including insisting on residency requirements for officers; the right of self-determination for Black communities to create new independent spaces or to maintain their right to their spaces in the face of "Negro removal"; mass transit that would help rather than harm Black communities; and the creation of community health centers, including the training of "street medics." While these were just some of the items listed in the 1972 Gary platform, previous platforms, especially local Black political conventions, had articulated a distinctively Black urban agenda that pushed beyond the boundaries of the postwar city.

But Black Power Urbanism was not simply a top-down political ordering developed by theorists, political activists, and others who met at conventions and compiled platforms and manifestos. Black Power Urbanism was built from the bottom up. The platform items and policy prescriptions that flowed out of foundations and community action agencies were formulated by the actions of everyday people in America's Black communities, especially the poor Black women who engaged in transcending the confines of the urban color line to create a better life for themselves, their families, and their communities.

Black Power Urbanism was created by tenants like Mary Smith of Newark, who lived in the Stella Wright Houses, just one of hundreds of shoddy and dangerous public housing complexes that were built in many cities as part of the urban renewal order to contain and control Black residents. Smith and others would lead one of the longest public housing rent strikes in the nation's history, ultimately forcing their local public housing authority to put Stella Wright under tenant management. Black Power Urbanism was also built by parents like Gertrude Wilks of East Palo Alto, who saw city school systems that treated children with disdain and indifference and who battled with administrators and teachers that were hostile to their now majority-Black and -Brown classrooms. Wilks and others would build alternative independent Black educational institutions—a primary school and a junior college—as desperately needed alternatives to the overcrowded and rundown facilities in their neighborhoods that pushed Black children out of the system and into underemployment, unemployment, or service in Vietnam, while white neighborhoods enjoyed new facilities and welcoming teachers.

Black Power Urbanism was built by individuals and groups like the Black Panther Party (BPP), which confronted one of the most visible and violent aspects of Black urban life: the police. The BPP's neighborhood patrols directly confronted the policing that worked to enforce the urban color line. These armed patrols were also accompanied by radical plans for the decentralization of the police into smaller precincts under community control, as well as the deployment of alternative modes of community engagement and accountability that would shift the focus away from top-down and anti-Black policing and toward community safety. Finally, Black Power Urbanism was created by residents who saw that their neighborhoods lacked stores that offered fresh, affordable food; clothing; and other necessities of urban life like parks and playgrounds or safe sidewalks. These residents would in turn create new spaces in which urban life could take place.

From Order to Locality

Black Power Urbanism, or the new forms of governance being developed, can be seen in the "concrete demands," the "urgent needs, things asked, and questions raised," that everyday people addressed to state—and more specifically city—governments.[29] City governments were seen as both sites of oppression and sites of opportunity from which power and resources could be diverted to Black people and Black spaces so that lives of dignity and peace, "communities of possibility," could be imagined and put into place.[30] In short, to understand Black Power Urbanism and how city governments grappled with demands raised by activists and residents, the specific context of the policy in question must be investigated; simply measuring program funding or personnel diversity as previous research has done is not enough to understand the complexity of this movement. A political developmental approach offers a useful path toward uncovering these new meanings and paths toward instantiation of these "new forms."

In a political developmental approach such as the one undertaken here, space, history, and more specifically timing, matters. Black Power Urbanism can be understood in socio-spatial terms as a "metonymic coalition" (for example, urban Keynesianism); it is a political order that is embedded within multiple layers of governance, as well as within spaces/territory. To understand the rise and fall of Black Power Urbanism is to see that it exists across different levels or "scales" (local, state, federal), but also, that it exists as a set of "nodes and paths that organize the linkages between resources, presentation, leadership, and the exercise of power."[31] This framing is helpful as it moves the study of urban political development, and more specifically, urban Black politics, beyond "methodological localism" and the fixed specificity of place.[32] The case-study approach allows for both specificity and generalizability.

Looking at three of the pillars of Black Power Urbanism—housing, education, and policing—I trace the impact of Black Power Urbanism on the ground and its attempt to reshape Black urban life.[33] By comparing and contrasting several cities across these three pillars, I show that despite local differences, Black Power Urbanism was a broad political and social ordering that occurred similarly in different places. At the same time, the paths that Black Power Urbanism could take, as well as paths that were foreclosed, were shaped not only by individual actors but also by local, state, and national political structures and institutional arrangements.

The four case studies pursued here challenge how we study Black Power and Black political mobilization in cities. One common approach studies Black electoral politics by paying deep attention to the ways in which Black Power supporters battled with other Black and white political interests in pursuit of political office as a means to control Black communities. Across many cities, Black Power supporters met with a range of successes and failures, with success largely defined as the election of the first Black mayor. The investigation of the three social pillars used in this book shows that an electoral-based analytical approach is not enough to explain the divergent paths of these cities.

I use an in-depth analysis of these pillars within the framework of Black Power Urbanism as an organizing order to trace the role of local, state, and federal institutions and institutional arrangements, as well as political alignments and coalitions, in shaping each city's Black Power developmental path. By looking at the policy instantiations of these three pillars—housing, education, and policing—I investigate the impact of Black Power Urbanism on the ground and its attempt to reshape policy understandings toward Black Power outcomes. By policy understanding, I mean the ideas and organizational structures that comprise the substance of a policy. With this approach, hypotheses about BPU outcomes can be assessed and tested.

The case studies in this book reveal the complex political development of the Black Power Urbanism order. First, they show the ways in which initial pathways (stylized as time one, or t_1) were shaped by existing political, institutional, and socio-spatial arrangements and understandings (PHI_1) and how they intersected with existing patterns of Black urban political development ($BUPD_1$). Early patterns of heightened Black political development were in each case met by the establishment's attempts to change the "rules of the game." For example, each of the cities investigated show a pattern of deliberate changes from above: from at-large to district elections (and vice versa) to changing the capacity and scope of local political or administrative structures (weakening public control to shifting patterns of service delivery). These changes did not go uncontested. Resistance—by Black Power insurgencies, their allies, and their opponents— would influence the subsequent shape (stylized as time two, t_2) of local Black political development ($BUPD_2$) (see figure 1.1). More generally, the specifics of Black Power insurgencies and local instantiations of Black Power Urbanism would lead to contestation, reconstitution, and even replacement of existing political and organizational structures and arrangements as new ideas and understandings, interests and organizations emerged in their wake (PHI_2).

Second, the case studies allow us to trace the ways in which specific political, institutional, and socio-spatial arrangements and understandings shaped different kinds of Black Power Urbanism instantiations, specifically in the areas of housing, education, and policing. For example, in cities where political and historical configurations leaned toward strong machine environments coupled with a strong degree of Black urban political development, Black Power urbanist instantiations were more likely to be co-opted or siloed (see table 1.1).

The case studies make it possible to understand the conditions under which these instantiations were more likely to become institutionalized durable policies as seen in Newark and to some extent East Orange. By contrast, in reform cities marked by weaker levels of Black political development such as Oakland and East Palo Alto, symbolic or episodic instantiations of Black Power Urbanism

TABLE 1.1 Instantiating BPU: Policies and institutions

STRUCTURE	CITY	POLICY PILLARS		
		HOUSING	EDUCATION	POLICING
Machine	Newark	Regime/durable ——————————▶		
	East Orange	Co-opted/siloed ——————————▶		
Reform	Oakland	Coalitional/fragmented ——————▶		
	East Palo Alto	Symbolic/episodic ——————————▶		

were more likely to appear. Indeed, local instantiations of Black Power Urbanism reflected the fragmented coalitional and contingent nature of reform environments. The case study approach used here demonstrates that neither protest nor urban insurgency models, nor traditional "Black mayors" electoral-based analytical approaches, are sufficient to explain each city's developmental path. While some scholars have argued that Black Power (Urbanism) was irredeemably flawed and fated to be co-opted by the broader political system, there is strong evidence that this co-optation was a two-way street.[34] Urban governance was by its very nature changed as Black Power Urbanism redefined the possibilities of urban life, even as those possibilities were—for a time—defunded, co-opted, or repudiated.

From Space to Place, From Theory to Case

If there were two cities that most exemplified the Black Power movement, then Oakland and Newark would be the top contenders. In 1966 Oakland was the birthplace of the Black Panther Party, whose revolutionary rhetoric, aesthetics, and Ten-Point survival programs served as inspiration for Black and Brown communities across the United States and the world.[35] Newark was a center of the Black Arts/Black Nationalism movements, the place where the first major Black Power convention took place amid the smoke and ashes of the nation's largest urban rebellion, and the place where the first Black mayor of a major northeastern city was elected.[36]

During the first half of the twentieth century the two cities shared other similarities. Newark and Oakland were vibrant though decidedly secondary cities within their greater metropolises. Each suffered from the problem of "no there-ness" that civic leaders would spend the twentieth century battling. During this same period, both were industrial cities whose growing population of migrants (domestic and non-American) contested and reshaped the socio-spatial and political structures of each city (see figure 1.3). In particular, each saw a rapid increase in the number of Black residents during the first part of the twentieth century, particularly during the Second Great Migration era (1940 to 1970).

Newark and Oakland can also be differentiated by the set of political and institutional arrangements that emerged as different groups battled over the contours of urban democracy and citizenship.[37] For example, the political system in Newark, like other older northeastern cities, alternated between a weak coalition of reformers and ethnic-based political machines. Newark's political system changed from mayor-council to commission to mayor-council over the course of half a century as each side, particularly the reformers, sought to make Newark a city in their own political image.[38] Newark's white elites and ethnic political machines cautiously used municipal government to reshape their city. Their efforts would eventually dovetail with the rise first of New Deal urban liberalism, and later the "spatial fix" of postwar Keynesian urban renewal. Indeed, by 1950

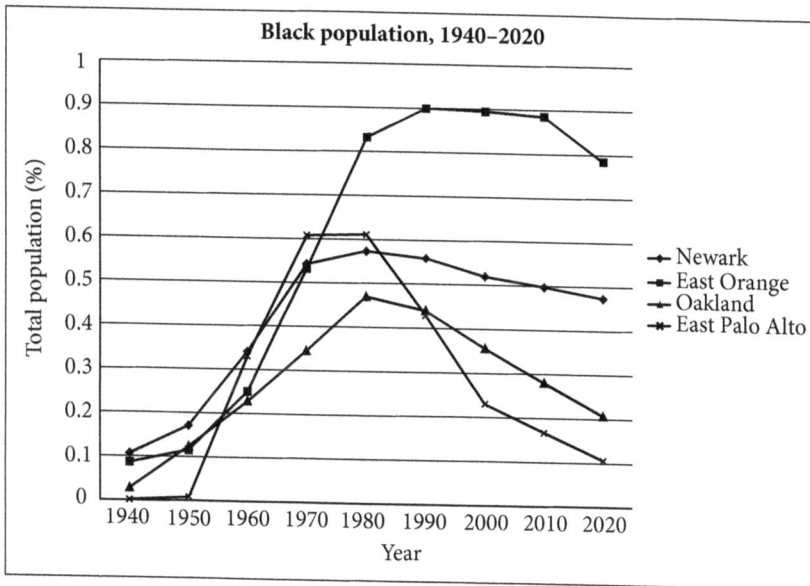

FIGURE 1.3. Black population growth, 1940–2020

Source: Data from Social Explorer.

For the years 1940 to 1990: Campbell Gibson and Kay Jung, "Historical Census Statistics On Population Totals By Race, 1790 to 1990, and By Hispanic Origin, 1970 to 1990, For the United States, Regions, Divisions, and States," Population Division Working Paper No. 56 (US Census Bureau, September 2002), https://www.census.gov/content/dam/Census/library/working-papers/2002/demo/POP-twps0056.pdf; "Negro Population in Selected Places and Selected Counties," Series PC(S1)-2 1970, Census of Population, Supplementary Report (US Census Bureau, June 1971).

For East Palo Alto and Oakland, 2000 to 2020: "Bay Area Census," Association of Bay Area Governments and Metropolitan Transportation Commission, 2025, https://census.bayareametro.gov/population.

For East Orange and Newark, 2000 to 2010: New Jersey State Data Center, "Black or African American Population: 2000-2010, New Jersey Municipalities," New Jersey Department of Labor, March 2001, https://www.nj.gov/labor/labormarketinformation/assets/PDFs/census/2kcensus/pl94/cnty/black.PDF.

For East Orange and Newark, 2020: New Jersey State Data Center, "Black (or African American) Population: Census 2010—Census 2020, New Jersey Municipalities," New Jersey Department of Labor and Workforce Development, August 2021.

Newark would be in the top five of American cities in the per capita use of federal renewal funds.[39] Oakland, by contrast, was a "morning glory," a western city in which Progressive Era reformers, inspired by visions of clean, effective government, free from the strife of ethnic and partisan politics, devised governments that were easily captured and run by social and economic elites. This issue was particularly acute for elites as the resurgence of the Ku Klux Klan in the 1920s, the rise of organized labor, and an increase in in-migration threatened local power arrangements.[40] Oakland's elites responded to these threats with a reform movement that introduced a more constrained role for municipal government, which fit the Republican Party sympathies of many of their members. By the 1950s, however, elites of both cities would turn to urban renewal and more explicitly "Negro removal" as the tool that city leaders hoped would return their city to a bright future (and increasingly a mythic past) of urban prosperity. It was the "root shock"—the psychic, financial, and political harm inflected on residents—of "Negro removal" that caused each city's path of Black urban political development to take a decisive shift toward Black Power Urbanism.[41]

Black Power Urbanism was not only present in large cities, it also swept across smaller Black places.[42] Black places—both large and small—were embedded in larger metropolitan socio-spatial arrangements. By looking at smaller cities such as East Orange, New Jersey and Palo Alto, California, it is possible to add points of analysis to help show how Black Power Urbanism was shaped broadly by space, political and socio-spatial arrangements, and the specificity of place. Across the three pillars of housing, education, and policing, I demonstrate the complex reality of chocolate city suburbs in a majority-white metropolis. By looking at Black suburban spaces, I trace how the spatial imaginary of suburbia, of the "crabgrass frontier," was shaped by the forces of exclusion, segregation, and suburban urban renewal, which by the 1960s was attempting to either block or remove Blacks from these suburban spaces.[43] Contestations over space, and the timing of these contestations—at both the macro- and micro-level—played a key role the shaping of Black Power Urbanism.

Critical (Spatial) Junctures

Three inflection points or critical (spatial) junctures would shape the rise and fall of Black Power Urbanism: the Keynesian postwar "spatial" fix; the institutionalization of the political economy of the segregated metropolis; and the installation of Reaganomics, the first wave of neoliberalism.[44] These point were "critical" in the sense that they indicated moments when an "existing authority [was] disrupted and established 'paths' [were] redirected as more authority was rearranged."[45]

The first critical (spatial) juncture was the postwar Keynesian urban order, which rested on the "spatial fix" of city (re)building.[46] This juncture would set the broad parameters under which Black Power Urbanism emerged. The Keynesian spatial fix of urban renewal, mass (white) suburbanization, and core city disinvestment—from the Housing Act of 1949 to the Federal Interstate Highway Act of 1956—took as its basis the removal and dispossession of Black and Brown urban communities.[47] Politically, the top-down federal investment in cities was coupled with an emergent normative belief in pluralism, most famously described by Robert Dahl's 1961 analysis of New Haven, in which he portrayed a political system where elites and policymakers believed that Black and other marginalized communities would have a fair say, and a fair share, in the fruits of the postwar city.[48] The reality proved quite different as urban renewal, the interstate highway system, and mass white suburbanization upended and dismantled the industrial city of the early twentieth century and in particular targeted and destroyed the hard-won and painstakingly constructed sites of Black communal life.

Between 1955 and 1966, urban renewal affected over eight hundred localities and directly displaced around an estimated three hundred thousand families (and indirectly tens of thousands more individuals).[49] These removals and demolitions were concentrated in the neighborhoods where Black residents had forged spaces of urban citizenship marked not only by the physical infrastructure of churches and small businesses, of places to pray and to play, but also by dense associational ties that reached across lines of gender, class, and migrant status. Urban renewal would shatter these communities: the existing political structures of these cities offered no meaningful way to engage in widespread resistance to the federal bulldozer. By 1963, in the wake of this massive spatial disruption and what Mindy Fullilove describes as the "root shock" of urban renewal, a new era of urban rebellions had commenced. Affected communities increasingly believed that their neighborhoods and spaces had been targeted as a form of urban genocide (see figure 1.4).

The broad contours of what would become Black Power Urbanism would emerge because neither the programs and policies of community action programs, which some critics dubbed "riot insurance," nor the broader Great Society could adequately repair or replace what had been lost under "Negro removal."[50] Instead, Black activists, intellectuals, and even some politicians developed an idea of Black spaces as colonial spaces poised for redemption and independence, which served as powerful alternative political formations of Black urban life.

The second critical (spatial) juncture was the rise of the segregated metropolis. Black Power Urbanism emerged not only in cities shaped by the urban Keynesian spatial fix, but also within a post–New Deal racially segregated metropolitan

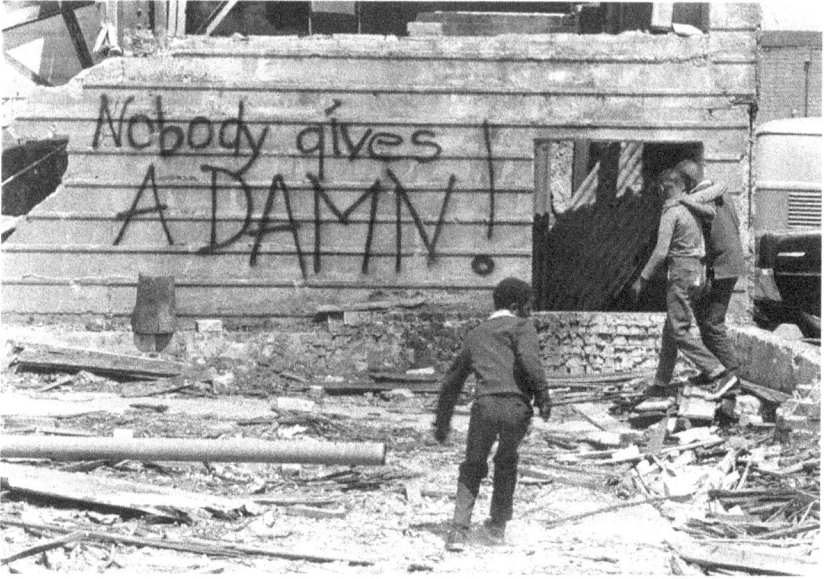

FIGURE 1.4.   Urban renewal in Oakland

Source: Redevelopment Agency demolition in Oakland, Bob Fitch Photography Archive, Department of Special Collections, Stanford University Library.

order in which citizenship rights were linked to particular spaces. The policies that made up the metropolitan color line obscured racial inequality and exclusion behind a seemingly race-neutral screen made up of private sector economic arrangements and mechanisms, as well as public sector regulatory and bureaucratic structures and rules embedded within and across multiple local, state, and federal jurisdictions.[51] These policies sharply delineated an increasingly "Black" city (urban space) from the "white" suburbs (suburban spaces). For whites, these divided spaces were attached to increasingly beneficial political, economic, and social goods. Meanwhile, on the other side of the metropolitan color line, the withholding of these goods became public policy. To paraphrase the writer Ta-Nehisi Coates, "the [Black City] was public policy."[52]

If the Black city was public policy, so too were "the suburbs." The "suburbs" were not simply spaces from which non-whites were excluded; they were political, economic, and cultural spaces as well. Politically they were the location of a new "suburban politics" that emerged from the early 1960s onward. The new suburban polity was characterized not only by the decisive shift of white middle-class Americans from central cities to suburban areas, but more importantly, by their residential shift from the Northeast and Midwest to the suburbanized Southern and Western regions of the United States. In the last third of the twentieth century, the suburban "sunbelt" became the chief battleground in national politics. Key to the suburban transformation was a multilayered response to the complexity of metropolitan racial inequality. This response was tempered by the belief of some white Americans that the moral and financial value of their "places" were under attack. Indeed, as a range of scholars have shown, these white spaces, particularly in the suburbs, would take on racialized political meanings and lead to the political mobilization of suburban counterreaction.[53]

Black Power Urbanism's struggle to dismantle this metropolitan state of racial disparity and exclusion revealed the racialized basis of these policies and the widespread support they attracted from those on the powerful (and non-Black) side of the postwar metropolitan color line. For example, Black Power urbanist–imbued demands for equalization of educational funding, for the construction of inclusionary housing, or even for the demands by Black citizens that police officers meet residency requirements sparked white suburban counterreaction. At the state level, these demands produced unexpected effects such as the passage of California's Proposition 13 and other "taxpayer bill of rights" legislation that imposed structural austerity budgets on majority-Black and -Brown jurisdictions. Suburban counterreaction included early proposals for the state takeover of urban (that is, majority-Black or -Brown) school districts in order to forestall meaningful school funding equalization, as well as new forms of anti-growth and carceral politics designed to reinscribe and strengthen racial and economic segregation.

The combined effects of suburban counterreaction would shape the viability of Black Power Urbanism. The complex territorial story in which Black Power Urbanism was embedded could be seen, for example, in the federal, state, and local level's surveillance, disruption, and violence targeted toward the Black Power movement and the unfolding of harsh and racialized "law and order" rhetoric. As Elizabeth Hinton shows in her work, the social programs of the Great Society (some of which Black Power Urbanism attempted to co-opt into new forms) would be replaced by a "criminalization of social programs" and the communities of color that they served.[54] The use of these case study cities allows us to develop a more detailed understanding of the making and unmaking of racial and urban political orders.

The third critical (spatial) juncture that would bring Black Power Urbanism to an end was the election of Ronald Reagan in 1980. His administration initiated multiple "wars" on Black and Brown communities and on the policy instantiations that made up Black Power Urbanism, including a massive expansion of the ongoing "war on crime" and the rapid growth of mass incarceration via a new "war on drugs."[55] These "wars" aided in the destruction of the material, political, and intellectual foundations of the New Deal/Keynesian city, which facilitated the roll out of a new spatial fix, the neoliberal metropolis.[56]

A clear understanding of the critical (spatial) junctures that formed the broader periodization in which Black Power Urbanism emerged also entails an understanding of Black urban development. The pathways of Black urban development, both within and across the specificities of place, have shaped the imaginings and the constraints that were attendant upon the formation of Black Power Urbanism.

Spatializing Black Urban Development

As W. E. B. Du Bois proclaimed, the problem of the twentieth century was the color line, and indeed the color line was the defining characteristic of much of twentieth-century urban history, politics, and space.[57] As the brief sketches of current-day Oakland and Newark have shown, the contours of a twenty-first-century color line are now also apparent. The metropolitan color line exists not just as a historical artifact but as an ongoing though mutable feature in the late twentieth-century neoliberal American metropolitan landscape.[58]

The durability of this color line was not inevitable. As Charles Mills argues, the problem of regulating Black citizens became acute in the post-emancipation moment; the end result of these efforts was a clear connection between race and space with political, social, and cultural consequences. As Mills suggests,

> The norming of space is partially done in terms of the *racing* of space, the depiction of space as dominated by individuals (whether persons or subpersons) of a certain race. At the same time, the norming of the individual is partially achieved by *spacing* it, that is, representing it as imprinted with the characteristics of a certain kind of space. So this is a mutually supporting characterization that, for subpersons, becomes a circular indictment: "You are what you are in part because you originate from a certain kind of space, and that space has these properties in part because it is inhabited by creatures like yourself."[59]

While the vast increase in urban Black populations in many major northern cities and their metropolitan areas during the First and Second Great Migrations (1914–70) would provide the demographic basis for the Black city, it was the *creation* of Negro ghetto(es)—and the dual processes of the spatialization of race and the racialization of space—that created one of the building blocks of Black Power Urbanism.

The creation of the (first and second) Negro ghetto(es) in cities like Newark and Oakland did not go uncontested by Black citizens, nor did it preclude political and social organizing both within Black enclaves and outside of them. Earl Lewis and others would also make the case that Black residents formed "congregations" and a sense of place in the spaces allotted to them by the urban color line of segregation.[60] Indeed, as Katharine McKittrick argues, rather than seeing these "black geographies" as damaged or "lifeless spaces," Black urban life should be more generally understood as a product of "particular spaces of otherness."[61] Black city residents, through formal and informal means, claimed urban citizenship that, while often unheeded by white-dominated cities, was always of importance to Black city residents.[62]

But how and why does the norming of space and race matter? Along with the work of Mills and McKittrick, that of Clarissa Rile Hayward and others can be useful in thinking about the role of race in urban space.[63] Hayward, following the lead of other social and political theorists, advances the argument that "space is not just 'where politics happens,'" nor is space a "'container' within which social and political relations are situated"; rather spaces and places are "prior grounds . . . which distinctively shape social and political relations of power."[64] As David Harvey argues, "places, by extension, are the specificity of space. Places are socially produced spaces—they are constructed by both insiders to whom a place has meaning and attachment, and by outsiders who see those places as external to their own. Second, since places are socially produced and not naturally given, they are subject to being changed through social action."[65] Urban geographies of space and place generate powerful positive as well as negative forces that influence individuals and communities. Indeed, both Hayward and Todd Swanstrom would argue that in the case of the United States, these urban geographies produce "thick injustices."[66] For Harvey and other advocates of the "right to the city," while injustice and oppression are built into urban geography, these spaces can become the springboards and organizing forces around which activism can take place.[67] Place and race can thus be understood as powerful forces shaping not only state development writ large, but also the development of the metropolitan spaces where most American urban life and urban citizenship takes place. Black Power Urbanism was a struggle to govern space and place and transform Black spatial interests into just spaces.

Periodizing Black Urban Citizenship and Political Development

In early twentieth-century ideas of the city and urbanism, Black people were seen as fundamentally alien to cities: newcomers who had no prior claim or connection. This ahistoricism was then buttressed by the "Chicago School," which popularized the notion that Black urban populations and their continued migration was akin to the threat posed by "invasive species" and would harm native ecology (that is, the urban fabric), if special mitigation efforts were not undertaken to fix Black pathology.[68] Scholars like W. E. B. Du Bois in his work *The Philadelphia Negro* and Horace Cayton and St. Clair Drake in *Black Metropolis* confronted and in some ways elided these conceptions of Black urbanites as fundamentally un-urban; each of them made the case for a robust and long-standing Black "city within a city."[69]

Mitigating urban Blackness would become central to how white politicians, social welfare theorists, and planners would see the future of cities. As Robert Weaver argued in his book, *The Negro Ghetto*,

> Ghetto patterns of residence are of relatively recent origins in this Nation. They were initiated, perpetuated and popularized by certain institutions. And there was a strong motive of special economic advantage undergirding the initiation. Perpetuation of the ghetto is no less responsive to special economic interests both outside and inside the area itself. This is not to imply that the ghetto is indestructible but rather to indicate that like most institutions, it generates vested interests for its continuation.[70]

Racial zoning became one type of state-sanctioned means for reasserting control over where and under what conditions Black people could live.[71] Though initial attempts to enact explicit forms of racial zoning failed as a result of *Buchanan v. Warley* (1917), the reproduction of both old and new types of racialized spaces continued as the twentieth century unfolded. Modern zoning became one such tool for implicitly advancing racial zoning, especially in the wake of *Village of Euclid v. Ambler Realty Co.* (272 U.S. 365 [1926]). Ostensibly used to control the spread of apartment buildings, zoning quickly became a means of indirectly spatializing race through mechanisms such as exclusionary zoning and other forms of land regulation.[72] Additional types of spatialization of race emerged as the result of "vested interests." Racial covenants and other institutional mechanisms like the Home Owners' Loan Corporation (HOLC) and the Federal Housing Administration (FHA) risk rating system offered a series of legal means for controlling the metropolitan color line.[73] The institutionalization of American planning also played a role in the continuation of racialized spaces. Indeed, Oakland, Newark, and East Orange are notable not only because they each adopted racialized zoning at around the same moment (circa the 1910s), but also because these cities (along with hundreds of jurisdictions) would each employ the planning and engineering firm of Harland Bartholomew to carry out urban renewal/highway construction plans that targeted each city's Black and/or minoritized communities.[74] The role of the firm in shaping a standardized approach to racialized city clearances would be noted by one scholar as a form of "administrative evil."[75]

Ongoing political and legal challenges would eventually eliminate some race-based spatial control mechanisms thanks to organizations such as the NAACP (as well as local groups), which battled federal, state, and local structures and more broadly zoning itself. In some cases, such as Oakland and East Orange, grassroots Black activism successfully pushed out hostile planning directors in favor of new ones that took community concerns somewhat more into consideration.

In the face of these highly racialized spatial interventions, and indeed, despite them, constructions of Black space occurred across all four sites surveyed in this book. As Du Bois showed in his work on Philadelphia's Seventh Ward, Black people were not strangers to American cities. From enslavement to emancipation, Black people had been intrinsic to the racial capitalism undergirding settler colonialism. Indeed, Newark's Plane Street Colored Church, which was established in 1832, was an organizing site for Black antislavery activism and a stop on the Underground Railroad.[76] Within these spaces, researchers from Du Bois to Cayton and St. Clair to Weaver would note the significant differences among Black residents, including class, gender, age, religious affiliation, and migration status, which complicates any assumption of a monolithic Black community. This diversity would come to bedevil Black Power/Black Power Urbanism advocates who sought to create a so-called unified front framed as "Black Consciousness." Later, as the neoliberal metropolis emerged, the ephemeral nature of "Black Consciousness" would complicate attempts by some Black activists to invoke what Michelle Boyd calls "Jim Crow nostalgia" in order to smooth over sharp intragroup differences among Black residents about the future of Black life in these spaces.[77]

The Deep Roots of Black Urban Citizenship

Newark stands as one example in terms of tracing the roots of Black urban citizenship. Black Newark was present even in the early days of European settlement, with Black residents in the pre–Civil War era taking active and leading roles in the abolitionist and anti-colonization movements, pressing for restoration of free Black male suffrage, and later acting as a conduit for the Underground Railroad. Black churches, colored schools, lyceums, saloons, and other instantiations of Black communal life were constantly being created and adapted to present socio-spatial demands.[78] By the early twentieth century, a modern Black Newark had developed on top of this earlier Black place. While some of the members of Black Newark's small middle class engaged in brokerage politics with white elite reformers, a substantial faction of working-class Black residents vied to make inroads into the city's ethnic-based machine politics.

While Newark had some of the oldest roots of these Black Power cities, since the late nineteenth century a small but politically and socially visible Black community also resided in suburban East Orange. It contained spatially distinct "congregations" of churches, small retail and service businesses, fraternal lodges, and even a settlement house that encouraged Black communal life. Booker T. Washington, who visited the city on one of his last northern tours, recognized the city's identity as the home of Black suburban respectability.[79] The presence of Black residents as well as other racialized populations (for instance, Italian immigrants) spurred the city to become one of the first to adopt Euclidean zoning in the wake of *Buchanan v. Warley* and the failure of racial zoning. In response to the rise of nearly explicit racial segregation in the city's schools (as well as across many northern cities), Black middle-class residents led one the first successful resistances to its spread.[80] By the late 1920s, these same middle-class residents would elect New Jersey's first Black state legislators who would go on to sponsor the state's postwar antidiscrimination laws. By 1962, East Orange could proudly tout its integrated schools and its single-family housing as evidence of its standing as a "model interracial city."[81]

By the 1920s, Oakland was vying for the title of "Harlem of the West." The city's Black community—complex and far from monolithic—was a part of the city's urban fabric, but largely centered in West Oakland and near the railroad terminus that employed a Black male workforce of sleeping-car porters and other laborers.[82] All the formal markers of Black communal life were established within the shadow of the Oakland color line, including civic and uplift organizations, churches, small retail shops, and restaurants. Mobilization for World War II and Oakland's emergence as the arsenal of the West would triple the city's Black population and begin to upend the internal accommodations and alliances that had constituted prewar Black Oakland. By the postwar era, a "charitable landscape" largely built and led by Black middle-class club women during the early part of the century would be demolished by urban renewal.[83] At the same time, the labor militancy of Black rail workers vied with the liberal integrationism of a Black middle-class political leadership that dubbed themselves "the men of tomorrow," as each group sought to remake Black politics in a city that was actively erasing significant parts of Black Oakland.[84] None of these groups had strong linkages to Black youth like Bobby Seale and Huey Newton, who confronted the devastating impact of "Negro removal" and political dispossession of the city's poor and working-class Black and Brown communities.[85]

East Palo Alto's Black community was the most fragile of all of these sites of Black life. Black Palo Alto was created within spaces marked by dispossession and exclusion. The incarceration of Japanese Americans who had resided there would lead to the "opening" of this seized property to postwar suburban real estate development.[86] Located on the margins of then-emergent Silicon Valley, this property was scooped up by developers who built "blue collar heavens," or housing geared to working- and lower middle-class whites, who assured that a full panoply of racial tools would be used to maintain these spaces as white only.[87] These assurances would fail. By the late 1950s, Black migration to East Palo Alto had increased as the last wave of the Great Migration made its way to a semirural landscape that resembled Louisiana and Texas. Other migrants arrived as a result of displacement from urban renewal in San Francisco and Oakland. Coinciding with and deepening this spatialization of race was the expansion of the state's interstate highway system, which created a "concrete curtain" that sharply separated multiracial and multiethnic East Palo Alto from predominantly white Palo Alto and its institutional center, Stanford University. Black communal life and political activism were shaped by the confluences of space and race. Grassroots efforts to address inequalities in education, housing, and policing were shaped by East Palo Alto's lack of political autonomy due to its unincorporated status. In addition, its location as a working-class racialized space left it in a weak position within the political economy of the segregated (suburban) metropolis. At the same time, the community's location adjacent to Stanford University would embed local activism into local (Bay Area) and national Black Power networks. The search for sovereignty—from the symbolism of renaming the city "Nairobi" to formal political incorporation—would characterize East Palo Alto's Black Power Urbanism.

"I Got No Country": Negro Removal

James Baldwin's interview with a young Black man vividly brings to life the ways in which Black urban citizenship claims were challenged as urban renewal in its many guises first fractured existing Black neighborhoods and then, in its wake, created new Black spaces into which those subjected to urban renewal and racialized predation (often multiple times) were hastily moved:

> A boy last week, he was 16 in San Francisco told me on television, thank God we got him to talk. Maybe somebody else ought to listen. He said, "I got no country, I've got no flag." Man he's only 16 years old. And I couldn't say you do. . . . I don't have any evidence to prove that he does. They were tearing down his house because San Francisco is engaging as almost [all] northern cities now are engaged in something called urban renewal, which means moving the Negroes out. . . . It means negro removal; that is what it means. And the federal government is . . . an accomplice to this fact.[88]

These massive dislocations called forth a distinctive range of responses in Black communities. During the summer of 1963, the first of the race riots in urban areas that came to be known as "long hot summers," revealed through violent racial unrest that Black and Brown young people understood that white-controlled city-wide political institutions, politicians, and ameliorative organizations were unable or unwilling to create a city in which Black and Brown people could not just survive, but also thrive.

While liberal integrationism had created opportunities for some, "Negro removal" had shown that the Keynesian city's vision of opportunity for all for was a vision in which Black people and their communities could be easily sacrificed. Indeed, as Preston Smith and others have shown, this spatial disruption placed some Black elites and local Black politicians in uncomfortable and increasingly politically untenable positions as their initial support for urban renewal was found wanting after the scale of disruption, demolition, and displacement of Black neighborhoods became increasingly clear.[89] Their powerlessness was only magnified as it became apparent that the token liberal integrationism they offered was no solution for the worsening conditions in Black neighborhoods.

"Negro removal" was only one of the issues that dramatized the limits of Black urban citizenship within the existing Keynesian urban political order. As Reverend Martin Luther King Jr.'s experience in Chicago vividly demonstrated, the Civil Rights Movement in the North had seen multiple and often failed campaigns to integrate schools and neighborhoods, to expand economic and employment opportunities for poor and working-class Blacks in "downtown" service jobs or public services, and to dismantle the segregated skilled trades unions.[90] Most significantly, decades of protest against oppressive and brutal policing at the hands of largely white police forces seemed to have had no effect at all. The metropolitan color line described by Du Bois and others proved to be surprisingly durable.

Black Power Urbanism was a new challenge to this urban/metropolitan color line. By the mid-1960s the possibility of a Black Power city seemed to be on the verge of reality. Much of this story of the rise of the Black city is well known through a causal narrative that rests on white flight, ethnic succession, and deindustrialization. Now nearly forgotten by the functionalist accounts of the rise of Black urban regimes is the alternative vision of Black Power Urbanism.

Dreams of a Just City

Black Power Urbanism was both radical and (im)possibly romantic.[91] Grace and James Boggs' essay, *The City Is the Black Man's Land*, was one of the first fully articulated discussions of Black Power Urbanism.[92] Published in 1966, the Boggs' essay argued that the election of Black faces in city government was not enough given the crisis facing urban Black communities. In a prescient analysis, the Boggs focused on the impact of the "cybercultural revolution" and increased automation, which would make Black industrial workers as "obsolete in advanced North America as farming with a stick already is in Asia, Africa and Latin America."[93] To address these crises, Black Power Urbanism should not—and indeed they would argue *could not*—follow in the footsteps of "ethnic succession" politics. Rather, the Black majority and their leaders should be "prepared to reorganize the structure of city government from top to bottom."[94]

The Boggs were not the only ones arguing that the Black Power city could not simply follow an earlier path; neither could it follow earlier pluralist models due to the unique position of African Americans in the urban North. The Boggs' essay was prefaced by a statement put forth by the Organization for Black Power in May 1965.[95] The group critiqued the limitations of the Civil Rights Movement, arguing that as it "originated in the South [the Civil Rights Movement] cannot address itself to these problems of the Northern ghetto which are based not upon legal (de jure) contradictions but upon systematic (de facto) contradictions. It remains therefore for the movement in the North to carry the struggle to the enemy in fact, i.e., towards the system rather than just de jure toward new legislation."[96]

Black Power Urbanism thus rested on a rejection of the limitations of the more narrowly conceived integration project of the early Northern Civil Rights Movement.[97] It also reflected the reality of white resistance to liberal integrationism, which ranged from a spatial "exit" from cities to a political "exit" of partisan realignment that rested on white suburban hostility to "race, rights, and taxes." These exits were all neatly encoded in the word "urban." Alongside white resistance and exit (and perhaps facilitating it) was the slow collapse of the urban Keynesian city during the 1960s as it was devoured by the "spatial fix," and the transformation of the particular pluralist-tinged Black urban citizenship that accompanied it.

Black Power Urbanism would center on creating a new city that embodied the aspirations of poor and working-class Blacks for a just urban citizenship, and more pointedly on creating a movement to transform Black neighborhoods and spaces. People trapped within Black enclaves and ghettos would battle "out of America's prison walls" and out of their colonial status to become a "nation within a nation," with indigenously created and controlled political, economic, and communal institutions.[98] More concretely, Black Power Urbanism, led by left and progressive groups, civil rights activists, certain politicians, and ordinary citizens, would focus on reversing, rather than just ameliorating, the worst of the inequities imposed by the urban renewal order and the metropolitan color line that accompanied and buttressed it.[99]

The Afterlives and Legacies of Black Power Urbanism

That Black Power was strongly connected to Black urban politics, especially during the 1960s and 1970s, seems obvious. *Dark Concrete* tries to excavate the fact that the obviousness of this connection is both true and also deeply distorting. Retrospectively Black Power has been recast as a mostly nationalist cultural politics that was oddly, unsuccessfully, and temporarily fused with the urban pluralist struggle. Indeed, in its most optimistic conception, Black Power came to mean the election of Black officials (particularly of Black mayors) and the creation of Black urban regimes, as well as the necessity for teamwork between residents, activists, and politicians as they grasped the opportunity to finally address the challenges and possibilities of America's Black cities (see figure 1.5).

FIGURE 1.5.   Newark's Black Power urban renewal

Source: "Newark Model Cities" (report), May 20, 1971, RiseUpNewark.com, accessed April 15, 2025, https://riseupnewark.com/wp-content/uploads/2020/10/Model-Cities-Program-min.pdf.

The study of Black Power in cities often means studying Black electoral politics with particular attention paid to the ways in which Black Power supporters battled with other Black and white political interests as a means to control Black communities. The optimism of Black Power activists was met with mixed record of accomplishments. However, the inability of the "first Black mayors" and then Black urban regimes to live up to the optimism of formal political incorporation and to forcefully resist the state's assault on Black cities led to a perception of Black urban politics as a quest for a symbolically rich but substantively poor "hollow prize."[100] Black Power—at least as delineated in these "hollow prize" accounts— couldn't and didn't save the cities. Indeed, critics like Adolph Reed argue that Black Power was simply a convenient fig leaf for the transference of power from whites who were abandoning the cities to a self-interested and corrupt Black leadership class who took power as neocolonial representatives of the state. In this view, Reed and other "hollow prize" supporters joined neoconservative and revanchist recodings of some cities, especially ones with contentious politics, as "Black cities." Black urban regimes were charged with maintaining order in these so-called "unheavenly" and "ungovernable" but undoubtedly Black cities.[101]

Rather than seeing Black Power as simply a convenient political tool and rhetorical ruse to install neocolonial Black administrations, this book looks at the ways in which Black Power Urbanism challenged what a "right to the city" could look like and demonstrates how attempts to instantiate these new claims offered a path—however incomplete—to envision and put into place more affirmative and just urban spaces for Black Americans. This "just city," a Black city, would be not only a city for Blacks, but a city—as well as a metropolis—in which all groups— especially those marginalized and oppressed by the color line, could share an equal claim to urban citizenship. By looking at what Black Power Urbanism did, both in rhetoric and in practice, the Black city that emerged by the end of the 1970s can and should be better understood as a place of deep contestation over who and what a Black city was for. Of course, it cannot be denied that American cities faced fundamental challenges in the 1970s and onward. What I am suggesting is that Black Power Urbanism was a path embraced by a wide cross section of activists, politicians, and ordinary citizens. Whether they failed in this embrace is certainly a legitimate question; however, I wish to go beyond an "archeology of failure" to question and interrogate the erasure of the political possibilities and struggles of Black Power Urbanism of the 1960s and 1970s.[102]

This erasure of political possibilities and struggles in turn has led to a definition and denigration of Black urban politics as a hopeless task that continually deludes Black Americans into believing that politics and even protest could ever be enough and that offers instead a vague call to "revolution" led by a perennially weak and disorganized Left. Indeed, in some ways the critics of Black urban politics are closer to blaming the victims of the state's assault on Black cities than to seeing the failure of those engaged in governing the city, which was heavily conditioned by a multifaceted attack on Black cities and Black citizens. By neglecting what Black Power Urbanism attempted and simply accepting the claims of failure put forward first by advocates of racialized urban austerity and then subsequently by proponents of urban neoliberalism, we fail to see how the contestation over America's cities both shaped and reflected other struggles occurring across and within other multiple political orders. By excavating what Black Power Urbanism potentially (and actually) did effectuate, I hope to reframe what we know about Black urban politics during the 1960s and 1970s, the turbulent wake of the Black Power movement, and more generally how we understand the urban political development of the last sixty years.

While the mark of political orders is their durability—that is, their ability to effect ideational, coalitional, and/or institutional change over time—political orders eventually become weakened by their own internal sources of fragility and the tensions between overlapping, intercurrent, and emergent new political orders. Such was the case with Black Power Urbanism. Ideas or policies, individually or collectively, may eventually be discarded as unworkable or rejected as politically or socially untenable. Thus, in cities where Black Power Urbanism appeared, its local instantiation would eventually fall or be forced into strategic adaptation and retreat, while the order(s) that replaced Black Power urbanism—whether the Black urban regime, the urban growth machine, or the neoliberal city, rested partially upon a repudiation of the forms—ideas, interests, and institutional arrangements—that had come before it. Like political orders before it, Black Power Urbanism's coherence is perhaps only visible in retrospect as scholars look at what preceded as well as followed it.

BLACK POWER URBANISM
Imaginings, Insurgencies, and Instantiations

> **Black people must seek audacious power—the kind of power which cradles your head amongst the stars and gives you the security to stand up as proud men and women, eyeball to eyeball with the rest of the world.**
>
> —Adam Clayton Powell, 1966

In June 2022, the New Jersey Center for Performing Arts (NJPAC) announced that as part of a multimillion-dollar redevelopment plan, it would demolish Cathedral House, which had formerly belonged to the Episcopal diocese (and was a protected landmark).[1] Cathedral House was notable for hosting the 1967 Newark Black Power Conference days after the Newark rebellion. Cathedral House was where Adam Clayton Powell's 1966 call for Black people to seek "audacious power" was given an organized structure (see figure 2.1).[2] Over a thousand delegates (many paying a twenty-five dollar fee) "representing 286 organizations and institutions from 126 cities and 26 states" attended the conference.

Some delegates, like Amiri Baraka (aka LeRoi Jones), appeared with fresh bruises inflicted by the police; others arrived after going through a gauntlet of National Guard soldiers who had arrived to lethally subdue the rebellion. Delegates included Reverend Dr. Nathan Wright, a Black Episcopalian religious worker and scholar who organized the 1965 pre-meeting and then chaired the 1967 conference. In September 1967, Wright gave an interview in which he offered a core aspirational definition of Black Power Urbanism. The purpose of Black Power, Wright argued, was "not to destroy America but to do great things for America, to move things forward; yes, to control part of America like all other ethnic groups, to help direct the affairs of America, to be creative American citizens; yes, to destroy the bigots, the social ill, political ills, the economic ills, and to drive then from the shores of America."[3] This aspiration to treat

FIGURE 2.1.   Ideas and manifestos: (*seated center to left*) Gloria Richardson, Omar Ahmed, Jima Tayari, and others. Black Power Conference, July 22, 1967

Source: Associated Press Photo / John Duricka

the new Black city as liberated territory would be the subject not only of subsequent conferences, but also of numerous attempts to put these ideas into practice in Newark (which Amiri Baraka would rename "New Ark") and other Black spaces, all in service to building a new Black "nation within a nation." Indeed, Amiri Baraka referred to the city as "New Ark" to emphasize its revolutionary potential.[4]

By 1980, this nation-building moment had come to an end. Cathedral House had long since reverted back to its core function as the diocesan headquarters. In 1997, the building was sold to NJPAC as part of a new arts center complex designed to lure suburban residents back to downtown Newark (see figure 2.2).[5] As part of its reuse, the façade was painted with a colorful mural by the graphic designer and artist Paula Scher, who had been asked to turn a "dowdy old building into something that's bright and appropriate for a school."[6]

In 2022, despite the building's iconic status, NJPAC argued that its demolition was necessary to allow for more functional loading bays and additional parking to entice its largely suburban customers to the art center's events.[7] It further justified the demolition by contending that it would restore the urban fabric that had been destroyed by the city's postwar foray into urban renewal. Coincidentally, the demolition would allow NJPAC to reconnect a "finely knitted tapestry of

FIGURE 2.2. Newark's Cathedral House: Site of 1967 Black Power Conference

Source: Darren Tobia / Jersey Digs

streets," not just for the sake of the city, but also to support the redevelopment of its "eight-acre campus into a walkable neighborhood with townhomes, ground-floor retail, and public space."[8] Local historic preservationists, community activists, and veterans of the city's Black Power movement condemned the plan and vowed to block it.

NJPAC did not have a strong track record in acknowledging Newark's history. The complex had been built on top of a former African American burial ground that NJPAC officials argued was not "real."[9] In addition, several other historical buildings under its remit had not been maintained or demolished despite assurances to the contrary.[10] By September 2022, NJPAC had agreed to save parts of the façade as well as the colorful mural. Mayor Ras Baraka sent a message of support for this compromise, noting that his "father [Amiri Baraka] was one of the thought-leaders who convened the Conference, which was all the more significant as it was held in the days following the Newark Rebellion."

In the end, a piece of Black Power history was saved, although the near miss was a result of the logic that had ruled Newark and other cities since the decline of Black Power Urbanism. Under Reaganomics and urban neoliberalism the city's interests—the perception of what constituted who and what a city was for—had shifted. Cities now needed to compete for residents and visitors to keep local urban economies afloat. NJPAC, built under the city's second Black mayor, Sharpe James, was designed to fulfill such a function.[11] The city's interests were not "Black interests"; rather the city's interests were its own, and among them was raising revenue by bring suburbanites back to downtown. Although a relic of Black Power Urbanism had been saved, few traces of Black Power Urbanism would remain after the redevelopment of this site.

As the threatened demolition of Cathedral House revealed, the emergence of the Black Lives Matter movement and other anti-racism and abolitionist movements such as the Occupy movement and police abolitionism led to a resurgence of interest in the Black Power movement. Recent histories as well as the popular media's treatment of the Black Power movement often focus on charismatic individuals like Amiri Baraka or Huey Newton, or on important groups like the Black Panthers.[12] Part of this focus rests on the aesthetics of groups like the Black Panthers and the broader Black Arts and Black Power movement, which have provided powerful and enduring symbols of Black resistance and Black sovereignty. Oakland—the home of the Black Panthers—was the city that was surely the most symbolic of the revolutionary Black Power of the 1960s. The images of unsmiling, armed young Black women and men wearing black berets signaled that a new era of Black politics and culture had arrived in Oakland, across the United States, and across the globe. The assertion of Black identity was even more striking given that Black Power was also embedded within, and saw itself as part of, a vanguard internationalist movement. Indeed, in this respect, the internationalist Third World and anti-colonial aspects of Black Power were both important in helping to articulate Black Power as a set of ideological and political mobilizations that were distinctive from older Black nationalist traditions. Yet, despite the current framing of the Black Power movement as a clear moment of radical solidarity and political possibility, its status at the time was much more uncertain and contested, as it stood uneasily adjacent but also in opposition to "Negro politics."

Negro Politics and Audacious Power

To modern post–Black Panther sensibilities, the image of Congressman Adam Clayton Powell Jr. standing behind a podium with then-chairman of the SNCC Stokely Carmichael/Kwame Ture sitting in the foreground is striking and unsettling (see figure 2.3).

FIGURE 2.3. Planning for Black Power: Kwame Ture (Stokely Carmichael) (*seated*) and Representative Adam Clayton Powell announcing a planning meeting for the Black Power Conference, July 27, 1966

Source: Bettmann / Getty Images

The image is from a press conference called by Powell to announce that he and co-convener Carmichael would "invite all Negro leaders to a Washington conference on 'Black Power'" over the 1966 Labor Day weekend.[13] The press conference itself would be the capstone of a tumultuous year for both Carmichael and Powell.

For Powell, this was the coda to his May 1966 commencement address at Howard University, where he was arguably the first elected Black official to give a "Black Power" speech.[14] Powell's speech, which called for Black people to "seek audacious power," was one that he had refined over a number of occasions, and by the time of commencement he had boiled it down to this: "To demand these God-given human rights is to seek black power—what I call audacious power—the power to build black institutions of splendid achievement."[15] Powell's speech, which was later published as "My Black Position Paper," outlined a definition of human rights that attempted to bridge Powell's past as a Harlem-based politico and a new future linked to the growing popularity of Black Power. To Powell, "[Black] life must be purposed to implement human rights." More concretely, human rights, in the context of Black struggle, mean "the right to be secure in one's person from the excessive abuses of the state and its law enforcement officials. . . . The right to freedom of choice of a job to feed one's family. . . . The right to freedom of mobility of residence. . . . The right to the finest education [the] social order can provide. . . . And, most importantly, the right to share fully the governing councils of the state as equal members of the body politic."[16]

Powell's fiery rhetoric was perhaps self-serving. Long a polarizing figure in an institutionally racist Congress, Powell had been increasingly attacked for his outspoken views on racial equality and his sometimes mercurial behavior.[17] As one of a handful of Black members of Congress in a chamber still dominated by conservative Southern Democrats, Powell was targeted through accusations that he had committed various alleged ethics violations. As the Black Power movement unfolded, the defiance of its stance dovetailed well with his own and the highly visible mobilization of its supporters was increasingly in alignment with his own struggle to remain in office and to remain politically relevant.

For Carmichael, the Black Power Conference would be the first Black mainstream connection to the vibrant call for "Black Power!" that he had proclaimed a little more than a month prior on Thursday, June 16, 1966, in Greenwood, Mississippi. For Powell, it capped nearly a year of thinking and political strategizing after he made what he would later call "the most important speech of my life." The "Black Position Paper" speech is now mostly relegated to the footnotes of histories of the Black Power movement and biographies of Powell. It is important, however, not only because it marks a curious turn for Powell vis-à-vis the emergent Black Power movement, but also because the speech was indicative of the fraught relationship that the Black Power movement would have with Black electoral politics, and by extension, the American political system.[18]

From the perspective of the early twenty-first century and in the wake of his long and sometimes flamboyant career in Congress, Powell's July 1966 embrace of Black Power is puzzling. Why would he ally himself with this nascent movement, given his role as civil rights crusader within Congress, and especially given the competing popular perceptions of Black Power (both then and today) as either an "unruly" dead-end rejection of the Civil Rights Movement, on the one hand, or as a failed revolutionary project, on the other? That Powell would be the first Black elected official to articulate a Black Power sensibility is unsettling to current historiography of the Black Power movement and also to our understanding of Black urban politics. This improbability is further underscored by Amiri Baraka's answer to the rhetorical question of "why Black power." Baraka's response was one in which the ideas, insurgencies, and instantiations of Black Power Urbanism were all inextricably linked together. Baraka's articulation went even further: Black Power (Urbanism) was gaining control of cities like Newark, with the goal of "nationaliz[ing] the city's institutions as if it were liberated territory in Zimbabwe or Angola."[19] Wright's and Powell's statements (not too dissimilar from Baraka's) are surprising as they came from figures that were still very much rooted in a mode of Black political life in which they, along with broader Civil Rights Movement, continued to press onward toward a practical articulation of what both the Civil Rights Act of 1964 and the Voting Rights Act of 1965 could or should mean.

By 1965, however, many younger Black activists and radicals saw "race leaders" like Powell and Wright, as well as "Negro politics" (and Civils Rights Movement activism in general), as "not only shabby and threadbare but also hopelessly decadent."[20] To them, Negro politics was just one of the elements that lay in the path of a more revolutionary upending of American politics and society. Notwithstanding his championing of civil rights legislation and the establishment of Johnson's Great Society, Powell's public persona only reinforced the perception of decadence, from his privileged background, his attendance at elite private schools, and his vacations in Europe, to his hedonism, symbolized by his multiple marriages and divorces and his frequent visits to his vacation house in the Bahamas.[21]

Powell's Black Power speech itself—which changed each time he gave it—is important because it shows the seismic, but still unnoticed shift that was occurring as the Black Power movement moved from the margins to the center of Black American political thought. Black Power, and more specifically Black Power Urbanism, would provide a model for a bottom-up understanding of what civil rights—reframed as human rights—could mean. The Washington Black Power Conference, where the speech would be given, was larger than expected. Secondary accounts show that by September, the call for a Black Power pre-planning conference had struck a chord, attracting "unexpected numbers of black young people" with "169 delegates from 18 states, 37 cities and 64 organizations" attending.[22] From the meeting a planning committee was put together that would plan a much larger meeting for the summer of 1967 in Newark, New Jersey. Reflecting the gendered hierarchy of the day, almost all of the committee members were men who would become highly visible in the Black Power movement. Newark's Dr. Nathan Wright Hare would be the point person for the second convention.[23] Unknown to the organizers at the time was that Newark in the summer of 1967 would become a site of Black rebellion.

Thus, the formal stage of the Black Power movement was born from a complex and uneasy alliance of ideas and interests that included support for anti-colonial struggles sweeping across the global South and anti-capitalist and liberation politics. Within the broader Black Power movement was the emergence of a distinctive new order, Black Power Urbanism. Reflecting its roots in the urban Black spaces outside of the South like Newark and Oakland, Black Power Urbanism was a collection of "ideas and understandings, interests and organizations" as well as an "interconnected pattern of institutional and ideological arrangements" that spatially and temporally cohered around a vision of Black urban life and distinctively shaped urban governance over a period of time.[24]

Like the broader Black Power movement alongside which it grew, Black Power Urbanism offered to activists, intellectuals, and everyday people a powerful analytical tool and political organizing mode, which shared durable and important linkages with long-standing modes of Black political thought, especially Black nationalism, Black citizenship, and racial uplift politics. Yet what made Black Power Urbanism such a radical political concept was not simply its articulation of Black political and cultural self-determination. The revolutionary potential of Black Power Urbanism was also that it saw people of African descent in the United States as not simply the objects of liberal integrationist "contempt and pity," but as subjects, as political agents whose bodies and spaces were imbued with inherent worth and beauty.[25] The assertion of African peoplehood was of course not new. What made this assertion revolutionary was its rebirth within the deeply spatialized context of the mid-twentieth-century Black city. While the most famous cry of Black Power was uttered in rural Greenwood, Mississippi by Stokely Carmichael in 1966, Black Power Urbanism was articulated in America's cities by a spatially embedded network of Black thinkers and activists affiliated with groups such as the Black Panthers in Oakland, California and Amiri Baraka's NewArk and Black Arts movements in Newark, New Jersey. This spatialization took place not only in Black cities like Newark and Oakland but also in Black metropolitan spaces such as the school boards of East Orange, New Jersey and the kitchen tables of East Palo Alto, California.

Theorizing Black Power (Urbanism)

Black Power as a domestic political program has been seen as a tragic failure despite its hopeful beginnings. Part of the failure was the result of political repression and deadly state violence carried out not only against members of the Black Panthers but also activists and groups associated with other Black Power/Black radical movements. The full scope of the repression of Black political mobilization in this era is still being uncovered by historians and journalists. COINTELPRO (the federal counterintelligence program), along with the enthusiastic assistance of state and local police forces, led to the imprisonment, exile, or death of well-known figures like Assata Shakur, George Jackson, and Mark Hampton, as well as other lesser-known local activists. The failure of Black Power as an alternative political force can also attributed to the hostility supporters faced from white society in general, which offered few concessions to the demands made by Black Power advocates unless faced with Black rebellion in the streets. While state repression was a key element in its failure, Black Power was also seen as highly susceptible to the very forces it attempted to subvert. Thus attempts to introduce radical community control and grassroots governance were quickly (in the minds of many critics) co-opted by bourgeois nationalism and ethnic politics. Efforts to attain community sovereignty, whether political, administrative, or economic, were frustrated by a variety of countermeasures such as Richard Nixon's Black capitalism policy or the rise of "community development corporations" and other entities that sidelined and bureaucratized local activists.[26]

Black Power theorists like Grace Lee Boggs and James Boggs argued that the divisions between the "Black Power advocates and the civil rights advocates" were inevitable within the Black freedom movement.[27] The latter, they argued, were "sponsored, supported, and dependent upon the white power structure, are committed to integrating blacks into the white structure without any serious changes in that structure. In essence, they are simply asking to be given the same rights which whites have had and blacks have been denied. By equality they mean just that and no more: being equal to white Americans."[28]

The Boggses were equally critical about divisions within the Black Power movement between "realists like themselves" and the "idealists or romanticists . . . [who] continue to talk and hope to arouse the masses of black people through self-agitation, deluding themselves and creating the illusion that one set of people can replace another set of people in power without building an organization to take active steps toward power, while at the same time agitating and mobilizing the masses." In the world of the Black left, Black Power could only work with a thoroughgoing but realistic rejection of old forms and the adoption of new forms—carefully insulated from co-optation and reform—by mass political action and accountability.

Over the course of a decade, from 1964 to 1974, using the catchphrase "unity without uniformity," Black Power supporters attempted to weld together a movement that bridged these competing ideas about Black empowerment. The successes and failures of the Black Power movement were also shaped by the movement's own internal complexities and contradictions that ranged across lines of ideology, ethnicity, religion, class, migration history, age, and gender. The Black Power movement, as many have noted, reflected important socio-spatial and historical lineages, from the militant labor-oriented strain that emerged in Detroit to the fusion of Marxism-Leninism and cultural nationalism that arose in Newark, and points in between (Harlem, Chicago, Los Angeles, and Oakland).[29] "Black Power" meant different things to different people—some subscribed to the ideology of the Marxist/leftist perspective of the Black Panther Party, others to the cultural nationalisms of rivals Amiri Baraka and Ron Karenga. Much of what is thought of as "Black Power" also rested upon imagined solidarities and homogeneities that minimized or erased the multiple cleavages that existed within heterogenous Black communities. Certainly these imagined solidarities and commonalities were facilitated by the fact that the Black Power movement drew powerfully from a deeply rooted Black American political tradition of masculinist, "bourgeois" Black nationalism.[30] Critics on the left certainly blamed the failure of the Black Power movement on the durability of Black bourgeois nationalism and the movement's adherence to liberal integrationism.

The 1972 Gary Convention was Black Power's political and cultural apex and perhaps the beginning of its decline, as the Black center signaled its distance from more radical calls for Black Power. The convention brought together a vast cross section of Black people, including a small number of international observers, reflecting the Black Power movement's internationalist concerns. In addition to charting a political program for Black empowerment and policy change, the convention's plan was to develop the foundations for a Black political party. The proposed party would meet grassroots concerns with accountable leadership. This leadership would also act on behalf of a cohesive (albeit imagined) Black community as a "third force" in American politics, providing a "balance of power" between the Republican and Democratic parties. Although organizers would celebrate "unity without uniformity," the existing political, social, and cultural schisms within the Black community challenged their ability to create a political party in which discipline and submission to a "leadership cadre" was accepted as the way forward. The formal founding of the Congressional Black Caucus in 1971 and its members' decision to back away from the Black Power convention movement and continue their participation within the confines of the Democratic Party doomed the prospects for a Black-led third party to emerge, particularly one that emphasized an incoherent mix of top-down ideological control and bottom-up democracy. Black Power, at least as reflected in the organizational disarray that emerged after the 1972 Gary Convention, was over.

For the most ardent supporters of Black Power, Black politics was "Negro politics": powerless, petty, corrupt, and beholden to white-controlled political institutions. The tension between Black Power (as a viable, legitimate, and necessary alternative) and the liberal integrationist path of electoral empowerment can be seen in the juxtaposition of Representative Adam Clayton Powell's convening of a one-day "Black Power Summit" in 1966, versus Bayard Rustin's 1966 essay, "'Black Power' and Coalition Politics," which rejected Black Power as it "not only lacks any real value for the civil-rights movement, but that its propagation is positively harmful. It diverts the movement from a meaningful debate over strategy and tactics, it isolates the Negro community, and it encourages the growth of anti-Negro forces."[31] Rustin was not alone in his initial rejection of the Black Power movement; his stance was echoed by many in the Civil Rights Movement establishment including national and local leadership within the NAACP and Urban League.

Given the resistance of mainstream civil rights leaders to Black Power, these younger and/or more nationalist/leftist critics believed themselves justified in their disdain for "Negro politics." The degree of Black disempowerment—both formal and informal—was substantial. In the early 1960s, activists in Oakland and Newark faced nearly intransigent white mayoral administrations that refused to cede anything more than token concessions in the face of the Civil Rights Movement that was by then sweeping much of the nation. Indeed, in the aftermath of the first wave of urban rebellions in 1963, when Black youth were asked why they rebelled, they often responded that it was the only way to make their grievances heard. "Negro politics" had done nothing to stave off the "Negro removal" regime that had successfully targeted Black neighborhoods, large and small, across the United States. Yet despite this disdain for conventional politics, activists could not ignore the political possibilities of the majority-Black city, which had been visible since the early 1960s as the Great Migration reached its peak. Carmichael's famous invocation of Black Power in Mississippi came on the heels of the Boggs' 1966 article ("The City Is the Black Man's Land"), which centered the Black city as the site for liberation.[32] Carmichael would spend years following his invocation with speeches attempting to clarify what exactly he meant by "Black Power." In a speech to an audience at UC Berkeley in 1966 (which he called the "white intellectual ghetto of the West"), Carmichael emphasized that among many elements making up the meaning of Black Power was the role of power and institution-building:

> How can we build new political institutions that will become the political expressions of people? How can you build political institutions that will begin to meet the needs of Oakland, California? The need of Oakland, California, is not 1,000 policemen with submachine guns. They need that least of all. How can we build institutions that will allow those people to function on a day-to-day basis, so that they can get decent jobs and have decent houses, and they can begin to participate in the policy and make the decisions that affect their lives?[33]

Carmichael would further refine Black Power as an operationalizable concept with the help of Charles Hamilton, a political scientist and lawyer.[34] Together they published *Black Power: The Politics of Liberation* in 1967, which argued for the real possibility of meaningful Black urban political empowerment.[35] The main question centered on which paths would be taken. For Hamilton and

Carmichael, the urban ethnic succession model was the wrong path. In their framing, Black empowerment "does not mean merely putting Black faces into office. Black visibility is not Black Power. Most of the Black politicians around the country today are not examples of Black Power. The power must be that of a community, and emanate from there. . . . The Black politicians must stop being representatives of 'downtown' machines, whatever the cost might be in terms of lost patronage and holiday handouts."[36]

Not all Black Power activists embraced Carmichael and Hamilton's approach; some believed *Black Power* and other work by Black political scientists drained the concept of its radical and transformative potential.[37] For many progressive activists, Black urban empowerment entailed the development of new forms—new imaginings, insurgencies, and instantiations—that would bring about a just and emancipatory city.

The Black Power Urbanism Archive

By the mid-1970s, Black Power Urbanism—never fully articulated as such during its heyday—had been recast as "grassroots" or progressive urban politics.[38] The "Blackness" of this right to the city—however defined—that had given it its impetus had been shorn away. The fact that this was done so easily is in part because the most consistent and detailed articulations of what Black Power Urbanism meant rested in the meeting notes, reports, and platforms generated by the many Black Power conferences held at the local, state, and national level. The historian Komozi Woodard calls these Black Power convenings the "Modern Black Convention Movement."[39] As these activists and their platforms receded into history and the urban crisis of the 1970s and 1980s took center stage, their focus on the city as the center of Black life and liberation was forgotten.

These platforms form the core of the Black Power archive (or method) that this book draws upon.[40] Rather than expressions of empty rhetoric and failed political strategy, these platforms are important articulations of an emergent set of robust imaginings and concrete ideas around what a just city for Black people and others could and should look like.[41] In addition to these platforms, other evidence of Black Power Urbanism can be discerned from widely distributed information issued by the Black Panther Intercommunal News Services or smaller local newspapers such as the *Flatlands*, published in Oakland during the late 1960s. The Black Power archive consists not only of manifestos and essays but also of plays, songs, and other written and/or oral work, in addition to things such as the compelling images created by the visual artist Emory Douglass or photos, posters, leaflets, and other ephemera.[42] Black Power Urbanism was taken up and documented via organizations such as the Institute for the Black World, journals such as the *Black Scholar* (and briefly, *Negro Digest/Black World*), and dozens of other smaller publications. A new class of professionals would take up the mantle of Black Power (and Black Power Urbanism) via new professional associations, from educators (the National Association of Afro-American Educators) and social workers (the National Association of Black Social Workers) to police officers (the Afro-American Patrolmen's League and the Council of Police Societies). Professionals organized new spaces to transform and rebuild the Black city, including architects and planners working in community architecture and advocacy planning organizations such as the Architects' Renewal Committee in Harlem (ARCH); Washington, DC's The New Thing Art and Architecture Center; and scores of local activists like Newark's Junius Williams, who led local community planning organizations.[43]

Meanwhile the instantiation of Black Power Urbanism could be seen in activists repurposing public spaces like Oakland's DeFremery Park as places where Black Power theorization and praxis lined up in the distribution of free food. Activists also sought to bring power back to the people through land, looking to recapture vacant areas created by urban renewal and dispossession and turn them into playgrounds, urban gardens, or spaces for public art.[44] Nascent Black Studies programs at colleges and universities, as well as a burgeoning network of independent Black primary and high schools created by parent and activists, were also places where Black Power Urbanism was manifested, and in the former case, institutionalized.[45] Finally, and most compellingly, the Black Power archives come from the prison writings of those targeted and imprisoned (and sometimes killed) by state repression.

Using these materials, I argue that Black Power Urbanism was a nascent "political order"—a set of politics, institutions, organizations, and understandings—that linked together disparate elements of Black urban communities (at the local, state, and national level) and their allies. While Black Power Urbanism uneasily presumed an internal solidarity, organizers and supporters also recognized the inherent tensions within it (acknowledged by phrases such as "unity without uniformity"). Multiple tensions ranged from class position/interests and gender and sexuality to connection to/rejection of electoral politics. The Black Power archives reveal that Black Power Urbanism was very much an ongoing political project, despite the unresolved tensions and bitter debates evoked in the conventions. The work of Black Power Urbanism happened in the streets, in the actions taken by community activists on behalf of and in partnership with a range of people within the Black community, including parents, students, public housing residents, women receiving welfare, the unemployed, factory workers, and members of gangs. Local institutions, organizations, neighborhoods, schools, parks, and other spaces became new geographies of repair and reconstitution in the quest to build a just and emancipatory city.

From 1963 to 1974, dozens of "Black Power" conferences, meetings, rallies, and other convenings were held across the nation and elsewhere, organized by local groups and student activists (see table 2.1). The most prominent of these Black Power conferences included Detroit's Grassroots Leadership Conference in 1963, where Malcolm X gave his famous "Bullet or the Ballot (Message to the Grassroots)" speech, the Powell-Carmichael Washington Black Power Planning Conference of 1966, and the groundbreaking Newark Black Power Conference in 1967.[46]

The Philadelphia Black Power Conference was held in 1968 following a year of political turbulence and amid increasingly violent confrontations between the Black Panthers and other groups of Black Power supporters and Black nationalists, as well as growing repression from state forces (federal, state, and local). Four years later, the 1972 Gary Convention—the largest gathering of its kind—was

TABLE 2.1 Black Power conventions, 1965–1974

YEAR	NATIONAL	LOCAL/NON-US
1963		Detroit's Grassroots Leadership Conference
1966	Washington Black Power Planning Conference	*Black Power and Its Challenges* (Berkeley)
1967	National Conference on Black Power *National Conference for New Politics*	
1968	Philadelphia Black Power Conference	Newark Black Political Convention Black People in Canada Conference & Montreal Congress of Black Writers*
1969	Regional International Black Power Conference (Bermuda)* *Black Panthers' United Front Against Fascism (UFAF) Conference*	Newark Black and Puerto Rican Convention *National Black Economic Development Conference*
1970	*Revolutionary People's Constitutional Convention (RPCC)* (Philadelphia)	
1971		National Conference on the Rights of Black People in Britain*
1972	National Black Political Convention (Gary) *Black Community Survival Conference*	
1974	Pan-African Congress	

Note: Conventions in italics are either aligned with BPP or with left/majority-white organizers. Asterisk (*) denotes international conference.

held. In between these major national conventions, which embraced—often uneasily—a wide swath of Black political activists and leaders, were a number of smaller national and local Black political meetings. These smaller conventions reflected the breadth of the Black Power coalition.[47] Other Black Power conferences occurred within or in contention with other sponsoring organizations such as the "Black Power and Its Challenges" conference sponsored by Students for a Democratic Society (SDS) in 1966. Finally, Black Power conferences (and the movement) were not limited to the United States. In 1969, organizers attempted to live up to the internationalist commitments of the Black Power movement by convening the 1969 Regional International Black Power Conference in Bermuda.[48] This conference was bookended by the Black Power conference held in Montreal, Canada in 1968 and the National Conference on the Rights of Black People in Britain, held in London in 1971.

Categorizing Black Power Urbanism's Manifestations

Seen holistically, these platforms encapsulate the political and policy aspirations of Black Power Urbanism and constitute a new understanding of race, space, and power. For example, the planning committee for the Newark Black Power conference reflected the complexity and evolution of "Black Power" itself, including movement theorists, activists, elected officials, and ordinary people on the ground who could agree on the unifying term of "Black Power" but would disagree about what "Black Power" actually meant. These differences were reflected in the 1967 Black Power Convention, which laid out a vision of Black Power rooted in the material reality of Newark and cities like it. It included fourteen workshops ranging from "The City and Black People," to "Black Power Through Black Politics," "Black Power Through Economic Development," and "Co-operation and Alliances."[49]

Newark was a key site for local Black Power imaginings. In 1968, two Baraka-allied groups, the United Brothers and Committee for Unified Newark, convened the Newark Black Convention as the "first step in the Black People's efforts to gain self-government by 1970."[50] The Newark platform of 1968 was explicit in its Black Power urbanist focus, calling for "a commuter tax on nonresidents, opposition to a proposed interstate highway that would divide standing black neighborhoods, community control of schools, and the development of community-police relations programs." The Newark Black and Puerto Rican Convention of 1969 took up not only the specificities of place—Newark as a post-urban renewal, post-urban rebellion city—but also the more emancipatory aspects. The inclusion of

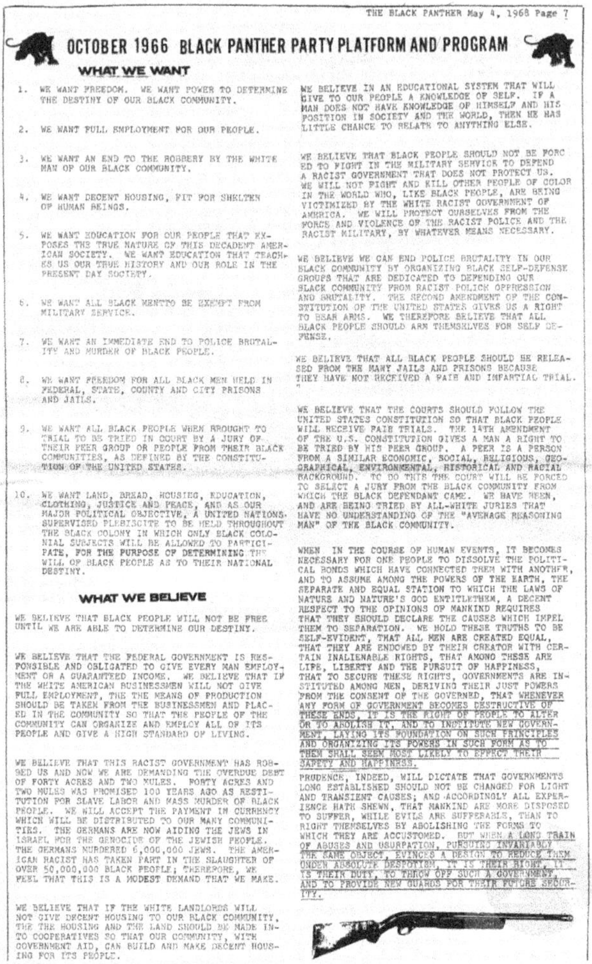

THE BLACK PANTHER May 4, 1968 Page 7

OCTOBER 1966 BLACK PANTHER PARTY PLATFORM AND PROGRAM

WHAT WE WANT

1. WE WANT FREEDOM. WE WANT POWER TO DETERMINE THE DESTINY OF OUR BLACK COMMUNITY.

2. WE WANT FULL EMPLOYMENT FOR OUR PEOPLE.

3. WE WANT AN END TO THE ROBBERY BY THE WHITE MAN OF OUR BLACK COMMUNITY.

4. WE WANT DECENT HOUSING, FIT FOR SHELTER OF HUMAN BEINGS.

5. WE WANT EDUCATION FOR OUR PEOPLE THAT EXPOSES THE TRUE NATURE OF THIS DECADENT AMERICAN SOCIETY. WE WANT EDUCATION THAT TEACHES US OUR TRUE HISTORY AND OUR ROLE IN THE PRESENT DAY SOCIETY.

6. WE WANT ALL BLACK MENTTO BE EXEMPT FROM MILITARY SERVICE.

7. WE WANT AN IMMEDIATE END TO POLICE BRUTALITY AND MURDER OF BLACK PEOPLE.

8. WE WANT FREEDOM FOR ALL BLACK MEN HELD IN FEDERAL, STATE, COUNTY AND CITY PRISONS AND JAILS.

9. WE WANT ALL BLACK PEOPLE WHEN BROUGHT TO TRIAL TO BE TRIED IN COURT BY A JURY OF THEIR PEER GROUP OR PEOPLE FROM THEIR BLACK COMMUNITIES, AS DEFINED BY THE CONSTITUTION OF THE UNITED STATES.

10. WE WANT LAND, BREAD, HOUSING, EDUCATION, CLOTHING, JUSTICE AND PEACE, AND AS OUR MAJOR POLITICAL OBJECTIVE, A UNITED NATIONS-SUPERVISED PLEBISCITE TO BE HELD THROUGHOUT THE BLACK COLONY IN WHICH ONLY BLACK COLONIAL SUBJECTS WILL BE ALLOWED TO PARTICIPATE, FOR THE PURPOSE OF DETERMINING THE WILL OF BLACK PEOPLE AS TO THEIR NATIONAL DESTINY.

WHAT WE BELIEVE

WE BELIEVE THAT BLACK PEOPLE WILL NOT BE FREE UNTIL WE ARE ABLE TO DETERMINE OUR DESTINY.

WE BELIEVE THAT THE FEDERAL GOVERNMENT IS RESPONSIBLE AND OBLIGATED TO GIVE EVERY MAN EMPLOYMENT OR A GUARANTEED INCOME. WE BELIEVE THAT IF THE WHITE AMERICAN BUSINESSMEN WILL NOT GIVE FULL EMPLOYMENT, THE THE MEANS OF PRODUCTION SHOULD BE TAKEN FROM THE BUSINESSMEN AND PLACED IN THE COMMUNITY SO THAT THE PEOPLE OF THE COMMUNITY CAN ORGANIZE AND EMPLOY ALL OF ITS PEOPLE AND GIVE A HIGH STANDARD OF LIVING.

WE BELIEVE THAT THIS RACIST GOVERNMENT HAS ROBBED US AND NOW WE ARE DEMANDING THE OVERDUE DEBT OF FORTY ACRES AND TWO MULES. FORTY ACRES AND TWO MULES WAS PROMISED 100 YEARS AGO AS RESTITUTION FOR SLAVE LABOR AND MASS MURDER OF BLACK PEOPLE. WE WILL ACCEPT THE PAYMENT IN CURRENCY WHICH WILL BE DISTRIBUTED TO OUR MANY COMMUNITIES. THE GERMANS ARE NOW AIDING THE JEWS IN ISRAEL FOR THE GENOCIDE OF THE JEWISH PEOPLE. THE GERMANS MURDERED 6,000,000 JEWS. THE AMERICAN RACIST HAS TAKEN PART IN THE SLAUGHTER OF OVER 50,000,000 BLACK PEOPLE; THEREFORE, WE FEEL THAT THIS IS A MODEST DEMAND THAT WE MAKE.

WE BELIEVE THAT IF THE WHITE LANDLORDS WILL NOT GIVE DECENT HOUSING TO OUR BLACK COMMUNITY, THE THE HOUSING AND THE LAND SHOULD BE MADE INTO COOPERATIVES SO THAT OUR COMMUNITY, WITH GOVERNMENT AID, CAN BUILD AND MAKE DECENT HOUSING FOR ITS PEOPLE.

WE BELIEVE IN AN EDUCATIONAL SYSTEM THAT WILL GIVE TO OUR PEOPLE A KNOWLEDGE OF SELF. IF A MAN DOES NOT HAVE KNOWLEDGE OF HIMSELF AND HIS POSITION IN SOCIETY AND THE WORLD, THEN HE HAS LITTLE CHANCE TO RELATE TO ANYTHING ELSE.

WE BELIEVE THAT BLACK PEOPLE SHOULD NOT BE FORCED TO FIGHT IN THE MILITARY SERVICE TO DEFEND A RACIST GOVERNMENT THAT DOES NOT PROTECT US. WE WILL NOT FIGHT AND KILL OTHER PEOPLE OF COLOR IN THE WORLD WHO, LIKE BLACK PEOPLE, ARE BEING VICTIMIZED BY THE WHITE RACIST GOVERNMENT OF AMERICA. WE WILL PROTECT OURSELVES FROM THE FORCE AND VIOLENCE OF THE RACIST POLICE AND THE RACIST MILITARY, BY WHATEVER MEANS NECESSARY.

WE BELIEVE WE CAN END POLICE BRUTALITY IN OUR BLACK COMMUNITY BY ORGANIZING BLACK SELF-DEFENSE GROUPS THAT ARE DEDICATED TO DEFENDING OUR BLACK COMMUNITY FROM RACIST POLICE OPPRESSION AND BRUTALITY. THE SECOND AMENDMENT OF THE CONSTITUTION OF THE UNITED STATES GIVES US A RIGHT TO BEAR ARMS. WE THEREFORE BELIEVE THAT ALL BLACK PEOPLE SHOULD ARM THEMSELVES FOR SELF DEFENSE.

WE BELIEVE THAT ALL BLACK PEOPLE SHOULD BE RELEASED FROM THE MANY JAILS AND PRISONS BECAUSE THEY HAVE NOT RECEIVED A FAIR AND IMPARTIAL TRIAL.

WE BELIEVE THAT THE COURTS SHOULD FOLLOW THE UNITED STATES CONSTITUTION SO THAT BLACK PEOPLE WILL RECEIVE FAIR TRIALS. THE 14TH AMENDMENT OF THE U.S. CONSTITUTION GIVES A MAN A RIGHT TO BE TRIED BY HIS PEER GROUP. A PEER IS A PERSON FROM A SIMILAR ECONOMIC, SOCIAL, RELIGIOUS, GEOGRAPHICAL, ENVIRONMENTAL, HISTORICAL AND RACIAL BACKGROUND. TO DO THIS THE COURT WILL BE FORCED TO SELECT A JURY FROM THE BLACK COMMUNITY FROM WHICH THE BLACK DEFENDANT CAME. WE HAVE BEEN, AND ARE BEING TRIED BY ALL-WHITE JURIES THAT HAVE NO UNDERSTANDING OF THE "AVERAGE REASONING MAN" OF THE BLACK COMMUNITY.

WHEN IN THE COURSE OF HUMAN EVENTS, IT BECOMES NECESSARY FOR ONE PEOPLE TO DISSOLVE THE POLITICAL BONDS WHICH HAVE CONNECTED THEM WITH ANOTHER, AND TO ASSUME AMONG THE POWERS OF THE EARTH, THE SEPARATE AND EQUAL STATION TO WHICH THE LAWS OF NATURE AND NATURE'S GOD ENTITLETHEM, A DECENT RESPECT TO THE OPINIONS OF MANKIND REQUIRES THAT THEY SHOULD DECLARE THE CAUSES WHICH IMPEL THEM TO SEPARATION. WE HOLD THESE TRUTHS TO BE SELF-EVIDENT, THAT ALL MEN ARE CREATED EQUAL, THAT THEY ARE ENDOWED BY THEIR CREATOR WITH CERTAIN INALIENABLE RIGHTS, THAT AMONG THESE ARE LIFE, LIBERTY AND THE PURSUIT OF HAPPINESS, THAT TO SECURE THESE RIGHTS, GOVERNMENTS ARE INSTITUTED AMONG MEN, DERIVING THEIR JUST POWERS FROM THE CONSENT OF THE GOVERNED, THAT WHENEVER ANY FORM OF GOVERNMENT BECOMES DESTRUCTIVE OF THESE ENDS, IT IS THE RIGHT OF PEOPLE TO ALTER OR TO ABOLISH IT, AND TO INSTITUTE NEW GOVERNMENT, LAYING ITS FOUNDATION ON SUCH PRINCIPLES AND ORGANIZING ITS POWERS IN SUCH FORM AS TO THEM SHALL SEEM MOST LIKELY TO EFFECT THEIR SAFETY AND HAPPINESS.

PRUDENCE, INDEED, WILL DICTATE THAT GOVERNMENTS LONG ESTABLISHED SHOULD NOT BE CHANGED FOR LIGHT AND TRANSIENT CAUSES; AND ACCORDINGLY ALL EXPERIENCE HATH SHEWN, THAT MANKIND ARE MORE DISPOSED TO SUFFER, WHILE EVILS ARE SUFFERABLE, THAN TO RIGHT THEMSELVES BY ABOLISHING THE FORMS TO WHICH THEY ARE ACCUSTOMED. BUT WHEN A LONG TRAIN OF ABUSES AND USURPATION, PURSUING INVARIABLY THE SAME OBJECT, EVINCES A DESIGN TO REDUCE THEM UNDER ABSOLUTE DESPOTISM, IT IS THEIR RIGHT, IT IS THEIR DUTY, TO THROW OFF SUCH A GOVERNMENT, AND TO PROVIDE NEW GUARDS FOR THEIR FUTURE SECURITY.

FIGURE 2.4A. Black Panther Party Ten-Point Program

Source: Black Panther Party, Ten-Point Program, Online Archive of California, UCLA Special Collections.

Newark's Puerto Rican community was not only a recognition of demographic reality and political necessity, but also of the idea that Black Power Urbanism meant a just city for all racialized and minoritized communities.

The city of Oakland and the Black Panther Party were also key ideational and organizational sites for the development of Black Power Urbanism. The Black Panther Party, as James Tyner argues, articulated a "politics of space."[51] "Defending the ghetto" meant not only confronting the police, but also addressing the political, cultural, and socio-spatial effects of exclusion and dispossession

FIGURE 2.4B. The 1967 Newark Conference: Manifestos and resolutions

Source: Nathan Wright, *Black Power Manifesto and Resolutions* (The Conference, 1967).

while also encouraging spatial consciousness and empowerment. Most notable in terms of the BPP's politics of space was the development of its Ten-Point Program, which affirmed the emerging tenets of Black Power Urbanism (see figures 2.4A and 2.4B). The ten points describe not just a generic political program, but a series of imaginings and ideas that were rooted in the specificities of the political and geographic space of the post–"Negro removal" city.

In addition to the Ten-Point Program were the sixty or so community survival programs put forward in various fashions by the Black Panthers.[52] These programs ranged from those that were well-known, such as the free ambulance, free breakfast for children, and free groceries for families to those that were less well-known but struck at the heart of everyday poverty: free clothing, furniture, and shoes. Programs like free busing to prisons and free commissaries for prisoners addressed the carceral state that enveloped Black communities. At the same time, the survival programs attempted to "defend the ghetto" from the brutal policing that plagued Black communities. In addition to their more well-known police patrols were the development of grassroots efforts to create new systems of community safety such as the Seniors Against a Fearful Environment (SAFE) program. The BPP also attended to health needs, offering dental care and encouraging a sustained focus on sickle cell anemia research.[53]

The Black Panthers' Ten-Point Program and Ture's and Hamilton's *Black Power* are just two of the objects in the Black Power archives that encapsulate the political and policy aspirations of Black Power Urbanism. Elements of the Black Panthers program relating to freedom, employment, housing, education, police brutality, the justice system, and racialized incarceration reflected the imaginings of a host of "new forms." Key to these imaginings was community control and reparative justice, with America's Black-majority cities (in the words of funk group Parliament) standing in as the symbolic and substantive replacement for the unfulfilled promise of forty acres and a mule. At its inception, the concept of community control did not mean simply "Black faces in high places," as it does today. It meant mass community participation, not only in administration but also in form and meaning. The terrain covered by Black Power Urbanism (as discerned by the Black Power archives) was quite vast and is not quite captured in the table below (see table 2.2). It ranges from reparations, sovereignty, abolition/decarceration, social welfare, health, jobs, economic development, and cultural development to community development and planning. It also includes housing, education, and policing—the three policy areas focused on in this book.

TABLE 2.2   Categorizing the multiple dimensions of Black Power Urbanism

IMAGININGS	IDEAS	INSURGENCIES	INSTANTIATION
Reparations	"40 acres and a mule"	Manifesto	Community development organization
Abolition/ decarceration	Fair policing	Protests	Youth diversion
	Impartial and fair justice system		Community justice councils
	Sentencing reform		Prisoners' rights programs
			Prison bus trips
			Legal clinics
Social/community care	Ending punitive welfare	"Welfare rights" activism	Welfare bill of rights/ due process
	Childcare		
"A chicken in every bag"	Food security	Buying clubs	Head Start
	Personal dignity: clothing, shoes		Black United Fund
			Free breakfast
			Food buying cooperative
			Clothing production

(Continued)

TABLE 2.2   (Continued)

IMAGININGS	IDEAS	INSURGENCIES	INSTANTIATION
Jobs/employment "We want full employment for our people"	"Local jobs for local people" Jobs for men/jobs for youth Community employment	Protest work sites BPP Employ- ment Referral Service Public employment	Minority set-asides/ municipal contracts Affirmative action Summer youth employment Comprehensive Employ- ment and Training Act (CETA) Community employment programs
Economic development "The black ghetto as internal colony"	Community-owned business Black capitalism	Activist- sponsored businesses	Community development corporations Corporate "urban coali- tion" partnerships Commuter tax
Community architecture/ planning "Building the just city"	Advocacy planning Black architects/builders	Local planning/ counter- planning Advocacy planning Community architecture Reprogramming public space	Architects' Commu- nity Design Center of Newark ARCH Architecture/planning as Black business DeFremery Park and Recreation Center Kuzuri-Kijiji
Health "Health for the people"	Community health clinics Drug treatment centers Lead paint Sickle cell anemia Dental care Free ambulance Optometry	Protests Sit-ins Education campaigns People's Free Medical Clin- ics (PFMCs)	Community clinics/com- munity hospitals Lead paint legislation Sickle cell "main- streamed" into science/research Local drug treatment programs

Calls for reparations and justice have always been a long-standing element of the Black freedom struggle. The Black Panthers' Ten-Point Program built upon this historic call by focusing their attention on the ongoing processes of dispossession and theft of Black people's labor and wealth via "Negro removal," as well as on the everyday realities of the ghetto economy in which exploitative prices for rent, food, clothing, and other necessities increased the difficulties of poverty, sustaining the saying that its "expensive to be poor." Thus the Ten-Point Program declared that "We Want An End to the Robbery By the Capitalists of Our Black Community." The Panthers were not alone in calling for reparations to address past as well as ongoing inequality and dispossession. At the first National Black Economic Development Conference held in Detroit in April 1969 and then at New York City's Riverside Church in May, James Forman delivered a "Black Manifesto" "demanding the overdue debt of forty acres and a mule" and making the case to the Christian church and to the white public that reparations were a fundamental necessity for any meaningful attempt to build a just city for Black Americans.[54] Forman's delivery of the speech at Riverside Church reflected the spirit of insurgency: Forman refused to stop his speech even as the senior pastor attempted to drown him out with the church's organ.

Calls for abolition and decarceration were also key to a reset of Black urban life. Black Americans, particularly Black men, were ensnared in an unjust system of brutal policing, an unfair and systematically racist criminal justice system, and highs levels of incarceration (even before the mass incarceration era of the 1980s). The repression and imprisonment of national and local Black Power activists highlighted these long-standing inequities. The Black Panthers' demands—"we want all Black people when brought to trial to be tried in court by a jury of their peer group or people from their Black communities" and "we want freedom for all Black men held in federal, state, county and city prisons and jails"—reflected the vision of a just city.[55] The instantiations of these imaginings and ideas were broad. They ranged from local communities creating the precursors to youth-led restorative justice councils to the establishment of local legal clinics, especially for help with evictions. The BPP sponsored a free busing to prisons program enabling families and friends to visit their loved ones who were incarcerated far away from Black communities. The party also sponsored a "Free Commissary for Prisoners Program" that "provide[d] inmates with basic necessities such as toilet articles, clothes, and shoes." This program was designed to defy a system in which "the prisoners' right to live and function like human beings has been cruelly relegated to the level of 'privileges' by the state."[56] These were highly prescient understandings given the massive expansion of the carceral system in California (and other states) during the 1980s and 1990s in what Ruth Wilson Gilmore calls the "golden gulag."[57]

Black Power Urbanism's demand for self-determination and self-reliance was inextricably linked to what activists argued was the precarious, "colonial"-like position of many poor and working-class urban Blacks. As Hamilton and Carmichael note, "virtually all of the money earned by merchants and exploiters of the black ghetto leaves those communities." Not only did resources leave the Black communities, but as James and Grace Lee Boggs argue, Black workers in an emergent age of urban deindustrialization and "cybernetics" were in danger of becoming an excess population.[58] Meaningful jobs and employment opportunities were needed in order to build and support Black communities and provide purpose and dignity to individuals.

From the beginning of the urban renewal era onward, Black workers and activists protested white-only work sites and continuously pushed to open up discriminatory trade unions. Black Power Urbanism continued these efforts but also emphasized the need to create jobs and opportunities within the community. Building housing, engaging in communal care and community safety, and providing schooling and education were all means for redeveloping and redirecting human capital and resources within Black communities. In addition, Black Power urbanists considered more concrete forms of Black employment, supported (and co-opted) small businesses—at least symbolically—through Nixon's Black capitalism program, and created community development corporations as an alternative mechanism for more directed and concerted efforts at local job creation.[59] Local groups also started small scale-business ventures: shoe and clothing manufacturing, restaurants, and bookstores.

"A chicken in every bag" symbolized the Black Panthers' approach to communal care. Hunger was one of the ways in which Black life had been demeaned and dispossessed (see figure 2.5).

The Panthers' free breakfast programs for children and free groceries for those in need addressed this fundamental lack. Communal care also extended to early childhood services including safe, affordable childcare, with the Head Start program as one of the instantiations of this Black Power imagining. Communal care, especially around issues of what we now call food security, was also part of Black Power urbanist imagining. Local groups started food buying clubs, opened cooperative grocery stores, and established urban food gardens in vacant lots. Communal care also recognized the intersectionality of community needs. Thus, the Panthers and other Black Power–allied groups endorsed the welfare rights movement, affirming that "we recognize the role of the National Welfare Rights Organization" and "we call for ten million dollars to assist in the organization of welfare recipients." Indeed, activism in the welfare rights movement was one way that women entered into Black Power urbanist spaces.[60]

Communal care also extended to health care, with the BPP asserting its belief "that the government must provide, free of charge, for the people, health facilities that will not only treat our illnesses, most of which are a result of our oppression, but that will also develop preventative medical programs to guarantee our future survival."[61] This call for care led to the provision of services to those in need via free people's health clinics that supplied dental as well as optometry services. Black Power Urbanism was also responsible for the creation of emergency

FIGURE 2.5. "10,000 Free Bags of Groceries" flier advertising the 1972 Black Community Survival Conference and People's Free Food Program, with promotion of the Black Panther Party's Angela Davis

Source: Collection of the Smithsonian National Museum of African American History and Culture, https://nmaahc.si.edu/object/nmaahc_2013.46.10.

medical "street units," the direct ancestors of today's EMT services, which are now a near-standard service offered by most local governments. Local medical institutions were pressed to provide medical care to populations that had been ignored. Indeed, in the case of Newark, the rebellion against a proposed new medical center would lead to a groundbreaking community agreement in which the medical center would be obligated to provided health care as well as employment to NewArk's Black and Brown citizens.

Health care for the people meant thinking about new ways to tackle threats such as the drug epidemic (especially heroin) flooding the streets of Black communities. The 1972 Platform asserted the belief that "mass health education and research programs must be developed to give all Black and oppressed people access to advanced scientific and medical information, so we may provide ourselves with proper medical attention and care."[62]

Visions of what a healthy community entailed resulted in treatment centers staffed by and for Black people, which in turn were seen as an alternative to incarceration for addiction. Meanwhile groups like the Young Lords and the Black Panthers were developing innovative treatments like acupuncture, now accepted by mainstream medicine.[63] The fact that the origin of these treatments was rooted in the Black Power and other emancipatory movements was, until recently, largely forgotten. New imaginings also meant forcing the medical profession and biomedical sciences to recognize and address sickle cell anemia, a disease that primary affects African Americans. And finally, community health meant addressing the urban environment and the toxic spaces into which Black and Brown residents had been forced and pushing for recognition of the dangers of lead paint and asthma as especially pernicious results of urban environmental racism.

The physical construction of a just city was another element central to Black Power urbanist imaginings that was taken up not only by professional architects and planners, but also by local citizen planners and community groups. For Black Power urbanist architects, urban renewal's impact on Black communities had been nothing short of catastrophic. As the Black Panthers' community survival program asked: "Where's the land? In a crowded inner city, where does one find or create open space? The immediate and most obvious answer is perhaps seldom considered or seen for its potential use—the blighted, unsightly vacant lots that dot our cities. These lots can be acquired from their absentee landlords and developed into much-needed miniparks, tot lots, community gardens, and cultural or recreation centers. This provides future job development possibilities as well."[64]

Organizations like ARCH emerged to reprogram and design spaces that promoted the "use value" of Black communities and that celebrated and encouraged Black placemaking and communal life.[65] Planners—both those that were formally trained and grassroots practitioners—argued that self-determination and community control over how Black spaces were developed could only come about through the replacement of "white planners with Black people" and via a "rejection of all the white programs and proposals that are not designed in the best interests of Black people and their community."[66] At times these plans for building a new just city went beyond the ghetto and approached the utopian, such as Floyd McKissick's Soul City in North Carolina.[67]

Whether these designs were built and plans were realized depended on mobilizing a new kind of insurgency. In 1966, "Fighting the Blight Or Urban Resistance to Authoritarian Social Change," was circulated to Newark community groups mobilizing to fight against the city's medical school urban renewal project.[68] This massive 150-plus acre project would serve as one of the sparks for the 1967 rebellion. The brochure offered instructions for how to engage not just in advocacy planning, but also in resistance. Instructions included not only refusing to testify that an area was blighted, but also to attack the arbitrary nature of the designation itself. Opponents were encouraged to point out the political nature of these renewal projects, "expose the discriminatory nature of these plans," and "demand to see all of the evidence." Building a just city meant mounting a resistance and gaining power; it meant "slow[ing] down the steamroller and the bulldozer, to gain time, to force changes in what's going on. . . . And hopefully, through proper work and organization, to gain power—real power—to sit in the right places and make the right decisions for the people who've always been on the short end."[69]

The Pillars of BPU: Housing, Education, and Policing

Where a Black person resided was subject to the interplay between Black place-making on the one hand, and on the other, the white political and institutional structures that determined where, how, and in what conditions Black people could live. Education (or schooling)—whether for empowerment or for economic sustenance and advancement—was linked to where one lived, but where one lived also determined who taught, what was taught, and what educational resources were available. Finally, issues of safety (and their role in enforcing the urban/metropolitan color line) impinged on the day-to-day quality of life of Black residents where brutal policing (likened to the techniques of an occupying army) made the actions of "living while Black" fraught with anger and fear.[70]

The Black Power urbanist understanding of housing was rooted in a Black spatial imaginary based on "use value not exchange value" (see table 2.3) in which community members had the right to live in safe, clean, and welcoming homes. As Bertha Gilkey, a public housing tenant activist from Saint Louis, stated, "We're a neighborhood, not a project." Even residents of public housing had the right to live in a "community, not the 'projects.'"[71]

These imaginings over the right to housing generated ideas about how to bring them about. Thus, the Black Panther community survival programs argued that if "the White Landlords will not give decent housing to our Black community, then the housing and the land should be made into cooperatives so that our community, with government aid, can build and make decent housing for its people."[72] The Black Power urbanist strategy stimulated a range of ideas (both old and new), including instituting tenant protections such as rent control/stabilization, code enforcement, and eviction protections. Other proposed policies included the establishment of community land trusts, cooperative and/or

TABLE 2.3   Housing, education and policing: Ideas, insurgencies and instantiations

IMAGININGS	IDEAS	INSURGENCIES	INSTANTIATIONS
Housing "We want decent housing fit for the shelter of human beings"	Cooperative housing Tenant management of public housing Community-owned and -built housing Affordable housing Homes for large families	Rent strikes Tenant takeover/ squatting Anti-eviction protests	Pest control Community tools chest/community home maintenance Tenant/eviction legislation Community planned/ controlled affordable housing Tenant management Rent control laws Tenant protection/ eviction laws Community Reinvestment Act Community land trust
Education "(Re)education for empowerment, not miseducation"	Community control not integration/busing Cultural competence, not just credentials Education as knowledge and praxis Culturally relevant education	Parent takeovers Student strikes Disruption of board meetings PTA activism Black Studies campaigns (high school/ college) School decentralization protests	Culturally relevant/ sensitive administrators/teachers/ paraprofessionals Black whole child development programs Decentralized administration Freedom/liberation/ community schools Independent Black schools Black Studies programs (high school/ college) Black community colleges AAVE/Ebonics pedagogy

(Continued)

TABLE 2.3   (Continued)

IMAGININGS	IDEAS	INSURGENCIES	INSTANTIATIONS
Policing/commu- nity safety "We want an immediate end to police brutal- ity and the mur- der of black people"	Armed, self-defense Community patrols Eliminate police brutality/ harassment Fix arbitrary sentencing and punishment Stop spread of narcotics and other drugs (war on Black communities)	Safety patrols (SAFE) Creation/enforcement campaigns "Get clean campaigns"	Black cops and Black leadership Review board (accountability) Professionalization/ training Local reconciliation "Youth" boards Residency requirements Neighborhood watch Drug (marijuana) decriminalization Prisoner's rights Juvenile justice diver- sion programs Legal aid

resident-controlled housing, and anti-redlining/credit access reforms so that the freedom to improve and stay, or to leave, would be available to all. Rent strikes, tenant takeover of buildings, and anti-eviction protests were all used as insurgency methods to push for these concrete changes. The instantiation of these new ideas was impressive. Across many majority-Black spaces, including the four case study cities, Black Power Urbanism saw the enactment or adoption of the following new ideas: tenant protection legislation including rent control and eviction rights laws, the enactment and enforcement of the Community Reinvestment Act, and the adoption in a few scattered places of community land trusts.[73]

Education was one of the most politically explosive issues for Black Power Urbanism. The position paper on education submitted to the 1968 Black Power Conference stated that "the present educational system, dominated and controlled by racist concepts and values is dehumanizing. The present educational system has failed to achieve its own goals which include literacy and the development of marketable skills for the masses of American youth. The only viable solution to the problem facing Black youth is that the Black community must exercise the power to control the education processes through local community control." The issue of community control over pedagogy was most famously aired in New York City's Ocean Hill-Brownsville controversy, where in May 1969 Black and Puerto Rican community activists, educators, and parents battled with the city's teachers union (the United Federation of Teachers) over the firing of nineteen white teachers by the new community board.[74] However, concerns over who should teach Black and Brown students, and what they should teach, had already been an issue of long-standing concern to many local activists and parents.[75] Indeed, East Orange is notable in that Black community mobilization had limited the city's attempts to thoroughly segregate its public school system in the early 1910s.[76]

Community control over education meant not only control over *who* taught African American students, but also *what* was taught to students. It meant increasing the number of Black teachers, specialists, and administrators, and expanding the boundaries of education and educators to include Head Start nurseries, classroom paraprofessionals, and after-school programs. It also meant controlling the content of education—from providing traditional classroom approaches to offering explicitly Afrocentric curricula in some schools.

But community control also meant control over who *maintained and built* those educational facilities: control of construction jobs and contracts was part of ensuring that the jobs and income derived from the city's inhabitants stayed within the Black community (broadly conceived). Thus, Black urban leaders continued their push to open up exclusionary trade unions and protective services unions to minority men and later to all women. Minority contracting set-asides were seen as recirculating scarce city dollars back into the "Black city" rather than into the white-flight suburbs. Although both then and now many deemed Black control over the education of Black children as self-serving "patronage" and "corruption"—in terms of teaching, control over administration and funding, and control over pay and performance evaluation—Black Power urbanists saw this control as essential to community development and uplift. Qualified and culturally competent Black teachers not only addressed the special needs of Black children in a racially unequal society, but their income, higher levels of education, and professional organizations provided valuable scaffolding for community empowerment and mobilization.

Control over school operations—from funding to expenditures to hiring—was seen as inextricably linked to issues of pedagogy. Control of over funding determined who was hired and what resources were available. As Eve Ewing has argued, schools are foundational elements of Black communities and Black placemaking.[77] Community control meant having a decisive say in pedagogy and operations, in the selection and naming of schools, and in the schools' design and construction. As evident in the cases of Newark and East Palo Alto, parental control of schools not only meant controlling individual schools and transforming the school board, it also meant creating a network of "liberated schools" that expressed the priorities of Black Power by flying the Pan-African flag, renaming themselves in honor of Black freedom fighters like Marcus Garvey and Harriet Tubman, or taking more explicitly Black Power names such as the African Free School or Nairobi Day School. Schools could be designed as places of connection and inquiry like Newark's Springfield Avenue Community School or East Orange's Storefront Middle School, or they could be designed as proto-carceral spaces like New York City's windowless I. S. 201, an intermediate school that was designed to be a "fortified refug[e] from a decaying city."[78] This New York City school was designed without windows in order to encourage racial integration, aid in bolstering student concentration, and prevent vandalism and broken windows. However, the design was so egregiously bad that integration attempts failed and Black and Brown parents attempted to seize control of the school so they could at least hire a Black principal and staff equal to the needs of the students. The controversy over these attempts added fuel to New York City's increasingly bitter and polarizing fight over community control in Brooklyn's Ocean Hill-Brownsville School District.[79]

"Defending the ghetto," or the realm of policing and community safety, was the third and most contested of the pillars of Black Power Urbanism. The Black Panthers were clear and direct about their demands: "We want an immediate end to police brutality and the murder of Black people."[80] Police forces had always been an important mechanism in creating and enforcing the urban color line. Black Power Urbanism envisioned a world in which the occupying forces of the urban police were removed from Black neighborhoods and replaced with alternative modes of community safety. Today, we would call the more radical of these imaginings "police abolition," while others might fall into the category of "defunding the police."

The insurgencies brought about to realize these ideas and imaginings included (sometimes armed) self-defense patrols deployed by the Black Panthers and other groups, which at times included confrontations in front of courts and police stations. Alternative forms of community safety programs were also created, such as services for escorting senior citizens, community restorative justice councils (sometimes run by and for youth), and "get clean" campaigns for people with addictions.

While many of these abolition-like insurgencies were instantiated, more often it was elements of the reform/defunding approach. Black Power Urbanism would lead to increasing the racial diversity of urban police forces, activists would press for imposing and enforcing residency requirements for police, and there would be repeated efforts to establish civilian-controlled police review boards that would hold the police accountable for their actions. Debates over what path Black/civilian control of the police should take reflected both local Black urban political development and established political and institutional arrangements and structures. One Black Power urbanist approach—as argued in the Newark Black Power platform of 1968 and pursued in East Orange—centered on using political power to seize full control of the police and restructure their organization to reflect a city's needs and its demographics. Black activists in places like Oakland and East Palo Alto wondered whether attempts to "defend the ghetto" should take the shape of administrative decentralization, given that the Black population was a highly spatially concentrated minority group in a deliberately fragmented political and institutional environment in which political influence and administrative accountability was low.

Whatever methods were chosen to enact change, these three policy pillars of Black Power Urbanism make it possible to understand the imaginings, insurgencies, and instantiations that occurred during its rise and fall. Although this is true for all four case cities, as Kenneth Gibson would proclaim, "Wherever the nation's cities are going, Newark is going to get there first."

NEWARK

Self-Government Is Possible . . . Let's Do It Together!

A new era in community health screams to be born. The people of Newark are unselfish mid-wives who have offered their homes and their hopes. But without whole community participation, there cannot be a new beginning in the improvement of health services. Nor can there be genuine progress without medicine making its boldest commitment. . . . The low-income and disadvantaged sectors of the community cannot be held responsible for the present state of public health in Newark. They are, however, prepared to share responsibility for the future, and there cannot be a meaningful future for the health professions without their partnership.

—"Agreements Reached Between Community and Government Negotiators Regarding New Jersey College of Medicine of Dentistry and Related Matters"

In 2018, reports surfaced that babies were dying of infection in Newark's University Hospital.[1] The hospital—born "screaming" out of the city's 1967 rebellion—was failing its patients and Newark's underserved "low-income and disadvantaged" communities who had "offered their homes and their hopes" in order to midwife a "new era in community health."[2] Mayor Ras Baraka, facing a public health crisis, called for a state monitor to oversee an overhaul of the hospital's management and improvements in the deplorable conditions in the complex.[3] Baraka's criticism of University Hospital was based upon his belief that the hospital had "fail[ed] to live up to the Newark Agreement negotiated when the hospital was created."[4] Mayor Baraka followed this condemnation with calls for action. First, he asserted, "the hospital needs to become more responsive to the people it serves and sensitive to their needs. This requires more community input with new leadership, including a new board with adequate representation of Newark residents and a new President/CEO with a history of sensitivity to community." Second, Baraka argued that "state and federal investment is needed to enable University Hospital to become the first-class teaching hospital that it was intended to be, including an overhauled emergency room, a world-class trauma center, and more outpatient clinics to meet the undeserved medical needs of the people of Newark."[5] The hospital admitted that the infant deaths were "stark reminders that an overhaul of the quality of care" and new leadership of the hospital was "urgently needed."[6]

Baraka's condemnation of University Hospital and the basis for his call for repair rested on the activism and rebellion of Black and Brown Newarkers as Black Power Urbanism catalyzed the city, its people, its politics, and its institutions. In 1968, Black Newark won a historic challenge to the city's largest urban renewal and dispossession scheme: the construction of the New Jersey Medical School complex, which would have cleared 150 acres and displaced thousands of poor and working-class Black Newarkers.[7] Activists won an agreement with city, state, and federal officials "to create a top-notch medical facility with community involvement and oversight in perpetuity." As a result, University Hospital became the state's only publicly owned acute care hospital and an institution upon which thousands of poor and working-class Newarkers depended. A range of activism also grew out of this agreement, including pushing public health researchers to focus on the lead poisoning crisis among the city's Black and Brown children.[8]

Despite this auspicious start, decades of mismanagement and disinvestment would lead to a slow decline in the hospital's services and physical plant. University Hospital's decline could be connected to many sources. To be sure it was partly rooted in mismanagement, but it could also be due to the shifting fortunes of Newark in the post-Keynesian world and to the dispiriting tale of urban crisis and failure that confronted Black mayors, who were left with the "hollow prize" of urban governance as Black control of cities led to limited material gains because of continued political and economic disinvestment.[9] Failure could also be blamed on the more contemporary crisis of inequality and dispossession that characterizes today's neoliberal metropolises. Yet, Baraka's invocation of the 1968 agreement coupled with community mobilization forced the hospital to recognize its historic role in the city. Indeed, the hospital's new leadership, in its "Letter to the Newark Community," acknowledged the "unique, historical role of University Hospital within the fabric of structural racism," while recommitting itself to act "as an anchor institution in our community."[10] Nearly sixty years after the rebellion, the crisis of University Hospital symbolized the complicated but enduring legacy of Black Power Urbanism. The development of Black Power Urbanism reflected both the long-standing Black urban citizenship that had characterized Newark since the nineteenth century and the post–World War II mixture of migration, urban renewal, activism, and rebellion that reshaped the city.

Black Power Urbanism emerged in Newark as part of the quest of Black and Brown Newarkers for sovereignty—for Black Power—for control over their neighborhoods, schools, housing, employment, and so on. This search for sovereignty was shaped by the distinctive patterns of Black urban political development, the broader urban political orders that shaped the city of Newark, and the explosive and destabilizing critical juncture of urban renewal, which shattered the city's ethnic neighborhoods and its social and organizational structures and hastened the decline of the city's economic base. Black Power Urbanism emerged at the center of these clashing political and economic developments.

The search for sovereignty was most visible through electoral politics, although Black Power Urbanism was more than that. Through coalitions that crossed significant ideological, class, and ethnic divides, Black and Brown Newarkers achieved one of the nation's "firsts" in the election of Kenneth Gibson as Newark's first Black mayor—one of three big-city Black mayors elected by 1970. However, Black Power Urbanism in Newark would also be led by politicos like George Richardson and activists like Junius Williams and Amiri Baraka (Ras Baraka's father). It included the leadership of many women, like Amina Baraka, who led the women's division of CFUN (Committee for a Unified Newark), and Marion Kidd, who not only was the head of the Welfare Committee of the People's Action Group, but also helped organize a consumer's buyer's club for welfare recipients.[11] These women played a significant role in articulating Black Power Urbanism, both on a theoretical level and in its day-to-day instantiation. Black Power Urbanism emerged from the everyday experiences and actions of these Black and Brown citizens—and many others—who challenged the urban renewal regime that had destroyed their homes and neighborhoods. This resistance would lead to the 1967 rebellion. The aftermath of the rebellion would most famously result in the Newark Community Agreement, which made the well-being of Newark's most marginalized citizens a key focus of the redevelopment plan. The search for new forms for a new Newark would take place across many often overlapping domains, including the three pillars of this study: housing, education, and policing.

Housing as community lay at the heart of the most visionary embodiments of a new Black city and arose as part of Black Power Urbanism: One example was Amiri Baraka's embrace of Kawaida, a "political doctrine of black nationalism and cultural revolution" that inspired his vision of building a "new NewArk."[12] The unsuccessful attempts of Baraka and his allies to build a new city within a city upon the land scraped bare by urban renewal offered both an inspirational as well as a cautionary tale about the potential and limits of Black Power Urbanism. Alongside of the drama of Baraka's vision of a new city within a city was the grinding years-long struggle led by Black women to take over Newark's infamous public housing—those carceral high-rise ghettos—and refashion them into spaces where their families could live in freedom, dignity, and safety. This struggle for control laid bare the twisted roots of the public housing order in the United States, in which the public housing authorities and the federal government approached their tenants with a combination of pity, contempt, and carceralization. Black women in Newark, Oakland, Saint Louis, and elsewhere would challenge these actors, making the case that they could refashion new life from these spaces. In Newark, the initial success that these women were able to achieve despite institutional resistance was threatened in the 1990s by federal programs like HOPE VI, which offered local public housing authorities funding to demolish housing developments without replacing all of the units lost.[13] Newark officials were early participants in this program, which destroyed almost all of Newark's high-rise public housing for families. Despite this, housing activists drew upon the groundwork laid by earlier activism, securing for future poor Newarkers the right to affordable housing and a "right to the city."

Education was the second domain in which the struggle to birth a new form took place. Black and Brown Newarkers (like those in Oakland, East Palo Alto, and more famously in New York City's Ocean Hill-Brownsville neighborhood), would lead the way in pressing for community control of schools.[14] Community control meant not only Black and Brown teachers, principals, and staff, but also the adoption of Black Power pedagogies that included teaching assistants and classroom aides who came from the community and the students' families. These new pedagogies called for culturally relevant education not just for Black children and youth, but also culturally competent and bilingual education for the city's large Puerto Rican community. These new forms were envisioned in public or publicly funded institutions like the city's public schools and Head Start preschools as well as in private Black-controlled spaces like the Chad School and Baraka's African Free School.[15] Black Power Urbanism would initiate decades of activism in relation to the city's schools, and parents, teachers, students, community activists, and politicians would struggle—sometimes viciously—over the stakes of public education in Newark. The echoes of the nexus between Black Power Urbanism and the city's struggle over education can be seen in the city's long fight to free itself from the state's takeover of the public school system in the 1990s. This struggle for community control intensified in 2010 when a "transformative" $100 million gift to the city by Facebook founder Mark Zuckerberg during Mayor Cory Booker's neoliberal administration funded controversial reforms such as increasing the number of charter schools while also closing neighborhood schools. Activists, parents, and students led community opposition to these reforms.[16] Mayor Ras Baraka would play a highly visible role in the struggle to reassert community control of Newark's public school system.[17]

Policing was the third pillar of Newark's Black Power Urbanism. With the consolidation of most of Newark's Black population into the city's Third Ward by the 1920s, the city and the Newark Police Department (NPD) had created a landscape marred by the interlocking violent mechanisms of hyper-policing, surveillance, and violence (linked to regulating Black mobility and citizenship claims) and chronic under-policing and predation (in support of police corruption and exploitation of residents by landlords and local businesses). Violent policing was the spark that unleashed the 1967 rebellion, and the first wave of protests centered on the Central Ward and the First Precinct police station. Policing is where Newark's Black Power Urbanism would fail. Newark's Black Power urbanists failed to imagine a broader world beyond the one that earlier generations of moderate Black leadership had focused on. Their goals encompassed expanded civil control of the police, including police accountability; an end to police corruption; and an end to vicious everyday street-level policing. Activists and Black party allies offered a limited redefinition of "community control" that challenged, but did not fundamentally displace the central role of the NPD in policing Black Newark. This led to decades of failed attempts to assert operational and political control that was durable enough to remake the NPD into a department that would not play the role of occupying force in the Central Ward, as it had during the 1967 rebellion and for decades afterward.

FIGURE 3.1. Black Power Urbanism in Newark

Source: Black Newark 1, no. 1 (April 1968): 3. Rutgers University Libraries.

Indeed, instead of reimagining existing policing practices and investigating whether they should be abandoned rather than adapted in the quest for a more just city, many members of the city's Black Power urbanist coalition asserted that effective community control could be achieved with a careful political and ideological takeover of existing political and institutional structures (see figure 3.1). This ethos—exemplified by the slogan "let's do it together" from a flyer for Kenneth Gibson's groundbreaking mayoral election—provided the basis for a multiracial/multiethnic working class that upended Newark's machine politics to pave the way for a search for "new forms." In the long run, a new equilibrium emerged that exposed the durability of long-standing political and institutional arrangements within the city and outside of it, and that at times reduced periodic searches for "new forms" into an updated model of ethnic succession politics.

Making Black Newark and the "Roaring Third"

Black Newark (enslaved and free) existed from the moment the city was established on lands previously held by the Lenni-Lenape people. By the late nineteenth century, Black (free and formerly enslaved) Newarkers had created a rich associational life that ranged from active antislavery/anti-colonization movements and organized support for the Underground Railroad network through churches and individuals to the founding of a "Colored" public school in 1856.[18] At the beginning of the twentieth century, Black Newark was a small enclave in the mosaic of nationalities that comprised the city (see figure 3.2).

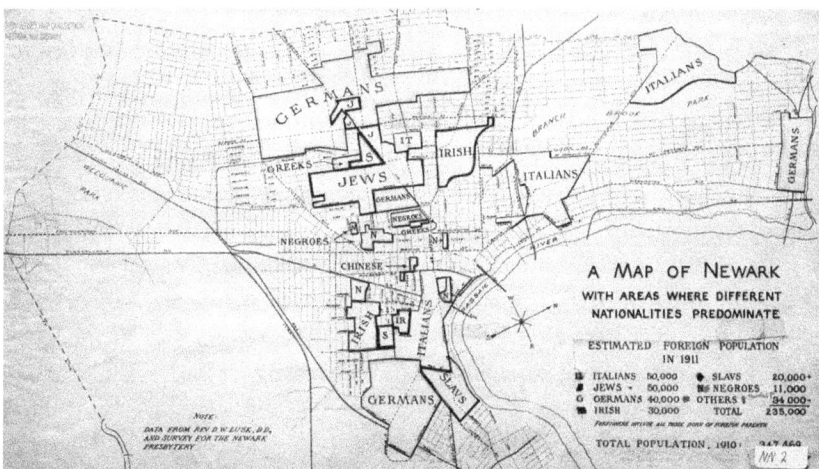

FIGURE 3.2. Newark is a city of nationalities.

Source: John P. Fox, Charles F. Cummings New Jersey Information Center, Newark Public Library, 1911.

The Great Migrations of the twentieth century fundamentally reshaped Black Newark and ultimately the city itself. Between 1910 and 1940, the Black population grew from around 9,500 people (or 3 percent of the city's population), to 45,760, around 11 percent of Newark's population. Migration hastened the consolidation of Black Newark into what would become known as the "Roaring Third Ward."[19] A new, albeit small, Black middle class emerged out of the institution-building that developed during this moment of spatial consolidation.[20] These Black-run organizations (often organized under the auspices of interracialism) included the Court Street YMCA and the Friendly Neighborhood (settlement) House. Other markers of Black segregated life included the establishment of Kenney Memorial Hospital to attend to the needs of Black patients and doctors who were barred from Newark's hospitals.[21] Another visible symbol of Newark's arrival as a part of the broader landscape of new Black metropolises was the 1917 founding of its Urban League by William Ashby, the state's first Black social worker.[22] By the 1920s, Newark's Black middle class understood themselves to be intermediaries between working-class Blacks and white Newark. Black Newark's leadership was largely forced to engage in interracialism, in which Black community concerns were addressed via special commissions and committees where Black representation was limited, while the policymaking ability of Black participants was largely advisory and mostly ignored.[23] Complicating this picture of community leadership were the myriad local political operators and "little plants," as the historian Clement Price called those who straddled the city's often intertwined criminal underworld. They included mob leaders such as Abner "Longie" Zwillman and "Dutch" Schultz, who allegedly "ran" the Third Ward and its political structure. The intertwining of organized criminal networks and the city's political operations—and reformers' persistent efforts to disentangle the former from the latter—marked both white and Black Newark's political history through most of the twentieth century.[24] This duality also marked Black urban political development, with one path characterized by patron-client relations tied to white reformers and social welfare organizations, and another path characterized by small-scale clubhouse politics, as Black politicos attempted to translate votes into patronage.

The second wave of the Great Migration massively increased the city's Black population, and the scale of migration meant that the everyday life of Black Newark would bear an increasingly Southern working-class stamp. The "roaring" Third Ward would come into its own as Newark's core Black neighborhood. Black entrepreneurs controlled a small slice of the neighborhood's retail and service economy, mostly small grocery stores, hairdressers and barbers, auto repair shops, and bars. In addition to a slew of small storefront churches, Black Newark hosted a full range of social and fraternal clubs. The city was part of the jazz and entertainment circuit in the Northeast that featured native Newarkers like Wayne Shorter, Sarah Vaughn, and Dionne Warwick. Sports entertainment included a thriving "Black Fives" Black basketball league and the Newark Eagles, a Negro League baseball team whose players included Larry Doby and Satchel Paige. Beyond these formal spaces, Newark also had its undercommons.[25] The need for entertainment and pleasure helped support the "scores of blacks [who] depended on the streets, bars and informal groups to bolster their economic position." Organized crime and the police battled over the vigorous "numbers industry" or lottery that was part of this street life. During Prohibition, Blacks built local stills and opened "blind pigs," or underground bars and saloons. As a result of this informal economy the Third Ward was increasingly viewed by white Newark as a place of immorality and danger whose inhabitants should be heavily policed and separated from whites.[26] The fear of Black crime led Newark police to forbid "interracial mingling" in the Third Ward, stating that "no one white person in a hundred has any business in the colored section."[27] For Blacks within the districts, Newark police engaged in "billy club justice," as all "black social activity in the streets . . . was tantamount to loafing and mischief."[28]

Changing the Rules

By the late 1920s, the rapid pace of Black spatial consolidation and population growth in the Third Ward raised the possibility that an African American could be elected to the city council, a key marker of formal political incorporation. As was the case in a number of cities that experienced a rapid and concentrated growth in Black residents, political leaders in Newark took quick action to avert that outcome. Civic reformers, in league with members of the city's declining ethnic majority of German and Anglo-Americans, came together to push for charter reform and a commission-style rather than a ward-based government in order to stave off a racial and ethnic realignment (of Blacks, Italians Americans, and Jews) within the city's political structure.[29] Reformers achieved their goal—in place of the ward system, a five-member board of commissioners was created, each member elected at-large on a non-partisan ballot. The mayoralty was reduced to a ceremonial position, selected by the commissioners.

At the time, Newark and Oakland had similar political structures. As new ethnic and racial groups grew in size, both cities averted threats to the political status quo by carrying out "good government" reforms that catered to the needs of those currently in power. The order in each city maintained its dominance differently. Post-reform Oakland was characterized by an "apolitical" and "quiet" politics controlled by a small elite, while in Newark, a different kind of political sensibility—consisting of systemic corruption and ethnic spoils—took hold. Under Newark's new commission-style city government, corruption would become even more rampant as each commissioner was given a virtual policy fiefdom to rule over.[30] The central concern of Newark's white ethnic machine politicians was to protect the political and socio-spatial fabric of Newark and their community's place within it, based on their understanding of Newark's government and the millions of dollars it controlled as a prime source of individual and community enrichment. For Newark's growing Black population, "good government" reform made Black urban citizenship tenuous by transforming Black spaces and Black voters into "non-political entities in city elections."[31]

By the end of World War II, the city had begun to transform under the impact of a nascent civil rights movement that arose out of Black mobilization under the Double-V campaign and a new demographic mix due to growing Black and Puerto Rican migration, the decades-long collapse of European immigration, and the concomitant assimilation of these older groups of immigrants.[32] Between 1940 and 1950, the city's Black population rose sharply from about 45,000 to about 75,000, and by 1960 to 138,000. Black residents went from 11 percent to 34 percent of the city's population. By contrast, the city's white population fell from 384,000 in 1940 to 363,000 in 1950, and then to 267,000 by 1960. Official anxiety over this transformation was reflected in many of the city's planning documents, which carefully noted the neighborhoods where Black and Puerto Rican populations increased while the white population decreased. This demographic transformation was spatially uneven, with Black residents largely consolidated into the city's Third (now Central) Ward (see figure 3.3).

Daily life in the Third Ward was subject to different kinds of predation, from high rents for small, overcrowded, and rodent-infested apartments to the many stores that sold shoddy, overpriced goods. Schools in Black areas were massively overcrowded, often running on double shifts and making do with poor-quality supplies and decrepit facilities.[33] While wartime spending had temporarily buoyed the economic fortunes of many Black Newarkers, offering them access to higher paying and higher skilled jobs, the postwar contraction and the reimposition of a labor color line set the stage for new struggles. Reports conducted by the city as well as census data provided empirical evidence of the dire conditions, especially in the realm of housing. The 1940 census would reveal that "within the five census tracts having the heaviest concentration of blacks . . . only twenty-one of the 6,333 dwellings units were owned by black occupants."[34] Overall, only 5 percent of Black Newarkers owned their home, compared to nearly 28 percent of whites. Almost all of the Black residents of the

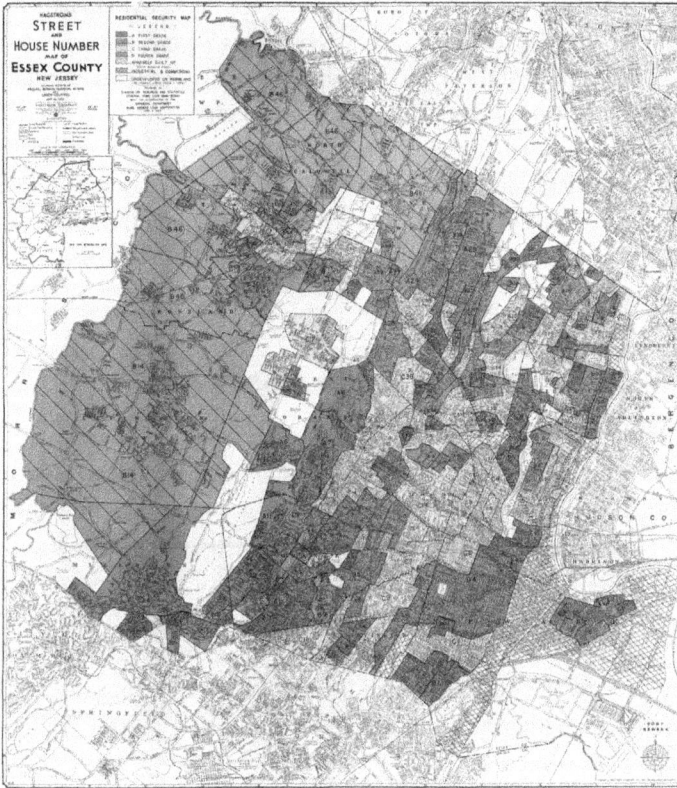

FIGURE 3.3. Bounded by race and class: Newark and Essex County HOLC map

Source: Robert K. Nelson et al., "Mapping Inequality: Redlining in New Deal America," in *American Panorama: An Atlas of United States History,* 2023, https://dsl.richmond.edu/panorama/redlining.

Third Ward were tenants in buildings owned by individuals who lived outside of the area.[35] The city's major Black newspaper, the *Herald News,* publicized community campaigns against absentee "slumlords" and highlighted the city's arbitrary enforcement of city codes, which allowed dangerous housing conditions to remain unaddressed by landlords.[36]

City officials and other elites were also complicit in other kinds of economic dispossession. Arbitrary regulatory power, punitive code enforcement, and a corrupt and exclusionary political and economic system made it difficult for Black entrepreneurs to set up new, legitimate establishments that could compete with stores and bars operated by the area's earlier residents. Corrupt policing also blocked Black Newarkers from fully realizing the profits from the city's illicit economy of "banking and playing the numbers," as well as illegal bars and stills.[37] By the 1940s, presaging the Black Power Urbanism that would emerge two decades later, Black Newarkers were beginning to identify outsiders who exploited the Third Ward as the source of their economic and political dispossession. Prosper Brewer, who emerged out of Newark's Black labor unions and later became the Republican district leader, offered a stern warning to outsiders: "It is time for us to let these people know that we are the majority in the Third Ward, and that we are going to control business in the ward from now on."[38]

The "New Newark" and the Postwar Keynesian City

To address their anxiety about Newark's economic future in the wake of postwar demobilization, in the early 1950s a small group of predominantly white corporate and civic elites led a campaign for a physically and politically "new Newark." To achieve this, Newark's corporate and good government elites initiated plans to wrest control of the city's political future from the growing power of the city's ethnic political machines. One of their campaigns for political reform, led by the newly founded Newark Citizens Committee of Municipal Government, agitated for the introduction of a new charter.[39] This charter would replace the now discredited and corrupt commission government with a strong mayor and a nine-member city council (five elected from wards and four elected at large).[40] The new structure would allow for the election of a Black city council member, a symbolic development that had been derailed during the 1930s charter reform. A broad range of good government groups supported the new charter measure and it earned cautious endorsements from the NAACP, the Urban League, the Congress of Industrial Organizations (CIO), and the New Jersey Negro Labor Council.[41] In attempting to clean up Newark's city government, the reform coalition played a role in incorporating Black politicians into the city's Democratic, white political machine, with the election of Irvine Turner to the city council. Despite their success in getting charter reform passed, reformers were unable to change Newark's political culture and its institutional and organizational structures, which mutually reinforced an insular political system in which ethnic membership determined political power. The remaining civic reformers and citizen groups had little ability to push back against an all-encompassing machine. The corporate interest that remained would eventually be led by the Prudential Insurance Corporation and other insurance and service firms, and it would be focused on, and fundamentally limited to, protecting the city's downtown core.

The campaign for a "new Newark" was more successful in making the case that the city needed to forcefully address the conditions of "slums and blight," especially in the Third Ward (rechristened the Central Ward under the new charter) as a means of saving the city. Planning for the "new Newark" began in 1943 when Mayor Vincent Murphy established the Central Planning Board (CPB). By 1947, the CPB (with the assistance of Harland Bartholomew & Associates, the premier urban planning firm of the postwar era) had issued several reports calling for a near full-scale redevelopment of Newark.[42] The CPB asserted that "sporadic efforts to reclaim small areas will not solve the problem. . . . It must be done on a comprehensive basis as a part of a long-range program of municipal improvements."[43] The CPB's call for massive urban renewal had been preceded by that of the Newark Housing Authority (NHA), which had published a report in 1946 detailing the "costs of slums" to Newark, ranging from tuberculosis deaths to "fatal home accidents."[44] Demolition and containment would be part of the answer as city officials proclaimed a comprehensive $250 million slum clearance project.[45] The postwar availability of federal funds made these new city dreams a reality, but urban renewal would make quality housing, adequate schools, and public safety even more difficult for Black Newarkers to obtain.[46]

The federal government's postwar role in institutionalizing and hardening the racial segregation and exclusion of Black and Brown Newarkers from most of Newark's suburbs left Black Newark trapped in a "white noose."[47] The city's elites initiated "soft" urban renewal by pushing for stringent "code enforcement" as a means to "clean up the city" and to indirectly force the displacement of problem populations like Newark's Black residents, many of whom were recent arrivals due to the second wave of the Great Migration.[48] With the assistance of Harland Bartholomew, the campaign for a "new Newark" made the case that the city had to embrace "hard" urban renewal in order to forcefully address the conditions of "slums and blight," especially in the Third Ward, as a means of saving the city.[49]

Urban renewal, Newark's version of liberal integrationism, and the rollout of the federal Community Action Program (CAP) occurred under the aegis of white civic reformers affiliated with the ethnic political machine. This coalition assumed that fundamental control over policy and funding would flow through the mayor's office.[50] Politically minded and moderate Blacks were expected to defer to white reformers affiliated with the city's Gray Areas project, funded by the Ford Foundation, as well as to the city bureaucracies that administered social welfare programs. The city's white political machine assumed that it would determine the scope and scale of Newark's urban renewal/community development apparatus, while allowing Black politicos and social welfare administrators to occupy the status of junior partners.

Hugh Addonizio's mayoral election in 1962 was an encouraging sign of burgeoning liberal integrationism due to the broad coalition of "white liberals, disaffected members of the Democratic machine, and black Newarkers" that organized behind his candidacy.[51] Addonizio's election initially raised hopes that the liberal integrationist path taken in the late 1950s would result in a softening of urban renewal's destructive path and a greater focus on the needs of Black Newark. Despite these hopes, Addonizio's first month in office showed that nothing had changed. Although some Black political figures like George Richardson (who had been one of Addonizio's campaign managers) received high-profile positions, Newark's political lifeblood—patronage—was not offered to rank-and-file Black political supporters. Part of the reason for this was political calculation on Addonizio's part—he had realized that the growing numbers of Black Newarkers posed an existential threat to Newark's current ethnically stratified political system. Indeed, some Black politicians had seen Addonizio as "a means to an end . . . a step toward the eventual (and inevitable) election of a predominantly black city administration."[52]

Barringer High and the Collapse of Liberal Integrationism

The first sign that this consensus around liberal integrationism was not shared and indeed was not acceptable to Black activists who were not aligned with machine politics occurred at the Barringer High construction site. The construction site demonstrated the near total exclusion of Black workers from construction jobs and the skilled trades, but more generally from much of Newark's economy. In a city where between 1950 and 1960 the Black percentage of the total population had increased from 17 to 50 percent and where Black and Brown students constituted well over 50 percent of the overall school population, the city's bid to rebuild majority-white Barringer High School with an all-white (albeit union) labor force quickly became a volatile flashpoint. As George Richardson would remark, "Imagine—a northern city like Newark without a black anything: no black sales clerks, no black bus drivers. We needed something to confront that."[53]

A coalition of Black (and white) activists and political leaders, including Richardson, gathered at Barringer to protest the limits of Newark's liberal integrationism, which rested on the raw political power of the city's white machine and its disdain for Black Newark. The protesters were met with violence—from the white construction crews and from the Newark police. For moderate Black Newarkers, the protest against the exclusionism displayed at Barringer and the causally indifferent violence deployed against an interracial group of protestors was the critical event needed to link the postwar Northern freedom movement with the ongoing mass Civil Rights Movement and hesitantly welcome the nascent emergence of Black Power Urbanism.

Police brutality in response to the demonstration fueled renewed calls to create a civilian review board, although they were quickly shut down by the Addonizio administration. The city's refusal to address the issue would lead Richardson to exclaim to a hostile Addonizio: "I'm not against you. . . . I'm against a pregnant woman getting beaten up by the cops."[54] After that protest Richardson resigned and set a course for Black political independence.[55] He established a new political organization, the United Committee for Political Freedom, which planned to run a Black candidate as an alternative to the local Democratic Party ticket. Richardson's break was the result not only of a refusal by the Addonizio political machine to see Black politicians and their constituents as equal partners, but also of the limits of liberal integrationism.

Richardson's break with the machine would be accompanied by other dramatic shifts in Newark's political terrain as new groups emerged in a now more fluid political context. As Mark Krasovic shows, while some community reform groups were seeded by the Ford Foundation's Gray Areas project in Newark, others, like the United Community Council (UCC), were either born and/or bloomed in the burst of funding and energy unleashed by the War on Poverty and its requirement for "maximum feasible participation" of poor residents in the planning and administration of federal projects.[56] In Oakland and East Palo Alto, as well as other cities, community action agencies like the UCC became the object of intense political struggle between some Black community leaders who saw in them a chance to build an independent political base and service delivery mechanism as an alternative to an indifferent if not hostile city government versus some Black politicians who believed that these agencies provided a more advantageous entry into existing political arrangements. To white politicians like Addonizio and later critics like Daniel Patrick Moynihan, these community action agencies and the requirement for "maximum feasible participation" struck at the heart of white-dominated urban political structures and ethnic/racial hierarchies. Newark's UCC was an example of this, as the organization showed a remarkable ability to "organize the unorganized," engaging thousands of participants from area boards down to neighborhoods and even "antipoverty block associations that stretched the administrative state even further onto individual streets." Even more importantly, as Krasovic shows, "to the thousands of members involved in this work, community action not only provided jobs and services . . . it also offered a political space in which they developed new leverage to affect their own lives, to confront the urban crisis in their own way."[57]

The Black leadership of these organizations was not passive, but pushed back vigorously against attempts to co-opt or take over these windows of political opportunity and organization-building. For example, Cyril DeGrasse Tyson, the UCC's first director, completed a seven-hundred-page publication that meticulously documented the targeted campaign by the Addonizio administration to push out the existing UCC leadership and transform the agency into another source of patronage, undercutting the democratic promise and accountability that was built into the community action program. This attack on the UCC and the undermining of local neighborhood democracy, Tyson argued, had "sowed the seeds of its own catastrophe"—Newark's 1967 rebellion.[58]

New Left groups like the Students for a Democratic Society (SDS) also organized within Newark. SDS's Economic Research and Action Program (ERAP), established under the banner of the Newark Community Union Project (NCUP) and led by an interracial group of activists including Tom Hayden, focused on helping residents organize against the increasingly brutal conditions in Newark's Black spaces. Although initially the NCUP focused on jobs, conditions on the ground and the activism of everyday Black women moved the project away from its "masculinist and producerist orientation," which concentrated on jobs for Black men, and toward a grassroots politics and mobilization that centered "rent strikes, tenant organizing, [and] confrontation with private slumlords."[59] The activism facilitated by NCUP overlapped with the emerging welfare rights activism of Newark's Black women, who began by organizing grocery-buying cooperatives to wrest their dignity and control of their family's food from neighborhood merchants charging high prices for dismal goods, and ultimately confronted Newark's "largest slumlord,'" the Newark Housing Authority.

But it was Amiri Baraka who led the most visible battles over Newark's Black future. A Newark native, Baraka returned to the city in 1965 to establish the first beachhead of his "New Ark," the Spirit House Movers and Players. Their cultural center would be the first of a network of organizations created by Baraka and other Black nationalists both within and outside of Newark.[60] In addition to cultural and educational groups and organizations, Baraka played a key role in the rise of specifically political groups such as the Committee for a Unified NewArk (CFUN) and United Brothers. Finally, Baraka, along with Newarkers like the Reverend Nathan Wright, helped organize what Komozi Woodard calls the Modern Black Convention movement, which contributed a broad range of ideas and instantiations to the process of bringing about a Black Power city.[61] Underlying all of these endeavors was Baraka's embrace of Kawaida and his vision of "New Ark"—the idea that Newark could stand as an example of community control and self-determination. While Baraka's vision of New Ark was the most explicitly spatial and political of the new Black Power mobilizations occurring in Newark, the spatial disruption of "Negro removal" and the hyper-predation that ghettoization produced were the starting point for the struggle over Black Newark and its future. To achieve a better Newark, the containment, exploitation, and erasure of Black Newark would have to be undone. This would be a vast and perhaps unsolvable task.

Newark's "Negro Removal" and the NHA Bulldozer

With the aid of federal money provided by the Housing and Urban Renewal Acts of 1937, 1949, and 1954, urban renewal and the construction of public housing acquired their own momentum in Newark.[62] One reason for the seemingly unstoppable pace of urban renewal was the leadership of Louis Danzig, the executive director of the Newark Housing Authority (NHA). Danzig created a position isolated from direct political control and oversight.[63] Until the 1970s, due to the demands of tenants and housing activists in the wake of the Stella Wright rent strike, the NHA ran the city's urban renewal program and built and maintained its vast public housing projects. The two worked hand in hand: "urban renewal" cleared "undesirable" people and neighborhoods for "higher and best uses," while public housing rehoused those who were cleared along with the new migrants that continued to move into the city. The scale of the NHA's programs also helped Danzig minimize political opposition outside of affected neighborhoods. In a city in which the purpose of politics was generally seen as the opportunity to acquire spoils, the NHA was a gold mine for New Jersey–style graft and corruption: "By 1949, [the] NHA was, with the exception of the Board of Education, the largest spender of funds and the largest dispenser of contracts in city government."[64] By 1965, most of Newark's central core was covered by one urban renewal plan or another (see figure 3.4).

Two urban renewal areas are of particular interest. The first is the downtown business core, over which planning officials expressed anxiety and trepidation about the future. While many white-collar jobs in the insurance and business services industry remained, Newark was slowly deindustrializing. The second area was the medical school complex located in the city's Central Ward, a 183-acre site where the planned development would displace approximately twenty thousand mostly Black residents. What made this vast displacement even more infuriating to Black Newarkers was that in a desperate bid to attract the medical school and other affiliated facilities, the city (and primarily the NHA) offered far more land than the medical school leadership had requested. The offer rested on the city's wholesale declaration of "blight" on the still viable, but now majority-Black neighborhoods located in the renewal area.

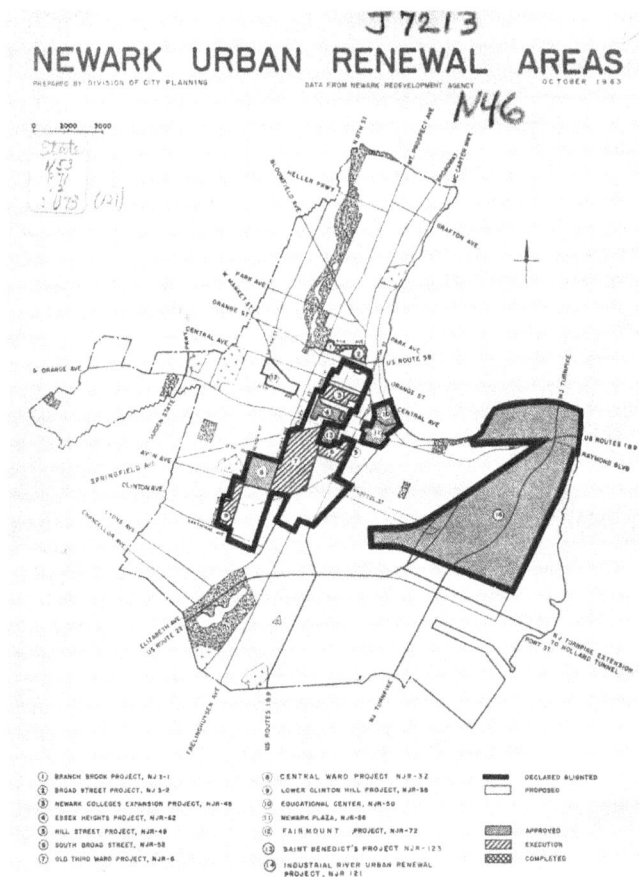

FIGURE 3.4. All (of Newark) in for urban renewal, 1963

Source: Housing Authority of the City of Newark (New Jersey); Newark Division of City Planning, October 1963.

Newark's ambitious urban renewal program attracted considerable interest from both the popular press and from urban planners. One contemporary account praised the NHA's professionalism, arguing that officials made decisions on "technical rather than political criteria" and that the NHA's policies "have not been the result of open conflict among local interest groups. . . . The work of its staff has been shielded from random interference by local interests."[65] The reality was quite different. Since the 1937 legislation, it had been an open secret among city officials and local media that organized crime groups were deeply involved in securing NHA contracts.[66] Meanwhile, many of the NHA's top leadership and staff lived in suburbs outside of the city, reflecting the top-down planning and implementation of NHA projects. The combination of private graft and official aloofness led to an erasure of the residents of affected neighborhoods, who were either displaced by or who lived in the new projects. These two processes contributed to a deep alienation among most average Newarkers, Black and white, and over the long run contributed to disengagement and deep-seated anger toward city government. The destruction of the physical markers of Black Newark's urban political development were examples of the push to achieve the "new Newark." For example, one of the city's oldest Black churches, the Plane Street Colored Church (established 1836), which served as a center for antislavery activism and a node in the Underground Railroad, would be demolished by Newark's "Negro removal" in 1957 and replaced by an athletics field for Rutgers University–Newark.[67] Over the course of twenty-five years, the NHA built a vast container for poor Black and Brown people (see table 3.1). The nine low-scale complexes built before 1950 were dwarfed in size and scale by the vast complex of grim high-rise projects built during the 1950s and 1960s. With few exceptions, like the neighboring Black enclaves in East Orange, Newark's white neighborhoods and suburbs, with the support of the FHA and local officials, were implacable in their intent to maintain a "white noose" around Black spaces.[68]

In light of these pressures, Danzig hoped to forestall or at least slow the pace of Black displacement to white neighborhoods and (indirectly) integration by speeding up the building of "Negro projects" in the city's Central Ward.[69]

In this instance, Danzig was supported by Black politicians like Irvine Turner who continued to compete for substantive power within Newark's political machine. Turner saw the construction of projects in the Central Ward as doing double duty. New construction would satisfy an almost insatiable demand for

TABLE 3.1   Newark public and publicly assisted housing, 1920–1980

DECADE*	NEWARK HOUSING AUTHORITY (NHA) SITES / UNITS	NHA ELDERLY SITES / UNITS	NON-NHA LOW/MODERATE INCOME DEVELOPMENTS SITES / UNITS
1920–1939		n/a	2 / 1,163
1940–1950	8 / 3,084	n/a	n/a
1951–1960	5 / 6,864	n/a	n/a
1961–1970	n/a / 826	10 / 2,476	12 / 3,223
1970–1980	8 / 543	7 / 1,009**	32 / 4,325**

Note: *Year of project based on date project authorized. **Includes Section 236 and Section 8.

Source: Public Housing in Newark (Newark Housing Authority, 1944); "New Public Housing Projects, 1969–1970," Summary of New Public Housing Projects (Newark Housing Authority, 1970); Robert Notte, Summary of Properties and Projects 1970–1976: Urban Renewal, Commercial, Industrial, Public, Residential (Newark Redevelopment and Housing Authority, December 1976); Official Statement: Housing Finance Corporation of the City of Newark (Newark Housing Authority, 1979); Public Housing Master Plan Newark, N.J. (Newark Redevelopment and Housing Authority, 1985).

modern quality housing for Black Newarkers locked out of the private market. Meanwhile the consolidation of these residents solidified a future voting base for Turner and other Black politicians as the city moved toward revamping its ward system.[70] Finally, Turner and others argued that the new projects simply reflected racist reality: "Few whites could be induced to live in the Central Ward anyway; anything built there would have to be Negro housing."[71] Turner's "win" would come at a cost. The redevelopment of the Central Ward, which resulted in the construction of thousands of new public housing units, also entailed massive disruptions. Overall, given the reluctance to relocate those displaced by construction into white neighborhoods, the NHA estimated that 8,500 Black families had to be relocated within the ward. This relocation led to the respatialization of a hyper-concentrated Black community.

But while public housing units were poured into the Central Ward in an attempt to contain the rising Black population, Danzig and the NHA continued to work with private developers to build moderate and middle-income housing in the city's surrounding white neighborhoods in a bid to stave off further white flight (see figure 3.5).

By 1960, the NHA faced the fundamental dysfunctionality of the urban renewal order in trying to meet the objectives of fighting blight, removing slum housing, and saving downtown. Danzig argued that neither the Federal Housing Administration nor private developers would finance or build middle-income housing (nor would whites, the intended residents, live there) if the project was in the "midst of a hard-core slum or a Negro ghetto," thus negating one of the goals of urban renewal, which was increasing the number of middle-income residents in blighted areas.[72] Because middle-income housing could not be built in blighted areas, Danzig was forced to admit that public housing was the only possibility for construction in areas of severe blight; while this would reduce a certain number of units of slum housing, the impact of demolition and displacement within the same area would lead to new projects being "rapidly inundated by the surrounding blight." "Negro removal" was understood as critical to urban renewal, but strategies of containment such as public housing would trigger even more displacement and disruption, making the prospects of successful urban renewal even harder to achieve.

The spread of slum housing in Newark and the inability of tenant organizers to achieve widespread changes in the system can be attributed to the combined actions of the government and private interests. Rapid changes in neighborhood population coupled with the uncertainty of where and when the urban renewal bulldozer would strike next led to a rise in landlordism, as property owners in changing neighborhoods sought to maximize what they believed were declining property values or to maximize profit from a captive market. The pace and spatial

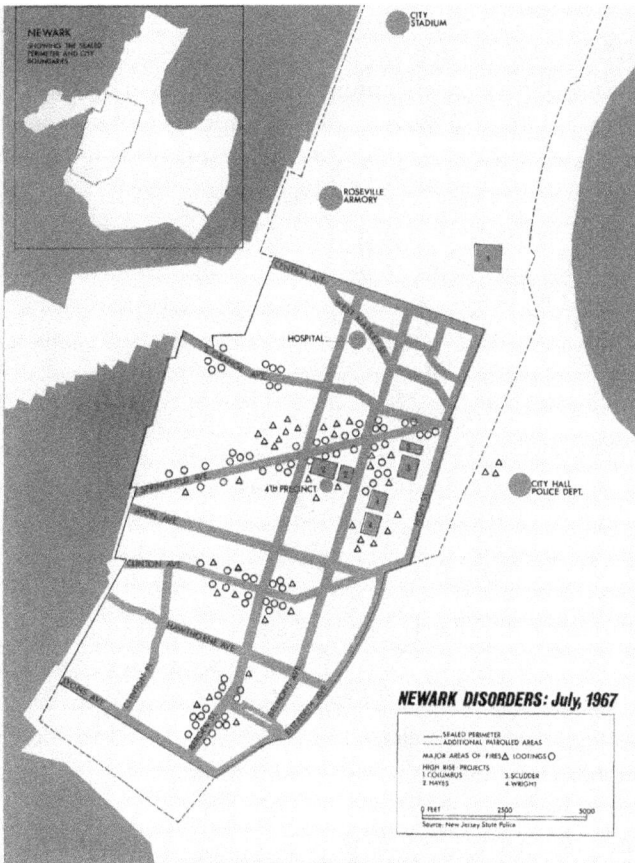

NEWARK DISORDERS: July, 1967

II. The Disorders

FIGURE 3.5. Nexus of rebellion: Stella Wright and the architecture of containment

Source: New Jersey Governor's Select Commission on Civil Disorder, *Report for Action* (New Jersey, 1968), 103, www.ojp.gov/pdffiles1/Digitization/69748NCJRS.pdf.

scale of urban renewal and public housing also triggered further abandonment and decay. In order to keep costs down, the NHA persuaded city inspectors to avoid vigorous enforcement of the city's housing code since well-maintained buildings would command a higher buyout price than "blighted" buildings.[73] The cost of continual tax hikes for owners coupled with the uncertainly of whether their neighborhood or an adjacent one would be declared an urban renewal area (thus triggering a sequence of further blight and abandonment) meant that Newark's residential and commercial market gradually ground to a halt. Without the ability to sell, owners used a variety of means to capture some of the fading value of their properties.

One popular way for owners to extract value was to use the tax system. As George Sternlieb explains in his classic work *The Tenement Landlord Revisited*, given the rising illiquidity of their properties, tenement landlords as well as ordinary property owners used the tax system to extract remaining values.[74] Apartments or buildings were rented out for as long as the building could support it, while the owners refused to put additional money into proper upkeep and maintenance. Value could also be extracted through nonpayment of property and other city taxes. Once the property fell into such disrepair that it could no longer be rented, the owners would "allow" the city to take the property over. This process initiated a further sequence of neighborhood deterioration. Cities like Newark and Oakland, overwhelmed with rising numbers of city-owned properties, were unable to secure the buildings, opening these spaces up to squatters and vandals. Abandoned properties proved to be infectious: as the number of these grew on a particular street, block, or neighborhood, it fueled even more decay and abandonment as remaining property owners saw declines in their property values. The market for tax liens sent quiet signals about the long-term health of Newark's real estate market.

By 1961, nearly 70 percent of all tax liens had been bought by the private market. By 1965, "*at least two years before the eruption of racial confrontation in central core locations*" (italics in the original), the market for tax liens had precipitously dropped and had collapsed by 1970.[75] Property owners began to walk away from their properties, with the city taking control of them in lieu of unpaid taxes; other property owners may have engaged in arson. Abandoned residential buildings were likely to be vandalized or experience fires; while commercial properties in some neighborhoods were damaged during the 1967 Newark riots This process of slow abandonment was clearly apparent in the aftermath of the riots, with whole blocks of empty properties in the affected neighborhoods damaged by fires or vandalism.[76]

The aftermath of Newark's 1967 rebellion made visible to those outside of the city what Black, Puerto Rican, and even working-class white Newarkers had already seen happening: the vast physical destruction of Newark's urban fabric and its ethnic neighborhoods. The public housing projects, especially the high-rises, were grim symbols of "Negro removal" and containment. As *Ebony Magazine* noted, "All of these projects are high-rise silos stacking human beings like so many ears of corn. All have little if any play areas, poor maintenance and even worse security."[77] The Hughes Report, issued in the wake of the rebellion, described the city's Central Ward, home of most of the city's virtually all-Black housing projects, this way: "Some 18,000 people are now crowded into an area with a radius of about a mile and a half. There is little grass or open space around the project grounds. There are no lavatory facilities on first floors or near playgrounds. It is virtually impossible in densely populated vertical silos for parents to supervise their youngsters, for maintenance workers to keep up with their chores, or for policemen to do their job adequately."[78]

The dire housing conditions—both public and private—for Black and Brown Newarkers was one of the key elements discussed during the Black and Puerto Rican Political Convention held in November 1969. The platform on housing was direct, arguing that a

- complete over-haul of [NHA] staffing must follow this board reorganization. Public Housing authority must be divided into two separate agencies, Public Housing and Urban Renewal;
- Public officials must stop land acquisition for non-priority items. This means an absolute moratorium on projects such as useless school expansion, and highways and commercial projects;
- Neighborhoods in good condition must be preserved. Rehabilitation money must be made available as a remedy against advancing deterioration;
- Money must be obtained from the Federal Government and used effectively to bring up the physical and social standards of the Public Housing Projects; and,
- Recreation facilities must be made available to young and old.[79]

Newark's chapter of CAP (Congress of African People), which was heavily influenced by Amiri Baraka, would put the stakes for housing and community control even more starkly as it made the case for its own vision of Black-controlled urban development. Urban renewal, the group argued, was "traditionally . . . an arm of white supremacy, where the Black community is uprooted at the whims of white people." Using HUD's new public participation process, Baraka's group helped to establish a Project Area Committee (PAC) as a means to challenge the NHA's control over redevelopment and housing. The purpose of the new PAC was to reflect a "broad based popular movement of Africans in the Central Ward of NewArk, revolting against the traditional urban renewal process. [PAC] has become the most successful model for community control of land in NewArk and one of the strongest voices in housing on the city. It is a black nationalist alternative to the white supremacist policy of urban renewal."[80]

Baraka would go forward in his plans to build a new NewArk with the construction of Kawaida Towers, a proposed apartment building for two hundred families on a site located in a white-majority neighborhood in north Newark. Beyond providing housing, plans for the building included a "300-seat theater . . . a lounge, wood shop, hobby shop, day care center, and public kitchen; and rooms for art display, reading, and arts and crafts."[81] In keeping with aspirations for community empowerment, the plan envisioned Black contractors and apprentices working alongside white contractors so that Black builders could develop the qualifications needed to subsequently work on other community projects.[82] The plan ended in anger and disappointment for Baraka and his allies, as white opponents mobilized mobs of protestors and white police officers to block construction while Mayor Kenneth Gibson stood by—unwilling or unable to stop the violence and obstruction. Eventually the combined opposition of white city council members, the NHA, and state lawmakers forced the shutdown of the project and the withdrawal of other urban renewal sites from Baraka's control. The failure of Baraka's expansive vision of rebuilding Newark along black nationalist and cultural revolutionary grounds would lead to a sharp and bitter break between him and Gibson.

Despite the acrimonious battle over Kawaida Towers, many Black and Brown Newarkers engaged in ongoing protests about the terrible conditions of the city's housing stock (especially its housing projects) and neighborhoods. Kenneth Gibson's mayoral campaign and Amiri Baraka's "NewArk" movement strove to force local government accountability and responsiveness as well as to advance the larger vision of tenant empowerment and community development. Gibson's campaign promised the complete reorganization of the Newark Housing Authority, including the establishment of a separate division for public housing and better maintenance of public housing units with the provision of increased janitorial and security services. For Newarkers in private market housing, Gibson promised to strictly enforce housing codes in order to preserve older housing units. In addition to housing conservation, Gibson also proposed affordable housing preservation through a "dual program of rent supplements to poor renters and tax incentives to landlords who preserve and repair their properties."[83] This call to a new vision of urban renewal and housing would be taken up by the women of the Stella Wright Houses.

A "Fight for a Bare Standard of Living in the Most Affluent Society in the World"

The promises made by Gibson and the vision set out by Baraka were embraced by many residents in Newark's public housing. From 1970 to 1974, tenants in the Stella Wright Houses along with the Hayes and Scudder Houses—all highrise projects located in the city's Central Ward—would form the backbone of the nation's longest rent strike.[84] The rent strike, conducted mostly by women residents and their families, successfully challenged Newark's approach to public housing, which had been rooted in an ethos of demolition, displacement, and containment. The women who lived in Stella Wright represented a new hope for public housing and its residents: that these complexes would not simply be de facto places of containment and carceralization, but rather, places where Black families could survive and thrive with autonomy and dignity.

Stella Wright's tenant activism rested on a recognition of their lived conditions, while also drawing on a long history of rent strikes and tenant organizing in Newark.[85] Although the NHA's public housing projects dominated the new landscape of the Central and South Wards, most Black Newarkers lived in private rental housing. A report released by the city noted that while the majority of the city's white neighborhoods had "substantially sound" housing, most of the city's Black and Puerto Rican areas were deemed "blighted."[86]

In 1963 and 1964, tenant organizers and groups like NCUP organized a wave of rent strikes against private landlords, not only in Newark but also in Harlem, San Francisco, and Saint Louis.[87] In Newark, the NCUP used the slogan "Rats, Roaches and Ridiculous Rents" (see figure 3.6). For people who were often invisible to the

FIGURE 3.6. Rent strikes, roaches, and ridiculous rents. Clinton Hill Neighborhood Council, 1964

Source: Stanley B. Winters Scrapbooks, Charles F. Cummings New Jersey Information Center, Newark Public Library.

political system, especially poor Black women and their families, these rent strikes were an important source of community voice and mobilization.[88]

NCUP organizers used a variety of techniques, from filing complaints with city departments to picketing recalcitrant slumlords at their suburban homes.[89] There was little improvement as City Hall was largely uninterested in providing protection against evictions or improving conditions (or powerless, as was the case of the city's newly established Human Rights Division). As a result, the battle against Newark's massive private slums would take on a new urgency as Black Power Urbanism unfolded across the city. The battle for housing justice by tenants and organizers found a focal point in publicly owned spaces like Stella Wright (see figure 3.7).

FIGURE 3.7. Stella Wright Tenants Association, "The New Stella Wright Handbook," 1975.

Source: Rise Up Newark, https://riseupnewark.com/wp-content/uploads/2020/09/The-New-Stella-Wright-Handbook-1975.pdf.

Newark's public housing rent strike was not an isolated event. The "fight for a bare standard of living in the most affluent society in the world," as one SDS-ERAP tenant organizer put it, occurred across the United States.[90] As Rhonda Williams and others have shown, the fight for "respect, rights, and power" came from tenants themselves, who understood that changes in their living conditions could only come through direct confrontation with the city governments and public housing authorities that had created the architecture of containment within which they lived.[91] The new activism of these groups relied upon the direct political mobilization and action of the low-income Black and Latinx women whose families lived in the now-decaying public housing complexes and the surrounding neighborhoods.[92]

By the early 1970s, the fight for tenant rights had developed important linkages with the national welfare rights movement as well as with the more diffuse "poor people's movement," and activists in many cities were engaged in broader struggles for economic and political empowerment. The fight for these rights was dramatically highlighted by a wave of public housing tenant strikes starting in Saint Louis (1968), followed by strikes in Baltimore, Boston, San Francisco, Newark, and Philadelphia.[93] Support for these tenants came from a variety of sources, ranging from local SDS-ERAP chapters that operated in Newark, Saint Louis, and other cities, to support coming from Black Power–aligned groups such as CORE (the Congress of Racial Equality) and SNCC (the Student Nonviolent Coordinating Committee). Great Society funding also facilitated tenant activism through the establishment of local organizations funded by the Community Action Program (CAP), VISTA (Volunteers in Service to America), and the Legal Aid Society.

In all of these rent strikes, the tenants' initial demands focused on immediate issues such as fixing the dangerous and decrepit physical condition of these housing complexes. Later, tenant activists would begin to articulate a more wide-ranging set of demands as they attempted to negotiate with hostile and indifferent housing authorities who paid lip service to requests for better services and safer buildings while claiming that lack of federal funding and "bad tenants" and "problem families" were responsible for the dangerous conditions that residents faced. Tenants increasingly demanded that they, not the public housing authorities (PHA), should control their destinies. Experience had shown them that local housing authorities were geared toward building projects and displacing people rather than maintaining projects and supporting communities. Certainly, the lack of responsiveness indicated that many PHA leaders and employees increasingly viewed the tenants as undeserving as the population of urban housing projects became increasingly feminized and racialized. Bertha Gilkey, who lived in Saint Louis's Cochrane Gardens, one of the epicenters of the tenant strike movement, reflected that racialization (and feminization) had led both the housing authority and the city to neglect not only her housing complex but also the neighborhood that surrounded these complexes. For residents like Gilkey, the rent strikes were not only to better conditions in the buildings they lived in, but to also reassert their urban citizenship rights, including the right to live in neighborhoods as residents with a "bare standard of living."[94]

"Towers of Frustration": The Stella Wright Strike

Newark's vast containers for the Black and Brown poor were largely constructed between 1955 and 1962.[95] As in other places such as Saint Louis and South Side Chicago, Newark's architecture of racial containment was largely shaped by a history of racialized space, inadequate funding, shoddy construction, and malign neglect. Stella Wright Houses, a complex of seven thirteen-story buildings with 1,200 units, was one of these places of racial containment. Built in 1959, Stella Wright quickly became a vertical ghetto where nearly five thousand people lived in quickly deteriorating conditions.[96]

To Stella Wright's northeast were the neighboring Edward Scudder Homes with eight thirteen-story buildings and 1,300 families. Scudder was just as massive as Stella Wright, and perhaps more dysfunctional since it shared many of the "cost-saving" architectural features that had once been lauded at Saint Louis's infamous Pruitt-Igoe housing project: skip-stop elevators, long gallery hallways, multiple entry points, and inadequate and/or dangerous communal spaces.[97] Completing this triangle of containment, to the west of Stella Wright was Hayes Homes, a massive complex of ten buildings of twelve or thirteen stories, with 1,452 units. All of these complexes had a predominantly Black or Puerto Rican tenant population.

The Wright-Scudder-Hayes nexus was emblematic of the racial containment architecture created by the NHA and the city's white politicians and construction interests. While patterns of police brutality and government neglect have long been seen as the key contributors to the rebellion, other factors played a role, including the massive "root shock"—the "psychological trauma, financial loss, and rippling instability"—caused by the transplanting of Black and Brown Newarkers due to near-constant urban renewal initiatives.[98] Long-time residents were uprooted from other parts of the Central Ward or from other neighborhoods, while arriving Southern migrants faced limited housing supply. Although many of the original residents of these complexes saw them as spaces of community and connection, to outsiders they presented a dangerous, desolate "moonscape" where government stinginess had created a space devoid of playgrounds, parks, trees, grass, stores, or other kinds of urban necessities, let alone amenities. The complexes were all built around the same period of time, and tenants could see that due to the NHA's lack of maintenance their units were increasingly falling apart, with complexes suffering from vermin infestation, vandalism, and crime. All three complexes lay adjacent to the Fourth Precinct—the police station at the epicenter of Newark's 1967 rebellions.[99]

Tenants certainly perceived the carceral aspects of these spaces—one resident of Stella Wright called the complex a "hellhole" and a "concrete concentration camp." By the mid 1960s, a decade after it was constructed, life in the red-brick complex had become a daily trial for its occupants: "Elevators failed; incinerators poured smoke and soot into hallways and apartments; the roof leaked; rats and roaches were uncontrollable; junkies occupied vacant apartments, and mugging, rape and break-ins became a constant fear."[100] A short documentary made at the time, *Towers of Frustration*, featured residents recounting their anger, fear, and frustration with living conditions.[101] While some of the tenants' anger was directed at other "problem tenants," most was reserved for the NHA, which, the tenants claimed, treated them with indifference and contempt.

While the architecture of containment led to alienation, the advent of Black Power Urbanism offered the possibility of transforming segregation into solidarity. Although the Wright-Hayes-Scudder projects were technically integrated in 1962 (via federal and state laws), by the time of the strike there were only nineteen white families among approximately four thousand units, leaving these complexes a place where predominantly Black and Brown tenants shared the same squalid conditions.[102] Like the activists in Saint Louis and elsewhere, Newark's tenant activists and their allies understood the problems facing public housing tenants through an intersectional lens: the NHA's neglect was due not only to mismanagement but also to the indifference and hostility that the agency showed toward poor Black (and Brown) women.

In retrospect the public housing rent strike over declining conditions should not have been a surprise, at least to NHA insiders and some politicians. In 1965, Danzig noted that the rents did not cover the expenses—especially as poorer tenants replaced higher-income tenants. The NHA failed to respond to increasingly vocal tenant complaints as well as broader criticisms coming from Black Power activists. Danzig blamed the agency's mismanagement and burgeoning maintenance issues on the tenants themselves, arguing that rising levels of vandalism and crime were the result of their actions rather than the failure of the city and the NHA to proactively recognize and address their own internal problems and to develop effective techniques to combat these issues. Indeed, it was not until the early 1970s—as a result of the rent strike—that the city agreed to provide police patrols in and around the complexes. Until then the NHA relied on an understaffed security force.

Part of the NHA's inability and unwillingness to improve conditions in the projects lay in the structure of the organization and the corrupt political milieu within which it operated. It was largely an autonomous agency over which the mayor had little to no power. From the start of Danzig's tenure, the director had established a quid pro quo with the city's power brokers. They did not stand in the way of his largely successful quest to capture urban renewal funds for the city, and in return he turned a blind eye to the practices of those who won contract awards and the quality of the materials and buildings that resulted. From 1960 to 1970, the "process of deterioration [of the city's housing projects] accelerated rapidly" amid multiple allegations that organized crime–related activity during the construction and maintenance phases resulted in shoddy workmanship and materials.[103]

The day-to-day management of the NHA became an important source of patronage for Newark's mayors and the city's ethnic machine. The placement of public housing projects reinforced the city's ethnic lines while providing political benefits to neighboring politicians. For example, "a public housing application with local political connections was able to secure a public housing unit, prevent eviction from a project, secure a unit in a better project, or have the NHA reconsider his rent, if he had the right sponsor at City Hall."[104] Corruption was so pervasive that when former Newark mayor Hugh Addonizio went to prison on sixty-four counts of conspiracy and extortion, it was alleged that under his administration "virtually every contract signed by the city in recent years had been inflated by ten percent to allow for 'kickbacks' to city officials."[105] Danzig's quid pro quo arrangement extended the reach of corruption into the agency itself. A 1974 HUD study found that the NHA was "excessively top-heavy" in terms of executives, with its employees "boasting the highest salaries, the shortest working week and the most generous expense accounts in the city administration." In addition, NHA employees "were allowed to maintain their own enterprises or outside business contracts."[106]

The NHA's shaky budgetary position, that is, the gap between expenses and revenues, was exacerbated by the enactment of the Brooke Amendments in 1968 (and later in 1970 and 1971), which capped rents based on tenant income.[107] Pushed by Senator Edward Brooke (R-MA), the first Black senator since the end of Reconstruction, this new rule limited public housing rents to 25 percent of income. Deductions for dependents lowered the total amount of income used in calculating the overall rent. While this cap meant lower rents for tenants, it also meant lower revenues for housing administrators. It was not until 1981 that the cap was lifted to 30 percent of total income. With a decline in tenant rent, a steady decline in federal subsidy money, and uncontrolled graft, public housing authorities faced a growing gap between revenues and expenses, furthering a cycle of neglect.

The Strike

In April 1970, tenants in Stella Wright, who already had experience from several years of tenant-led organizing, went on a rent strike with the support of VISTA and the predominantly Black Queen of Angels Catholic Church, as well as other church groups outside of and within the city.[108] Kenneth Gibson's successful but contentious mayoral campaign, as well as the fact that his coalition won three out of nine city council seats, indicated that there was also the potential for political support for the strike.

Stella Wright's rent strike was quickly taken up by tenants in Hayes and Scudder. The strike was led by project residents Constance Washington and Toby Henry, with the assistance of Tom Comerford, a Catholic priest who was by then the only white resident of Stella Wright. Washington and Henry were the two most visible members of a large group of Black mothers, who like their peers in Saint Louis and elsewhere, seamlessly combined tenant activism with the emerging welfare rights movement. The initial goals of the strike were limited—the rollback of a fifty-dollar rent increase and a demand that the NHA address the thousands of housing code violations and dangerous conditions that plagued the three complexes.

Because the NHA believed that the condition of the complexes was due to "bad tenants" rather than bad funding policies and bad management, it was reluctant to negotiate. The rent strike made the issues even worse as the unpaid rents—though insufficient—were still important to NHA functioning. The tenants' initial success in blocking eviction attempts by the NHA gave way to a stalemate between the tenants and the NHA.[109] The tenants were disappointed to find that Gibson refused to mediate the dispute, despite his campaign promises and his seeming agreement with Newark's Black Power manifesto. Gibson was by then locked into bitter political battles with a multitude of actors. On one side he faced the remaining Italian American council members and the ethnic political machine of the North Ward who remained implacably hostile toward Gibson and his attempts to shut down what they saw as their fair share of city patronage. On the other side lay the increasingly vocal disenchantment of Baraka and the city's Black nationalist wing who claimed that Gibson was a not only a disappointment but also a sellout. There were other rifts: although Gibson ran on a unified

Black platform, this platform only temporarily masked the divisions between Gibson and other Black machine politicians. The limitations of Black political power—for the city and for Gibson—became apparent the following year (1972) when Gibson's attempt to nominate a new executive director of the NHA was frustrated by tenant hostility to the proposed nominees and by the formal rejection of the still white-dominated city council. In the end Gibson was forced to accept the nomination of Robert Notte, who allegedly had a "cloud of suspected Mafia connections hanging over his head," to the position of executive director of the NHA.[110]

Demolition as Solution

HUD remained conspicuously absent; it did not intervene in negotiations over Stella Wright (nor over Kawaida). Although the NHA blamed HUD for the lack of funding for maintaining public housing, HUD's position was that operational issues were the domain of local PHAs. HUD was increasingly silent about the future of already existing public housing due to the changing stance of the federal government on the subject, with Nixon eventually declaring a funding moratorium in 1974.[111] With HUD and Gibson absent, and with the NHA now in the hands of Notte, who in all probability did not feel beholden to Gibson, the NHA took an even more aggressive stance. In an effort to force the tenants to pay, the NHA turned off the heat and electricity and announced that they would be shutting down these buildings.[112] Although the courts ordered the NHA to turn the heat and electricity back on and to desist from plans to close the projects, the NHA engaged in a stealth demolition campaign through neglect and displacement. Vacant apartments were sealed or left open to the elements to decay. Meanwhile basic maintenance, as well as security measures like replacing missing front doors, were ignored. By November 1973, conditions had deteriorated to such an extent that the Essex County Court, in *Housing Authority of the City of Newark v. Aikens*, found in the tenants' favor.[113] The judge ruled that the tenants could not be evicted and also reduced all back and current rent until "necessary repairs" had been made by the NHA. In July 1974, with the assistance of Gustav Heningburg, a local civic leader and "community fixer," a final settlement was reached between the tenants' group and the NHA.[114] This agreement, which led to limited self-management and periodic infusions of emergency funding from the NHA, reflected the policy limbo of public housing in the United States and the inability and unwillingness of some of the nascent Black urban regimes like Gibson's to take responsibility for the crumbling remains of the segregated metropolis.

On a positive note, the wave of rent strikes that swept across Newark and the rest of New Jersey (and across the nation) led to the creation of the New Jersey Tenants Association, which pushed for a "Tenant's Bill of Rights." Enacted by the New Jersey State Legislature in May 1970, the bill was the catalyst for a wave of tenant activism that resulted in 110 municipalities (including East Orange) adopting rent control laws.[115] Among the statewide rights that tenants won were the establishment of an "implied warrant of habitability" and the right to withhold rent if conditions for habitability were not met. For tenants of public housing in Newark (and other cities), the ability to withhold rent did lead to positive action. Despite these protections, in the long run, housing authorities like Newark's could point to the Nixon-induced structural budget crisis and the diminishing funds available for public housing from the federal government as the reason for the lack of repairs or maintenance. Demolition by neglect was a federal as well as a local project.

From Dignity to Empowerment: Tenant Management

Stella Wright's tenants won the right to remain in the face of the Newark Housing Authority's ongoing abandonment of its public housing units and its threatened shutdown of Stella Wright during the first year of the strike. The tenants also gained control of the complex through the establishment of a tenant management program and won the appointment of a "public housing high-rise tenant" as a member of the NHA Board of Commissioners. In keeping with the "social, economic, educational and political goals" of the rent strike, tenants acquired the right to replace on-site NHA employees with newly trained (and paid) tenants and to have better access to NHA employment opportunities. Finally, in addition to these changes, the Department of Housing and Urban Development committed $1.3 million to the complex for "repairs, improvements and security."[116] The inclusion of tenants as paid employees was key to the resolution of the Stella Wright strike as well as other tenant strikes and reflected its womanist origins. Julia Rabig argues that tenant employment recognized the tenants' "implicit asser[tion] that the uncompensated labor of poor and unemployed women was indispensable to the community's stability. Tenants sought to transform women's traditionally unpaid work—child and elder care, the maintenance of common spaces, the supervision of recreation, and mediation of interpersonal disputes—into paid positions."[117] Stella Wright's new tenant council reflected these aspirations in the introduction of its *New Stella Wright Handbook*, which begins: "A Dream, a desire, and a hope for poor but dignified tenants and prospective tenants."[118]

The agreement in Newark to create a tenant management council (TMC) for Stella Wright was similar to TMC agreements reached in other cities.[119] This document was an optimistic vision of empowerment. In places like Stella Wright, tenant activists envisioned spaces where residents could take over housing authority functions while developing employment for tenants as maintenance workers, cleaners, and security guards. Other possibilities included residents staffing on-site day-care centers for residents and others. Yet it was not easy to sustain Stella Wright control over these functions. For many of Stella Wright's residents, jobs with the NHA were seen as a step up and a way out of poverty and into the unionized working class—and more importantly— out of the projects.

For the NHA, tenant management at Stella Wright was a distraction from the conclusion that the NHA and other housing authorities had increasingly come to embrace: high-rise public housing was falling apart and these settings did not work for tenants or neighborhoods. Much of this belief rested on the erroneous "Pruitt-Igoe myth," which alleged that the design flaws of high modernism had led to the decline of complexes like Stella Wright.[120] The reality was that bad public policy in the form of day-to-day neglect and mismanagement of the buildings coupled with widespread shoddy construction—the latter a reflection of increased federal hostility to public housing—made these places increasingly unlivable. Early on in the protracted negotiations during the rent strike the NHA made the claim that public housing did not work and also that the NHA—and by extension the city—could simply no longer afford these types of housing projects nor the poor people who lived in them. As early as 1973, the NHA proposed the demolition of high-rise public housing in Newark. Periodic infusions of HUD funding into Stella Wright during the Carter administration through the HUD Capital Modernization Program led some activists to believe that a serious commitment to public housing renewal would reverse the Nixon administration's almost complete shutdown in funding for additional public housing projects. The reality looked bleak for Newark's other high-rise public housing projects. Complexes like Scudder Houses and Hayes Homes—also participants in the rent strike—experienced scattershot renovations, usually in response to a publicized emergency. The NHA's neglect of its building stock and increasingly dire conditions was the result in part of its own weak management, which was exacerbated by the authority's independence from the mayor and the insidious impact of New Jersey's political culture of patronage politics. The level of vacancies increased in the complexes as the NHA, lacking a viable (and funded) plan for relocating tenants, attempted to indirectly empty the complexes through its policy of "demolition through neglect."

In 1982, Harold Lucas was appointed as the first Black director of the NHA (twelve years after Newark elected its first Black mayor) and was almost immediately forced to enact massive cuts. Authority staff was cut in half from 1200, leaving 600 people managing 13,000 units, with twenty-eight security people "armed solely with sticks."[121] The Reagan administration provided additional leverage to the NHA in its quest to demolish public housing, stating that the "whole attitude that the Federal Government can solve all the housing problems of this country—those days are over," and backing up that rhetoric with massive budget cuts to the remaining public housing programs (with the exception of housing for the elderly and disabled).[122] By 1985, the anti–public housing consensus at the federal and local level had shifted in the NHA's favor. As Michael Leo Owens and others have shown, the demolition of high-rise public housing also had the support of middle-class Black residents, particularly in cities with high levels of Black municipal empowerment.[123] While Stella Wright continued to operate under tenant management, the NHA moved forward with the actual demolition of its high-rise public housing projects. The NHA's move was not without opposition. The tenant groups and housing advocates that had come together for Stella Wright regrouped again. In 1987, the Newark Coalition for Long-Term Housing filed suit to stop the demolition.[124] The coalition won a consent decree in 1989, in which the NHA agreed to build 1,777 units to replace the 1,559 lost to demolition and was also required to repair and rent more than 1,500 vacant units. Despite the coalition's efforts, by 1992, the NHA had successful managed to abandon and empty many of its buildings through its indirect strategy.[125]

By 1999, Stella Wright was in the crosshairs of the NHA, with the authority planning to use $35 million in HOPE VI funds to demolish the complex's 1,179 units. Under the new punitive, neoconservative federal housing regime, tenants were offered the opportunity to relocate to the new development, but they had to comply with new behavioral rules and criminal background checks.[126] In 2002, the last of the Stella Wright buildings was demolished. It was replaced by a low-rise town house–style development.[127]

When presiding over the city's demolition of Hayes Homes, Mayor Sharpe James (Gibson's successor) declared that its destruction was "the end of an American dream that failed."[128] His disdain for high-rise public housing would be echoed by Andrew M. Cuomo, the Clinton-era secretary of housing and urban development, who would state that "when public housing makes the statement of exclusion and isolation, President Clinton has said, 'Tear it down and don't repaint it, put in new windows or new fences.' . . . It had the wrong intent from the beginning and should be replaced with smaller, low-rise, low-density places where people want to live."[129] The dream of Stella Wrights tenants that public housing could be a place for families and communities to grow and thrive had died a painful death. Perhaps the expectations of tenant self-management were unrealistically and perhaps deliberately set too high, but in the context of Black Power Urbanism, tenant control seemed to offer a path for housing where families could live in a safe and just space.

Newark: The Prize of Urban Education

In 1972, in a move led by seventeen-year-old member Larry Hamm, the Newark Board of Education agreed to the display of an African liberation flag in all of the city's classrooms "where black students were in the majority."[130] For Hamm and his enthusiastic supporters this victory "signal[ed] a new day of black consciousness and pride among the black students of Newark," as well as "a greater allegiance in themselves."[131] While flying the Pan-African flag may seem to be a small symbolic gesture, it marked the culmination of over a decade of open and sustained struggle over the state of Newark's schools and their maltreatment of the city's Black and Puerto Rican students. Critics—including Mayor Gibson—derided the symbolism and argued that the move did not address the deep issues within the school district, including low test scores, lack of classroom resources, a hostile workforce, and a crumbling physical plant.[132] Despite this criticism, the symbolism did reflect a deeper shift toward a new educational system that would be consistently—though not always correctly or competently—held accountable to the "people." Education in post-rebellion Newark was and would continue to be a source of political spoils, but also a contested site for community control and empowerment. As the Barringer High School construction protests had demonstrated, Black Newarkers pushed for greater accountability from city government and the quasi-independent Newark Public School (NPS) system in terms of where resources and funding were allocated, especially as federal Title I funds became an important source of school funding. The emergence of Black Power Urbanism added a new dimension to these demands for accountability as activists agitated for a school system whose structure and curriculum engaged rather than alienated the Black and Puerto Rican students, who by the time of the 1967 rebellion made up the majority of the Newark Public School system's student body.

By 1960, the majority of Newark's Black and Brown students faced a public school system that was in a decades-long funding crisis that had led to crumbling buildings and inadequate resources.[133] It was a system whose administration was dominated by Italian Americans—the ethnic group then in power—and that was staffed almost exclusively by white teachers, whose attitudes toward the growing Black and Puerto Rican student population ranged from indifferent to outwardly hostile. The systemic discrimination and exclusion within Newark's public school system became increasingly untenable as the city's demographics rapidly shifted.

Even as whites continued to leave the city, the ongoing Great Migration and Puerto Rican migration had swelled the city's school population by twenty thousand students over five years. In 1961, 55 percent of Newark's pupils were Black and 4 percent were Spanish-speaking; in 1966, the ratio was 69 percent Black and 7 percent Spanish-speaking. The effect of this rapid demographic change on NPS was striking. One example was Weequahic High School, which for decades had been seen as a "college prep" school for the city's aspiring Jewish middle class. From 1961 to 1966, the Black student population grew from 19 to 70 percent of its total student body.[134] The increase in the number of Black and Brown students exacerbated the issue of space. Like other cities the Great Migration touched, Black children were more likely to be placed in overcrowded and essentially segregated schools, often run on double shifts, than in underutilized schools in white neighborhoods. One report noted a shortfall of approximately six thousand spaces in 1961 and nearly ten thousand spaces in 1967.[135] The educational facilities of the NPS, especially in majority-Black and -Brown neighborhoods, were in dire shape after decades of underfunding. Rehabilitation or replacement costs were estimated at about $200 million.[136]

This rapid and massive shift in student population posed particular problems for the city's overwhelmingly white teaching force (only 1.4 percent of the city's 3,500 teachers were Black). Sixty to 70 percent of the city's teachers lived outside of the city (this included 25 percent of Black teachers). Before 1968, there had been no Black principals and only one Black vice principal. One-third of the teaching staff were substitutes (a significant number were classified as long-term "permanent"), and many of them were Black. The inability to secure a permanent position was due to written and oral exams that deemed many highly educated Black teachers unqualified. Often these tests were unfairly administered, results were ignored, or in the case of the oral exam, speakers with a "Southern" accent were judged to be ineffective communicators.[137] In May 1967, the Organization of Negro Educators (ONE) was formed to address these disparities in the teaching force and the district's administrative staff.

Activists and parents argued that the majority-white teaching force had a negative effect on student performance. Studies found that some teachers in newly majority-Black and -Brown schools saw the new students as not only alien, but also "more difficult to teach . . . unruly . . . unmotivated."[138] Other studies found that in poor-performing majority-Black schools, teachers were often late or absent, with "one in six teachers" leaving each year.[139] The poor performance on standardized tests by Newark's Black and Brown students supported a belief among some teachers that the students were uneducable. Newark's Black and Brown students ranged in ability and background; some were recent migrants with uneven educations, while others had been educated in Newark's de facto segregated schools. Many suffered the trauma of life in Newark's metastasizing hyper-predatory ghetto neighborhoods.

Challenging the "Quiet" Status Quo

Under the city's ethnic machine, debates about personnel selection and school management, not to mention substantive educational reform, were not aired during board of education meetings. Instead, as one report noted,

> Public meetings of the Board . . . were found to tend toward assuming the trappings of formal social settings, where with due ritual, ceremony, and institutional deceit, those affairs of the community directly or indirectly were managed quietly by the representatives of the white community. Black participation was near or at the zero point: an occasional Black individual attended silently . . . in a semi observer role; the stilted presentation of the arranged-beforehand request or statement alleged to represent the concerns of the Black community . . . exhausts the extent of Black participatory roles.[140]

In general, the board refused to acknowledge demands for greater communication, consultation, and accountability, even as Newark's Black and Puerto Rican population increased. Parents, neighborhood groups, and Black Power and Puerto Rican activists continually (and increasingly) pressed school administrators over the declining condition of the city's schools and the quality of education. In the run-up to the 1967 Newark rebellion, dozens of groups packed school board meetings. In order to be heard, Black parents and activists would "intentionally break the rules usually observed at public meetings," and in turn disrupt the "norms of parliamentary and essentially white personnel formality, status distinction, privilege, secrecy, and bureaucratic ritual."[141]

The mobilization of dozens, if not hundreds, of Black attendees at the board of education meetings accomplished a variety of goals. First, confrontational participation leveled the playing field, communicating a refusal to act deferentially toward a body that was seen as either self-serving or venal. Second, the more theatrical the confrontation, the greater the possibility for communicating grievances, concerns, and ideas in a system designed to minimize and/or ignore the Black and Brown parents and students. The most important durable effect of this process was a form of resocialization that created and shaped Black political behavior. School board meetings became a way to enhance intracommunity solidarity or unity by allowing public testing of possible ideas and coalitions. For individuals or groups, performances at board meetings were a means to visibly develop and demonstrate leadership aspirations.[142] The emergence of Black Power Urbanism upended the participatory and performative characteristics of the white urban regime.

The demands for quality education for children in safe buildings staffed by caring and committed teachers grew even more fervent as the board and the teachers demonstrated their indifference and hostility. One symbol of this hostility, coming days before the rebellion, was Mayor Addonizio's appointment of a politically connected, white high school graduate to a high-level board position in place of Wilbur Park, an education advocate who was also the state's first African American CPA. The old regime was slowly destabilized with the rise of a new demographic reality in which, by 1966, Newark's student body was nearly 75 percent Black and Puerto Rican. The employment and professional prerogatives claimed by Newark's majority-white teachers, administrators, and staff increasingly seemed to be in conflict with the demands and needs of Newark's new majority. Black Power Urbanism challenged these prerogatives, seeing them as a collective barrier to achieving a just city for Newark's Black and Brown students.

Crafting Black Power Education

The articulation of Black Power education in NewArk was laid out during the Black and Puerto Rican Political Convention held in May 1969.[143] The more important of the two platforms drawn up during in the convention was written in a workshop led by four educators: Newarkers Eugene Campbell, vice president of the Afro-American Teachers Association (AATA) of New Jersey; William Holden, an NPS school administrator; and outside consultants C. Herbert Oliver, chairman of Brooklyn's Ocean Hill-Brownsville School District, and Lester Campbell, another New York City educator-activist who was a member of the AATA of New York.[144] The second educational platform was written by the youth committee. There was considerable overlap between the workshops, with participants' recommendations largely focused on three key areas.

The first set of platform items suggested "radical and revolutionary changes" to the public school curriculum and structure.[145] In keeping with the priorities of Black Power Urbanism, curricular changes were foremost. While the resolution called for the system to focus on education through the prism of a

Black curriculum, this was not its only aim: it included a call for centering the experiences and needs of Newark's Puerto Rican students in the curriculum. In the context of post-rebellion Newark, Black Studies was a broad umbrella, encompassing Black and Puerto Rican history but also adding "Swahili and Spanish languages to the curriculum of all public schools." The need for bilingual and ESL teachers and services for Puerto Rican students was also stressed. The new curriculum would be written by Black and Puerto Rican educators with changes approved by the community. In keeping with BPU's belief that independent knowledge production came out of people's lived experiences and alternative modes of knowledge, professional criteria were not specified for pedagogical innovation or community approval. Other systemic changes included supporting the African Free School and other independent schools as models for the public system, as well as other innovations such as an all-day program for prekindergarten children. The group also called for Newark to adopt a community-school model in which neighborhood schools would offer free lunches, medical services, recreation, social agencies, and entertainment to children and families. Rather than spaces where children were miseducated or pushed out, NewArk's schools would act as places of guidance for children and centers of support for families and neighborhoods.

The second set of resolutions from the platform were proposals for maximizing community control over public schools through elected community boards, which would also have representation on the central board. These boards would have control over hiring and promotion. Unsurprisingly, given the tensions within the school system, the platform called for teachers to be subject to the direct accountability of the community and required that teachers "live or have background related to the community in which they are teaching."[146] One measure that would have resonance decades later in the context of Newark's neoliberal educational reforms was the call for the district to tie teachers' salaries to pupil achievement in order to attain greater accountability from teachers and school systems. Those measures of student achievement would be developed by the community, not by education specialists. Community control and curricular control were of particular interest to the youth workshop. While many of the recommendations they made echoed the main working group, youth participants highlighted the need for Black and Puerto Rican guidance counselors and relevant vocational education. Members of the youth working group also called for a city-wide elected student council and community service opportunities for youth. Reflecting the disparate treatment in school discipline that disproportionately punished Black and Brown students, the youth group also focused on creating community control over school discipline issues.[147]

The third set of resolutions focused on addressing the systemic needs of the city's schools. Meaningful change could not happen in the context of low salaries for unmotivated and culturally incompetent teachers; lack of resources including updated books, materials, and other supplies; and a crumbling physical plant, especially in the majority-Black schools of the Central and South Wards. Getting Black and Brown Power education to NewArk meant challenging the state's "foundation" plan, which shortchanged increasingly poor and majority-Black and -Brown school districts like Newark and Trenton. Indeed, given the multiple unmet needs and the decades of neglect and underfunding, workshop participants called for the state and federal government to take over education and welfare spending, and in particular, issued a call for funds to support "meeting the basic necessities of the citizens of Newark." Undergirding all of these recommendations was the acknowledgment that none of these resolutions could be implemented or sustained unless there was a "mobilization and politicizing [of] community residents to fight or work toward applying any or all pressure necessary to bring about essential changes in the public school system."[148]

Black Power Meets Union Power

The rebellion underscored the urgency of balancing the demands for educational reform and community control against the desire of the teachers unions for professional and economic benefits. In response, the NPS initiated a number of changes that were implemented beginning in 1968. For example, ONE proposed an alternative for the many Black substitute teachers seeking permanent status, suggesting that teachers could substitute three years of experience and satisfactory ratings from their principals as a route to state certification rather than taking written tests. The board also proposed suspending the promotions list and basing principal and assistant principal appointments on criteria other than examination scores.[149] The two teachers unions, (the Newark Teachers Association [NTA] and the Newark Teachers Union [NTU]), though in favor of more Black principals, raised somewhat disingenuous concerns that "currently qualified candidates" would be discriminated against. The board subsequently appointed ten Black people as acting principals and vice principals in the elementary, junior high, and senior high schools. The board also abolished the system of written and oral examination for the promotion of administrators. The rapid move caused alarm among white council members and teachers. One council member argued that the board's actions were "a clear violation of due process, the sanctity of contract and the civil rights of the promotional candidates involved [and that] there were legitimate vacancies that existed and should have been filled by persons who had passed the Board's own examination procedure, rather than by persons selected by a method clearly not impartial."[150] A group of white teachers then filed a federal lawsuit against the board seeking damages for what they argued was a deprivation of their rights, as well as a preliminary injunction to bar the board's appointments.[151]

Growing Black political mobilization and confrontation with the board, as well as the board's willingness to walk away from what the teachers unions saw as hard-fought achievements over reforms in hiring and promotion, came into explosive contact with the inter-union competition between the NTU and the NTA. Each entity tried to position itself as the means by which the white teaching majority could secure their gains, increase their compensation and other prerogatives, and carve out a sphere of jurisdictional autonomy free from Black control.

Two back-to-back teachers' strikes caused severe and long-lasting antagonism and distrust between the city's then majority-white teaching staff and Newark's Black parents and community activists. The first strike occurred in 1970 during the last year of the Addonizio administration. Teachers organized in response to conditions in Newark. The decline in Newark's schools was reflected not only in its failing physical plant, but also in a central office more concerned with patronage and contracts than with the quality of education for students and the employment conditions for teachers. For aspiring mayor Gibson and his Black Power Urbanism allies, the leadership of the Newark teachers union by Carol Greaves, an African American woman, as well as the union itself, posed somewhat of a problem, as an aspirational belief in Black unity and labor solidarity clashed with Greaves's position. Despite Greave's visibility, Black activists, buoyed in part by the Black and Puerto Rican Political Convention, would develop an even more detailed call for Black community control of Newark's schools.[152]

Under the wider urban coalitions that typified urban Keynesianism, and as seen in the Barringer High struggle, most urban unions—skilled trades as well as teachers unions—stood as enforcers of racial and gender exclusion. Greaves's leadership and the early (though brief) support of the Black teachers' coalition, however, initially led to a muted support for the union from many Black activists and parents. Indeed, the union's initial claims could be read as strictly classroom control issues, of teachers against an overbearing and corrupt central office, as opposed to issues about the changing demographics of the school system and demands for more Black teachers and administrators. This struggle over conditions and the rising activism of Newark's teachers reflected the growing mobilization of teachers unions as well as the broader mobilization of public sector unions. However, in the context of demands for more community input and accountability during the era of Black Power activism, teachers unions were criticized for placing their majority-white members' interests (and their membership dues) ahead of the needs of poor children.

Black Newarkers voiced an early version of these criticisms during the second teacher's strike, which began in February 1971. While many of the issues remained the same as during the first strike, the players did not. The union's grievances were no longer persuasive to Black Newarkers and Black Power activists, in particular, decried the fact that aside from the leadership of Greaves, the union was largely made up of teachers who did not look like many of the students they taught and who went home to white suburban communities in which their students could not live.[153]

With the success of Gibson's election, Amiri Baraka was at the height of his influence. Baraka, along with some allies on the now minority-dominated school board, viewed the teachers' previous settlement in 1970 as a giveaway of district authority that essentially allowed white teachers to do far less in the classroom for far more money. Baraka and his allies saw the second strike as a means for the soon-to-be Black-dominated school administration to recentralize power. Presaging the moderate stances that he would take during his mayoralty, Gibson eventually stepped in to help settle the strike. In the process, he also appointed a task force that would recentralize school board authority. The two teachers' strikes resulted in a decades-long acrimonious and poisonous relationship between the city's teachers and its unions, and between the union and the city's Black political class and Black parents. The Newark teacher's strikes also recast community control much differently than in neighboring New York City and its Ocean Hill-Brownsville controversy.

The bitter context of the second teachers' strike was also influenced by the reconstitution of Newark's educational regime and the altered role of ethnic politics. Neither white political leaders nor their constituents disappeared after the rebellion and Gibson's election. Although Gibson had won the mayoralty and Black candidates had won more seats on the city council, this did not mean that ethnic politics in the city was dead. Italian American political leaders like Anthony Imperiale and Stephen Adubato would provocatively (Imperiale) or more quietly (Adubato) continue to make the case for the maintenance of "Italian power" in Newark. This animosity was demonstrated in high schools like Vailsburg and Barringer where fights and walkouts by Black and Italian American students continued throughout the early 1970s. In the younger grades, racial and ethnic antagonism became more muted as many Italian American families, including the family of former New Jersey governor Chris Christie, moved from Newark to suburban Essex County. Puerto Ricans (Newark's "other ethnic group") would also enter the stage, claiming that the board and the teachers were using their community as a pawn in the dispute. In 1974 the Puerto Rican community would stage its own rebellion. Many of their demands echoed those made by African Americans but the Puerto Rican community made the case that under the city's newly empowered Black regime their position had worsened. All of these divergent interests: the political/ideological divisions between Gibson, other Black politicos like George Richardson, and Black nationalist activists such as Amiri Baraka; the unwillingness of the Italian American bloc to work in coalition with the ascendant Black ethnic bloc; and the tense relationship of Puerto Ricans with both Italian Americans and African Americans, all made for a bitter labor dispute and a school board that was contentious and at times paralyzed in its response.

Gibson was limited in his ability to solve the near paralysis of the board. Part of this lack of power was structural. Like many of New Jersey's school boards, the Newark board was appointed, and as a result it was difficult for Gibson to change the board's composition. Even when he was able to appoint more Black candidates to the board, the political ambitions of individual Black board members did not necessarily harmonize with Gibson's political calculations. The slow collapse of the Newark economy in the wake of the 1967 rebellion affected the city's finances. Indeed, by 1975, this paralysis and slow-moving chaos had led to a school system in crisis, with a $35 million deficit. For the first time since 1968, the state raised the specter of a state takeover of the district. Although the threat was dropped, it was a signal that Black-controlled school districts would be subject to a higher level of scrutiny than majority-white districts, especially as the state of New Jersey was embarking on a new way of equalizing school funding across the state's school districts.[154]

Creating Zones of Education for Liberation

Black Power Urbanism not only challenged the educational status quo, it also nurtured a host of new educational spaces, networks, actors, and alliances that helped to reform and reconstitute Newark's educational regime. One of the most visible results of these reform attempts was the school board's 1965 decision to employ teacher's aides, or "indigenous nonprofessionals."[155] Taking inspiration from both Mississippi and New York City, Newark's advocates believed that "hiring local residents—primarily mothers of schoolchildren—would improve classroom instruction, connect schools to their surrounding neighborhoods, and create jobs and careers in education."[156] In Newark, teacher's aides would help to address the lack of teaching and staff support needed relative to the district's changing school population and to bridge the deep gap between teachers and the students, as these aides would be hired from the neighborhoods similar to those in which students lived. The patronage network also benefited from the hiring of this group. With support from Black politicians and activists waning and Gibson positioning himself as a credible candidate for the mayor's office, Addonizio saw jobs for poor and working-class Black Newarkers as a way to shore up support for the machine and his reelection. The status of the teacher's aides as proto-paraprofessionals was ambiguous: in contracts talks for the 1966–67 academic year the NTA proposed hiring 240 teacher's aides, who would "relieve regular teachers of clerical duties, [and provide] improved medical care and other services."[157] The NTA came close to achieving its goal: at the end of the next school year the district reported that it had hired 225 aides "who were drawn from local neighborhoods, [and who had] receiv[ed] certificates of achievement. School systems throughout the country have been reported following Newark's lead in utilizing and training teacher aides."[158] In the proposed contract for 1967–70, one of the sticking points was that the union wanted to ensure the continued involvement of at "least 214 teacher aides to alleviate such non-teaching routine duties as lunchroom supervision, playground duty, bus duty, etc."[159]

The NTU supported the introduction of teacher's aides for several reasons. NTU leaders and some teachers believed that "parents [would] support the teachers if they strike because teacher aides from the community would persuade the community of NTU's position."[160] Once introduced, the presence of teacher's aides would come to be seen as a necessity as well as a symbol of Newark teachers' professional status. Indeed, at some of the city's schools like South Eighth Street (renamed Martin Luther King Jr.), teachers' insistence that they would not perform nonprofessional chores triggered intense acrimony between the teachers and many Black parents and community activists. This demand by teachers remained a sticking point in contract negotiations until the bitter end of the 1971 strike, when Gibson and the union finally agreed that "non-professional chores [would] be limited to leading children from building entrances to their classrooms and monitoring high school corridors between classes [while] substitutes and aides [were] responsible for all other non-professional chores."[161]

Newark's Black Power Urbanism movement also led to the development of new educational spaces that hearkened back to the nineteenth century and the Newark Colored School. Indeed, a headline in *Black Newark*, the city's Black nationalist newspaper, would proclaim "Black Education—No Liberation Without It!!" while offering brief reports on the new Black Power–inspired educational spaces (see figure 3.8).

FIGURE 3.8.   Instantiating Black Power Urbanism education in Newark

Credit: *Black Newark* 1, no. 9 (September 1972): 1, 4.

Two independent Black institutions, the Chad School and the African Free School, were established during this Black Power moment. The Chad School was created by a local organization loosely affiliated with the Black Panther movement. Originally started in 1969 as an afternoon program, it had expanded by the following year to occupy five converted row houses on Clinton Avenue on the eastern edge of the Central Ward. Adopting the reigning philosophy of independence and self-reliance, it did not accept government funding and maintained an all-Black teaching and administrative staff. The second institution was the African Free School, which Amina Baraka and other members of CFUN's women's division started in 1965 as a preschool located in Spirit House, CFUN's headquarters.[162] The elementary school program was located in the Robert Treat School, on the edge of the medical school urban renewal area. By 1970, the elementary school program had been formally incorporated into the Newark public school system.

Within the public school system, a small number of semiautonomous educational spaces were created in the ferment of Black Power Urbanism.[163] The Springfield Avenue Community School, located in the city's Central Ward, was one such space. Founded by the Newark Day Care Council (NDCC), Springfield was the state's first public community school.[164] The school building was a former furniture store whose renovation, designed by a Black architect, was structured around a pedagogical approach that demanded intensive involvement of parents as teachers and learners. Black mothers seized control of the school from the NDCC and the New Jersey Early Childhood Learning and Development Center.[165]

The school—once under the control of parents and led by educators like Edna Thomas—underwent a significant redesign of the curriculum to an Afrocentric approach that unapologetically embraced "Black culture." In addition, students were spatially, educationally, and culturally embedded in a particular place: "Newark—A City of Progress." To these educators and parents, schools like Springfield and their students should not be resigned to the "doom-and-despair" that characterized most accounts of Newark, but rather should embrace the emancipatory possibilities of progress. To the members of the Springfield Avenue community, there was "nothing humorous or visionary" in that assertion of progress. Indeed, it "merely forecasts a condition they believed [was] realistic, and [were] working hard to attain."[166]

Springfield Avenue Community School was not the only example of the spontaneous grassroots assertion of local community control, in which parents, and at times local political leaders and neighborhood activists, would seize control of their schools in order to force change. The assertion of this control was achieved through temporary actions such as boycotts and sit-ins as well as through sustained organizing and protests both at the schools and in front of the board. From 1964 through 1971, these actions mostly took place at schools where parents had protested for years about overcrowding, split sessions, and dangerous and unhealthy conditions. At some schools these actions were designed to push out undesired teaching and administrative staff, as well as to impose a parentally devised and controlled curriculum. By 1972, local control had been permanently established at a cluster of schools in the Central and South Ward, including the African Free School. For some schools, this assertion of control involved renaming as a reflection of their new status as places of education for Black liberation. Robert Treat, home of the African Free School, was renamed Marcus Garvey School. The South Tenth Street School was renamed the Harriet Tubman School, while the South Eighth Street School, which had a past history of local activists and parents issuing and carrying out semi-violent threats, was renamed the Martin Luther King Jr. School. Thirty years later, in the context of the state's proposed takeover of the system, the Harriet Tubman School would be celebrated as an "island of excellence" that succeeded where other Newark schools did not by "insulating the classrooms from the drag of a stifling bureaucracy by going outside the system for money, equipment and other kinds of support."[167]

After the Revolution

The resolution of the teachers strikes and the emergence of alternative spaces of educational liberation did little to address the uncertainty and divisiveness that continued to plague the school system. This sense of crisis was heightened when Gibson was forced to reveal that that the board faced a $35 million deficit with no new sources of funding in sight. With this revelation the state threatened a district takeover for the first time since 1968, although it did not proceed with it. Instead, the state senate appointed an auditor general to review the district's fiscal affairs. The auditor "stress[ed] that he was not part of a state takeover," but simply an "objective appraiser of the quality of board business operations."[168] City officials, including Gibson and the school board, as well as Black education activists, were all skeptical of the state's assurances that the Newark Board of Education still "maintain[ed] its integrity as a semi-autonomous body."[169] Indeed, presaging the criticism to come when the state actually did take over the system in the 1990s, one board member denounced the state-appointed auditor as a "white overseer."[170] While the move to appoint an overseer of district expenditures may have been motivated by concern over the district administration, the state's interest in the finances of poor school districts was also triggered by the recent ruling in *Robinson v. Cahill*, which mandated that the State of New Jersey address the significant fiscal inequality across the state's school districts with a plan for equalization.[171] Despite state intervention and the promise of better funding for the city's troubled schools, Black middle-class families and increasing numbers of working-class families continued to leave the system, which meant that it would serve an even poorer student body.

Newark's Black Power urbanists, who saw Black leadership as a means of organizational change and political empowerment, were instrumental in the 1973 appointment of the city's first African American superintendent, Stanley Taylor. Taylor's appointment, however, could not overcome the system's deeply contentious politics and the structural issues it faced in terms of the poverty of its students and the real physical decay of the city's schools. The school system went through a series of superintendents over the next decade or so, each of them leaving once they realized that they could not achieve the impossible—high quality, culturally competent education in a financially disinvested and physically crumbling school system. Moderates like William Ashby, a Black political leader since the 1930s, voiced their frustration with the city schools and their skepticism over the growing influence of Black Power pedagogies, arguing that somewhere along the line someone has to say "Stop," This is it. We are not doing a good job, professional educator or layman, and say these are the facts. Until such a time as these reading levels and arithmetic levels come up, there isn't anyone who can say in the city of Newark, professional or otherwise, that we are doing a good job because these children just can't read and do arithmetic. . . . I think we are going to have to call a sharp halt to all the camouflage that has gone on for the past 10, 15 and 20 years.[172]

The inability to solve the growing crisis of Newark's schools through a change in superintendents or a change in mayoral leadership suggested to some activists that a deeper structural change was needed. One of the key reforms they advocated was a push for an elected rather than appointed school board on the theory that board members would be more responsive to parents if they were not beholden to the mayor, contending ethnic groups, or the teachers union. Some scholars suggest instead that the referendum for an elected school board was "engineered by a strongly union-backed group of citizens."[173] Whatever the case, frustration with the state of the hyperpoliticized and ethnically polarized school board, and Gibson's seeming powerlessness to control its activities, led to the activists winning the battle for an elected board in 1982. The switch to an elected board, which many community activists hoped would lead to more responsiveness, did initially result in the "'most productive period' in Newark school history," with significant increases in district-wide math and reading scores.[174] This improvement proved to be short-lived; rather than academic improvement, the elected board led to a significant growth in school staff. According to Wilbur Rich, during this period the union consolidated its control over the board, securing a 23 percent pay increase for teachers as well as pay increases for members taking union-run classes, and gaining the right to exclude school administrators from teaching observations.[175] Part of this huge growth in staffing was due to the fact that by the late 1980s both voters and local officials recognized that the schools were one of the few public institutions left at the neighborhood level that offered a modicum of social and economic security and possibly mobility to struggling residents, and votes for the politicians who delivered these jobs.[176]

In the end, an elected school board did not solve Newark's ongoing educational issues. Indeed, the existence of an elected board; ongoing and highly publicized petty corruption on the part of administrators, teachers, and parents; and a lack of clear measurable success would all help to feed into and justify the narrative of institutional and political failure that had been developing in relation to urban school districts like Newark since the early 1970s. City schools had become "urban" schools. In the face of this emerging narrative of "failing urban schools" and the real failure of the system that lay before them, Black Newarkers continually pushed back at the notion that a state takeover would be in the city's best interest. Newark's public schools served many of the city's poorest neighborhoods as spaces around which important community-building and sustaining activities took place, as well as a politics that both challenged and supported Gibson's political machine. In 1989, citing the "academic bankruptcy" of the Newark system, Republican governor Thomas Kean set in motion the long-threatened state takeover of the Newark system.[177]

Newark schools seemed to be trapped in a permanent state of failure, with perennially low test scores, high dropout rates, and a crumbling physical plant. The system itself had seen over four decades of near continuous reforms, which had been adopted and then discarded as administrators followed the current educational trends. On top of these setbacks, Newark's school administration was beset by patronage, graft, and incompetence—the jobs and contracts controlled by the schools had been considered "the prize" for much of the twentieth century—whether the city was under reform, ethnic (that is, Irish or Italian), or Black control.[178] While poverty rates and fiscal stress explained some of the system's failures, the inability of Black administrators to "fix" these schools was a betrayal of the hopes of those who had struggled for community control of schools and of Black Power Urbanism. The state takeover of the Newark school system in 1992 seemed to be a definitive repudiation of Black Power Urbanism, yet its imposition did not go uncontested. The legacy of Black Power Urbanism meant that the state's oversight of the system was continually contested by activists, parents, and students who held onto a belief in the necessity for "[m]obilization and politicizing [of] community residents to fight or work toward applying any or all pressure necessary to bring about essential changes in the public school system."[179]

Begin As You Mean to Go On: Newark's Urban Policing

By 1909, Divers Coleman, "the only colored man on the Newark Police Force," had spent nearly twenty-five years assigned to Newark's First Precinct (located in the city's Third, now Central, Ward).[180] A newspaper article about him noted that Coleman, or "'Uncle Tom,' as he is familiarly called by his colleagues . . . has been a credit to his race, and will leave behind him a record unstained by a black mark." It reported that he was appointed (along with two other Black officers) in 1885 "through the influence of Aldermen Thebold and Hickey, who represented his [Coleman's] ward at the time." Coleman's position in the Newark Police Department (NPD) reflected the subordinated position of Newark's Black community. Coleman was lauded for his faithful service, his "kindly disposition," and his "cotton-colored" hair. He was also praised for his notable arrests, especially of "desperadoes," as well as his standing as the "real bogeyman for the law breakers who crossed his path."[181]

For the half century or so after Coleman's retirement, Black police officers were a rare sight in the ranks of the NPD. They included Carlton B. Norris, hired in 1930, who developed a reputation as "'not a friend to the (black) folk [due to his] 'heavy handed' use of the 'Billy club.'"[182] As the Black population of Central Ward increased, the NPD would increasingly see the Black residents of the First Precinct not as fellow citizens with a sprinkling of "desperados" and "lawbreakers" in their midst but rather as a suspect population to be brutally surveilled, controlled, mistreated, brutalized, and sometimes killed at the hands of the police. Throughout the first two-thirds of the twentieth century, the NPD would essentially act as an occupying force in the Central Ward and wherever Black citizens found themselves in the city. During the same period of time, members of the NPD, a wide swath of Newark's ethnic machine politicians, and a plethora of organized crime groups viewed the Central Ward and other Black and Brown neighborhoods as sites for predation, corruption, extortion, and violence. The police would serve as the focal point and conduit for the multiple forms of violence and trauma imposed upon Black Newark.

Black Newarkers during World War II and the postwar period engaged in local civil rights activism around urban renewal, housing, education, and more importantly "police-community relations"—a euphemism for the violent and degrading relationship between the almost all-white NPD and the Black and Brown communities of Newark. This latter issue forged strong bonds of cross-class solidarity within Black communities as both poor Black teens and Black community leaders and activists were subject to the NPD's urban policing. By the end of the 1950s, the local Black press had documented multiple reports of police brutality, which were invariably addressed through police cover-ups or outright denials. One example of NPD's brutality that indicated a lack of respect for class lines was the beating of Edward Taylor, director of New Jersey Labor Council. This beating and others so enraged the Black community that they "sparked a forum of 250 [Black] ministers and businessmen. Although [a white newspaper] reporter was present, the story never ran [in the white newspaper] because the editor 'decided that story was too inflammatory.'"[183]

The brutality of the NPD, its involvement with organized crime, and its participation in other forms of bribery and payoffs was no secret to Black Newarkers. Indeed, a 1959 report found a huge difference in Black and white

Newarkers' opinions about the police.[184] The report found "stories about police discrimination—physical abuse, unfair arrests, and, to a lesser extent, laxness in the protection of Negroes—are widespread and have been heard by almost half the Negro community," while "less than a tenth of the whites have heard such stories, and even fewer believe them to be true. Furthermore, most of those [white residents] who have heard these stories believe there is at least some truth in them."[185]

The recommendations that the report put forth reflected the chasm between white and Black Newark. Thus the report found that "belief in stories about mistreatment of Negroes at the hands of the agency whose primary function is to protect citizens, the police, is so widespread among Negroes as to present a very real problem for the City of Newark." The solution the report suggested was not to change the system that inflicted daily harm on Black Newarkers, but rather a "thorough investigation to learn whether these charges have any foundation, . . . followed by a public relations program aimed at assuring the Negro community either that their fears are unfounded or that proper steps have been taken to insure their equal rights before the law in the future. The Commissioner or the Police Department may want to consider the advantages of consulting the various public and private agencies in Newark concerned with the field of human relations in order to develop an adequate program to deal with the situation."[186] Despite the urgings of this report and the protests from community activists, denial, delay, and minute symbolic concessions became the response of the city administration to the violence of urban policing.

The city and more indirectly the NPD responded to the crisis of police brutality in ways similar to other cities. First, it made weak efforts to adopt the "police-community relations" model that had been developed in cities like Oakland during and after World War II as Black migrants challenged prewar socio-spatial boundaries.[187] Second, with the election of Addonizio, it embraced a limited liberal integrationism as the city's final reform movement faltered and a revitalized ethnic machine acceded to power. Addonizio was elected to office with the clear support of Black Newark's politicos, who had encouraged Black Newarkers to support him. As a reward, Black Newark received some additional patronage as well as a limited opening up of municipal employment to Blacks residents. The NPD was one place where this occurred. In 1955, out of a thousand-member police force, the NPD had a total of twenty-seven Black police officers, with five recently promoted to sergeant.[188] Under the leadership of Dominic Spina, by 1965 the department had established "salt and pepper" patrol units of Black and white officers riding together, had hired more Black offers (without getting rid of discriminatory hiring rules like height requirements and "character investigations"), and had pushed through the promotion of more Black officers to sergeant (but not to higher ranks).[189] By 1963, Spina would declare that the NPD was "completely integrated."[190] None of these moves fundamentally altered the antagonistic relationship between the NPD and Black and Brown Newark.

Tensions remained high between the police and different sectors of Black and Brown Newark up until 1966. In 1960, Newark's CORE chapter held a thousand-person rally against police brutality. In 1963, Barringer High protests would lead to Black political activists, including mayoral appointee George Richardson, being roughed up by police. The status of the NPD and to whom it was accountable was made clear in the wake of the Barringer High protests. Richardson, called in by Mayor Addonizio to explain his actions, said, "I am not picketing against you, I am picketing the police." Addonizio responded to Richardson's argument with a naked assertion of power: "I'm the mayor. They are my police. That's me."[191]

Two years later, this denial and lack of accountability would again be on display with the death of yet another Black man, Lester Long. The trauma of the killing was exacerbated by the decision of the district attorney to decline laying charges, even though the officer involved gave wildly conflicting accounts of the shooting. Once again, the Black leadership of CORE and other groups repeated their demand for the establishment of a civilian review board. The killing of Black citizens with impunity was the most visible aspect of the NPD's violent and corrupt policing of Black Newark, which particularly affected Black and Brown youth. A documentary made at the time gave voice to a young Black man who matter-of-factly described daily ongoing abuse by the NPD: young men were regularly picked up for "loitering," beaten, and then released; it was simply part of the system.[192]

The several deaths that occurred at the hands of the police between 1964 and 1965, including that of Lester Long, coupled with the daily violence of Newark's urban policing, revealed the hollowness of Addonizio's liberal integrationism. Once again CORE led a massive rally in support of a civilian review board (see figure 3.9), and, once again Addonizio and Police Chief Spina refused to countenance any discussion of it.[193]

Addonizio embraced a police-community relations model, launching the Newark Police-Community Relations Training Program as a way to satisfy rising criticism.[194] Meanwhile, Spina claimed that there was no police brutality issue, stating that "only 28 complaints" had been lodged in the past five years, even in the face of one hundred thousand arrests.[195] Critics countered this claim, saying that Black Newark "couldn't trust anything the police told them."[196] Indeed, the legitimacy of the NPD, and by extension Addonizio and his machine, plummeted as critics (both Black and white) argued that the police force was "shamelessly crooked" and "shockingly friendly" with

FIGURE 3.9.   Whose police? The struggle for a civilian review board for Newark

Source: "CORE protest, 1965," box 2, folder 4, Fred Means Papers, MG Nwk Means-(Main), Charles F. Cummings New Jersey Information Center, Newark Public Library.

organized crime.[197] By the end of 1967 local Black leaders—from moderate to militant—were predicting that Newark was a powder keg and that the NPD's behavior was the "one big danger" in determining whether Newark would join the list of cities experiencing "long hot summers" of urban unrest.[198] In July of 1967, Newark joined that list and the Newark Police were one of the precipitating factors of both the rebellion and the police riot that followed. The Newark rebellion lasted from July 12 to July 17, 1967. Twenty-six people were killed; seven hundred people were injured; and over $10 million in property damage occurred, most of it concentrated in the city's Central Ward.[199]

The immediate aftermath of the rebellion provoked several conservative responses including piecemeal symbolic reforms by the Addonizio administration, the rise of "law and order" politics and vigilantism by Italian Americans (the city's last large white ethnic group), and the increased militarization of the NPD and other local and state police forces. Addonizio tried to deflect blame by promoting Lieutenant Edward Williams, a fourteen-year police veteran, to captain of the First Precinct, the epicenter of the Newark rebellion.

White police officers violently protested the promotion both in front of City Hall and on police radios, "disparaging the city and its 'first n[-----] police captain.'"[200] Local, state, and federal authorities responded to the rebellion with more militarization of the police and less lip service to notions of police-community relations. Indeed, in 1968 the mayor would once again refuse to consider the establishment of a civilian review board.[201] More alarmingly, once his support from Black Newarkers had largely evaporated, Addonizio reached out to whites in the city's North Ward who formed neighborhood vigilante groups in the days during and following the rebellion and subsequently embraced urban "law and order" politics. The police were theirs, and they were the police's.

In the Black community, the rebellion only fueled Newark's own Black Power Urbanism. The first full-fledged Black Power Conference happened only days after the rebellion ended and the attendees and the conveners of the conference, from Amiri Baraka to Nathan Wright, were profoundly shaken and radicalized by their firsthand experiences. Indeed, the Black Power Manifesto and Resolutions issued by the conference not only called for community control of the police but also condemned the so-called "Riot Bill" as "unconstitutional . . . infring[ing] upon the rights of free speech and assembly and . . . propos[ing] to stifle Black Power and Black Liberation."[202] The Black Power Conference also adopted a resolution "deplor[ing] the totally unnecessary brutality to Brother LeRoi Jones [Amiri Baraka] and other Black people of Newark. We also demand that they be compensated for their injustices by the City of Newark."[203]

The Newark rebellion infused further energy into the quest for Black sovereignty and the fight to rein in the NPD. Unlike the Black Panthers' Ten-Point Program, the 1968 *Platform of the Black and Puerto Rican Convention* eschewed revolutionary and abolitionist rhetoric in addressing the policing issue and adopted a more reformist approach that saw Black Power as deriving from control of political institutions. The reformist aspect of the platform reflected the flavor of Newark's Black Power Urbanism. In included the declaration that "it is our intention to elect a black mayor in Newark. We feel that through his powers, the court will be more responsive to community needs. To remove that power from the mayor and place it in the hands of the governor would be a mistake."[204]

Other reformist elements suggested by the platform included adding more Black and Puerto Rican officers to the force by changing recruitment requirements and standards; enforcing a residency requirement; and offering higher salaries, tuition assistance, and in-service courses to provide police officers with more culturally competent training (for example, coursework in areas of urban sociology, psychology, and criminology). The systemic corruption within the ranks was addressed with calls for "promotions in the police department . . . [to] be based on examinations which include areas of urban sociology," while the "assignment of personnel [should be] on the basis of merit and without favor or partisanship." Two structural changes were suggested. One was the "establishment of an effective police review board to investigate and hear community complaints concerning police activity"; the second, the "abolition of the police director's position and the establishment of a civilian's board of police commissioners to assume the former functions of the police director. It is hoped that by having commissioners selected from the community that the police department's policies will reflect the wishes of the community."[205]

The final set of recommendations barely touched on the explosive relationship between Black and Brown youth and the NPD. The convention called for the establishment of a "youth aid bureau in every precinct" and for the creation of community groups that would "work in close cooperation with local youth aid bureaus and with the administration and the residents in the Essex County Youth House." Newark's Black convention did not come close to truly confronting the NPD's abusive policing.

In Newark, Black Power urbanists believed that control of the city though elected office (the mayor and city council) would subsequently lead to the power to reshape the NPD and the local criminal justice system. Black Newarkers aiming for a NewArk thought that ceding power to the state—whether in the realm of policing or education, both of which had been proposed by Governor Hughes in the aftermath of the rebellion—would ultimately stifle Black Power. But Black Power Urbanism supporters also focused on reforming the carceral apparatus that had emerged out of corrupt ethnic machine politics. Black Power Urbanism supporters shaped their demands based on their knowledge of Black Newark's negative experiences with the Ford Foundation–backed Gray Areas program, which targeted Black and Brown youth under the aegis of "juvenile delinquency," and the realization that the city's own tentative postwar embrace of police-community relations policing in a quest to shore up the liberal integrationism of the city's more liberal citizens had been a failure.

The first test of Newark's Black Power urbanist approach was Gibson's election as mayor in 1970 and his seemingly inexplicable refusal to name a Black police chief. Gibson's selection of John Redden (a white man) was especially galling to activists like Baraka since there were senior Black law enforcement officers in the ranks, and more crucially, the Black and Puerto Rican Convention platform and the Gibson campaign had advocated community control of the police via the establishment of a civilian-controlled board of police commissioners and the establishment of a civilian review board. Some accounts of the period suggest that Gibson's appointment of Redden was neither inexplicable nor a betrayal, as Baraka and his allies asserted. Rather Gibson was taking into account the political difficulties and extreme back-lash that Carl Stokes of Cleveland (who had been elected a few years before him) had faced in Cleveland when he appointed a Black police chief to run an almost all-white and hostile police force.[206] Closer to home, Gibson was also faced with the difficult task of solidifying his control over an adversarial, entrenched white bureaucracy that resented his victory and feared for the jobs and perks they had obtained under the city's Italian American–dominated ethnic patronage system. At the same time, he had to work with a city coun-cil that was, by a slim majority, controlled by white city council members who represented the majority-white neighborhoods that had decisively voted against him during the city's racially polarized mayoral election.

Gibson also had to contend with an emergent white "law and order" vigi-lante group in the city's North Ward led by Anthony Imperiale.[207] Imperiale's group, as well as his later successful bid for political power, stood as a stead-fast force against any attempt by Gibson to meaningfully reform the police. Indeed, their implacable opposition to reform and their ability to influence other parts of the New Jersey's byzantine machine politics, ranging from the county executive to the statehouse, forced Gibson into the position of having to appoint a white director of police, to the absolute fury of Baraka and Black Power supporters. When Baraka and his supporters clashed with Imperiale's forces over the building of Kawaida Tower in the North Ward, the police once again showed their true allegiances. Redden refused to interfere with the vigi-lantism of the off-duty white cops, who physically blocked and assaulted the Kawaida workers and supporters in order to stop construction and allow time for rulings to come down through the machine-controlled courts. The physical confrontations between white residents aligned with the police and Black and Brown Newarkers spilled into the high schools as well, with fights breaking out across the city's "integrated" high schools.

Yet Redden was not a passive victim caught between Black and white political activists and a weak mayor. Redden was fundamentally unwilling to press for any substantive transformation of Newark's police force, its toxic relationship to Black and Puerto Rican Newark, or its commitment to abusive policing. Instead he focused on upgrading the force's infrastructure and using federal and state funding to modernize the department in the belief that improved policing would come through more and better equipment and buildings. Redden's equivocal response to continued white police brutality and Imperiale's assertion that "the police belong to us" undermined and critically weakened the premise that Black Power Urbanism would lead to a just city by taking over "old forms" rather than rejecting these old forms in favor of new ones.

After Redden's resignation Gibson was finally able to appoint a Black police chief, Edward Kerr. Kerr's nomination was blocked by white city council members four times, leaving Kerr with only an "interim" status. Eventually, the council gave in and allowed Kerr to be permanently appointed, although by the time they had done so Kerr had decided to leave. In the wake of Kerr's departure, Gibson appointed Hubert Williams as the city's first Black police chief. Williams would serve from 1974 to 1985, becoming Newark's longest-serving police chief and architect of the department's brief golden age, when he seemed to be successful in diversifying the force along with modernizing and professionalizing it to stamp out corruption and abuse. A shift in demographics occurred as the number of Black and Latino officers holding higher ranks increased as a result of efforts, including litigation, that pushed for faster promotion of Black officers. Yet despite William's efforts, as in many cities, a pervasive "fear of crime" came to dominate the attitudes of both Black and white Newarkers, both of whom fomented waves of police populism, that is, support for the police by working classes, including people of color. Gibson reflected this trend when his father was mugged and beaten, angrily exclaiming: "There have got to be some changes."[208]

While Williams attempted to assume control over the still hostile majority-white NPD, the department did not pull back on its provocative policing. The next crisis would occur 1974 when the NPD's mounted police attacked members of the Puerto Rican community who were attending the Las Fiestas Patronales celebration in the city's Branch Brook Park. In response, the Puerto Rican community rebelled, with activists and leaders focusing their collective anger on the continued high levels of police brutality directed at their community, although there was also growing anger because they believed that they were excluded from the Black urban regime that was being constructed in the wake of Gibson's election. Puerto Rican activist Sigfrido Carrion, a member of the Puerto Rican Socialist Party, along with Amiri Baraka, formed the People's Committee Against Police Brutality and Repression (PCAPBR), which once again pushed for the creation of a civilian review board. The PCAPBR argued that this was the "one progressive change . . . needed to insure equal enforcement of the law and justice to the oppressed people here in Newark."[209] A Black face in City Hall had not resulted in just policing for Black and Brown Newarkers.

With the Gibson administration lacking the will or the ability to push forward on police accountability, the PCAPBR allied with other groups to establish an interim committee for a civilian complaint review board.[210] The PCAPBR and Baraka's CAP formed a broad coalition with "community organizations, ministers, students, tenants, [and] workers."[211] The goal was to collect enough signatures to place the creation of the board on the ballot as a public referendum.

While organizers worked to collect the needed signatures, the coalition held two "Peoples' Courts," which allowed ordinary Newarkers to testify about their experiences with police brutality and harassment. The PCAPBR brought members of the Puerto Rican community into explicit coalition with these groups, which were mostly located in the majority-Black Central Ward. By 1975, the broader coalition had collected over twenty-five thousand signatures, although massive numbers of signatures were disqualified by the still machine-dominated local courts, leading to yet another failed attempt at forcing the creation of a civilian review board. With this defeat and as part of its move away from Black Power Urbanism and toward a more doctrinaire Marxism, Baraka's CAP began to push for a broader engagement with the issue of police brutality with its national "Stop Killer Cops" campaign.[212] This was a decisive move away from the belief from less than a decade earlier that Black control of policing would lead to transformation. Instead Baraka and CAP would argue that

> the people should be in control of the police, not the police in control of the people. The police, the courts, jails, city government are all part of the state mechanism set up to suppress the people. We understand that even if the Police Review Board is established in Newark [or in any other city], this will not be an end in itself. Because finally the only way the people can control the police is that the people must take control of the government and rip it out of the bloody claws of the rich criminals that control the world. The Civilian Complaint Review Board is a reform that will be used to mobilize people and expose the class nature of the police, the courts, jails and the state, and thus will heighten the level of struggle.[213]

Despite continued organizing in Newark's Black and Puerto Rican communities for police reform, there was little success in curbing the abusive practices of the Newark Police Department. While Black and Puerto Rican communities struggled for police reform both locally and nationally, the federal government was working feverishly throughout the 1970s and 1980s to strengthen local and federal law enforcement agencies under the banner of "law and order"—which would have disastrous consequences for Black and Brown communities.

Fiscal Crisis: From the Newark Experiment to Stop and Frisk

From 1975 to 2014, Newark would reflect most of the trends of policing after the civil rights era. From 1968 to 1982, the Federal Law Enforcement Assistance Administration Act (LEAA) sent millions of dollars to the city, but it was spent not on community policing nor any of the items set forth in various Black Power manifestos (including Newark's own), but on enhancing the lethal capacity of the NPD, building a new headquarters and jail, and purchasing modern communications equipment.[214] To the extent that money flowed to "the community" it went to small programs embedded in the city's dysfunctional school system (itself roiled by attempts to assert Black control) and to North Ward community groups headed by Anthony Imperiale and other white ethnic power brokers.[215] Meanwhile the city would be one of the test sites for the experiments that would form the basis for the "broken windows" policing that would drive criminal justice from the 1980s until today.[216] The irony of the Newark experiment was that the perception of crime felt by city residents—though real, as seen by the mugging of Gibson's father—was heightened due to the NPD's efforts to block police layoffs in the wake of the 1975 cutbacks in federal funding. Like its neighbor to the east, the NYPD, the NPD would stage a "Fear City" campaign in order to embarrass the Gibson administration and stop police layoffs. Hubert Williams's departmental leadership and his participation in the Newark police experiment was not only a clear rejection of BPU-oriented community policy or accountability, it was also a signal that the NPD's focus under a Black mayor would be the surveillance of unwanted (Black and Brown) people to secure space for downtown's commuting workers and the last vestiges of the city's remaining department stores and other middle-class retail. Williams's commitment to "modern police" and police reform would eventually lead to his appointment as the head of the national Police Foundation.

The War on Drugs and the crack epidemic hit Newark particularly hard. The mass incarceration that ensued further hastened the physical decay and political paralysis that had begun to grip the city as Gibson's administration sputtered to an end and new machine politicians like Sharpe James were poised to take control. James ran for office on a version of Black penal populism, warning that "Newark is now Fear City and Dope City, with the prostitutes and drug pushers operating all over the city at all hours."[217] Newark's Black Power Urbanism, with its hope for reimaging a just and better life through reform and control, had largely disappeared.

Even as Black Power Urbanism as a political organizing force was disappearing from Newark, activists like Baraka and Larry Hamm (a leader of the local People's Organization for Progress) remained active in local politics and organizing. In 1992 after yet another police killing (in this case, two youths in a stolen car), Baraka and Hamm once again led a coalition demanding the establishment of a civilian review board.[218] With the city firmly in the hands of Black and Latinx politicians, the time seemed to be ripe. Yet even Mayor James's support was not enough to withstand the massive resistance from the

NPD and the state police unions. Several years later, the issue was raised again under neoliberal mayor Cory Booker. Support for a civilian review board received mild support from the city council as well as from Booker, who supported the need for greater "transparency." However, Booker called for more study of the issue as a way to delay consideration of the proposal even as he appointed a white police chief and continued to support a "stop-and-frisk" policy that targeted Black and Brown youth, much like the NPD's anti-loitering policing of the 1950s and 1960s.[219] Larry Hamm's analysis of Booker's conflicted position reflected the reality that confronted most mayors in the post–Black Power/mass incarceration era: "The police are a political force as well as a paramilitary force. And any politician that takes on the police to stop police brutality or violations of constitutional rights—they're going to incur the wrath of the police."[220]

Ras Baraka's election in 2014 signaled a clear change from Newark's adherence (reluctant or not) to the punitive policing that undergirded the mass incarceration state. Following in the footsteps of earlier community activists like his father, and having himself experienced the devastating effects of violence on the city's Black and Brown neighborhoods, Baraka campaigned against police brutality but also for finding and embracing community-based approaches that would not simply decrease crime but also address the trauma created by violence. Baraka's efforts to reshape Newark's policing were ironically bolstered by the overreach of the NPD, which by 2014 was under Department of Justice monitoring. Even with the federal monitoring, it was not until the massive demonstrations in the wake of George Floyd's death that Baraka was able to make good on the long-promised establishment of a civilian review board that truly had the means to deliver some oversight, accountability, and justice to Black and Brown NewArk. Newark's Black Power Urbanism had failed but its attempts to reimagine policing, accountability, and control found a successor in the Baraka administration.

In 2010, Newark's school system made the domestic and international news. In a calculated rollout, Oprah Winfrey, flanked by Governor Chris Christie, Mayor Cory Booker, and Facebook founder and CEO Mark Zuckerberg, dramatically announced that Zuckerberg was going to donate $100 million to the Newark Public School system. The donation caused a firestorm of notice and approval. For Zuckerberg it was a timely maneuver in the face of a critical biographical movie that had just been released, but for Booker it also was a timely and well-executed plan, brought about by his charisma and deep connections to wealthy and powerful neoliberal educational reform groups and Wall Street techno-philanthropy circles.

The gift's provenance also reflected the urban neoliberal order of the late twentieth and early twenty-first centuries. Booker, an Ivy League good govern-ment reformer who grew up in integrated New Jersey suburbs in the wake of the Civil Rights Movement, had developed an unlikely alliance with Republican governor Chris Christie, whose family had left Newark in the 1960s for subur-ban Essex County. Christie was in the midst of establishing himself as a moder-ate yet "tough" blue-state Republican. Supporters as well as skeptics of the gift wondered whether it would prove to be a game changer not only for Newark, but for other "failing urban schools." Zuckerberg's gift promised to short-circuit this seeming durable cycle of failure. Grant money could be targeted in ways that state equalization funding could not. Meanwhile, Booker, with Christie's backing, could push for a restructuring of school instruction with the rapid expansion of charter schools and closing of traditional neighborhood schools. With private money and charters, a new Newark school system could emerge that would break the lock that the Newark "school cartel" had had on to the system and on the city's children. Charter schools would empower parents to pick the best schools for their kids, while charter performance would be subject to "market-like" incen-tives and sanctions. Individuals, not neighborhoods or communities, would be newly empowered under this new "data-driven" system.[221]

The Zuckerberg gift revealed an acrimonious battle over the role of commu-nity control and the nature of school governance and accountability. Attempts to leverage the funds into a "school reform" takeover of Newark failed as Cami Anderson, the new superintendent, who had been brought in to implement this transformative vision, attempted to close neighborhood schools and open up more charter schools. After years of organizing and protest against the state takeover, the spirit of Black Power Urbanism and its organizational instantiations could be seen in this moment.

With the support and intense political activism of ordinary Newarkers, espe-cially high school students, networks of organizational support and a strong and raucous legacy of political activism around educational policy emerged to suc-cessfully push back on this Zuckerberg initiative. Ultimately the superintendent resigned; Booker left for the US Senate, and Christie—focusing on his nascent presidential campaign—moved to get Newark off the state's hands. Mayor Baraka led Newark to beat back education reformers and regain mayoral and board con-trol of Newark's schools. As in the case of University Hospital, the echo of Black Power Urbanism made a brief, but important appearance, pulling the city's edu-cational system back from the neoliberal brink. Fifty years or so after its difficult birth, the unfinished business of Black Power Urbanism continued to unfold in NewArk.

EAST ORANGE

Black Power Urbanism in a Model Interracial Suburb

> **I think it is better to talk about the "respectable class" rather than a middle-class. In these black New Jersey neighborhoods, there are upper middle-class people living next to people who project respectability and who have some of the trappings of middle-class society but are not necessarily economically well-to-do.**
>
> —Sheila Rule, "Middle Class Is a State of Mind, Not Money," *New York Times*, June 24, 1979

In 2016, Mayor Lester Taylor proclaimed that East Orange, New Jersey was on the cusp of revival due to his administration's radical step of publicly embracing "the concept of [an] 'urban' identity in order to strip the term and East Orange of its negative connotations." For decades the Black political leadership of this city had remained committed to trying to convince itself and the rest of the state that the city was only a few lucky breaks away from regaining its former status as the home of the "Fifth Avenue of the suburbs." Taylor would jettison this conceit and proclaim that while "in New Jersey and other cities around the country, when stories are written about 'urban,' they're always about blight," East Orange embraced "urban as a positive lifestyle." By the 2010s, spreading real estate investment and speculation had finally reached East Orange, where, " people being priced out of the east, whether in New York, or Hoboken and Jersey City, [are] moving further west. And we're seeing people from the west wanting to move from the suburbs back into areas that are more convenient and accessible without having to drive a substantial distance."[1]

Seventy-five years after the city issued its 1950 master plan, the goal of East Orange's white planning officials to transform a faded Progressive Era genteel suburb into an "urbane suburb" was finally embraced by Black elected officials and other civic elites who succeeded them. Since 1969, when the city's first Black mayor had been elected, subsequent mayors (all Black) had touted the city's imminent revival even as it became one of the poorest majority-Black cities in the state. Given East Orange's racialization as a Black suburb during the city's

"Negro removal" era, local Black leadership and especially middle-class Black residents could have embraced Black Power Urbanism. Instead, the city's leadership adhered to the logic of postwar American suburban political economy, engaging in a constant struggle to lower residential property taxes, increase commercial ratables, improve local schools and public safety, and encourage more middle-class homeowners to move into the city while dissuading lower-income residents (especially renters) from staying.

This logic was overlaid with an additional logic of Black suburban respectability. East Orange's future would be secured by a class of people who not only cared about lifting up those who were struggling, but who also had a very distinct understanding of their socio-spatial position. As one resident noted, "I'm not a black man, I'm a proud black man. . . . And that pride doesn't come from giving the black power sign but, like the others . . . in trying to make a difference, in trying to show we care."[2] As this resident said: "I think it is better to talk about the 'respectable class' rather than a middle-class. In these black New Jersey neighborhoods, there are upper middle-class people living next to people who project respectability and who have some of the trappings of middle-class society but are not necessarily economically well-to-do."[3]

This suburban respectability, though dominant, was not unchallenged. The city's poor and working-class residents continually pressed the city to respond to their needs whether through tenant protection laws, after-school activities, or a community policing model with a police force that reflected the city's residents and acted more as a partner than an occupying force. Taylor's election marked a turning point in East Orange's socio-political spatial imaginary that moved away from embracing a suburban ideal and toward a model of Black suburbanism that prioritized building a just community for all residents.

In East Orange, Black Power Urbanism intersected with the long legacy of Black suburban respectability politics and the unfolding of Northern suburban civil rights movements.[4] As a center of Black middle-class suburban citizenship since the early twentieth century, the Black Power Urbanism of other cities such as Newark and Oakland made little impact on the overall process of Black empowerment and political succession within the city. Despite the efforts of some progressive Black East Orangers, the influence of Black Power Urbanism as a means to create a just city for all of its Black residents was muted at best. Part of this silence was the immense strength that preexisting hierarchies and structures of past suburban racial orders held in the city. This suburban racial order thwarted even modest attempts to build "new forms" that could respond to the concerns not only of its Black middle class, but also of its much larger population of working-class, poor, and Black immigrant residents. Meanwhile, the state saw the emergence of a metropolitan (white) backlash against Black empowerment, which challenged its postwar white spatial imaginary of consumer citizenship in which mass consumption in support of suburbanization equated to good citizenship.[5] Like in Newark, Black Power Urbanism had an impact on education, housing, and policing, although these interventions were challenged by the metropolitan "frontlash" of the 1970s through 1990s, when a statewide Republican coalition of white suburbanites tried to thwart efforts in housing and education that threatened to weaken the metropolitan color line. These efforts included attempted as well as actual takeovers of East Orange's finances and its school district while delaying, obstructing, or subverting court-ordered polices to expand housing and educational opportunities for Black households and children. By the early twenty-first century, the last vague echoes of the city's brief flirtation with Black Power Urbanism would come to its final quiet end. The city, with the aid of HOPE VI public housing demolition funding, would demolish its two publicly owned and/or subsidized housing projects for families while leaving intact senior citizen housing, originally built for elderly whites during the 1950s and 1960s era of (sub)urban renewal.

A Model Interracial City

Black Power Urbanism arrived in East Orange in the fall of 1966, when James Sherman, a Black teacher at East Orange High, was dismissed from his student advisory position for his sponsorship of a "Negro poetry reading" from a "Negro anthology" at a school assembly.[6] The white principal charged that the "provocative" poems had caused "an undercurrent and overcurrent of unrest." The principal was not alone: several white teachers had walked out of the assembly. Sherman asserted that while the poems "may have lacked polish," they addressed the immediate concerns of many of the school's Black students, who made up over 70 percent of the student body: "These kids live right in the middle of the struggle. Of course, they feel deeply about it, but it wasn't 'Black Power' poetry. . . . If it pointed up any racial division, it was only because it was there all along. It blew away the topsoil."[7] After a threatened five-thousand-person march and a five-hour emergency session of the school board, the Black teacher was reinstated.[8] However, the status quo of quiet liberal integrationism had been challenged by students and by the Black working-class residents of the city.

The poetry reading, the walkout, and the threatened protests demonstrated that the situation in East Orange was a far cry from four years earlier. In 1962, the *New York Times* had proclaimed that East Orange was a "Model Interracial City."[9] Mildred Barry Garvin, appointed in 1961 as the first Black member of the

Board of Education, shared this belief, along with many middle-class Blacks.[10] Garvin stated that the school district was "on the whole . . . well integrated." This peaceful integration was due to "communication before any bitter attitudes were allowed to build up." Some middle-class Blacks also claimed that this peaceful integration was due to the fact that "Negroes moving into East Orange [were] of the highest quality."[11]

The belief in East Orange as a town of respectable interracial citizens was one that was interwoven into the city's foundational myth. The authors of the city's centennial history stated confidently that East Orange had a proud tradition in which it "sought out the best in self-government . . . a refusal to abide with the shoddy, the makeshift, the expedient." Even as some Blacks and whites were congratulating themselves on this interracial comity, these self-congratulations were overshadowed by a suburban imaginary shrouded in nearly a century of quiet conflict. The governance of East Orange was heavily influenced by attempts of the white majority to use new techniques of racial spatialization like zoning and school attendance boundaries to control the movement of undesirable groups who threatened to breach the suburban color line. Meanwhile, Black citizens of East Orange were challenging decades of second-class citizenship even as middle-class leadership wrapped these challenges in a cloak of suburban respectability politics.[12]

East Orange: The Progressive Suburb

East Orange epitomized the prototypical Progressive Era suburb and the fragmentation of the American metropolitan landscape.[13] The city was incorporated in 1899 after its secession from Newark. The establishment of a trolley car system radiating out from Newark and later, commuter rail, turned East Orange into a commuter suburb filled with prosperous citizens who worked in Newark or New York City. Although its economic livelihood was intimately tied to Newark, East Orange's political and civic leadership envisioned the new city as a safe alternative to Newark's physical decay, industrial pollution, and ethnic politics. Though a part of the greater Newark area, East Orange developed a fortress mentality that was rooted in geographic reality. East Orange was not in fact an island unto itself as "[the] streets of East Orange [were] continuous with those of the surrounding communities along each of its boundary lines."[14] Political, racial, and ethnic divisions also played a role in creating this fortress mentality. Many of the town's white residents had been heavily influenced by the growing temperance and nativist movements of the late nineteenth and early twentieth centuries and shared a deep suspicion of Newark's politics and its growing population of immigrants, which they saw as a threat to the broader social and cultural order.[15]

East Orange's civic leaders adopted Progressive Era government and administrative structures designed to ensure elite control of local politics and to protect the town from the "various problems" that came from the "arbitrary line of demarcation between East Orange" and its neighbors (especially Newark). The town's governance structure reflected its origins as a Progressive Era "morning glory." Its political structure was designed to keep power in the hands of the dominant elites, predominantly white Anglo-Americans, who were a mix of "amateur democrats" (that is, nonpartisan but policy-engaged residents) and local small business owners.[16] While the city adopted a mayor-council system, it also employed a city manager. In true Progressive Era fashion, municipal power was even further fragmented with the creation of multiple boards overseeing municipal departments.[17] The dominance of one-party rule and the presence of an ethnic/economic elite, coupled with a hybrid mayor-council/board of commissioners government structure, offered few paths of entry into local politics and governance for the town's two largest racial/ethnic groups: Italian Americans and a small but historic Black community that predated the city's incorporation.

Civic leaders took further steps to consolidate their vision of East Orange as a fortress against the threat of Newark's problems and a genteel suburb. One of these steps was to adopt a master city plan in 1917; East Orange was one of the first cities to do so. Like many city plans of the era (and since), it demonstrated a deep suspicion of apartment buildings and other multi-residence dwellings. The 1917 city plan, for example, proclaimed that the town "began to be seriously invaded ten or fifteen years ago by apartment houses and garages."[18] East Orange's elites, like many other Progressive Era city leaders, viewed apartment buildings with suspicion, as they were possible vectors for introducing residential transience (and undesired populations) and degrading property values. One of the key purposes of the East Orange city plan was to develop and implement a zoning plan that would control future growth in the city, and more importantly preserve property values and the right population mix.[19] A section of the city plan highlights these issues: "The chief point of present congestion is in the rapidly growing apartment house section near the center of the city. There are two Italian sections in the southern part of the city and four scattered, small groups of colored people near its center. The Italian sections show the highest birth rate of any part of the community."[20] In keeping with these concerns, the town's planning department periodically monitored not just how many of each group's population lived in the town, but also where they lived. In 1917 the city created a surveillance tool: a map with the title

"Distribution of Colored Population in City and Italian Population in Ward III" (see figure 4.1). The map (later updated in 1926, 1927, and 1931) showed at the lot level where the city's Black and Italian American residents lived. The map was not only a surveillance tool; it also reflected the belief of many of the town's elite leadership that these two groups were not fellow citizens—both were framed as civic and spatial problems.

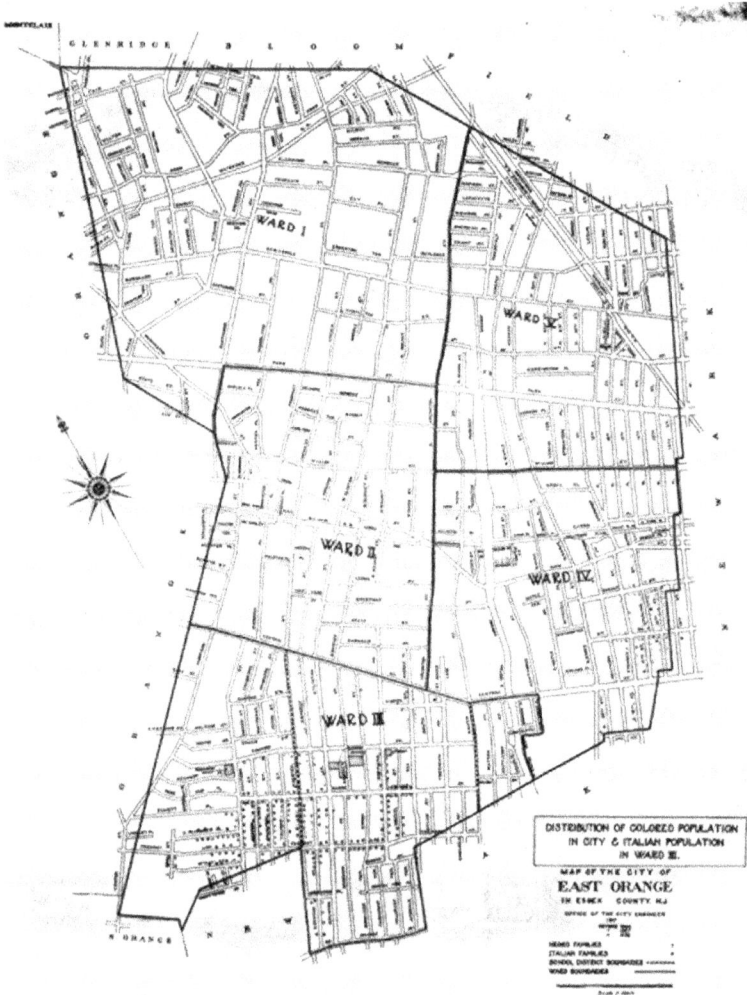

FIGURE 4.1. Race surveillance map: African Americans and Italian Americans, East Orange, 1928

Source: *Map of the City of East Orange in Essex County, N.J.*, Office of the City Engineer, 1932.

A Place of Their Own

Black East Orangers created a space of their own despite this socio-spatial prob-lematization. The town's Black neighborhoods were home to "colored churches" like "fashionable Calvary," "respectable Mt. Olive," and Saint Paul's African Meth-odist Episcopal (AME) Church. Although East Orange was a domestic service suburb for African Americans, it (as well as neighboring Montclair) was also a residential suburb for those individuals who could afford to leave Newark (or New York City) and were in search of higher-status housing and suburban living.[21] Middle-class Blacks tended to move into single-family or multifamily housing in the town's southwest quadrant. While some of this housing was the result of "filtering" (that is, other groups moving out of older buildings, making way for Black occupation), some of the houses were newly built and marketed to Black families through African American newspapers like New York's *Amsterdam News*. By the 1940s, Black East Orange had built up a dense network of social organizations and civic uplift institutions (including interracial and race relations groups) that Black Newark would not be able to replicate until decades later. One example of this was the East Orange Settlement House (later Lincoln Houses).[22] As result, East Orange became a center of Black suburban life, and consequently one of the host cities for Booker T. Washington's last tour before his death.[23] This associational life allowed the suburban Blacks of East Orange, Orange, and Montclair to organize themselves sufficiently to participate in local Republican and Democratic politics.

The reform-style structure of East Orange's government created a bifurcated political environment for Black East Orange. Within city politics, it led to the creation of a patron-client relationship between some middle-class Blacks and whites, especially in the arena of women's activism around social welfare issues. However, Republican party politics during the early twentieth century had pro-vided a limited entrée into state- and county-level political institutions and organizations and made possible the creation of Black political clubs. While Newark did not elect its first Black politician until the 1950s, Black suburban-ites (led by East Orangers), with Italian and Jewish support, managed to elect six African Americans to the state assembly between 1922 and 1932 (Orange in 1921 and 1922; East Orange in 1923; Orange from 1926 to 1928 and from 1929 to 1930). The sixth representative (and last Republican) elected was J. Mercer Burrell to the state assembly in 1932, even as nationwide African American voters began to vote overwhelmingly for Franklin Roosevelt and the Democratic Party.[24] The coalition in support of Burrell's candidacy reflected the robust Black political life outside of Newark. These groups included the Belleville Colored Political Club, the Fourth Ward Women's Republican Club of

East Orange, and the Third Ward Colored Republican Club.[25] Burrell's election is notable because he proposed and later led the enactment of the Burrell Labor Bill, which prohibited labor discrimination in the State of New Jersey, and in 1951 he served as one of the lawyers for the Trenton Six, a "trial that became known as the "Scottsboro case of the North."[26]

The postwar era and the emergence of the Northern Civil Rights Movement raised the stakes for local Black empowerment. Jane Rick, a local white social worker, observed that while Black suburban residents experienced "a new feeling of self-sufficiency [was] brought on by wartime employment in essential industries," they now had a "chip on the shoulder attitude" in the face of token government representation and municipal services that were inferior to those they had received for decades.[27] The city's middle- to upper-middle class Black residents were also becoming more assertive in challenging white East Orange's thin commitment to suburban interracialism. While their claims were often cloaked in suburban respectability politics, this Black leadership would vigorously pursue the rights of full suburban citizenship. This new assertiveness rattled the exiting social hierarchy of the city and its white power structure. As the postwar era unfolded, as would be the case for many older, "inner-ring" suburbs, East Orange's white politicians and civic leaders would cast about for solutions to restore its social hierarchy and its threatened status as a desirable suburb. For East Orange, the solution meant embracing a new identity for itself as an "urbane suburb." This new identity would be facilitated by the unfolding urban renewal order and its commitment to "Negro removal."

Postwar Anxieties, The (Sub)Urban Renewal Order, and the Revanchist Suburb

By end of World War II, East Orange possessed many of the ingredients touted today as essential for sustainable suburban development: dense apartment buildings catering to families with few children, an upscale and walkable shopping district, mass transit access to multiple major cities (Newark and New York City), and an institution of higher education that added students and faculty to the town's population mix. Though many of the town's leaders acknowledged the town's strengths they also saw some worrisome trends in the changing demographics of the town and what they saw as its lack of modern suburban amenities like easy highway access or shopping malls. They saw the embrace of urban renewal and highways as a sure way to make a secure place for this older suburban city in the postwar suburban era.

As the United States emerged from World War II, East Orange officials were worried that their town would not be able to retain the prominent social position it had achieved in the first part of the twentieth century. This concern was echoed across many older cities and suburbs, which had a significant decline in investment during the Depression and subsequent war. In response to this concern and with an eye toward dealing with wartime demobilization, Congress looked to infrastructure projects like urban renewal to keep the economy going. For cities, especially those controlled by Democrats, urban renewal would become an important element in cementing their role in the postwar Keynesian urban renewal order, which married targeted federal spending on cities with aggressive spatial restriction.

East Orange made two key moves to adapt to the perceived challenges of postwar (sub)urbanism. First, in keeping with their reliance on "experts," the city created a true city planning department. Second, the city hired a planning firm, Harland Bartholomew and Associates, to intensively study all aspects of the town from its physical infrastructure and its housing and educational needs to possibilities for revitalizing its shopping districts and businesses. Hired by dozens of cities including Newark and Oakland, Harland Bartholomew would play a significant role in shaping postwar cities and suburbs. Key to the firm's approach was an aggressive focus on transportation and urban renewal as the means by which cities could eliminate "blight" in order to retain or attract middle-class residents, downtown shoppers, and office workers. Creating a new "urbane" city or suburb would theoretically enable these places to stay competitive and experience new suburban growth.[28] An important part of that assessment was a growing and at first explicit concern about the spread, control, and correction of "blight." For the white East Orange leadership "blight" could be measured in a number of ways, from the lack of new commercial and residential development to the growth of East Orange's Black community. The city's master plan of 1950 was an attempt to address these pressing concerns about local economic development and the threat to East Orange's white suburban imaginary posed by Black racialization of East Orange's white spaces.[29]

Anti-apartment attitudes had softened by the 1940s. East Orange was now known for its elegant apartment buildings and for the upscale shopping areas that surrounded them. Central Avenue, which ran from Newark westward through the Oranges, was the most notable of these shopping areas and was christened as the "Fifth Avenue of the suburbs" with the opening of upscale New York City–based retailers such as Best & Co. and B. Altman & Co. By 1965, the city that had been known for its grand houses was also home to 460 apartment buildings that housed approximately half of the population. Indeed, the town became known as a place for residents of suburbs located further out to downsize to a more manageable and "urbane" location. The relocation of Upsala College to the town in 1928 also boosted East Orange's reputation. According to the town's 1964 centennial history, Upsala was one of the "finest colleges in the east," which gave the town "an asset for which there is no exact accounting."[30]

Businesses seemed to respond to this mix of urban services and suburban access. Although Newark had long been the regional center for the life insurance industry, between 1949 and 1963 East Orange's real estate developers were able to lure more than fifty insurance companies away from Newark to East Orange. Three other large companies also relocated to East Orange: Dun & Bradstreet, Otis Elevator, and the Aluminum Company of America.[31] These corporate moves were accompanied by the movement of a slew of service firms such as law firms and title and mortgage companies. A spate of building construction accompanied this increased number of office and professional firms: between 1950 and 1962, forty-three new office and professional buildings were constructed with a valuation of approximately $6.9 million.[32] Despite this growth, town officials eyed their suburban competitors nervously. Compared to the new suburban office parks and shopping malls, East Orange's downtown and neighborhood shopping areas seemed shabby, drab, and not car-friendly. To fix these problems the city focused its energy on three solutions: urban renewal, "Negro removal," and highway construction.

"Segregation Because of Color and Income"

"Negro removal" would come first. East Orange eagerly embraced the state's newly passed Preiser Act of 1944 (and subsequently the federal Housing Act of 1945 and the much expanded 1949 Act). Almost immediately, state chapters of the NAACP, local Black political and civic groups, and the Black press all criticized the weaknesses of the state's redevelopment act, chief of which was the lack of "provision for the rehousing of persons dispossessed from the blighted areas."[33] In addition, under the law, the blighted areas could be sold to private developers who would also benefit from a twenty-year tax exemption (on the excess over current valuation).[34]

The city's housing plan of 1945 (which was a detailed subset of the city's overall master plan) reflected its desire to use urban renewal as a means of excising the town's Black population. An early version of the plan showed two separate maps: one demonstrating where the Black population was concentrated, while the other revealing the areas targeted for urban renewal and rezoning (see figures 4.2A and 4.2B). The rezoned areas were located primarily in the Black working- and middle-class area made up of single-family homes. The housing plan proposed that an area of the city (the Amherst neighborhood in the city's southwest ward), which was filled with Black middle-class homeowners (as well as Italian

Americans and Jews), should be extensively rezoned for "garden apartments" that would be restricted to "upper income groups able to pay $75 to $80 per month." By contrast, the average rent in the city was $52.69 per month. According to an analysis by the local NAACP chapter, the proposed rezoning would lead to the displacement of 55 to 60 percent of the town's Black population.[35]

To add insult to injury, the city offered an as yet unbuilt, small low-income housing project to house some of the displaced. For middle-class homeowners, this was not an acceptable solution. Not only was the city trying to erase Black homeownership, which was presumably a source of community stability and amicable relations between the races, but the plan would also reduce the amount of available housing for middle-class Blacks. Not surprisingly, Black residents were furious. The mainly middle-class residents of the Second Ward quickly mobilized in collaboration with the local NAACP as well as the American Jewish Congress and other liberal groups to push back against what they called the city's intent to implement "segregation because of color and income."[36] After hundreds of residents showed up at a planning meeting to demonstrate that they would "take the case all the way to the Supreme Court," the city backed down from its attempt to enact explicit racial rezoning.[37] This early battle over the city's attempted "Negro removal" served to warn other Black communities of what urban renewal would come to mean for their neighborhoods.

In the wake of this defeat, the city embraced a more racially neutral (sub)urban renewal. Under the guise of urban renewal and highway construction, the city was able to split the Black community. The areas of town housing working- and middle-class Blacks residents in single-family homes were left alone, while the Fourth Ward, the commercial and retail heart of Black East Orange, was sacrificed for highway construction. The "blighted" remains were then given the "treatment" of urban renewal. The goal of removing at least part of Black Orange remained a serious concern for the city government, although it was couched in careful bureaucratic language after the fiasco of the 1945 housing plan. In a town whose Black population had risen from 15 percent in 1950 to 35 percent in 1960, the policy tools of highways and urban renewal allowed the city to shift the Black population as far away as they possibly could—hopefully out of East Orange to some other jurisdiction.

Making the Suburban State: Highway Construction

In its brochure, *An East-West Freeway for Essex County*, the Joint Council of Municipal Planning Boards proclaimed a new right for the "fed up" taxpayers of New Jersey: "We believe a man bound from Morristown to Newark should be entitled to a fast, comfortable and safe trip all the way—rather than traveling

easily to the West Orange line, then bucking a Chinese Wall of traffic congestion the rest of the way to Newark."[38] Further, the Joint Council declared that it
was "time to abandon the policy of building fine broad highways up to the city
limits and then letting the municipalities worry about how their inadequate city
streets will accommodate the huge flood of traffic poured into them by the State
Highway System." Cities, according to one expert cited, were "sick," and "efficient
transportation" via "modern expressways" was the only cure. The right to the
highway and the right to access the new postwar suburban lifestyle was central
to the development of a postwar consumer citizenship.[39]

The expansion of the Garden State Parkway by 1954 and then the construction of Interstate 280 in the early 1960s fundamentally changed the nature of East
Orange and particularly its Black spaces.[40] While a limited Essex Parkway had
long existed, the decline in the popularity of parkways, especially in dense urban
areas, and the ambitions of the state's highway engineers combined to create a
plan to expand the parkway into a much larger project spanning the northern
and southern parts of the state. While the debate over the construction of an
expanded Garden State Parkway was muted, the debate over Interstate 280 was
not. Indeed, while city officials seemed to embrace the proposed highway, "more
than 1,000" residents angrily denounced the plan.[41]

Although it had been on the agenda of various state and local planning boards
for thirty years, the highway was finally realized with the enactment of the 1956
Highway Act. The project had a wide base of support, including the state's highway department; a coalition of downtown Newark business interests; residents and
developers in outlying suburban and semirural areas who would now have quick
access to the city; and residents of more affluent towns like Montclair and Glen
Ridge (located on East Orange's northern borders). These two towns may have seen
East Orange as an ideal buffer area that would absorb highway disruption, while
affording easy highway access to their residents. Newark's boosters, like many downtown boosters during this era, believed that having multilane highways would keep
or bring more people into the city, although in fact they acted as massive funnels
draining both residents and businesses from the city. The state highway department
was able to deter opponents by cobbling together a route that used existing state and
railroad rights of way. The use of these rights of way meant that instead of being
shifted though the southern part of town, the new route hewed closely to the town's
main train line and its historic Main Street to the north, cutting the city in half.

With highway construction looming, East Orange residents began an active
and public opposition. While much of the opposition came from residents and
small businesses (both Black and white) that would be displaced by the highway,
other residents opposed the state highway department's initial proposal, which
was for a cheaper elevated highway that would loom over neighborhoods, further

depressing adjacent property values. Presaging the highway revolts that would take place across the United States nearly a decade later, local activists decried the "folly of an elevated road, causing property depreciation in areas where the federal government was going to spend money to rehabilitate older sections of the city."[42] Citizen activists were victorious in beating back the state's proposed "cheaper" elevated highway, which resulted in the alternative submerged cut through the city. According to the town's official history, "in addition to the State highway department, almost all of the big newspapers . . . were against the idea

FIGURE 4.2A.   (Sub)urban renewal is "Negro removal": East Orange housing plan, 1945

Source: Harland Bartholomew and Associates and East Orange (N. J.) City Planning Board, *Land Use and Zoning: Third and Fourth of a Series of Reports [to] the City Planning Board*, East Orange, 1945, East Orange Public Library Local History Collection.

of depressing the road."[43] Despite this establishment support, local activists, led by the town's newspaper, the *East Orange Record*, "carried the fight [against the proposed roadway] all the way to Washington" and won.[44]

Despite the victory of achieving a submerged highway, the city's future prospects were uncertain. The impact of the two highways on East Orange's small footprint (four square miles) was significant. The juncture of the Garden State Parkway and the new Interstate 280 would take 5 percent of the town's land, which would, in the words of the mayor, "alter beyond recognition the present

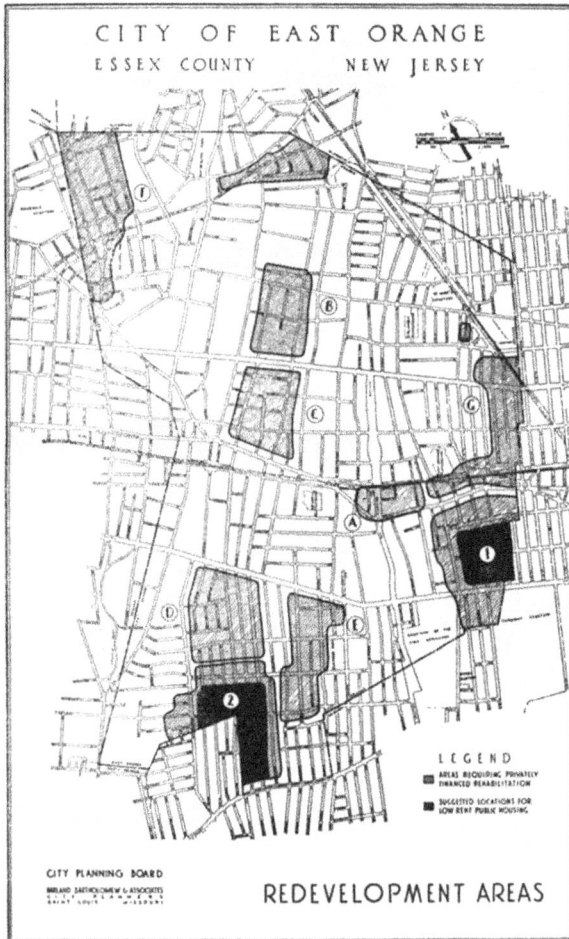

FIGURE 4.2B.   (Sub)urban renewal is "Negro removal": East Orange housing plan, 1945

Source: East Orange (N. J.), *Housing and Zoning* (The Author, 1945).

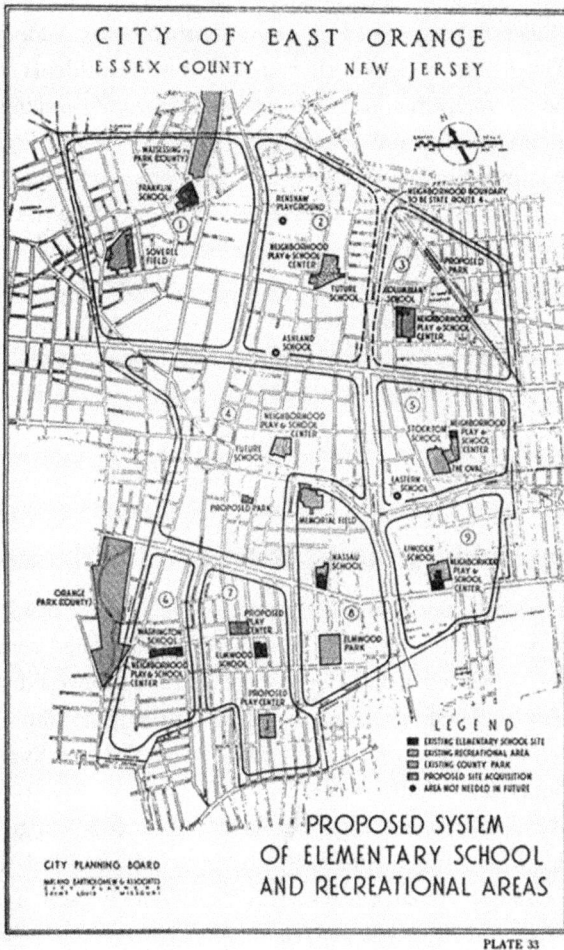

CITY OF EAST ORANGE
ESSEX COUNTY   NEW JERSEY

LEGEND
EXISTING ELEMENTARY SCHOOL SITE
EXISTING RECREATIONAL AREA
EXISTING COUNTY PARK
PROPOSED SITE ACQUISITION
AREA NOT NEEDED IN FUTURE

PROPOSED SYSTEM
OF ELEMENTARY SCHOOL
AND RECREATIONAL AREAS

CITY PLANNING BOARD

PLATE 33

FIGURE 4.2C.   (Sub)urban renewal is "Negro removal": East Orange housing plan, 1945

Source: City Planning Board, *The Master Plan for East Orange, New Jersey* (City Planning Board, 1950).

residential neighborhood; also a commercial area will be wiped out and a new one must be created."[45] The two highways cut the city into quarters and in the long run devastated its main street, which ran parallel to the highway's northern edge. Despite these drawbacks, the city attempted to put a positive spin on the new spatial reality by advertising East Orange as the "crossroads of New Jersey."[46]

Initially, better highway access seemed to provide economic benefits, as businesses continued to relocate from Newark to East Orange, but this was only a short-term effect. The availability of cheaper land and the lure of federally sub-sidized and (indirectly) segregated modern suburban housing continued to lure Newark's, and later East Orange's businesses and its white residents further west.[47]

While some saw highway construction as an opportunity and others as some-thing forced upon the city (and a development that it had to make the best of), civic leaders continued to believe that urban renewal was a net positive good for the city. Urban renewal in East Orange served three purposes. In the immediate postwar era, town leaders turned to urban renewal tools as a way to fix the town's changing demographics. By the late 1950s, with two highways bisecting the town and the rise of new suburban areas to the west (facilitated by one of these high-ways), town leaders turned again to urban renewal as a way revitalize the town's fading main street shopping areas and help the city recover from and capitalize on the otherwise destructive highway construction.[48]

Suburban Renewal and Differential Citizenship

East Orange's urban renewal plans centered around three areas: Brick Church commercial zone, the city's historic and somewhat dilapidated commercial and civic center; the Doddtown urban renewal area in the northwest quadrant of the city; and the Fourth Ward urban renewal area. For the Brick Church area, town planners hoped to use the new highway that ran parallel to it as a linchpin for retail and commercial revitalization.

In the Doddtown urban renewal area the city planned to "upgrade" a mixed Italian American and African American working-class area bordering the adja-cent town of Orange.[49] Finally, the Fourth Ward—the historic home of Black East Orange—was directly in the path of the two highways that would bisect the city. The urban renewal plan for this area called for a rehabilitation of whatever remained of the town's historic Black neighborhood.

The city's treatment of the residents and business in two of its urban renewal areas reflected the differential citizenship rights that existed in East Orange. The Doddtown renewal plan was one of the first cooperative joint renewal plans with a neighboring municipality (Orange) in the nation.[50] It called for the demolition of deteriorated properties and some rehabilitation. According to 1962 testimony offered by Mayor James Kelly, approximately 975 households (or about 2,000 individuals) would be displaced by the Doddtown project; a high proportion of these residents were elderly whites. The promises of robust relocation assistance by the mayor and council and a commitment by the city to build subsidized housing for the elderly brought the city considerable acclaim.[51] The town and the mayor were true to their word: a senior citizens' housing commission was created

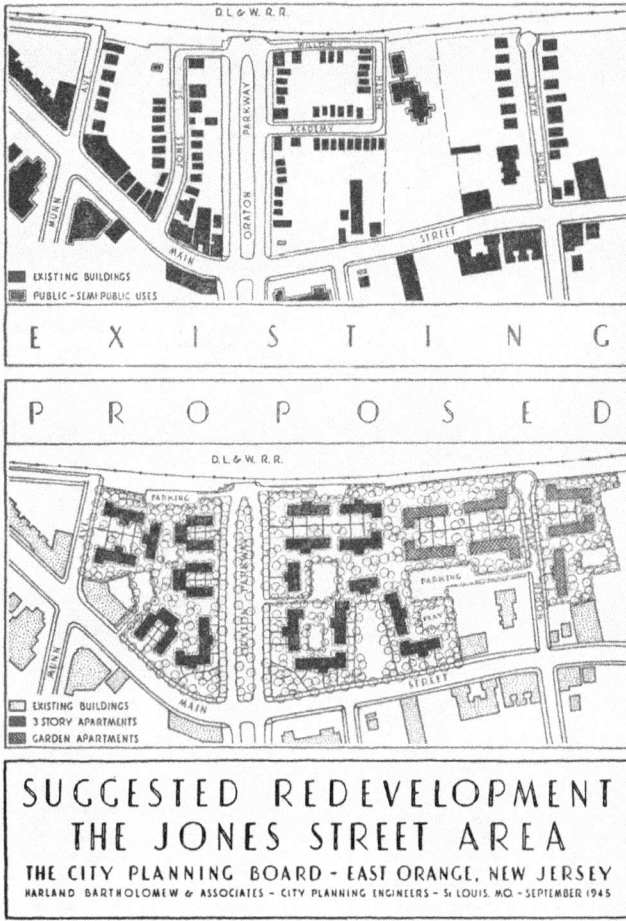

E X I S T I N G

P R O P O S E D

SUGGESTED REDEVELOPMENT
THE JONES STREET AREA
THE CITY PLANNING BOARD - EAST ORANGE, NEW JERSEY
HARLAND BARTHOLOMEW & ASSOCIATES - CITY PLANNING ENGINEERS - St LOUIS. MO. - SEPTEMBER 1945

56   PLATE 22

FIGURE 4.3A.   Jones Street neighborhood/Fourth Ward and "Negro removal"

Source: City Planning Board, The Master Plan for East Orange, New Jersey (City Planning Board, 1950).

to handle the displacement of the (white) elderly, which led to the construction of two subsidized residential towers for seniors in the Doddtown area. Public housing was finally available in East Orange, but only for the elderly and, although it was left unsaid, for whites.

The treatment of the Fourth Ward urban renewal area provides a striking contrast to the Doddtown plan (see figures 4.3A and 4.3B). This area of Black settlement had also been targeted by the city in its 1945 housing plan as well as the 1950 master plan and the city was more explicit about its desire to subject this neighborhood to urban renewal treatment than in Doddtown. According to the

REDEVELOPMENT AREAS

Plate 21 shows that approximately one-quarter of the city's area could be razed, reassembled and rebuilt to the benefit of the city as a whole. The deterioration of the areas needing rebuilding tends to spread into adjoining neighborhoods. This emphasizes the importance of an early start on a long range program. Timing of redevelopment is important. It is not anticipated that every substandard portion of the city can be eliminated. The reasonable approach is to rebuild the areas which are doing the most damage. Each such improvement will have a separate and distinct beneficial effect on all property values. The recommended order of the redevelopments is indicated by the lettered symbols on the plate. Probably 30 or 40 years will be required for the consummation of the projects. Possible treatments of the earlier improvements within the twenty to thirty year range of the plan follow.

THE JONES STREET AREA

The worst housing conditions in the city are found in the area lying on both sides of Jones Street and of Oraton Parkway between Main Street and the Lackawanna Railroad. This area not only constitutes an economic liability, but has arrested the normal development of Main Street commercial property. There would be many advantages in its restoration, and residential property in the vicinity would benefit thereby.

The location is ideal for an apartment development. It is near transit lines and the Lackawanna Station, and convenient to shopping facilities.

Plate 22 shows existing buildings and a study of a possible layout for complete redevelopment of the area into three or four story apartments and garden apartments. The plan could be so designed that the whole rehabilitation could be done either at one time or in two or three stages. It will be apparent that the business property in the vicinity would immediately be improved and become source of increased tax revenue.

THE CLINTON - HAMILTON AREA

Between Park and Springdale Avenues and Prospect and North Walnut Streets, lies an area over half of which is still vacant land. This area separates two of the finest home neighborhoods in East Orange. Plate 23 shows the existing development as well as its suggested rehabilitation.

The North Walnut Street, Prospect Street and Park Avenue frontages have not yet appreciably deteriorated. The remainder of this section is valued at only $444,000 for tax purposes, and returns an annual sum of about $22,000.

This section is more suitable for single-family homes than for any type of apartment development, and by re-subdivision into spacious lots, using as much as possible of existing streets and utilities, it could be effectively rebuilt as a large scale operation.

Urban redevelopment in the form of single-family homes is a new concept but there is no reason why it should not be feasible in East Orange.

Other measures, such as suggested traffic, zoning and school improvments could assure the residential future of a majority of all properties in this area.

THE ASHLAND - CARLETON AREA

Plate 24 shows a study of a possible redevelopment of this neighborhood. There are seventeen existing commercial and apartment properties which could be made to fit into the new design. This redevelopment could be quite spacious and would consist of three or four story apartments in the portion nearest Main Street and garden apartments in the remainder. Present development on Park Avenue could be left largely as it is.

THE ELMWOOD PARK AREA

One of the most pressing needs of the city is a place where younger people can afford to buy homes and raise families. The easterly area shown on Plate 25 might well be the answer. It is designed around Elmwood Park and the existing apartment and garden apartment developments north

54

FIGURE 4.3B. Jones Street neighborhood/Fourth Ward and "Negro removal"

Source: City Planning Board, The Master Plan for East Orange, New Jersey (City Planning Board, 1950).

planning board, "the character of the buildings and the stagnation of improvements immediately contiguous to that district are such as to call for replacement irrespective of ownership (whether Colored or White)."[52] Most of the middle-class Black leadership consented to the decision to place the city's low-income housing project in that neighborhood, as many of them were focused on saving their own neighborhoods from urban renewal. The area would receive a "combination treatment of clearance and rehabilitation" and the city would "re-plan complementary land use around (the highway)." The treatment, including the land used for the parkway and the interstate, would cover over 175 acres and demolish around one thousand dwelling units and the historic associational heart of Black East Orange. The city's feeble efforts on behalf of poor and work-ing-class Blacks reflected the shattering of local community structures within the Fourth Ward and the lack of desire among middle-class Blacks to come to their aid. Unlike the Black middle-class residents of the Amherst Street neighborhood that had been targeted in the 1945 housing plan, the residents of the Fourth Ward were unable to resist the federal and state bulldozer of highway construction.

Nearly a decade after clearance and despite the obvious devastation and need, the area lay cleared and adjacent areas became blighted, remaining that way until the late 1960s. As Robert Weaver and Catherine Bauer each noted in their evaluations of urban renewal, the treatment inflicted on the Fourth Ward meant its destruction, and no amount of rehabilitation could bring back a destroyed and virtually erased neighborhood. Although the city in its Fourth Ward urban renewal project plan stated that it would provide relocation assistance for house-holds and business displaced by the construction of Interstate 280 and the Gar-den State Parkway, these promises proved to be largely empty. Most residents found housing on their own, sometimes in worse condition, while most small businesses closed. By 1970, local Black empowerment, Black Power Urbanism, and the Model Cities Program would come together in a vain attempt to recon-struct a shattered neighborhood.

Black Suburban Empowerment Meets Black Power Urbanism

White East Orange had long prided itself on being a bastion of suburban good government, with local politicians and the people who staffed the city's many boards and commissions continuing the city's traditional reliance on "amateur democrats." The rise of the Northern Civil Rights Movement and the claims for full (sub)urban citizenship on the part of East Orange's Black population called this self-regard into question. The political establishment of East Orange imper-ceptibly bowed to this emergent new reality. Mayor James Kelly, elected in 1958, was the first Democrat in the city's history to hold the mayor's office. Though a relative newcomer, Kelly was part of a political and civic elite who believed that the salvation of the city lay in managing the city's racial populations by spatially concentrating some Black residents entirely and displacing others from the city while bringing in a better (that is, whiter and more affluent) population. Kelly's election was preceded by another tremor in East Orange's political firmament: the 1956 election of the town's first Black council member, Thomas Cook. This was followed by the election of two additional Black men to the city's nine-person council in 1962.[53] Part of this wave was linked to the demographic changes that white political and civic leaders had feared. By the 1950s, the Black community comprised about 25 percent of the town's population, although the new residents were younger, less educated, and had a lower income than white residents. Many of them were working- or middle-class Blacks who had moved from Newark to East Orange or who were part of the still-ongoing Great Migration. While the new Black residents were poorer than the whites, this did not mean that they were nonpolitical.

The election of the city's first Black council members, as well as the seemingly peaceful and decades-long integration of the city's schools, appeared to provide substance to East Orange's status as a "model interracial city."[54] However, this rosy picture of benign interracialism would falter as the influence of the Northern Civil Rights Movement and later Black Power Urbanism came into clearer focus. The city's response to the growing (albeit polite) Black demands for substantive power (against the background of state- and county-level machine politics) was to change the rules of the game. In 1963, the city council took up and passed a charter reform law that increased the term lengths of the town mayor and the current city council members, thus weakening future Black political incorporation while extending the dominance of white politicians into the late 1960s even as the city's white population rapidly decreased. In addition to these structural challenges, the city council took care of an immediate political threat to the establishment by making sure that William Hart, a leading local Black politician, was offered a position in the Democratic governor's administration. These moves blunted a direct challenge to the local political establishment by Black community activists and leaders who aimed to restructure the city's housing, education, and urban renewal policy away from Black displacement and toward Black empowerment.

By 1962, when East Orange had been deemed a model city, the Civil Rights Movement was no longer simply something happening in the South; the Northern Black freedom movement had also begun to shift into high gear. Though Black East Orange had some symbolic political and civic representation, it did not have substantive power until Black Power Urbanism swept over East Orange. By the late 1960s the city's rising Black political class had rejected the top-down "amateur democrats" of white East Orange and were pressing for a city that was responsive to and inclusive of the needs and concerns of not just "taxpayers" (the coded language that white city council members would increasingly use to refer to white residents), but all residents—Black or white, homeowner or renter. In 1967, East Orange's white political and civic establishment seemed poised for a serious challenge with Black candidates running for office and the existential shadow of Newark's rebellion. The first sign that Black political power was on the rise was the election in 1967 of Thomas Cook as city council head, along with the election of four other African Americans to the city council: Alfred Brown, Harold Smith, William Holt, and William Hart (who had been elected as the first Black member of the council in 1960). In 1969, William Hart would win the mayor's office, defeating longtime mayor James Riley.

The end of white East Orange's hegemony was dramatically shaped by the city next door: Newark. The promise of peaceful integration marked by civility and moderation that was shaped in part by the expert consensus of elite reformers was undone on July 12, 1967 when the city of Newark erupted in rebellion. The Newark rebellion was not a faraway event; it was on East Orange's doorstep. As early as July 8, according to the Hughes report (a review of the Newark rebellion conducted by a commission appointed by the governor), "a fight between 15 Negroes and the East Orange and Newark police on the Newark/East Orange border further heated emotions."[55] As the rebellion in Newark increased in intensity, East Orange police (like police forces in other adjacent municipalities) blocked off streets leading to Newark. This blockade also included "stopping and searching all vehicles with out-of-state license plates" as there were rumors that "outside agitators" were involved. East Orange firefighters assisted in putting out the fires raging in Newark. By July thirteenth the rebellion had spread to the edge of East Orange in the area around North Fourteenth Street. The circumstances of the altercation in East Orange—who was involved and why—remain unclear in later reports. The East Orange police claimed to have arrested nineteen people who "identified themselves as Black Muslims."[56] Central Avenue, which extended from Newark to East Orange's "Fifth Avenue of the suburbs," experienced significant destruction, as did Springfield Avenue, another major commercial artery.[57]

East Orange's residents may have withstood the physical upheaval and displacement caused by two major highway projects, coupled with urban renewal, but the closeness of the rebellion to East Orange had a profoundly negative effect on its white residents. The urban crisis was now next door. By 1970, East Orange's white population had dropped to 30 percent of the total population. Yet, perhaps white out-migration was unavoidable regardless of the conditions in Newark. As East Orange's officials and planners worryingly noted, by the late 1950s the city's population was divided by race, but within racial categories it was divided by age. The city's white residents were old: they were 14.3 percent of residents over 65. Of these seniors, 61 percent were women. According to local historians, these women tended to live in working-class areas of Doddtown, which had been targeted for urban renewal, or in the grand apartment buildings that made up East Orange's "urbane suburbanism."[58]

The pace of this demographic transition hastened in the immediate after-math of the riots. As one oral history recounted: "When the dowagers died and the WASPS fled quickly, there was a glut of housing and rental and sales prices fell dramatically. Even my relatives (who were of the wrong religion and ethnic group [Italian Americans] were suddenly able to get apartments."[59] However, the decaying physical environment of some parts of East Orange may have also pushed younger white residents, who had access to FHA mortgages and did not face a segregated suburban housing market, out of the city. The physical blight and psychic "root shock" caused by urban renewal and highway construction during the 1940s and 1950s may have also been a major factor in East Orange's transition. By the early 1960s, several urban analysts had noted that the "dispo-sition problem" of urban renewal programs seemed to create rather than cure "blight." Urban renewal powers allowed city governments to quickly declare an area "blighted," which then gave them the ability to follow up with land clearance. Cities, however, were not able to start the new construction process as quickly as they had done for the destruction process. Thus, while the town was success-ful in clearing "blighted" property in its three urban renewal areas in a relatively short period, much of the cleared land stood empty for years while city officials persuaded private investors to build. Indeed, the presence of these open spaces actually seemed to repel investors as adjacent areas lost their property values and attractiveness once neglect and decay crept in around the redevelopment sites. In the case of Brick Church, the town's downtown area, major portions of cleared property remained empty well into the 1990s.

Finally, there was another transformation that occurred during East Orange's transition from a "model interracial" to majority-Black suburb. With the dis-appearance of its white citizens, a particular kind of civic continuity and civic capital based on "amateur democrats" was lost, as was elite control of the policy agenda. By 1974, almost none of the civic groups listed in East Orange's centen-nial history of 1964 were still functioning. In the new East Orange, Black Power Urbanism coupled with older forms of conventional and respectability politics led to the creation of new kinds of civic and social capital. Not surprisingly, the Black middle class—or what remained of it—now controlled the city. Subsequent Black mayors turned to top-down urban renewal as a mean to bring back the glory days of the "urbane suburb."

Making a (Suburban) Model City

The city's belief that it had maintained itself as a fortress against Newark was shat-tered by that city's rebellion. The Fourth Ward reflected Newark's encroachment:

despite the impact of the reduction in housing units due to urban renewal and highway construction, the neighborhood had become the new home of "low income . . . problem families" pushed out of Newark.[60] Acknowledging this new reality, East Orange officials were persuaded to submit a joint application for the federal Model Cities Program with the city of Newark. However, in the aftermath of the long hot summer of 1967, the program was a political statement by the federal government that it was addressing the urban crisis, which meant that given the scope and visibility of Newark's rebellion, the government would press for a program that highlighted Newark alone.[61]

Although East Orange's joint application was rejected because the city was not "seedy enough," it did receive a Model Cities grant in 1968 for the Fourth Ward urban renewal area.[62] The city's "Negro removal"/urban renewal plan of 1950 had led to the shattering of this neighborhood, so much so that one planning report described the current "economy of the neighborhood [as] so lop-sided as to be non-existent . . . there is lacking a merchant or industrial middle-class or base upon which a strong community can be built."[63] While the Model Cities Program encouraged community participation and involvement, East Orange's version of the program was shaped by the city's longer tradition of top-down governing and planning. The grant application did not meaningfully engage with the residents of the Fourth Ward; it was mostly written by the city planning director and a team of faculty and students from Upsala College.[64] Anne Foerster notes in her study of the program in East Orange that to the extent that Fourth Ward residents were involved at all, input was limited to a post hoc community survey and a contentious advisory board.[65]. As a result of this top-down approach, Black middle-class empowerment would be pitted against a diminished though still influential white power structure with the ethos of "amateur democrats."

A "Beautiful Village": Rebuilding the Fourth Ward

By the late 1960s, urban redevelopment reflected the imperatives of local economic development, the influence of Great Society programming, and the emergence of East Orange's particular style of Black Power Urbanism. Black Power Urbanism in East Orange sprang from the political pressure placed on the city council by the ascendance of Black city council members, the planning stages of William Hart's run for mayoral office, and the significant growth in the town's Black population, including poorer Blacks displaced by "Negro removal" in Newark. War on Poverty funding, including the Model Cities Program, coupled with and directed by pressure from the Black community, forced the town to shift some of its focus away from downtown development and to finally address the destructive impact of highway construction on the historic Fourth Ward. Black Power Urbanism changed the debate around urban renewal and gave far less deference to the town's planners and the city's remaining white elites. Indeed, with white leadership and federal funding lagging, the conflict over the development of the Fourth Ward marked the penultimate struggle between the older white leadership and the ascendant Black political class.

The city responded to the louder political voice of the middle-class Black community, including Hart's mayoral candidacy, by focusing on (re)building some civic infrastructure in the area, including replacing a firehouse, building a library addition for a local junior high school, and erecting a new public library to replace the obsolete early twentieth-century Carnegie library. The city also sold off six properties (that had been acquired via urban renewal) for commercial development. Projects built included an office showroom, two small office buildings, and a gas station. The most notable commercial investment was Sussex Mall, a $1 million, 165,000-square-foot strip mall. Facing a largely unfunded displacement, Calvary Baptist Church, one of the city's oldest Black churches, relocated and built a new sanctuary after its old one was demolished as part of the highways' construction.[66]

Rehousing the Displaced

Three housing developments also played a key role in the rebuilding of the Fourth Ward. While the city built and/or sponsored two of these projects, the third would come about at the behest of community activists who challenged East Orange's long tradition of top-down planning. In keeping with the city's employment of differential citizenship when it came to affordable housing, the first project was the construction of a 127-unit high-rise building for low-income elderly on the eastern side of the Garden State Parkway. The second project, Arcadian Gardens, was the low-income project first proposed in the 1950 master plan. The 212-unit townhouse-style development was in keeping with the city's suburban spatial imaginary, and was also in compliance with new federal regulations regarding the design of public housing for families. East Orange's public housing would be a lower-scale alternative to Newark's dense high-rise projects like the Stella Wright Houses.[67]

The third project, Kuzuri-Kijiji, was where Black Power Urbanism left its mark on East Orange. The project's name, which was "Swahili for 'beautiful village'" was chosen due to "the need for a strong name representing the black heritage" as opposed to the "usual type of corny project names, such as Sussex Meadows."[68] The 247-unit project was designed by a local Black architect,

Edward T. Bowser Jr., and built by an activist group led by Jesse Jefferies, a local realtor. According to Robert Bowser, mayor of East Orange from 1997 to 2013, Bowser Jr. and members of the Upsala College Black Student Organization "read the old urban renewal laws and found that if families were displaced, and a group of the people got together they could, they could put 10% of the estimated costs of the project they would have first rights to redevelop the property. And they did that here in East Orange."[69] The group put together a development proposal and submitted it to the city and to the state housing finance office. The Kuzuri group pressed for cooperative ownership; as a result they faced resistance and delays from state and federal officials who wanted a more conventional ownership structure. Edward Bowser and others repeatedly traveled to the state housing agency to confront officials about their chronic delays in approving the requested funding. In the end, the agency acceded and state provided funding for the project.

Although it secured state funding, the group made the decision to forgo a request for a tax exemption. Other Black-led or endorsed projects, both in East Orange and in Newark, had sought tax exemptions, which had led to acrimonious debates by the white members of each of the city councils. The issue of tax exemption had been especially difficult in the case of Amiri Baraka's contested Kawaida Tower development. In the context of East Orange, Jeffries argued that tax exemption was "a burden on the local black taxpayer, the majority of whom were least able to afford to subsidize the lower income received by urban blacks in the present society." Accordingly, Kuzuri-Kijiji would "pay taxes proportional to those charged in other apartments in East Orange."[70] The project's operational support would come from co-op payments from residents as well as federal Section 23 rental subsidies, which had proved wildly popular in Oakland.[71] The complex was built by the F. W. Eversley construction firm, one of the largest Black-owned construction firms in the New York City area. The firm's rapid growth during the late 1960s was testament to Black Power urbanist activism, which pressured local, state, and federal officials to give Black construction firms the first shot in rebuilding Black communities; and to the impact of Nixon's policy of Black capitalism, which provided financial support and technical advice to Black businesses.[72]

Kuzuri-Kijiji formally opened in October 1973 (see figure 4.4). It was celebrated in the *New York Times* as "one of the largest housing projects in the country developed by Blacks," in successful contrast to the "embattled Black-sponsored Kawaida Towers in neighboring Newark."[73] The opening ceremony featured remarks by Amiri Baraka and was presided over by Mayor William Hart. The complex would serve as the home of a stable working class-community until the co-op was dissolved in the 1990s and the buildings were emptied in 2015.[74]

Educating the "Model Interracial City"

East Orange's public school system had been legally integrated but de facto segregated since the turn of the twentieth century. Since 1899, the city had historically dealt with the problem of integrated education by deploying a mix of administrative moves, from crafting school attendance zones that mapped onto and solidified the city's deep-rooted residential segregation patterns, to academic tracking, which kept white (and some middle-class Black) students apart from most Black students in separate and unequal spaces within the city's school buildings.[75] By the early twentieth century East Orange's Black community was established enough that the leaders of local Black organizations and institutions formed the nucleus of the periodic opposition to white East Orange's semiofficial discriminatory treatment of Black children.

The institutional racism of East Orange's school system carried over to planning for the postwar era. Although most of the city's schools were old (built during the late nineteenth and early twentieth centuries), the city's 1945 building plans did not initially include the majority-Black schools (Ashland and Eastern). Five years later, the town's 1950 proposed education plan was designed to facilitate the town's long-standing attempts to re-sort its population.[76] As in the housing plan, town officials and city planners hewed to the belief that "homogeneous neighborhoods" were the optimal sites not only for living but also for delivering education and recreation.[77] The 1950 proposed plan arranged school attendance zones (for primary and secondary schools) that fit existing, as well as desired, racially segregated spaces (see figure 4.2C).[78]

In addition to an increasing level of undesirable (that is, Black) school-age children, school and city officials also noted another dire problem with the overall system. The oldest and most dilapidated schools were located in the Third and Fourth Ward where the town's historic Black population was located and where most of the town's population growth was occurring. To town officials, "renewing" Black areas by removing current residents and building single-family housing and apartment complexes for a "better sort of resident" was inextricably linked to school construction, and of course, school financing. Quality residents needed quality schools, but quality schools could not be provided unless quality residents (who presumably paid higher taxes) were on hand. Thus, the city proposed alternative plans for the school system, with replacement of old facilities generally contingent on seeing changes in the school system's demographics as well as—most importantly—new tax revenues that would support more than modest improvements in school facilities.

The 1950 plan presented the town with three options for upgrading its aging physical plant. Each scenario effectively kept the idea of neighborhood schools at the K–5 or K–8 level with attendance zones that would mostly adhere to existing

HOUSING

Blacks Open Housing Co-op In East Orange, New Jersey

It was almost two years to the date from the groundbreaking to the official opening of Kuzuri-Kijiji, the largest housing development in the United States developed by Blacks.

The event is historical and significant for many reasons. The complex, a cluster of two and three-story townhouses on 18.2 acres, is in a predominantly-Black area of East Orange, N. J., and is less than four miles from the site of Kawaida Towers in Newark, N. J., whose construction has been held up by months of picketing and court battles.

. Kuzuri-Kijiji, which means "beautiful village" in Swahili, is a $6.7 million project, designed for low and middle-income families, and which contains 150 three-bedroom townhouses, 73 two-bedroom townhouses and 24 one-bedroom apartments for the elderly.

Black architect Edward T. Bowser designed each townhouse with its own individually-landscaped yard and the buildings are constructed of masonry, with hand-hewn shingle eaves and spindrels, featuring balconies, patio doors and canopies.

The monthly maintenance, or rent, will range from $190 for the one-bedroom apartments. However, under the federal rent subsidy programs, the monthly rent charged can be reduced for the tenant to as low as $42 for the one-bedroom apartment and $138 for the three-bedroom apartment. Tenants will be required to make a $400 down payment and will receive proportional shares of ownership in the complex.

Like Newark, where Kawaida is to be constructed, East Orange has a Black mayor, William S. Hart. The city has approximately 80,000 residents.

Actor Ossie Davis and Imamu Baraka chat at opening of housing complex.

FIGURE 4.4. "A beautiful village": Black Power housing in East Orange

Source: "Blacks Open Housing Co-op in East Orange, New Jersey," *Jet Magazine*, November 1, 1973, 30.

racial boundaries. Further consolidation was planned for both proposed and new middle schools and for the city's two high schools. Modernized facilities would presumably make the maintenance of existing levels of racial "integration" acceptable to Black parents while keeping white parents within the school district. In practice, the 1950 plan meant that East Orange High—located roughly in the city's center and one of the district's oldest buildings, with a near majority-Black student body (around 50 percent)—would become a supermajority Black school by 1965 (71 percent). By contrast, Clifford Scott High School, located in the majority white northern ward of the city, retained a majority-white student body (from 96 percent in 1952 to 90 percent in 1964).[79]

A "Better Sort of Negro"

Until the late 1950s educational peace was maintained by a tacit understanding in which the school district allowed (some) middle-class Blacks—the "better sort of Negro" in Barry Garvin's words—into white academic spaces in return for middle-class Black acquiescence to the de facto segregation and inequality of the school system. The rapid change in school demographics put pressure on this understanding in ways that neither the white school and political leadership nor the established Black middle-class leadership would fully comprehend. While echoes of Black Power Urbanism would finally move Black East Orange to mobilize for equity and/or integration, the radical energy that it brought to other Black spaces was missing from this struggle over education. Unlike nearby Newark, or further afield in Oakland or East Palo Alto, East Orange did not see a flurry of educational experiments and confrontations take place. East Orange's path during the 1960s was markedly different.

While Blacks had long constituted a durable and vocal percentage of the school system's students, by the late 1950s the school system had a Black student body that was approaching 30 percent. This shift in demographics was not reflected among teachers, staff, or leadership. Despite the appointment of Barry Garvin to the school district council, only 11 percent of the city's teachers were non-white and none of the twelve schools in the system had a Black principal. In 1962, due to overcrowding in the majority-Black Stockton School, another school (Kentopp) was created and a new principal, J. Garfield Jackson Sr., was appointed, making him the first Black principal in the system.[80] By 1960, the possibilities of rebuilding the school system that had been presented in the postwar education plans seemed increasingly unfeasible. Though a flurry of new apartment and office-building construction had taken place during the 1940s, the number of Black families moving into the city was increasing, while white families were opting to move to suburbs farther out. By 1964, over 60 percent of the East Orange school system's ten thousand students were African American. Not surprisingly, the student population was not evenly distributed in terms of race. Schools located in the northern, majority-white neighborhoods had majority-white student bodies, while schools in majority-Black areas had majority-Black student bodies.[81] The East Orange school system, like many in "integrated communities," had been and still was a de facto segregated system.

Garvin and Jackson's appointments and the establishment of Kentopp were two small concessions offered by the city's white political and civic leaders; however, they did not change the demographic facts on the ground: the school system had transitioned to a majority-Black student body. In response, the town's political and school leadership made the surprising announcement that they would solve both the problem of integration and the school system's faltering finances by endorsing the creation of an "educational plaza" that would centralize all the city's students and do away with neighborhood schools.[82] The plan for the educational plaza had been formulated by Mayor James Kelly and newly appointed school superintendent Robert Seitzer.[83]

The questions before the city's educational and political leadership were how to maintain what they saw as the delicate balance of integration and to how to cope with the transformation of educational policy as it begin to focus on educational performance during the 1960s. The school district put off any real, substantive day-to-day change in how East Orange's existing schools were governed—in terms of teaching or pedagogy—and instead supported an "educational plaza" that would not only radically integrate the town's educational system, but also, through the plaza's form and function, the system's cautious leadership would somehow magically develop the capacity to embrace a whole new pedagogical approach. East Orange's educational plan of the future replaced a suburban system of small neighborhood schools with a K–12 educational complex that at one point was slated to also include a community college. This centralized system would largely be paid for by the federal government rather than the majority-white taxpayers of East Orange.

Keeping White Children

East Orange's bold "revolutionary plan to end school segregation" was heralded in both the Black and white press.[84] The city would build a "modern high-rise, centrally located complex that would take 15 to 20 years to complete."[85] This complex would be the center of a new "centralized school system [that] could employ new methods of team teaching, require only one major library and prevent duplication of services." As a result of this development, the city could "return other school property to the tax rolls."[86] This revalorization of public property from public use to market value would even include the recently renovated (1960) Clifford Scott High, which East Orange education officials suggested "could be used for office space."[87] The claims made by East Orange about the educational plaza rested on a subtext made up of issues—past, current, and future—concerning the nature of public education in a post–*Brown v. Board of Education* world in which Black people were no longer willing to acquiesce to segregated schooling either through remaining in segregated neighborhoods; quietly subjecting themselves to segregated school attendance zones; or accepting a tokenized, subordinate, and marginal position for Black students within the walls of so-called integrated schools.

East Orange was not the only city to publicly embrace educational plazas. Conceived in the 1950s as a modern alternative to what some educational experts saw as an outmoded form of education unsuitable for the "demands of the space-age," they became a possible solution for the post-*Brown* educational landscape. As Ansley Erickson notes, the idea of educational plazas like the one proposed in East Orange "drew the interest of local leaders and national networks of educators seeking to further desegregation but concerned about how to do so within the bounds of white resistance. Huge single- or multi-school campuses ... would draw students from broad geographical areas and facilitate desegregation. But in the design and location choices for these imagined (but often not realized) education parks, desegregation advocates revealed a spatial ideology of schooling that reflected both a rejection of racialized Black spaces and an anti-urban, modernist aesthetic."[88]

Across New Jersey, Black parents and civil rights advocates, inspired by the Brown decision as well as Southern resistance, began the pushback against de facto segregation by filing a flurry of lawsuits (with the help of the New Jersey NAACP and local branches) against New Jersey school districts in the early 1960s.[89] They initiated lawsuits right on East Orange's doorstep, suing the city of Orange immediately to the east and "liberal" Montclair, located on the city's northern border. East Orange's attempt to delay the meaningful desegregation of its schools was rapidly coming to an end now that parents had seen success in challenging de facto segregated systems. In an important 1961 case addressing segregation in New Rochelle, New York, the court found that "the *Brown* decision had clear application to Negro children and to public education and school boards outside the South."[90] Several years after that decision, the New Jersey case of *Booker v. Board of Education of Plainfield* (45 N.J. 161 [1965]) ruled that "a firm mandate was placed upon the state educational authorities to see that the children of this state, constitutionally entitled to a free public school education, had an equal opportunity, both in theory and practice, to obtain that advantage." The case not only affirmed the right of Black students to confront de facto systems, but the court also stated that the "Commissioner and State Board must take the positive action required in order to assure compliance with state law and policy."[91] This declaration had significant ramifications for the state commissioner of education, whose reluctant attempts to enforce desegregation on suburban districts was faced with legislator resistance, and he would ultimately be forced out of office.

To white school officials nervous about whether court-mandated desegregation would take place, the educational plaza concept appeared to be a viable and fairly painless solution to the post-*Brown* puzzle facing white-controlled school districts with rapidly increasing minority student bodies. Local officials confronted two questions: how could these districts integrate schools without "losing" the remaining white students, and how could districts address the building upgrades necessary to deliver a modern education without "burdening" deserving (white) taxpayers? Federal officials like Harold Howe and organizations such as the Ford Foundation saw educational plazas as a last chance, arguing that since "none of the other devices have provided satisfactory answers to big-city school integration, it now appears certain that educational parks will move into the forefront of civil rights strategy and educational experimentation."[92] For progressive educators, both around the country and in East Orange, the scale of these new educational spaces offered the possibility of delivering more individualized, better-resourced, and more culturally relevant education than was possible in the small, overcrowded, and segregated schools that many students were forced to attend.[93] Despite the enthusiasm of pro-integration advocates, some Black activists viewed these plans with suspicion, arguing that they were simply another attempt to shortchange Black students.[94] None of the plans contained any of the core tenets of Black Power Urbanism: Black control of schools that were staffed by Black teachers, staff, and administrators, delivering a culturally relevant curriculum with a pedagogy that addressed the needs of Black children and youth.

The East Orange Education Plaza

The plan released by Superintendent Seitzer was a surprise to both staff and parents as it was developed in secrecy.[95] This approach was in keeping with the city's reliance on outside experts and its predilection for keeping local decision-making in the hands of the town's civil elites via "citizen advisory groups." The plan was developed in conjunction with experts who touted educational plazas such as Robert Havighurst and with the support of federal officials like Commissioner of Education Harold Howe II. The Ford Foundation also played an important role in funding the expert research as well as the city's overall proposal.[96] Indeed, when Seitzer announced the plan he alluded to forthcoming federal and foundation support as key elements in its financing. His secrecy reflected official East Orange's unwillingness to directly address racial inequality, instead concealing its attempts at racial management behind a cloak of technocratic language. Hence it was reported that "although East Orange's 9,856 students are 60 per cent Negro, racial balance was not a prime issue."[97]

The educational plaza plan was an implicit acknowledgement that the alternatives laid out in the city's 1950 planning documents developed by Harland Bartholomew had been superseded by racial facts on the ground. The 1950 plan to enhance and protect the ideal of homogeneous neighborhood schools was no longer workable at the elementary level due to the rapid growth in the number of Black students and the concomitant decline in white students. In 1952, six of the district's eight K–6 schools were majority-white, while by 1964 only two of them were—both located in the city's remaining white neighborhoods. With political and educational leaders committed to holding on to the belief that "neighborhood homogeneity" was a necessary condition for the delivery of quality education, support collapsed for assistance to and upgrading of the now majority-Black schools. In short, without the need to maintain adequate facilities and restricted attendance zones to keep white parents in the system, the upgrading of the city's neighborhood's schools was reoriented toward creating a "quality education for the disadvantaged" at the least cost to the city's (white) taxpayers.[98]

The neighborhood school, which had been valorized as the bedrock of quality education during the post-*Brown* era, was quickly discarded in East Orange and elsewhere once most of the neighborhoods became majority-Black. According to an East Orange Board of Education press release, neighborhood schools "could no longer meet the complicated educational needs of the space age"; only an educational establishment staffed by experts could do so, with the added benefit that the "integration that would be guaranteed by centralization [was] a worthwhile 'extra.'"[99]

The plan for the East Orange educational plaza was not a complete deviation from the 1950 plan. What remained and became the basis of the plaza was a proposed new school that would have been built adjacent to an existing stadium in an area that was already slated for urban renewal (see figure 4.5). Although the proposed site was smaller than the ideal educational campuses envisioned by proponents of this concept, the planners of the East Orange campus turned toward an explicitly urban form to squeeze more usage out of the proposed site. This meant that instead of the suburban idyll of green fields and playgrounds proposed in the 1950 plan, the plaza would instead make do with a medium-rise resource tower, rooftop playgrounds, and underground parking.[100] The scale of the complex was naturally vast, given that it would eventually house all of the city's ten thousand students. Initial plans called for a "core structure with five or six wings," each of which would hold "600 to 900 students."[101]

While the imperatives of managing integration and stemming white flight underlay the planning of the campus, East Orange's superintendent publicly rejected the notion that racial change was driving district planning. Educational researchers and the many observers who came to look at the city's "detailed architectural renderings" privately observed that race was clearly central to its

FIGURE 4.5.   Managing integration: East Orange's educational plaza

Source: *The Syllabus*, East Orange High School, 1965, 8. East Orange Public Library.

motivation. While these thoughts went unaired in the city, others outside of the city certainly were aware of these unstated motives. For example, the consultant hired by the Berkeley (California) School District reported that

> in developing "the case" for the educational plaza, East Orange has emphasized the implications which it would have for the instructional program. These include increased specialization, better use of facilities, greater opportunities for innovation, etc. While the plan would achieve integration (which the Administration considers good), they appear to be mainly interested in the plaza as a means of developing a top-quality school system—one that would be so good that people would quit

taking their children out of the public schools and placing them into private schools.[102]

Through its proposed educational plaza, by 1966 East Orange, along with cities like Syracuse, New York City, and Berkeley, had emerged as one of the few places that were successfully coping with the "anxieties of desegregation." In addition to funding from the Ford Foundation, the city was able to tap into both Title I and Title III of Elementary and Secondary Education Act (ESEA) funding to develop plans for a proposed town-wide middle school—the first step toward the consolidation of the city's schools and planning for the larger educational campus. According to one observer, "federal support for an educational park project, if not an essential ingredient in that project's success, is a helpful addition, allowing the project to make 'tangible progress' as it moves along 'the right track.'"[103] Federal and philanthropic support, however, were not enough given the increased pressure for inclusion and the substantive power of the city's rising Black majority.

Like many New Jersey school districts, the city's board of education was an unelected body. Its five members were appointed by the mayor and served for a five-year term. Reflecting the city's "amateur democratic ethos," the board of education saw itself as a "strictly policy making entity"; the day-to-day running of the schools was left to the superintendent (who by 1964 had served over twenty years in the position), while final budget decisions were made by the board of school estimate. The board of school estimate also consisted of five members: two appointed by the board of education, two city council members, and the mayor. The board of school estimate presented the district budget to the city council, which then voted on whether to accept or reject. At no point was there any opportunity for the average citizen to directly participate in the budget process. In many ways, elites believed this was a positive outcome as the city's schools would be protected from the shortsighted "pressure of groups." In practical terms, this meant that the district was not focused on responsiveness to the concerns of Black citizens and parents, but on satisfying its majority-white teaching and administrative staff. This distance also allowed the board of school estimate to remain attuned and sensitive to the white taxpayers who increasingly saw the city's school budget as "bloated and wasteful" as the number of Black and "disadvantaged" students increased.[104]

Greater Black political representation after the 1967 council elections, the inevitability that Hart or another African American would win the next mayoral election, and the changing demographics of the school district would lead to Seitzer's retirement and the appointment of the city's first Black superintendent, Russell A. Jackson Jr., in 1968.[105] Outside of official channels, the spirit of the moment began to "blow away the topsoil" of East Orange's belief in itself as an "urbane suburb." The Newark rebellion had literally spilled over into East Orange, which was also home to a small number of Black nationalist/Black Power organizations. Meanwhile at East Orange High, the student assembly featuring "Black Power poetry" reflected this new era of empowerment that momentarily united poor, working-class, and middle-class Black East Orange.

In the five years between the announcement of the plaza and Seitzer's retirement, plans were dramatically scaled down to simply a "model middle school." The grander plans for a complex serving the entire district and encompassing a possible community college were abandoned as the Johnson administration's Great Society programs were defunded and white taxpayer resistance in East Orange and elsewhere grew. Harold Howe, the federal official most enthusiastic about the educational plaza concept, would leave his position in 1968.[106] Though the project had been scaled down, supporters of the middle school were now animated by new educational theories sweeping the country. A temporary "storefront" school that brought together approximately one hundred of the district's Black students from the town's majority-Black schools and one hundred white students from town's remaining majority-white K–8 school was opened to minor acclaim.[107]

As plans progressed to actually start building the delayed middle school, the new racial and political fault lines of East Orange would be revealed. In 1971, the city council passed on first reading an ordinance authorizing $10.3 million in school construction bonds. However, four council members, two white and two Black, raised questions about the construction costs and the impact of the bonds on taxes. They also had concerns about the plan's "educational validity."[108] On a second reading the council passed the ordinance with all the Black council members approving, one white council member opposing, and a second white council member abstaining. Concerns over cost remained heightened, leading the board of education to come back with a redesigned and less expensive structure. The council voted almost unanimously (with the exception of one white member) for this new design with a lower bond issue of $9.4 million. In a strange twist, after the plan had been approved and bids solicited, Hart proposed an alternate site with the reasoning that it would be cheaper to adapt an existing building than to construct the new building the city had planned on.[109]

East Orange's transformation into an outpost of the Black Power metropolis came into starker relief when Mayor Hart offered an "affirmative action" proposal. Hart proposed an additional $200,000 appropriation for minority employment training, which would be added to the $9.4 million bond issue. The ordinance needed six votes to pass; all four Black council members and one white member supported the bill, but the remaining four white members opposed.[110] White council members insisted that their opposition was based on fiscal grounds, with one white council member stating that "the taxpayers of this city are in revolt and I in conscience can't vote for this expenditure."[111] Still another white council member argued that though he "wasn't against the idea of an affirmative action program, [he's] against the expenditure. The burden on our taxpayers is getting heavier and heavier."[112] In response, one Black council member said that he "could not conceive how people can rationalize opposing" such a program, while another Black council member suggested that not only was it "sad" to have to "pass a resolution to insure equal opportunity," but that it was "incumbent on the council to provide this opportunity for the residents."[113] In the end, this opposition proved temporary as a new proposal that added additional funding for the building as well as for the affirmative action program was approved by the council's five Black members and one white member, for the majority vote.

The debate over school finances was also intertwined with Hart's attempt to build low- and moderate-income housing in the city. One white council member saw the struggles over school funding, minority employment, and public housing as radical steps toward Newark-style "Black power." Mayor Hart, the council member argued, "wanted to chase the last whites out of East Orange." For East Orange Blacks, Black Power meant a disruption of the white suburban imaginary. The city would no longer make a distinction between the "the taxpayer" and "the residents." Both groups would have equal standing. As one local Black official in New Jersey put it, "The problems [in the city] are such that when you talk about uplifting the city as a whole, it's going to uplift Blacks. But in terms of job opportunities and better education, it's going to benefit whites too."[114]

By 1972, East Orange had decisively broken with its past identity as a "model interracial city." Going forward the city council would have a Black majority. The board of education would have both a Black president (Mildred Barry) and a Black vice president, while Russell Jackson Jr. would continue his tenure as the district's first Black school superintendent. Planning for the middle school complex would reflect a more open, less elite-driven East Orange that briefly captured the spirit of both the Black Power metropolis and New Left urbanism.

"What a School Should Be"

Compared to the educational plaza, whose concept and initial design was shrouded in secrecy and announced via press release, the design process for what would be known as the East Orange Middle School (EOMS) complex was far more transparent and inclusive. Uniplan, the complex's architects, opened up the East Orange School Design Center (EOSDC), a storefront community design studio.[115] Funding for the storefront came in part from the Education Facilities Laboratories (EFL), which was funded by the Ford Foundation and had been established in 1958.[116] Like other initiatives in the community design/participatory planning era, the storefront planning center was envisioned as a place to solicit community feedback.[117] The community design office opened in August 1970 "with a public celebration, street closing, and mayoral ribbon-cutting—and a 'public welcome' policy."[118]

While many of the grander ideas of the educational plaza scheme had already been jettisoned as federal money proved illusory, as the project scaled down to a middle school some of the more prosaic elements, such as the 150-car underground parking garage, remained. However, by the early 1970s these elements were deemed unfeasible and too expensive. In place of the 1964 plan, the architects offered what they argued was a more site-sensitive design that acknowledged the residential neighborhood of one- to four-family houses in which the complex would be located, rather than "some early schemes [that] used less land, but [were] oppressive in scale when related to neighboring structures."[119] Indeed, "large sites can only be assembled through relocating families and demolishing their homes. It would clearly have been antithetical to the process to anticipate doing this."[120] Even more important to the planners was the participatory nature of the process. The design office was open every day with full and part-time staff, and it identified and reached out to thirty community organizations to solicit their input. The firm's goal was to "identify community hopes and ideals, and measure these against the realities of economic and technical constraints." Thus, the planning process was an ideational and physical space where "ideas proposed by a housewife, a student, a policeman, or that nice little old lady, were investigated while they looked on. This gave each the opportunity to see how architects work and to instantly understand the drawbacks and/or merits of their contribution."[121] Even more critically, the firm centered the needs of students, inviting East Orange's children to "explore in drawings what a school should be" (see figure 4.6).[122]

The design also reflected some of the new pedagogical thinking of the time, emphasizing a school oriented toward community, connection, and flexibility.[123] For the architects, and perhaps for the new East Orange, "the success of EOMS and EOSDC must be measured in such intangible terms as 'credibility' and 'community understanding.' The result will be less the traditional architectural monument, and more of an architectural-community solution."[124]

In the end, the middle school (later named after Hart) would be built and opened by 1975 with relatively little controversy compared to the

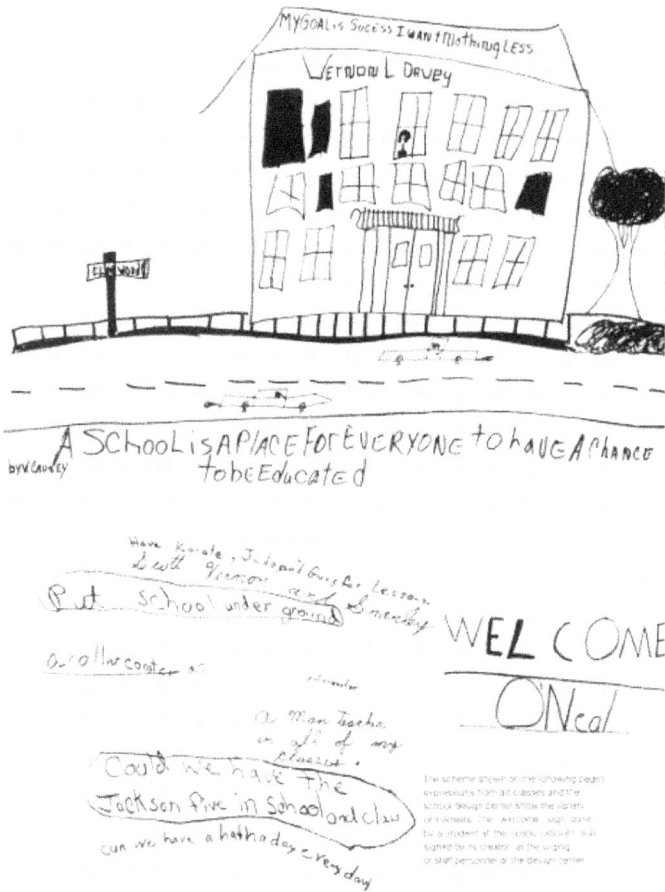

FIGURE 4.6. What a school should be: Community design for educational experimentation

Source: "By the People," *Progressive Architecture*, February 1972, 88–95, 89.

announcement for the educational plaza.[125] In place of an urban campus that denied the individuality of the student and the value of community in favor of a colorblind landscape was a school designed to fit into the mixed landscape of Black East Orange. Although this project was a success—even winning an architectural award—by the time it was finished the dream of East Orange as a "model interracial city" was over and so too was its attempt to create "integrated" and superior education.[126] Going forward, the city's federal grant applications would discuss the challenges of education in a school district with a majority-Black and increasingly poor student body and with a physical plant that aside from the new middle school had not seen any substantial upgrading or modernization since the early twentieth century. East Orange's teachers staged the city's first labor action in 1973 (Newark did the same) in response to a $2 million cut in the school budget as the Nixon administration's first wave of defunding urban and low-income areas took effect.[127] In that same year education advocates would win one of the country's first equalization lawsuits, *Robinson v. Cahill*, when East Orange joined with the city of Newark and some of the state's poorest and nearly all Black and/or Brown districts to force the state to assist the students left behind in newly segregated and dramatically underfinanced and underresourced districts. In response to this lawsuit and another (*Abbott v. Burke* [1975]), New Jersey would become one of the first states to begin aggressively overseeing "academically bankrupt" school systems and would subsequently push for state takeovers of these systems. East Orange and Newark would be some of the state's first targets.

Policing the Model Interracial Suburb

The Newark rebellion proved once again that East Orange was not an urbane suburban island unto itself. From July 8, 1967, when the first confrontation occurred between "15 Negroes" and East Orange police, through the state's subsequent state of emergency and the blocking off of all streets that crossed the Newark/East Orange border, the city was faced with a reckoning over the transformations that had occurred both in Newark and within its own borders. In later testimony, members of the Black Community Defense and Development Organization, a Black nationalist organization with links to Baraka's United Brothers, were identified as the "15 Negroes" who were involved in the confrontation with police.[128] This confrontation is notable not only because it preceded the full-blown rebellion that occurred the next evening, but also because of the police officers who were involved. The police contingent included East Orange as well as Newark police officers and among the latter group was an officer who had shot and killed an eighteen-year-old Black youth in 1965. Though the officer changed his justifications for the shooting multiple times, in the end a hearing found that he had not used excessive force. The officer returned to duty, but "his occasional assignment to Negro areas was a continuing source of irritation in the Negro community."[129]

The city's relationship between a still-dominant white power structure and the near-majority Black population could be seen in the composition of East Orange's police force. The 160-person force had only a handful of Black officers. Local activists would continue to push the city to diversify the ranks of police and fire departments and change the police commission's structure to allow for more community input.[130] Although the Newark rebellion shone a bright light on the state of policing in the city, it was two pieces of federal legislation, the Model Cities Act of 1968 and the Law Enforcement Assistance Administration (LEAA) of 1968 that would shape East Orange's perceptions of crime and disorder as refracted through both its now-challenged suburban spatial imaginary and the city's own brand of Black Power Urbanism.

The proto-carceral state apparatus that had emerged out of the Ford Foundation's Gray Areas studies programs in Oakland and Newark took a new turn in the wake of the urban rebellions that had swept across US cities during the 1960s. The Kerner Commission Report (also known as the National Advisory Commission on Civil Disorders) was published in 1968, after the summer of 1967 saw over 150 riots in the United States, including Newark's. The Kerner Report focused on police-community relations, and particularly on bad policing, as one of the key factors that explained the wave of urban rebellions. The most dominant response to assertions that bad policing was the culprit was that these rebellions were not purposeful, justified, or legitimate. Thus, the federal government offered LEAA funding to state and local governments for additional police measures to avert future rebellions and control what was increasingly seen as a surplus population of the ghetto. On paper at least, East Orange rejected that approach, stating that it was not interested in a "domestic arms race" that would create an "armament of riot control arsenal."[131] Nor did the city create a vast surveillance system to be deployed through school and housing projects as other cities did. Instead, East Orange embraced the softer (though no less controlling and/or punitive) "police reform" approach that was being put together under the leadership of the Police Foundation and funded by the Ford Foundation.

The city's response to calls for a new kind of policing reflected the struggle between Black and white residents and between Black Power urbanist aspirations for community participation and the city's traditional reliance on expert assistance. As was the case for education and housing, in the face of Black Power Urbanism and its focus on policing and the criminal justice system, the city's response to community activists' concerns over unfair policing was also limited and muted. While the city's police reform approach was taking shape, however, the Model Cities Program introduced (albeit briefly) a Black Power urbanist approach to policing. In keeping with the idea of community control over policing— or at least substantive community input into policing—the Model Cities Program offered a variety of new services that had never been offered by the city before, nor by many other cities. These included a legal services clinic as well as teen recreation and jobs programs that were understood to be more productive than traditional juvenile delinquency prevention programs. In addition, reflecting growing anxieties about a burgeoning "dope" problem within Black communities, there were calls for a drug abuse clinic and drug addiction prevention programs.[132]

The city's police reform approach was extended in 1970 when Mayor Hart agreed to allow students at John Jay College to conduct an external audit of the department. A *New York Times* article, which favorably reviewed the audit, revealed the ways in which politics, governance, crime, and drugs would become interrelated by the early 1970s in an early iteration of today's carceral state. The John Jay study called for the creation of a "single body . . . to handle all aspects of the drug problem and coordinate work that now is divided among the schools, health agencies, the Mayor's office and the police."[133] The second recommendation suggested that the city create "an office or agency completely separate from the Police Department to which addicts, their families and interested citizens can go for instant help." Third, it suggested "organiz[ing] a permanent rehabilitation center to help the city's 320 registered addicts and the unknown number of unregistered addicts." The article also offered a glimpse of the tensions between the "community" and the police as the 1970s-era War on Drugs began to escalate. Two members of the Model Cities Program articulated the conflict that lay within the community over the rise in drug use and the spread of the drug trade, with one approving of the separate facility because "these kids never go to the police because they'd be afraid of getting their friends in trouble."[134] The second member was more critical of the police and less sympathetic of drug users, asking "why does it take so long for the police to do something after they are told about drugs being used and sold in a certain house?"[135]

Black Power Urbanism, which had never been robust in East Orange, was pushed aside as the new Black leaders of the city grappled with their own (sub) urban crisis of cutbacks in state and federal funding, continued disinvestments, rise in crime and slumlordism, and finally the death of one aspect of the suburban spatial imaginary of safety. As one Black resident lamented, it used to be that "people walked the streets. They could leave their doors open. Only four years ago, my house was broken into by some joker."[136] By the late 1970s, the ongoing War on Drugs as well as an increase in crime crashed into East Orange and particularly the Fourth Ward, the most fragile of the city's neighborhoods. In 1977, Thomas Cook, who succeeded Hart, would declare that that the city was under a "siege of fear." Arcadian Gardens, one of the city's two multifamily housing projects and not quite a decade old, was considered the epicenter of the wave of violence. Residents complained that Arcadian Gardens had become a "haven for drug pushers and users." Cook—locked in a difficult reelection battle—gave a "tough on crime" response to his critics: "I'm giving fair warning to all lawbreakers that our public safety forces will be fully supported from this City Hall in carrying out their professional duties. If that entails cracking heads and kicking butts, that is what is going to happen."[137] Neither tough talk nor the expansion of the police force allayed a growing fear of crime (itself the result of a rise in robberies and burglaries). Middle-class residents' growing perceptions of public disorder were fueled by what they saw as a changing population mix. In addition to new lower-income residents arriving from Newark, East Orange and Asbury Park were the recipient of "several thousand ex-mental patients" who lived in hastily converted boarding houses.[138]

The city, once the recipient of multiple "cleanest city" awards—with the most recent in 1973—was increasingly seen as a place marred by trash, disorder, and vacant houses and retail stores. Over the next few decades the city's mayors would lead periodic "clean-up campaigns" urging tenants and landlords to take pride in their surroundings; and more pointedly would take to task nonresident landlords for failing to maintain their properties. One mayor would declare a "war on slums," stating that his administration would "rid the city of 'slumlords and slum tenants.'" These problem populations who lacked "civic pride" would have to "shape up or we're going to put them in jail." Particular ire was directed toward "landlords who live in the [other] suburbs" and who "solicit welfare clients" to rent their declining properties.[139]

At the same time that Mayor Hart and later Mayor Cook were lambasting "landlordism" and "problem" tenants, they also urged the local landlord association to work with the East Orange Tenants Association on managing these properties so as not to "tear down the city." The city went several steps further, first identifying especially egregious problem buildings (approximately thirty-five of them) and then encouraging tenants to take over the buildings of especially negligent absentee landlords. Tenants of one apartment building did so in 1980; the building became the city's first to be owned and managed by tenants.

The city's politicians as well as its Black middle-class residents believed that the city had experienced a sharp rise in low-income renters, which politicians had historically linked to disorder and crime. This was coupled with middle-class residents' fear of uncleanliness, and by extension their commitment to suburban respectability politics. Mayors would continue to evoke cleanliness as a key measure when assessing the state of the city. Indeed, in Taylor's 2016 state of the city address, he noted that the city "worked to motivate its business partners, as well as residential homeowners and renters, to clean up their city. East Orange was once known as the cleanest city in the country. . . . But we also had one of the lowest crime rates in that time frame. And we have this adage that a 'clean city [and] a safe city equals a profitable city.'"[140]

While "cleanliness" was one way in which the changing status of East Orange from "urban suburb" to "poor city" was measured, the city also employed other more traditional measures of public safety. The police department was recognized for the rapid and seemingly peaceful integration of its ranks, as white police officers left and new Black officers took their place. While the city experienced sharp reductions in income from the federal general revenue-sharing program that led to the layoff of 15 percent of the city's police force, during the 1980s the force itself had expanded from 160 to 300 officers.[141] The federal and state government's escalation of the War on Drugs led to growth in the size of the city's police force, but also to the city's embrace of new forms of community surveillance, especially the deployment of CCTV and neighborhood watches.[142]

In the early twenty-first century, the city hired an NYPD veteran, Jose Cordero, to lead its police force.[143] The new chief applied the full panoply of "broken windows" policing measures, including adopting a "Compstat on steroids" approach paid for with state and federal funds.[144] Problem blocks were shut down to vehicular traffic and put under twenty-four-hour surveillance. The surveillance included giving residents "computer programs enabling them to report suspicious conditions by pointing their [computer] mouses at street photos." The East Orange Police Department (EOPD) expanded other types of surveillance including "vertical patrols" in residential buildings (the practice of police patrolling private apartment buildings); a gunshot-detection sensor system; a license recognition system to track stolen or suspect cars; and a building monitoring program encouraging tenants to inform the police of suspicious neighbors. This new type of policing and these unprecedented levels of surveillance did not unfold without damage. Residents who lived in the approximately 140 buildings (whether private or publicly owned) that were enrolled in the "vertical patrol" program lost the right to privacy, while other residents accused the city's police force of engaging in racial profiling.[145] By 2011, Cordero and his deputy had left due to a simmering dispute between Cordero and the rest of the EOPD over his "alleged[ly] abrasive" managerial style.[146] In 2018, in a sign of the city's commitment to "broken windows," Cordero would be brought back for a limited period. Mayor Taylor justified this commitment to heightened surveillance and overpolicing of the city's poorest neighborhoods by invoking the racial inclusion of the EOPD: "Our police department is 80 percent African-American. . . . And that's why, not only are we one of the safest communities with our demographics in the state, if not the country, we also don't have a lot of the issues of alleged brutality that you see, in part, because our men and women who protect our community are aware of and respect the culture and the people they serve."[147]

Between Suburban Nostalgia and Frontlash

In 1970, William Hart triumphantly took office as East Orange's first African American mayor, proclaiming that he was not just a Black mayor, but a "mayor for all citizens." However, once in office, Hart found the city's finances to be a "hollow prize." The town's revenues had been decimated by the sudden and dramatic collapse of the town's white middle-class population and the exit of its insurance industry back offices to newer suburban office parks. The mayor's annual reports reflected the city's increasingly desperate financial conditions. Hart was not the only mayor who saw a Black urban crisis in the making. In the early 1970s he joined with other Black mayors to press for greater aid from both the state and federal government. This informal alliance led to Hart becoming one of the founders of the National Conference of Black Mayors, which attempted to develop a Black urban agenda during the Carter administration. Hart, along with other mayors, also attended national Black Power conferences.

Over the next four decades, East Orange's political leadership would embrace a succession of new redevelopment fads in order to regain the city's lost urbane character. In 1975, the city decided to develop Central Avenue—the past home of now-departed high-end department stores and boutiques—as a quasi-pedestrian mall, a fad then sweeping many declining small cities such as Allentown, Pennsylvania.[148] The project was unveiled in 1980 with a ribbon cutting and marching bands. Renamed Evergreen Arcade, the new space was publicized as "New Jersey's premier in-town shopping experience," where shoppers could enjoy a "safe, well-lit and well-patrolled" space under the plexiglass canopies.[149] While the plan was to lure nonresidents back, the mayor also exhorted local residents to support these remaining businesses. However, by the early years of the twenty-first century the experiment had been deemed a failure: stores catering to middle-class shoppers continued to close and were replaced by fast food and low-end retail. Meanwhile the remaining canopies created a depressing tunnel effect, deterring shoppers.[150]

In the 1980s and then in the 1990s, East Orange would go in and out of the state's Distressed Cities Program, which subjected its budget and spending to state oversight. The program was initiated in 1980 by Republican governor Thomas Kean, one of the nation's most visible "ed reform" governors. The program—which largely covered majority-minority cities like East Orange, Jersey City, Camden, and Irving—was a measure designed to force these cities to take "strong fiscal medicine." Cities were not only required to "open their books, but [also to] accept any financial reforms." Democratic administrations in the 1990s would reduce threats of state takeovers—whether fiscal or educational—while Republican administrations would increase the odds. In 1996 Republican governor

Christine Todd Whitman's plan to cut income taxes by 30 percent coupled with a cut to state aid to communities had a significant negative effect on East Orange's finances, forcing the city back into the Distressed Cities Program.[151] By 2003, a new mayor, Robert Bowser, had restructured the city's finances and enabled East Orange to become the state's first city to exit state oversight.[152]

These setbacks did not loosen the hold of suburban nostalgia that still animated some of East Orange's political leadership. In 2004, at the groundbreaking of an $18 million mixed-use and mixed-income development near the Brick Church urban renewal area, Mayor Bowser (who had previously served on the city's planning department) declared that the reason he ran for mayor in 1998 was to "restore the city to the status it used to have. We used to have the best school systems, the best of everything, the best shopping, the best housing."[153]

For Bowser, recapturing that past lay in rejecting East Orange's role as a place (along with Newark) where the county could move its poorest residents. He and other town officials believed that market-rate and "work force" housing were the future of the city.[154] Bowser argued that the city had become "way out of balance with affordable housing . . . so for the overall survival of the city, we have to bring it back into balance—we had to tear down the only public housing in the city. The naysayers are saying that we are chasing the poor people out of town. But the real deal is that you have to decide what's best for the city in terms of its survival."[155] Despite these high hopes of restoring Black middle-class homeowners as the future of East Orange, by 2008 it was clearly evident that the city's working- and middle-class Black residents had been targeted by predatory subprime loans.[156] East Orange would have one of the highest rates of foreclosures in the state as well as the nation. Unlike Newark, the city did not make a public effort to address the foreclosure crisis. Instead, in a sign of a new Black suburban imaginary, a commitment to communities where homes were places to live and not investments, a local nonprofit group stepped in to address the high numbers of foreclosed and vacant properties that dotted the Black suburbs of Newark: East Orange, Orange, and Irvington.[157] In 2012 the state moved to take over the Kuzuri-Kijiji complex as the final step in clearing out its remaining tenants; it then demolished the project in preparation for the sale of the site to private investors.[158]

The post–Great Recession years would demonstrate another cycle of stalled growth. For example, in the face of recession in 2009 the city once again announced a revival of the "avenue that used to be" with the restoration and opening up of a local movie theater. The theater would close less than a year later, leaving the city to once again come up with a plan to restore a now-invisible past. By 2015 investors were flocking to the city, spurred by a rising housing market in the region and historically low interest rates, which led to a rapid period of residential and commercial construction growth.[159]

East Orange's public school system was not spared the effects of suburban anger toward majority-Black and -Brown communities. This anger was unleashed first by threats to metropolitan desegregation and then by the *Robinson v. Cahill* ruling. This spread of state "oversight and accountability" was also apparent in the efforts of Kean's administration and those of subsequent Republican governors to take over local majority-minority school districts. Republicans in New Jersey, as in other states, developed a local school district takeover strategy in response to successful efforts by Black and Brown education advocates to force the state to create more equitable school financing mechanisms that shifted funds away from majority-white suburban districts to majority-Black or -Brown low-income districts.[160] East Orange had better luck than Newark in maintaining control of its school system. The extreme poverty of the town's almost 99-percent African American school-age population made the district eligible for coverage under the Abbott School Equalization Plan, the latest iteration of a school financing plan that the New Jersey Supreme Court had spent the decades since 1973 forcing on a reluctant majority-white and suburban state. To remain eligible for state aid, the district had to agree to a series of curricular and organizational changes. While the results of these changes were mixed, the Abbott ruling did unleash a flurry of new school construction that replaced many of the school buildings already deemed obsolete in the 1950 plan.

The crown jewel of this building campaign would be the rebuilding of East Orange High on the campus of the now-defunct Upsala College. A high school profiled in the *New York Times* as having outdated books and rundown facilities now looked like other suburban high schools that abutted it. The rest of the campus was purchased by a private developer who turned it into "a new upper-middle-class neighborhood called Woodlands at Upsala, composed of 51 three-, four- and five-bedroom homes and a row of 17 attached town homes."[161] The city not only reembraced its own suburban imaginary, it embraced a vision of the city in which the majority of its poor and working-class citizens were unable to afford houses whose prices started in the "low $400,000s."

Black Power Urbanism left faint traces in East Orange. The mild attempts to reshape race and space—through a community school, a housing cooperative, and community policing—would founder. In their place, Black political empowerment through the ethnic succession of Black people into East Orange's white political and civic spaces were the beginning and the end of any gestures toward the Black Power moment. The space for any radical reimagining was also limited by the roll out of New Jersey's suburban frontlash, as the suburban-dominated state legislature engaged in decades-long attempts to diminish and constrain the state's emergent Black and Brown spaces. Rather than a city for all Blacks—the poor, the working class, and the always dominant middle class—East Orange pursued a Black suburban spatial imaginary in which good schools, low crime, and a retail streetscape that hearkened back to East Orange's early twentieth-century gentility became the singular focus of its political class. As Mayor Taylor concluded in his 2016 state of the city address:

> I think we represent transformational leadership. . . . I think we represent how municipal government should be operated just like a for-profit enterprise that understands what business and service you're offering; finding out the best ways to deliver that service in a cost-efficient and expedient manner; and also evaluating what works and doubling down on it, and what doesn't work and being brave enough to acknowledge that there's a different and better way of doing things.[162]

OAKLAND
Organizing for Survival

> Our basic objective becomes this: politics is organizing and unifying
> the people around their basic desires and needs. You know, you get
> in these classes sometimes, "The Basic Socio-Economic Structures
> and the adverse conditions we are subjected to, and consider these
> particular sociological and psychological factors, etc., etc., etc.,
> etc.," . . . that's not politics. You don't go down the street talking
> to the people like that, talking about how they ain't got their minds
> together yet. They got their minds together, all right, I'm saying
> politics is organizing people around this, and teaching them through
> organization to control those institutions that control their very lives.

—"Oakland, Cal. Mayoral Candidate Bobby Seale:
You Can't Drop Out of the System," *Ann Arbor Sun*, April 23, 1973

> Charges have been made that we used to have a "white power struc-
> ture" made up of a wealthy elite, but that does not justify setting up
> a whole new government, for example, of Negroes.

—Chris Rhomberg, *No There There*

In 2020, the small Victorian-era house located on 2928 Magnolia Street became a symbol of the subprime disaster of 2008 that continued to metastasize in Black Oakland. Located in the historic heart of Black West Oakland about two miles south of Bobby Seale's childhood home, the Magnolia Street house embodied the twists and turns of Oakland's urban color line and decades of dispossession and racial capitalism (see figure 5.1). Several decades after white settlers established the city of Oakland on indigenous Ohlone lands, the house was built to house white workers. In 1941, the Japanese American family living in the house was forced to leave for an internment camp.[1] The following year, the house was bought by a Black family who were part of the Great Migration of Southern Blacks drawn to Oakland's wartime economy.[2] It remained in the family's hands for the next four decades, even after Oakland's urban renewal order and highway construction transformed the neighborhood surrounding Magnolia Street into a hazardous, unhealthy, and unjust landscape.

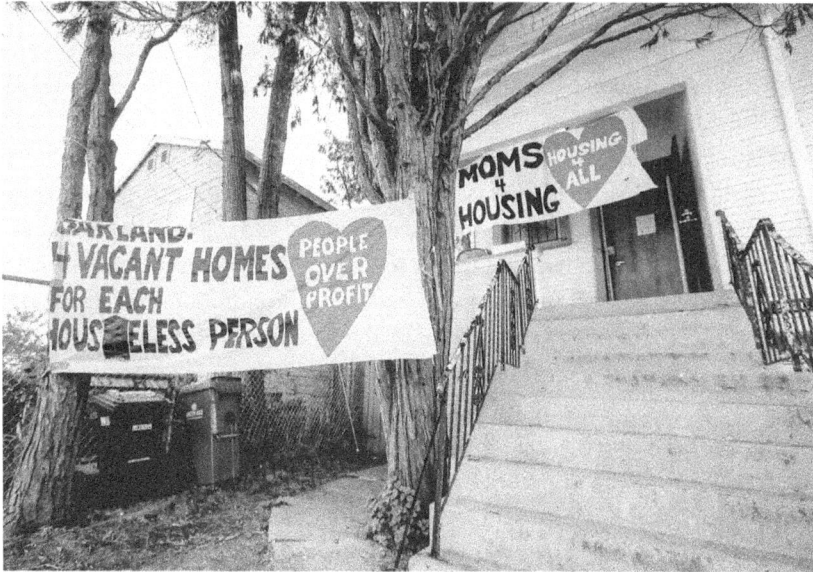

FIGURE 5.1.   Moms 4 Housing: Magnolia Street

Source: Associated Press Photo / Jeff Chiu

After the death of the owners, a private investment company acquired the Magnolia Street house. Several years later, in 1994, a Black woman bought the house using a subprime mortgage but lost the house to foreclosure in 1996. Once again, a private investor bought the property and sold it in 2019 to a real estate equity firm that focused on buying foreclosed and other types of "distressed" properties. There the property sat unoccupied until November 19, 2020, when Moms 4 Housing, a group of "unhoused working mothers," seized control of 2928 Magnolia Street.[3]

Moms 4 Housing's organizing statement concerning the city's houselessness problem was straightforward: "There are four times as many empty homes in Oakland as there are people without homes." Their answer to the problem was radically simple: "No one should be homeless when homes are sitting empty. Housing is a human right." For these activists, Oakland's housing crisis was the result of a system of structural dispossession and predatory inclusion that isolated individuals. The condition of "predatory inclusion," defined as the access of low-income or historically marginalized people to conventional real markets but on "more expensive and comparatively unequal terms," suggested to these mothers and other community activists that this crisis was not something that could be solved by individual people, but required solidarity.[4] Solving the problem of the unhoused would entail challenging a system based on individual predation and communal dispossession by "uniting mothers, neighbors and friends to reclaim housing for the Oakland community from the big banks and real estate speculators."[5]

The seizure of 2928 Magnolia did not go uncontested. Moms 4 Housing faced several months of legal battles as well as periodic physical attempts to take possession of the house, which was now the center of local and international attention. On January 14, 2021, a "heavily armed contingent of Alameda County Sheriff's Office deputies entered the home, pushed their furniture into the street, and arrested two of the women. By morning, the families had been fully evicted."[6] Despite their eviction, Moms 4 Housing won an important symbolic and substantive victory. Under pressure from a broad coalition of activists and community groups and from the city of Oakland, the developer agreed to sell the property and as many as fifty more of the houses that it owned to the Oakland Community Land Trust. These houses would be taken out of the ongoing cycle of predation and dispossession and made available to "working moms" and others who lacked homes for their families. More importantly, 2928 Magnolia Street and the other houses would serve as a symbol of renewed activism around the "right to housing" as a human right, as well as a symbol of the growing and vigorous "right to the city" movement. Moms 4 Housing's direct action hearkened back to an earlier era in Oakland's history when Black Oaklanders struggled for the right to decent housing, education, and public safety.

Black Power Urbanism unfolded in Oakland as Black Oaklanders, grappling with the new reality of dispossession and destruction in the wake of "Negro removal," searched for "new forms": for ways to resist and to rebuild a city that would be more just and equitable than the older Oakland that had marginalized, policed, and dispossessed them out of their hard-won spaces of congregation. The attempts to find "new forms" for Black Oaklanders emerged from three overlapping processes of political development: first, the development of the socio-spatial landscape of the city's prewar Black polity; second, the structural and political violence of the city's postwar urban renewal/"Negro removal"; and third, the hard limits of liberal integrationism as envisioned by the city's white elite power structure. A new, though fragile, Black Power Urbanism emerged in Oakland in the form of a multifaceted attempt to marry the revolutionary potential of the Black Power movement with the ongoing developmental project of Black political empowerment.

The formation of the city's prewar Black polity and its attendant internal contradictions and commonalities had an important influence on the rise of Black Power Urbanism. Mass migration linked to World War II followed by the postwar deployment of "Negro removal" (urban renewal plus highway construction) disrupted this older Black polity, setting the stage for a complex and contested search for new forms. This search was not easy: building a new Black Oakland involved an internal battle between multiple factions and the complicated relationship of Black Oakland with the multiracial/multiethnic world of postwar Oakland, where Chicano, Asian American, and Native American interests were also struggling to be heard.

This contestation is reflected in the three pillars of Oakland's Black Power Urbanism: housing, education, and policing. Housing policy aimed at the dispossession and erasure of Black Oakland; this was the goal of the city's "Negro removal" plans, at the heart of which was the expansive Acorn redevelopment plan. Acorn's first formulation was rooted in a Black elite politics of respectability and liberal integrationism, although the project was transformed and then demolished under the Clinton-era HOPE VI program. In terms of education, the rise in demands for equity in Oakland's public school system were a direct response to the socio-spatial inequalities faced by Black, Brown, and Asian parents in the city's flatlands, while the children of white elites ensconced in the city's hills were experiencing the postwar "golden age" of public education. In Oakland—well before the Ocean Hill-Brownsville struggle of 1968—the demands for community control and for a pedagogy rooted in Black Power Urbanism took place within pitched battles that began to occur during what had previously been "sleepy" and "non-political" board of education meetings. These struggles for community control took place in the schools themselves, as parents and students fought on the ground battles for safe, communal spaces that met educational, cultural, and developmental needs, rather than spaces that failed to educate them or worse, pushed them out onto the streets, into unemployment, or to the Vietnam War. Policing and communal/public safety was another vital issue for Oakland's Black Power Urbanism. While the emergence of the Black Panther Party and their claim to "defend the ghetto" shocked government policing and security agencies, it was a both a reflection and a clear realization of the ongoing daily struggle between Black Oakland and a police force that treated non-whites as noncitizens.[7] Against this backdrop of open contestation by the BPP, whether real or imagined by an increasingly paranoid and deadly police force, efforts to gain accountability and control over the Oakland Police Department (OPD) would repeatedly stall, while the everyday violence and extraordinary police killings would continue. Notions of "police abolitionism," that is, the possibility of the abolition of the police department or a fundamental transformation of policing laid out in the BPP's survival programs, remained unrealized as Black political actors and community groups repeatedly tried to reform the OPD, a force that remained remarkably intransigent and hostile to anything that challenged its prerogatives.[8]

Oakland's Prewar Black Polity

Commuters traveling westward on Bay Area Rapid Transit (BART) could mark their journey's progress by the appearance of the sign for Esther's Orbit Room, a jazz club located on Seventh Street, north of the Nimitz Freeway (see figure 5.2). Until its closure in 2011, it was one of the few remnants of everyday life in historic Black Oakland, which—in the shape of restaurants, bars, stores, and barber shops—coalesced around Seventh Street, the commercial and cultural heart of Black Oakland.

The emergence of Seventh Street reflected the ways in which race, gender, and class shaped the geography of Black Oakland. The early boundaries of Black Oakland were set into place as early as 1869, when the Pullman Palace Car Company began to require that all of its passenger porters had to be Black men and that they live within walking distance of train yards, with the boundary for residency set at Adeline Street.[9] By the late 1920s, approximately eighteen thousand people and a wide range of Black uplift organizations, churches, and retail stores, as well as a small professional class, had emerged centered on Seventh Street.[10]

FIGURE 5.2. Exterior of Esther's Orbit Room, 1987

Source: Courtesy of the African American Museum and Library at Oakland Photograph Collection, MS 189, Oakland Public Library, Oakland History Center.

The Seventh Street community was home to respectable entities like Beth Eden Church (founded in 1889) and the Baker-Taylor Funeral Home (established in 1919).[11] Local uplift organizations included a Negro Business League chapter, an Afro-American Council; an NAACP branch; the Local 188 chapter of the Universal Negro Improvement Association (UNIA), and a local Black newspaper, *The Sunshine*.[12] A Black charitable landscape also emerged, almost all of it built by Black women's organizations.[13] There were charitable organizations such as the Fannie Wall Children's Home and Day Nursery (established in 1918), a Home for Aged and Infirm Colored People, the Fanny Jackson Coppin Club, the Mother's Charity Club, an Art and Industrial Club, and a YWCA as well as the Linden Street YMCA (the "Colored Y").[14] Small restaurants like Slim Jenkins demonstrated the importance of Seventh Street as a space for Black leisure and play while clubs like Esther's Orbit Room were part of the area's rich nightlife. Indeed, Oakland, along with Los Angeles, would emerge as one of the centers of the West Coast Jazz scene. Over a dozen jazz clubs opened up in Black Oakland, including several "Black and Tan" clubs that catered to Black and white audiences.[15]

The existence of Seventh Street as both the symbolic and the spatial heart of Black Oakland papered over the very real divisions that existed within and across the community. "Black Oakland" was not a monolith—spatially, socially, or politically. The early twentieth century produced a particular kind of Black middle-class politics. The city's small Black middle class of small business owners, who were in many cases the leaders and members of its uplift organizations, like the Black middle class in other small prewar Black communities, was "limited [in] its potential for mass protest, and in their relations with white society, [B]lack leaders relied on their ties with white patrons."[16] For the Black working class, however, labor organizing would provide another path toward Black community-building and empowerment. Up until the wartime mobilization, railroad jobs were a way to achieve working-class stability. The Pullman Porters provided a distinctive political voice for Black Oakland while connecting the city to other parts of Black America. Former mayor Ronald Dellums claimed that the Pullman porters "'seemed like the astronauts of the Black community,' because they left the community and ventured into the world. Railroad men would return with stories of what they saw and learned."[17] Locating the West Coast headquarters of the Brotherhood of Sleeping Car Porters union in Oakland strengthened the importance of Black unions in shaping Black communal identity outside of the ameliorative uplift and religious organizations largely run by the Black middle class. C. L. Dellums (uncle of Ronald Dellums) served as the local's longtime leader. Under Dellums's leadership, the union, while collaborating with traditional middle-class Black organizations like the NAACP and churches, was also

FIGURE 5.3. Fighting blight to save the city: Seventh Street, before and after urban renewal. Apartment block, Seventh Street, West Oakland.

Source: Courtesy of the collections of the Oakland History Room, Oakland Public Library, Oakland History Center.

assertive in confronting the city's power structure in alliance with other unions and some white reform groups.

Black politics in Oakland contained a spectrum of Black political thought, from Booker T. Washington–style uplift and Garveyism in the first decades of the twentieth century to the Congress of Industrial Organizations (CIO) alliances of C. L. Dellums and the Pullman Porters. In an urban political system designed to fragment and diffuse power and authority, the city's Black civic elites repeatedly (though not uncritically) embraced the often token liberal integration offered by white Oakland, while the CIO unionism of Dellums engaged in coalitional politics with other progressive interests in the city. Oakland's complex and fragmented spatial, institutional, and social landscape produced two often competing strands of Black political development: the elite brokerage/patron-client politics of the middle class and the episodic coalitional politics of the working class and the poor.

World War II, the Second Gold Rush and the Emergence of Modern Oakland

World War II and the second leg of the Great Migration would upend the small close-knit nature of Seventh Street and the balance of power within Black Oakland as thousands of workers from the South migrated to Oakland and the Bay Area. The hegemony of the older Black middle class was upended as working-class Blacks and their children confronted a socio-spatial landscape increasingly designed to contain and constrain their aspirations that migration would lead to them to a new life, in a more just and equitable place than the places they had left.

Wartime mobilization spurred a massive drive to build ships and manufacture munitions and other war materiel, and triggered the emergence of Oakland and the Bay Area as one of the West Coast's "arsenals of democracy."[18] The employment needs of the city's wartime industries, such as the Kaiser shipyards, the port of Oakland, and the area's military bases, drew thousands of Blacks and whites to Oakland and its industrial suburbs. The impact of World War II on Oakland was tremendous, expanding and revitalizing the city's industrial base, especially as the Oakland port became a transportation and logistics hub. The city's population reflected this activity, growing from 302,000 in 1940 to 384,000 in 1950. Oakland's Black population nearly doubled, rising from 47,000 in 1940 to nearly 85,000 in 1950. This was a stunning development for a city in which the Black population had been a relatively small percentage before the war and in which the KKK had gained a tremendous amount of popular support among working- and middle-class whites during the 1920s.[19]

The tensions between the old and new Black Oakland, and increasingly between middle-class and working-class members of the community, would grow progressively more acute as Seventh Street and by extension much of Black Oakland was subjected to "Negro removal," even as postwar urban Keynesianism and proto–War on Poverty programs opened up new paths for Black middle-class ascendancy. In the mid-1950s the deployment of "Negro removal" saw the beginnings of the rapid destruction and erasure of historic Black Oakland and the subsequent respatialization of race. With a tinge of Jim Crow nostalgia, "residents reminisce[d] on the vibrancy of Seventh Street, how shoppers would walk down the street laughing and meet[ing] up with friends."[20] A new Oakland and a new Black Oakland would emerge as "Negro Removal" kicked into high gear, as Oakland's white elites increasingly saw Black Oakland as a barrier in their ongoing quest to reinvent the city.

Planning for a New City

Oakland's aspirations to regional preeminence emerged out the rubble of the 1906 San Francisco earthquake. By 1927, Oakland, like other cities, had embraced the new profession of city planning and like Newark and East Orange had employed the firm of Harland Bartholomew to restructure the city for the automobile age.[21] The "problem" of Black Oakland and other suspect areas of the city had occupied white city planners from the early twentieth century onward, with early city housing reports singling out Black homes and neighborhoods as vectors of disease and crime.[22] Indeed, a 1937 housing report bolstered support for a highway that would bisect Seventh Street by stating that the "housing advantage of this diagonal highway route is that it would segregate that portion of the district under discussion where non-white families are largely concentrated from that portion where they are relatively few in number. A plan of housing could take advantage of this physical division by providing a unit or units for mixed-race occupancy west of the East Shore Highway, and units for all-white occupancy east of the Highway."[23] This report both supported and was supported by the 1937 issuance of the Home Owners' Loan Corporation (HOLC) Residential Security Map for Oakland, Berkeley, and other surrounding areas. Not surprisingly, the map's redlined areas included not just the city's heavy and light industrial areas, but also areas inhabited by the city's diverse non-white citizens, including all of West Oakland and the Flatlands.[24]

Despite these nascent moves by city elites to fix the problem of Black Oakland through exclusion and further segregation, Dellums, along with Black and white union members, delivered some of the benefits of the New Deal to Black Oakland in the shape of public housing authorized under the 1937 Wallace-Steagall Housing Act. In collaboration with a more militant CIO and the League of Women Voters, Dellums led demonstrations in front of the city council to press for a resolution to build public housing under the act. This pressure, coupled with pressure from the federal government (via the Lanham Act) to provide desperately needed housing for defense workers, forced the city to give in. Two developments were built in West Oakland: Campbell Village (1941) and Peralta Villa (1942). The complexes, like other wartime worker housing, would remain racially segregated for over a decade until Dellums and his allies successfully compelled the Oakland Housing Authority (OHA) to offer integrated housing.[25] The locations of these two developments were an ominous sign of what was to come. Critics charged that not only were both proposed housing developments located in majority-Black neighborhoods but also that the buildings identified for demolition were not the most blighted in terms of housing quality. Instead of protecting quality housing in a racially mixed neighborhood, the city planned to demolish these buildings in order to make way for more segregation. Even more worrying, the developments (like the ones that followed three decades later) were located adjacent to undesirable and environmentally unhealthy areas.

With the wartime boom ending, official Oakland once again turned its attention to Black Oakland, which stood directly in the way of the city's postwar vision of itself as the region's "industrial garden."[26] Oakland's white officials quickly took advantage of widespread fears about a postwar slump. They laid the overcrowded conditions that for decades had been a source of continual protest by local Black leaders at the feet of Black residents themselves. Accusations of "rising crime and violence" were also deployed to justify the desire of city officials to designate Black West Oakland as "blighted" and thus open it up to "urban renewal treatment" (see figure 5.3). The "treatment" to turn Oakland into an "industrial garden" had the effect of displacing the city's growing Black population to other neighborhoods, or even better, out of the city altogether.[27]

White political and civic elites were dismayed by the rapid pace of Black in-migration and white out-migration (the latter consisting of residents, factories, and businesses). Black migrants, including Bobby Seale's parents, were buoyed by wartime earnings and continued access to jobs at Oakland's government facilities. As a result, well over half of incoming Black migrants bought houses after the war. Many of these houses were concentrated in West Oakland and other areas deemed open for Black settlement, and almost all of them were bought under exploitative conditions and with unequal access to mortgage financing. Indeed, one study found that there were very few conventional mortgages in these areas.[28] While the "white noose" of the suburbs kept most non-whites out, it readily let whites in. Working-class whites shared in the postwar bounty as generous federal subsidies and government-sanctioned discrimination led to the creation of hundreds of "blue heavens"—white working- and middle-class suburbs.[29] If white Oaklanders were dissatisfied they were able to vote with

FIGURE 5.4A.   Men of tomorrow: Beneficial Development Corporation's Acorn plan

Source: "'The Acorn Proposal,' Submitted by Beneficial Development Group in Conformance with the 'Goals and Objectives' Established by the Redevelopment Agency of the City of Oakland for the Acorn Project," December 1, 1964.

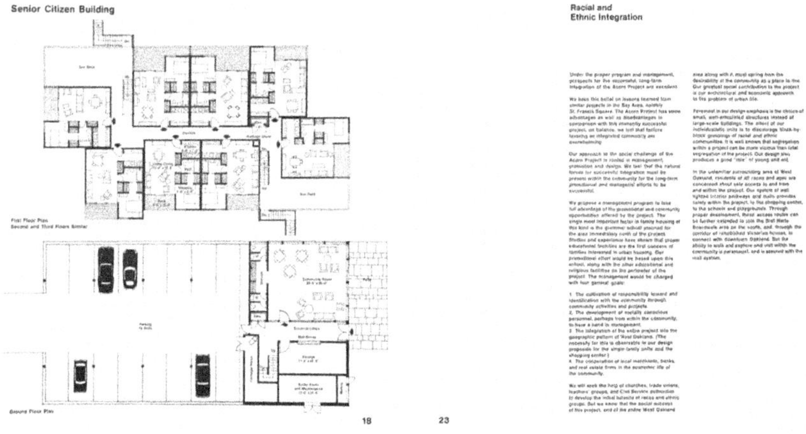

FIGURE 5.4B.   Men of tomorrow: Beneficial Development Corporation's Acorn plan

Source: "'The Acorn Proposal,' Submitted by Beneficial Development Group in Conformance with the 'Goals and Objectives' Established by the Redevelopment Agency of the City of Oakland for the Acorn Project," December 1, 1964.

their feet: between 1950 and 1960 about fifty-eight thousand left, many to the south suburbs of San Leandro and Hayward, which vigorously enforced the metropolitan color line. The next decade saw an additional fifty-seven thousand whites leave and then another eighty thousand left between 1970 and

1980.[30] These white suburbanites would eventually provide the votes for the "racial propositions"—especially around housing and education—that sought to freeze California's racial, political, and fiscal geography in favor of white, homeowning voters.[31]

Elite anxiety over the city's postwar future collided with the emergence of Black West Oakland as a space of political and social congregation. Rapid migration and the demands of the wartime economy stimulated the growth and militancy of the Bay Area labor movement. The coalition between the more civil rights–friendly CIO and Black labor leaders like C. L. Dellums would form the basis of a postwar liberalism in which the state legislature began to take up laws favoring fair employment and non-discrimination (with varied degrees of success).

In Oakland itself, this rising labor militancy and the broad coalition that it engendered would lead to the general strike of 1946, headed largely by women retail workers but supported by a wide array of unions.[32] On its heels, a new political front opened up based on a coalition of left/liberal white union members and Black Oakland activists and residents. In 1947, in a shock to the political establishment, the Oakland Voters League (OVL), a union/left/Black coalition (including Dellums and the Brotherhood of Sleeping Car Porters) won four of nine seats on the city council. Their platform was significantly progressive and pushed back against the hegemony of Oakland's white elites. The OVL called for "restructuring the city's tax structure which favored downtown property holders, . . . the immediate expenditure of $15 million in bonds already approved for streets, parks and playgrounds, and other city improvements; immediate open hearings on transportation needs; city planning for new industry and full employment; election of a board of freeholders to reform the city charter; planning for a 'full program' of housing including support for rent control and low-cost, low-rent, no discrimination municipal housing; and . . . impartial statesmanship in business-labor relations."[33]

By 1951, this challenge had been largely put down through anti-communist hysteria and an anti-OVL coalition made up of real estate interests (especially small apartment building owners), middle-class white homeowners, and small business owners. This coalition engineered a recall election as well as a general election to unseat the OVL council members. Behind this successful anti-OVL coalition lay the unseen hand of Oakland's majority-white political and civic elites. Faced with the success of a left/liberal/Black alliance, city elites once again pushed for changes in city council structure, this time opting for an at-large council that diluted the electoral influence of Black and working-class areas.

This restructuring continued the city elites' ongoing quest to quell political challenges. Both the city council and the school board became "self-perpetuating" entities.[34] For example, from 1931 to the late 1960s, only "3 members out of 23 . . . joined the [school] board initially through election." The noncompetitive and exclusionary nature of the city council was equally astonishing, as "in 48 contests over a 40-year period, only five non-incumbents were elected."[35] Meanwhile the city's mayors were largely figureheads. Oakland was a decidedly "morning glory" city, touting its Progressive Era government reforms with a government structure designed to fragment institutional power, frustrate minority group mobilization, and favor tight-knit elite control.[36] Presiding over the city's governance and development was the powerful Knowland family, which owned the city's main newspaper (the *Oakland Tribune*) and acted as leader of Oakland's political and civic elites.[37]

Oakland's "Negro Removal"

The 1950s marked the emergence and subsequent ascendancy of Oakland's urban renewal regime. The first step was the issuance of *Urban Redevelopment in Oakland*, the city's first postwar redevelopment plan, which identified West Oakland as the core of almost all of the city's "blighted areas."[38] The next step was fulfilling the intent of the city's 1937 Bartholomew plan by beginning the spatial reordering of Oakland with the construction of four new freeways. The majority of these began construction during the 1950s: the Nimitz Freeway was completed in 1952; the Cypress Street Freeway in 1957; the McArthur Freeway in 1966; and the Grove-Shafter Freeway in 1968. The images of the area cleared for the Cypress Freeway serve as iconic symbols of the violence of Oakland's urban renewal regime. West Oakland, especially parts of vibrant Seventh Street— the commercial and institutional heart of Black Oakland—was in one infamous case crushed by a Sherman tank, or in other cases literally scraped away by the Oakland Redevelopment Agency (ORA) bulldozers.[39]

After three years of lobbying by Oakland business and real estate interests, the approval of the General Neighborhood Renewal Plan (GNRP) of 1957, which would be overseen by the newly established Oakland Redevelopment Agency, cemented the second element in the city's spatial and racial reordering. The goal of the GNRP was "to save the remaining downtown merchants from total economic eclipse" and from the "galling" presence of "low-income, largely black and Chicano renters" who had replaced the middle-class white shoppers.[40] In keeping with the findings of the GNRP (as well as the 1949 redevelopment report), much of West Oakland, including the Magnolia Street house, lay in an urban renewal area designated as the Acorn Project. The GNRP envisioned the Acorn redevelopment area as a buffer zone that would limit the encroachment of Black residents on the downtown area to the east, while encouraging further industrial development in West Oakland that could capitalize on the highway infrastructure that was being put into place.

The Acorn Project area covered fifty blocks and was located in the parts of West Oakland that had been left untouched by highway construction. The ORA, like redevelopment agencies in Newark and other cities, used multiple strategies to displace and/or dispossess the people and areas being readied for urban renewal "treatment."[41] For example, the city adopted a new housing code and stepped up code enforcement in order to justify widespread condemnation or abandonment of properties by landlords or owners unwilling or unable to afford the changes demanded by the city. As Lillian Love, a Black homeowner in the area, would remark, no monies were extended (though technically available) for homeowners to pay for these new code requirements. By 1960, the city had condemned one thousand houses (many not "blighted" but simply occupied by Black and Brown people) and displaced nine thousand residents. The ORA clearance would be called the "most successful blight clearance project in the nation's history" as the agency had "purchased 90% of parcels, relocated 83% of families, demolished 75% of structures, [and] sold 4 lots for new plants."[42]

The GNRP's ambitious goal of clearing the area of "blight" was successful. The city had effectively contained Black West Oakland via a "wall of highways, state buildings, private business offices [and] high-priced restaurants or stores." Unsurprisingly, given the role of city police departments across the nation in policing the urban color line, Oakland's new police department was located "in a $14 million building on lower Broadway, put there, in the words of one long-time observer, to 'anchor lower Broadway.'"[43]

Remaking Black Oakland

While the ORA was attempting to forcefully imprint its own vision on West Oakland, pockets of resistance were emerging both in West Oakland and then in other areas of the city where Black and Brown Oaklanders lived as the city's racial lines were being redrawn. The most successful resistance was led by Lillian Love, who along with other working- and middle-class Black homeowners organized to save their neighborhood, Oak Center, from being declared blighted by the ORA and thus subject to demolition and erasure. Criticisms of Love reflected the class tensions cutting across Black West Oakland. One observer described Love—whose father had bought a house in the neighborhood area prior to the Second Great Migration—as "'an instant Negro' who owns property enough to make her comfortable, and who is chairman of the Oak Center Neighborhood Council of *home owners*. It is not a tenants association. She is Supervisor in the Welfare Department."[44]

Like Love, many of the Oak Center homeowners, including the Black couple that owned 2928 Magnolia, were members of the more economically secure segment of the city's working class. The fact that Oak Center Neighborhood Association agitated to save their neighborhood did not necessarily mean that were supporters of low-income housing for poor Black and Brown Oaklanders. Oak Center would have supported many aspects of the ORA's plan if it had led to the "recreat[ion] of a stable middle-class integrated community in the central city."[45] Other Black residents were less successful in defending their homes and neighborhoods from the ORA. One group went to court, unsuccessfully suing the city and the federal government with the argument that the Acorn Project "would deprive Negroes of their properties." Like other Blacks displaced by urban renewal across the United States, Oakland's Black residents knew that redlining, housing discrimination within Oakland, and the "white noose" of the suburbs made it impossible for them to relocate within the city. Like East Orange's Black middle-class citizens, Black plaintiffs were not wrong in making the argument that urban renewal "in effect, deprive[d] them of homeownership [as well as other residential options] because they have limited access to other residential areas."[46] They told the court that "they have no objection to urban improvement, but objected to being evicted from their homes without a place to go." The court ruled against them, allowing the ORA to continue its path of destruction while the city abetted its aggressive displacement and dispossession. The majority-white city council blocked attempts to increase the number of public housing units in the city to house the potentially displaced, arguing that no additional units were needed beyond the initially proposed 506 that the city had committed to provide.[47]

The Oak Center resistance is notable as it was one of the few successes in the face of the ORA's urban renewal "treatment." More common were the incommensurable losses experienced by Black Oakland, such as destruction of a Black charitable landscape that for decades had nurtured both working- and middle-class Blacks through individual and family services, recreation, and community activities. The Fannie Wall Home lost its Community Chest funding in 1957 and in 1962 was forced to accept a buyout offer for its building from the ORA for $34,000.[48] Other losses included the original Linden YWCA building (which became the West Oakland Center) and "several buildings used for the Market Street Branch of the YMCA, St. Joseph's Catholic Church and hundreds of other structures." Of this charitable landscape, only Saint Vincent's (which had originally been an all-white care institution) survived, as it was able to draw on the Catholic Church and the support of an "ambitious young politician named Ronald Reagan."[49]

West Oakland's Black cultural and commercial structures fared no better. With the exception of three structures—the historic Beth Eden Church, the Baker-Taylor Funeral Home, and one home that was being used as an agency field house—"urban renewal programs in the name of reform eradicated every other cultural institution" in the Acorn Project area.[50] Only once the violent destruction by bulldozer and tank had passed and the cleared lots remained "empty of homes and buildings but full of rats and sparrows" did Black Oakland see a token response from the city: John B. Williams, a Black city planner from Cleveland, would be appointed as the executive director of the ORA in 1964 and Love would be appointed to the ORA board in 1966.

The full impact of "Negro removal" on Black Oakland could now be discerned in terms of displacement of community institutions, closing of small Black-owned businesses like Slim Jenkins, and lost housing for thousands. At least fourteen thousand people were displaced. While most of those displaced were African Americans, at least 20 percent were Latinos.[51] In terms of housing, 7,250 units had been lost. These included the 1,400 wartime units, 4,000 units lost for the building of the Acorn redevelopment area, and 300 units lost for a post office facility. The construction of the multiple highways that converged through the area and the BART system also resulted in the destruction of a significant number of units: 600 houses due to Grove-Shafter, 500 to McArthur Freeway, and 450 to BART construction. For those who could stay, predatory inclusion—including what one observer called "capital starvation"—shaped the conditions under which residents could stay in their neighborhoods or create small business. Along with "Negro removal" it would contribute to the area's "accelerated decline," even as other parts of the city prospered.[52]

In the Wake: Post–"Negro Removal," Black Mobilization

"Negro renewal" acted as a catalyst in the search for "new forms" for rebuilding the city. This process included managing conflicts between multiple factions within Black Oakland, but also navigating the complicated relationship of Black Oakland in the multiracial/multiethnic world of postwar Oakland where Chicano, Asian American, and Native American interests were also struggling to be heard.[53] Within Black Oakland one side would be led by the newest and most active members of the community: the children of the Great Migration, mostly working-class Black youth that would fuel the growth of the

Black Panther Party and other activist groups from the early 1960s onward. In the middle, and comprising the vast majority of Black and Brown Oakland, were everyday people whose politics were shaped by quotidian interactions with the landlord, the store owner, the police officer, and the teacher. On the other side, a new postwar Black middle class of professionals, entrepreneurs, and other white-collar workers would quickly pivot to the new opportunities afforded by nascent government/social service employment in place of the declining segregation economy centered around the now-doomed Seventh Street community.

From this latter group, a new Black political class would emerge that sought to work within Oakland's political system while also pushing for greater political, social, and economic rights within the framework of postwar liberal integrationism.[54] This new class was epitomized by the Men of Tomorrow, a quasi–social club founded in 1954 that considered itself a "Black chamber of commerce." Largely made up of members of the Second Great Migration, the group comprised a "who's who" of Black elites in Oakland and the Bay Area. Notable members of this group included Lionel Wilson (the future first Black mayor of Oakland) and W. Byron Rumford, a state representative who would sponsor the Rumford housing antidiscrimination act.[55] Barney Hilburn, one the group's few Republican members, was appointed as the first and for many years the only Black member of the OHA board and was a member of the board of education.[56] The Men of Tomorrow's identity would be strongly tied to its roots in West Oakland where the group initially met at Slim Jenkins, "a little ghetto restaurant . . . down on Seventh Street."[57] Following older forms of Black politics, the Men of Tomorrow periodically though politely challenged the white Oakland power structure. At the same time, they adeptly contributed to and built upon the gains of the national and state civil rights/freedom movements, while developing a new postwar class of political leadership.[58]

In the late 1960s certain members would cautiously adopt some of the rhetoric of the Black Power movement, most notably calls for political power and sovereignty. More common were those members who, with the emergence of Black Power/radical politics, were increasingly co-opted into the existing system. Their faith in working within the system was based on the belief that "the Republican power structure [had slowly recognized] that they couldn't possibly survive with any stability in the community or energize black middle-class development unless they shared some of the governance."[59] The role of the Black middle class in politics would become problematic in the future as a "significant portion of Oakland's black political leadership in the sixties emerged from the ranks of social workers and administrators" who staffed Oakland's emerging surveillance and control system.[60]

The transformation of Oakland's Black charitable landscape, fueled by "Negro removal," was symbolic of the new kinds of class tensions emerging within Oakland's Black polity. West Oakland's Linden YWCA had been formally racially integrated in 1944 and its name changed to the West Oakland Center. By 1950, under the auspices of the Ford Foundation's Gray Areas program, the West Oakland Center would become one of the nodes of what Donna Murch calls a "proto-carceral apparatus," designed by white elites to surveil and control Black youth, and by extension Black Oakland. Murch argues that within this system the Black middle class was charged with the management of Black working-class youth.[61] While professional aspirations and economic mobility may have under-girded their contributions to this proto-carceral regime, middle-class Blacks were also enmeshed in this system due to their own beliefs in uplift and respect-ability, which directed them to help "maladjusted" Black youth and mitigate the threat they allegedly posed to transitioning neighborhoods. Under the direction of Wayne Thompson, the city's white liberal city manager, Black professionals like Norvel Smith aided in the creation of "district councils" designed to "social-ize these residents to prevailing values."[62] Liberal technocrats believed that creat-ing new forms of participation (assisted by the coordination of control entities like the school board, the Oakland police department, and the California Youth Authority) would help bring (Black) citizens' values in line with prevailing norms of governance.[63]

By the mid-1960s, the rift between the Black middle and working classes had become increasingly spatialized as communal Black spaces—like Slim Jenkins's restaurant—were demolished, along with the rest of historic Black Oakland's economic, social, cultural, and charitable landscape. Working-class and poor Black Oaklanders were pushed out of West Oakland to East Oakland and the Flatlands, while many middle-class Blacks had greater opportunities (though not easily accomplished) to join middle- and upper-class whites up in the Hills.[64]

In the wake of ongoing displacement and dispossession, as well as the demands of daily life in a city structured by deep levels of racial and ethnic inequity in housing, education, policing and other areas, space for new inde-pendent forms of political organizing was being created. One such space hap-pened with the assistance of the War on Poverty. In order to administer War on Poverty, Great Society, and later Model Cities funds, the city set up the Oakland Economic Development Council (OEDC). The amount of OEDC funding was significant—nearly $70 million (about one-third more than the city's overall budget)—as Oakland had become a hoped-for model of urban development and "riot prevention."[65] Many of the newly appointed OEDC board members (both Black and white) had sat on Oakland's Ford Foundation–funded Gray Areas Program and from its inception, it was clear that the OEDC was a subsidiary of the city government.[66] By 1965, the federal Economic Opportunity Act's mandate that local agencies were required to allow for "maximum feasible participation of residents of the areas and members of the groups served" made it possible for local activists to make a decisive move. As in Newark and other cities, the requirement of "maximum feasible participation" gave local organizers the means to wrest control of programs and more importantly funding away from city halls and to use it for communities of color.

The Black professionals like Norvel Smith who ran the OEDC envisioned a twofold role for themselves. They would assume a "tutelary role" vis-à-vis the Black poor, but would also continue to participate in liberal integrationist politics. They saw themselves as engaged in "responsible opposition" and "skillful negotiation" as a way to carve out a meaningful place for the OEDC in the city.[67] However, the OEDC's ambivalent position—a result of its need to appease city government as well as the West Oakland community—set the stage for confrontation to erupt between the community and the city. In 1966, when the city again applied for more federal funding, local activists noted that the millions of dollars that had been funneled into Oakland had not created new housing to replace the thousands of units that had been demolished, nor did the funding create more and better employment for the city's working-class and poor residents. In addition, as was the case in Newark, the mayor's office saw the OEDC's attempt to assume some measure of control over the organization as a threat to the administration's power. This perception of threat was heightened when the somewhat liberal city manager was replaced with a new city manager who was hostile to the emerging demands of West Oakland. The OEDC found itself in a moment of transition by 1966–67 as the militancy of the emerging Black Power movement and growth of the Black Panthers pushed the organization away from its formerly accommodating relationship with the city.

The end of the balancing act would come when the OEDC took on the issue of police brutality, which shaped the day-to-day lives of many Black Oaklanders. Since the 1940s, there had been several attempts by reformers working within Oakland's political system to try and create a civilian review board for more police oversight and accountability. In the face of these previous failed efforts, the OEDC proposed using Ford Foundation funding (not city or federal funding) to create a nonprofit "Police Affairs Committee" that would "hear citizens' complaints and provide assistance in using established channels to those with seemingly justifiable cases."[68] This mild attempt to create oversight of the police proved to be a radical step too far for both the city political establishment (the mayor, the city manager, and the city council) and the Oakland Police Department. Their outrage fueled a vigorous attempt to defund and dismantle the OEDC. These attempts, plus a recognition that the political and programmatic objectives of the group would never be realized while under city control, led the local activists who now dominated the OEDC to declare it an independent agency, OEDC Incorporated (OEDCI). The establishment of the OEDCI ended the OEDC's role as both broker and buffer between the city and West Oakland and the emergence of a public and decisive break in the silent struggle between them. Mayor Reading's fear that a "whole new government . . . of Negroes" was in the making seemed to be all too real.[69]

The OEDCI hired Percy Moore as the new executive director, contrary to what the more moderate Black leadership had expected. Working with a variety of activist groups, Moore shifted the OEDCI into a more confrontational position. With the introduction of the Model Cities Program, Moore now had the ability and opportunity to collaborate with a new organization, the West Oakland Planning Council (WOPC). The WOPC asserted the right of Black Oaklanders to direct the millions of dollars of federal funding that was flowing into Oakland port (then one of the largest and most profitable on the West Coast) and downtown to the benefit of the city's poorest and most marginalized residents.

Moore approached the pending Model Cities application as an opportunity to reset the relationship between West Oakland (and by extension poor Black and Brown Oakland) and city hall. The Model Cities Program allowed for a structural insertion of community control over federal funding in affected areas by encouraging the creation of local organizations that would directly coordinate with the federal government over contracts. More militant Black activists, some of whom had organized as the West Oakland Advisory Committee (WOAC), pushed for direct negotiations with the city and the federal government.[70] Key to the control of funds was the demand that the OEDC give community activists "fifty-one percent control" over the Model Cities board, which made it possible to bypass the OEDC leadership, and more say over the allocation of funding.[71]

Over the course of the next year, Moore, acting as both the director of the OEDCI and as a leader of the WOPC, along with fellow activist Paul Cobb, formed a broad coalition of almost 165 organizations to gather under the WOPC umbrella, including such disparate voices as the "West End Nursery and the Black Panther Party."[72] The WOPC would prove to be a pivotal player in establishing and asserting a spatialized and political dimension to Oakland's Black community. By 1969, Moore, Cobb, and other activists had secured "recognition of the WOPC as the legitimate spokesman for the West Oakland community," while also arguing that West Oakland itself should be considered a separate zone controlled those who lived there.[73] Though community control has often been equated with Black control—and indeed this was the stance of both Black nationalists like Newark's Amiri Baraka and some of the Black Panthers—in the landscape of multiracial Oakland, the idea of community control (and who was included) would be continually challenged and broadened. While Black actors were easily the most visible in the West Oakland coalition, in Moore and Cobb's formulation Black Power Urbanism translated into a vision as well as an agenda that would stretch the boundaries of "community" from just West Oakland to all of Oakland, especially the poor and the marginalized.

Rebuilding Housing for Black Oakland: From Public Housing to Affordable Housing

The calls of Moms 4 Housing and other groups for the recognition of the right to housing as a human right, as well as the right to community control over the ability to house its members, were directly linked to the Black Panther Party's Ten-Point Program crafted at the Seale's dining room table. The program's points included full employment, reparations, decent education, and ending racist urban policing and the carceral state. In addition, point 4 of the program read: "We want decent housing, fit for the shelter of human beings. We believe that if the White Landlords will not give decent housing to our Black community, then the housing and the land should be made into cooperatives so that our community, with government aid, can build and make decent housing for its people."[74]

This initial call for decent housing would be elaborated upon in the party's later Program for Survival (1968) and its Survival Pending Revolution programs (1974–80).[75] The updated programs first called for a "People's Cooperative Housing Program" where "with federal government aid, decent, low-cost and high-quality housing for Black and poor communities" could be built. Land banking (a precursor to community land trusts) was also raised as an important element in the party's survival program.[76] Housing was not just the provision of buildings, it also meant homemaking, or the provision and maintenance of safe and sanitary places where people could not only survive but thrive. Thus, the survival programs also called for services such the "People's Free Plumbing and Maintenance Program"; "Free Pest Control . . . for the extermination of rats, roaches and other disease carrying pests and rodents" (a problem noted by Newark's activists); and a "Free Furniture Program."[77] The Black Power city was a city of homes for people to live in, not just bare places to shelter.

The Black Panthers' platform calling for the right to decent, safe, and secure housing was not mere rhetoric; it reflected daily life in a city with a deep housing crisis linked to ongoing as well as historical structures of dispossession and displacement. In 1966, Mrs. Daisy Allen called for help in resisting her family's eviction by the police and her landlord. The reason for her eviction lay in her refusal to pay rent as her "landlord [had begun] to tear down the walls of her kitchen and bedroom and took apart her bed."[78] The landlord claimed that these repairs were needed in order to comply with the city's new housing ordinance (itself a tool of displacement and dispossession). Neighbors as well as "at least 15 representatives" of multiple organizations such as the Oakland chapter of the Welfare Rights Organization (WRO) and Western End Help Center came to Allen's aid.[79] Like the Black mothers who started Moms 4 Housing, Allen and the groups protesting her eviction saw these evictions as part of a longer-term pattern of "tenant terror" used by slumlords to exploit the poor. Rather than interpreting these actions as instances of individual moral failing, Allen and the groups blocking her eviction defined them as human rights violations. Not only had the landlord violated "public health standards and safety [but also] the dignity of people as human beings."[80]

Black Power urbanists saw housing not just as a source of shelter but as part of an overall system of domination, exploitation, and control. Organizations like the WRO advocated on behalf of women who were being evicted by unscrupulous landlords or who were stymied in their ability to secure safe and affordable housing by the capriciousness and low level of income support offered by the welfare system. The city's response to its self-induced housing crisis was sluggish at best and racist and misogynist at its worst. Black political mobilization would ultimately force the city to build the conventional public housing units that the OVL had secured commitments to in 1947.[81] Built in the low-rise townhouse style used in Oakland's wartime projects and reflecting West Coast disdain for high-rise projects, these developments were placed next to urban renewal areas, all forming the core of Oakland's "second ghetto"—a space created by the "public regulation and monies" of the postwar urban renewal order.[82] Some of these developments would be the first encroachment on the white working-class areas of the Flatlands.

Oakland's reluctant and flawed provision of low-cost public housing reflected the white city's belief that private market housing should hold a sacrosanct and privileged role in the city. Many white elites, as well as the OHA, saw the provision of public housing as an unwanted burden. It was the result of outside pressures by the federal government, who first insisted that the city build worker housing to address the dismal overcrowding caused by wartime mobilization, and then build public housing in exchange for urban renewal funds (see table 5.1).[83] The OHA, by design largely insulated from outside political

TABLE 5.1   Oakland public and subsidized housing, 1920–1980

YEAR	OAKLAND HOUSING AUTHORITY (OHA) FAMILY SITES / UNITS	NON-OHA FAMILY SITES / UNITS	OHA SENIOR SITES / UNITS	NON-OHA SENIOR SITES / UNITS	TURNKEY HOUSING UNITS (SCATTERED SITES)	SECTION 23 UNITS (PRE-SECTION 8)
1920–1950	4 / 915					
1940–1944	6 / 2,100					
1950–1968	3 / 400		1 / 100			
1968–1980	3 / 1,000	9 / 985**	2 / 101	16 / 1,720**	1,621	1,400

Note: **Includes Section 236 sites.

Source: Marilynn S. Johnson, *The Second Gold Rush: Oakland and the East Bay in World War II* (University of California Press, 1994): for figures for 1940–1944, see page 106; Theodore T. Tarail, *Housing Authority of the City of Oakland: Analysis of Housing Projects* (Council of Social Planning, Oakland Area, 1965); "Celebrating 80 Years of Progress," Oakland Housing Authority, accessed May 13, 2025, https://www.oakha.org/AboutUs/Pages/History. aspx; "Publicly Assisted Rental Units in the City of Oakland (Does Not Include Public Housing Units Owned and Managed by the Oakland Housing Authority)," Community and Economic Development Agency (CEDA), March 17, 2015, https://cao-94612.s3.amazonaws.com/documents/Directory-of-Assisted-Rental-Housing.pdf.

pressures, viewed its now majority-Black housing projects as symbols of failed government (that is, liberal) policies and the social and moral failings of Black people themselves. The low quality of the housing complexes that were built reflected the low value the city and the OHA placed on public housing. As for the mostly Black (women) tenants of the OHA's complexes, they were seen as problem tenants incapable of living decent, productive lives. The OHA was thus an organization that reluctantly built public housing and reluctantly managed it. The end result of OHA's organizational culture was housing that demonstrated their disdain for the poor and their desire to spend as little as possible.[84] Given these attitudes, the OHA was uninterested in managing their complexes in a way that improved the day-to-day lives of tenants or the neighborhoods in which these complexes were located.

By the late 1960s, Black activists had increased their pressure on city officials to address the housing crisis. This pressure coincided with a wave of tenant activism, especially among Black women. In Oakland, as in Newark, San Francisco, Saint Louis, Boston, and other cities, public housing became the site of Black women's political and community mobilization. Black women took the lead in mobilizing for more responsive public housing agencies that would treat them as citizens and tenants, not problems. This mobilization was not surprising in the case of the OHA, as the agency was known as an indifferent if not callous manager. For example, in both the Lockwood Gardens and Peralta Village complexes, tenants planted gardens and installed fences near their units in order to provide aesthetic pleasure, a sense of home, and a safe play area for children. Despite pleas and protests, the OHA uprooted these signs of community commitment as part of a "beautification" campaign funded by the War on Poverty.[85]

The OHA's institutional disdain and hostility would eventually extend to other types of housing policy. From the late 1960s and through the early 1970s the city took part in the Section 23 leased housing program (a privately owned but publicly subsidized program that was a precursor to the Section 8/Housing Choice Voucher Program) and the Turnkey Construction Program (both collectively known as "scattered site housing"). Mayor John Reading argued that despite their market-friendly aspects, these programs were essentially "low cost housing [that was] a drain on the taxpayers. It would be a gross injustice to use land which is two to three times more valuable than other land."[86] Reflecting this mindset, the OHA sponsored buildings (both conventional and turnkey/leased) that were shoddily built with few amenities. Given the huge displacement occurring in other parts of Black Oakland, these new developments were almost instantly overcrowded, and many of the units were occupied by large families.

For OHA public housing residents, the relatively affordable rents of "low-cost housing" protected them from a wildly expensive and predatory private housing market that repeatedly exploited renters like Mrs. Allen. Yet this affordability was also a reflection of the lack of value that the OHA placed on residents. Like Campbell and Peralta Villages, almost all of the new complexes were "located in close proximity to freeways or major surface streets," leading one social worker to report that "interior noise levels are so high that residents were almost required to yell to be heard."[87] It is not surprising that the massive displacement to environmentally harmful neighborhoods would lead some of Oakland's activists to coin the new term "environmental racism."[88] For these reasons, publicly owned housing was not the first choice for many in need of housing. Juanita Barnes, a Black woman living with her family in an OHA complex, was looking forward to being placed in a Section 23 unit. Barnes described living in the OHA complexes as "hard on the nerves." The project she left had "77 apartments with more than 300 children in our two block project."[89] The Section 23 program not only allowed her family to escape the heavy-handed paternalism and rigidity of the OHA, it was also the "the ideal solution, [with] smaller projects and the chance [for her] to raise a few flowers."[90]

Black organizations such as the Men of Tomorrow and the Black Panther Party attempted to achieve some control over the provision of housing despite the city's overall disdain and hostility toward public housing and despite the various barriers that federal regulations and funding placed in front of each attempt at Black housing development. The history of the Acorn development provides a glimpse into these ongoing struggles to build a new Black Oakland.

From Multiple Acorns, a New West Oakland?

The three phases of the Acorn Project have many tales to tell about Black Power Urbanism and community control, yet with the exception of temporary construction jobs, the long-term narrative is skewed toward the ways in which the middle-class inheritors of the Men of Tomorrow became perhaps the greatest beneficiaries of Black Power Urbanism. Phase one (from 1957 to 1972) shows how attempts by middle-class Blacks to offer a somewhat community-oriented redevelopment plan were ultimately rejected by the ORA in favor of an "integrated" project aimed at luring middle-class whites to West Oakland. The second and third phases of the Acorn Project (from 1970 to 1977) reflect the ascendancy of Black Power Urbanism in that the projects were designed by and for Oakland's Black residents. While the latter two phases could be seen as examples of successful Black Power Urbanism, the entire Acorn complex proved to be less than enduring. Decades of mismanagement by the ORA and then the OHA led to physical decline that was exacerbated by massive levels of disinvestment. This in turn was triggered by the federal government's gutting of funding for public housing and the rising levels of crime and lack of safety engendered by the nascent the War on Drugs and then the War on Crime. By the 1990s, the federal government's HOPE VI program, which provided funding for the demolition of public housing, would lead to the destruction of many of the units as permanent affordable housing; new units would be built as part of lower-density, mixed-income housing developments.[91] While those tenants who remained benefited from a much better living environment, the loss of hundreds of units and the discarding of the idea of permanent publicly owned housing would contribute to Oakland's twenty-first-century housing crisis.

The role of the Men of Tomorrow is a less well-known aspect of the struggle to build Acorn.[92] With Black activism and resistance to the city's massive "Negro removal" plan increasing, several members of the Men of Tomorrow formed the Beneficial Development Corporation and made the case that their group should lead the development of Acorn's planned public housing component. Officers of the group included W. Byron Rumford (president), Dr. Carlton B. Goodlett, Milburn T. Fort, and Samuel O'Dell. Willie Brown (future mayor of San Francisco) served as council. Reflecting their hopes for a multiracial integrationist future and possibly to ease the application process, Beneficial retained the architecture firm that originally designed the site plan, while also putting forward a rising

Japanese American landscape architect named Casey Kawamoto.[93] In keeping with its community oriented-ethos, the group also drew up a separate plan for financing to be provided by a new Black-owned bank.[94]

Beneficial's plan for Acorn Village reflected the aspiration for a public housing complex that was dramatically different from barracks-like, utilitarian projects such as Campbell Village or Peralta Villa (see figures 5.4A and 5.4B). The Beneficial proposal offered a "livable, attractive urban environment expressing a variety of character and diversity of activity. A great variety of visual experience and intrigue for the pedestrian should be stressed. . . . The urban character [will be] continued in the development of the small, convenience shopping center which preferably should be developed as a town square with a variety of activity, both commercial and non-commercial in character."[95] In its amenities and layout, the plan reflected the commitment by most of Beneficial's members to liberal integrationism. The proposed complex offered townhouse living similar to the city's other public housing developments. The proposal included a variety of housing types ranging from "single-family Sales housing to multi-family apartments and housing for the elderly" in addition to community buildings, all of which would form "pedestrian-oriented neighborhoods."[96] The proposal inadvertently underscored those things that had been destroyed by urban renewal: community, connection, and scale.

The Acorn plan proposed by the Men of Tomorrow lay in abeyance for several years due to the increasingly hostile struggle between the Oakland Redevelopment Authority (ORA) and Black residents of West Oakland. This struggle would eventually lead to the departure of the ORA's director, Thomas Bell, after he was accused (correctly) of not only misleading the residents of West Oakland about the impact of Acorn on their neighborhoods, but also being disrespectful and dismissive. In 1964, John Williams, an African American, was appointed as the head of the ORA. Williams arrived too late to stop the massive destruction that had already occurred or the budgetary commitments for highway and BART construction that were in the process of being expended. Williams attempted to mitigate the damage imposed on Black Oakland via the ORA; however, he recognized the limits of his power. He came to the position with a sober warning to his new constituents: "I do not pretend to come before you as the Messiah with a glib promise that urban renewal and Redevelopment is the cure-all for the problems and ills of Oakland. . . . We will either more forward or slide backwards—there is no standing still."[97] What Williams could do, however, was begin the slow process of bringing *some* Black residents (albeit moderate, middle-class ones like Love) into the bureaucratic machinery of redevelopment, and to move toward awarding the development of the Acorn housing component to Beneficial.

The building of Acorn Village (Acorn I), however, was delayed for another five years as the city wrangled with the federal government and the Beneficial group over funding. Not only did the majority-white city council demand "extra financial assurances before approving Beneficial's application," the FHA also signaled its "reluctance to guarantee the $7 million construction loan for moderate-income housing in a ghetto area."[98] Given the hostility of Oakland's white elites to Black assertion of control over any aspect of the redevelopment process, it would not be unreasonable to speculate that the long delay, using the city's famously fragmented political and institutional structures, was an effort to dislodge Williams and the Beneficial group's attempt to institute meaningful Black control over the redevelopment of West Oakland.[99] During this period of struggle and delay, the multi-acre site that would house the first phase of Acorn remained vacant, occupied mostly by "rats, ants, and sparrows."[100] The city ultimately rejected the Men of Tomorrow/Beneficial proposal and turned back to its earlier embrace of white-led organizations (and the awarding of "juicy contracts" to their contractors) to bring about the construction of the first phase of Acorn. By the time it had been completed in the early 1970s, the Men of Tomorrow had largely dissolved, with many like Lionel Wilson moving on to other political positions. Meanwhile, new groups like the West Oakland Planning Council (WOPC) emerged to lead the way.

A 1968 *Oakland Tribune* newspaper article, titled "Acorn Project Aims to Attract Whites," revealed the disjuncture between the aspirations of white Oakland and the on-the-ground realities of Black Oakland over the fate of West Oakland. While the ORA retained the development's original architects, the city forced the agency to award the building and operation of the complex to the Alameda County Building Trades Council rather than to a minority or Black-owned construction firm, as Beneficial had proposed. The selection of the trades council to bring about the city's vision for an "integrated" housing project was a particularly vicious irony as the council was bitterly resisting attempts to integrate the trade unions and open up employment opportunities in the construction trades to Blacks and other non-whites.[101] The November 1967 groundbreaking ceremony was presided over by Williams and Robert C. Weaver, the head of the newly created US Department of Housing and Urban Development. The project would open in September 1968 with 479 units at a total cost of $9 million.[102]

Though the new Acorn Village was seen as a decisive break from Oakland's bleak concrete public housing townhomes, the final design heavily resembled the Beneficial plan with its low-rise townhouses around community spaces. Yet, it differed from the Beneficial plan in that the ORA touted features that signified its desirability as a middle-income enclave, presumably for whites. First, only

10 percent of the units were set aside for low-income families, while the upper income limits for residents was set at $11,225, far above the poverty-level incomes of most of West Oakland Black residents. The ORA's attempt to lure more affluent and white residents was reflected in some of the design choices, from the "sleek white exteriors" of the units, to the decision that "art [would] get about 1 percent of the construction budget" and that "everything from trash receptacles to light standards and drinking fountains will be designed with art and aesthetics in mind."[103] In addition, the development offered residents "12-foot deep patios surrounded by tall wood fences."[104] This amenity was quite different from the ones offered to residents in the city's Peralta Village public housing complex, where the OHA tore down the fences that residents had put up at their own expense so they could carve out some privacy and a safe space for their children to play. For its "presentable as community housing projects go" design, the architects would win the 1970 Holiday Award for a Beautiful America.[105] The plan also reflected the development's disassociation from West Oakland. Dropped from the plan were a shopping center and other retail services to replace what the OPA bulldozer had torn down.

By 1972, the vision of an affluent, white development was largely gone. One of the ORA commissioners called the complex "a disgraceful mess" whose management "seems to be making no effort to encourage racial integrations. Tenants [are] mostly black."[106] The ORA in turn began discussions about replacing the management of the complex either with a manager already under its own aegis or someone completely new. Before construction the ORA had argued that its plan would succeed as it would not only draw upon a planned elementary school to be built in the area, but also seek the help of "churches, trade unions, teacher's groups and civil authorities" to develop racial and ethnic integration and ensure that Acorn Village became a "desirable place to live."[107] However, as Marta Gutman argues, the redevelopment of the Acorn site would not and could not replace the network of social care institutions and groups that had developed over decades.[108] The Acorn proposal had been a hopeful attempt to reseed a desolate moonscape created by Oakland's "Negro removal."

Begun in 1969, the second phase of the Acorn renewal area (Acorn 2) reflected the fractured ascendance, as well as the limitations and possibilities, of Black Power Urbanism. With Williams as the head of the ORA, the organization cooperated with a new group, MORE (More Oakland Residential Housing Inc.), led by John Henderson.[109] MORE was formed by an alliance of several community groups, including the WOPC, the Oak Center Neighborhood Association, and the United Taxpayers and Voters League. In addition to this neighborhood coalition, MORE worked with two Black architects, Robert Kennard and Arthur Silvers, who would go on to design an innovative middle school in West

Oakland.[110] Unlike the Beneficial group, which did not explicitly address the need for Black construction jobs, MORE was part of an effort to support Black contractors who were being organized by the newly established General and Specialty Contractors Association (GSCA), led by Joseph Debro and Ray Dones.[111] The GSCA sought to break the interlocking stranglehold of discriminatory trade unions and the large white-owned contracting firms that had destroyed and rebuilt the city's Black neighborhoods.

Again, in a sign of the city's discomfort with directly owned public housing, the new development of 375 units on 10.3 acres of land (between Seventh and Eighth and Market and Union Streets) was financed via the federal government's new Section 236 program and further backstopped by the Kaiser Urban Development Corporation (itself a creature of Kaiser Industries, one the city's largest and most powerful industrial firms). Despite this limitation, the project was Black-led, both in design and construction, and even more important, the director of MORE had pledged that mass meetings would be held so the community could "chart the shape the new housing project [will] take. . . . 'We want to take this total packet to the community and let the residents have some say on what they want on this land.'"[112]

Acorn 2 had multiple construction phases. The first phase consisted of a 126-unit townhouse development for about $3.7 million, while the second phase consisted of 341 units in three twelve-story towers.[113] While Oakland had never entertained the possibility of high-rise "projects" for subsidized/affordable housing, Williams saw the prospect of a high-rise built by and for Black stakeholders as a "real landmark for the West Oakland community." Other elements of phase 2 were the construction of the West Oakland Health Center, completed in 1969; the Martin Luther King Jr. Elementary School in 1972; and housing developments sponsored by local community groups like Taylor Memorial Methodist and Beth Eden Baptist churches.[114] Many of these projects were built by Ray Dones and his firm, Trans-Bay Engineers, Inc., which would become one of the nation's largest minority contractors.[115] Acorn's third phase was the construction of a small local shopping center, Jack London Gateway, which was a belated attempt to replace the neighborhood necessities—like a grocery store and other amenities and services—that had been almost wholly destroyed by the ORA's blight clearance project and that had been excluded from previous Acorn plans.

One of the most high-profile elements of the broader Acorn redevelopment scheme was the City Center Project. Despite the fact that Williams was at the helm from 1964 onward, the city and the ORA had continued their onward path of destruction and renewal. The City Center Project was envisioned as a replacement for the city's aging downtown business and shopping district. Key to the project was the destruction of fifteen blocks of housing. By 1973, Black Power Urbanism had transformed this project from one controlled by the ORA to a project that reflected an ongoing contestation over what and who constituted the city's interests. In May 1973, "attorneys for the Black Panther Party and the East Bay Legislative Council of Senior Citizens" used federal redevelopment regulations against the city by charging that Oakland had not fulfilled the requirement for constructing replacement housing for units lost to urban renewal or creating an adequate supply of low-income housing.[116] As the BPP noted in their newspaper, the move to block the business-as-usual redevelopment of City Center was a stunning achievement. The city council would spend the next few months attempting to remove the BPP-sponsored roadblock. The council maintained resistance in the face of Bobby Seale's 1974 run for mayor and the broad-based political mobilization being led by Black Panther Party members to support Seale and other candidates, but by September this resistance had crumbled due to this unprecedented pressure, as well as the ongoing mayoral race. The BPP and local activists had won.

Black Power insurgencies had achieved an "unprecedented replacement housing proposal" of $12 million. The proposal included three hundred affordable housing units, while in keeping with the BPP's platform the complex itself would be run by a nonprofit corporation "wholly controlled by community groups including a tenant's union [that] will retain collective ownership and policy-making control over the entire housing complex."[117] More concretely, the agreement included "developer commitments to 50 percent minority employment on project supervisory and property management staff, joint marketing with black real-estate brokers and 5 percent equity for a local economic development corporation created by the developer with nine minority co-investors."[118]

Black Power Urbanism had brought some Black interests to the ORA table. The construction of the City Center Project marked the successful incorporation of moderate Black organizations into the ORA orbit through Williams's strong advocacy of affirmative action. In 1972, the ORA "claimed a 62 percent minority employment ratio on all demolition, construction and rehabilitation work in the previous year. By 1974, the ORA claimed that $10 million in urban renewal contracts went to minority firms, with another $10 million to joint ventures between white- and black-owned companies." In terms of employment, between 1968 and 1972, "2,207 out of 3,484 jobs on redevelopment projects had gone to minority workers."[119] The project allowed for the further implementation of two programs. The first was Project Upgrade, which was designed to "help minority craftsmen with previous construction experience attain journeyman status," while the second program, PREP (Project Rehabilitation Employment Project), would provide construction experience to "minority youths unable to matriculate into union apprenticeship programs."[120] In addition to these two programs, the ORA reported that "66 percent of City Center construction work-hours were performed by minorities and 49 percent by Oakland residents."[121] This was a remarkable accomplishment especially given the refusal of other entities within the city such as the Port of Oakland or the construction trade unions to countenance any meaningful employment opportunities and/or contracting opportunities for Black workers. The gains made via the ORA should not be discounted simply because both working- and middle-class Blacks benefited. Indeed, Joseph Debro, who was responsible for bringing together the GCNA, argued that "the minority contractor is one of the most important agents in rebuilding the inner city ghetto. . . . Not only does he provide jobs for community residents, . . . he also gives a measure of control over the rebuilding of the community to its residents. . . . Jobs performed by minority contractors help to increase the dignity and self-reliance of the community."[122]

The election of Lionel Wilson as Oakland's first Black mayor in 1977 marked the ascendancy of Oakland's Black middle class even as some of those who had been its spatial architects passed on. The Men of Tomorrow had long since disappeared and in 1976 ORA director John Williams, who had presided over an uneven attempt to shift the ORA from removal to renewal, died of cancer at the age of fifty-nine. Black middle-class ascendancy stood in stark contrast to the extraordinary negative turn that had overtaken the Acorn complexes. By 1978, six years after its opening, parts of the Acorn projects were described as "vandalized, burnt out wreckage."[123] Perhaps it is not surprising, given its birth in the wake of violent erasure and root shock, that the spatial and civic community infrastructure built by historic Black Oakland and destroyed by "Negro removal" could not magically reappear to sustain these fragile new communities. The Republican war on cities and the War on Drugs provided another blow. By the 1980s, the Acorn projects had slipped into decline and in 1989 was the location where Huey P. Newton, the former Black Panther Party leader, would be killed by a drug dealer.[124] Far from containing the ghetto, Oakland's planners wanted to erase it, in order to re-form and re-spatialize the city's racial landscape.[125]

Despite these challenges, the residents of the Acorns—especially the Black women-led families who lived there—continued to press for accountability and change in their living conditions. By 1992, the complex was only half-occupied and known to be a center of gang activity and conflict. Black women tenant leaders like Janet Paterson and Mattie Witfield, following the lead of other tenant groups in places like San Francisco and Newark, began to press for tenant self-management and ultimately ownership.[126] HUD, under the management of Jack

Kemp, responded to this pressure and in 1995 promised to redevelop the complex and two others (Peralta Villa and Campbell).[127] In keeping with the new ortho-doxy surrounding the inherent flaws of public housing (and indeed its alleged crimogenic properties), critics pointed to the amenities touted in Acorn's ini-tial opening—the "semblance of suburban privacy to the city"—as major flaws, since the design "points front doors away from the street and breeds crime in its hemmed-in courtyards and alleys."[128]

By 1996, HOPE VI was in ascendancy. Rather than institute tenant control or ownership, as in Newark and elsewhere in Oakland, the OHA dramatically reshaped the Acorn project. Density was reduced by half—in some cases by removing extra floors from townhouse units—while reconfiguring the com-munal spaces into courtyards "with locked gates to limit access."[129] The next decade brought even more radical changes. Acorn 1 was almost entirely demol-ished and replaced by small two-story single-family houses. Acorn 2 and 3 were renamed, respectively, "Town Center Apartments at Acorn" and "Courtyard Apartments." The revitalization included the building of a "recreational center, a community building, tot lots, a pool and three basketball courts; a Com-puter Learning Center as well as a network connecting individual computers within each home."[130] While the new Acorn Town Center was saved, hundreds of OHA's affordable units for low-income families were permanently lost due to chronic and serious mismanagement and the neoliberal belief that public housing and other New Deal relics were inherently bad for families, neighbor-hoods, and cities.

We Can Wait: Education for Liberation

"We can wait," said Paul Cobb as the Oakland Board of Education once again refused to respond to demands from Black parents, activists, and even its sole Black board member to address the district's systematic discrimination against and disinvestment from majority-Black and -Brown schools in the district. While Black parents were waiting, rather than introduce measures to promote equity and investment, the Oakland public school district was playing an important role in developing Oakland's incipient carceral structures. In conjunction with the police, other law enforcement agencies, and local social welfare agencies, Oakland's public schools were critical sites in transforming Black and Brown students, as well as the communities in which they were embedded, into objects of surveillance, control, and containment.[131]

White students, by contrast, were experiencing the "golden age" of California education as symbolized by the newly opened Skyline High School. Located in the Oakland Hills, the $4.6 million state-of-the art school boasted fifty class-rooms, a library, a cafeteria, a gymnasium, an auditorium, and administrative offices. When attendance boundaries were announced, it was revealed that the city's newest school would be almost entirely white and serve the affluent families who lived in the Oakland Hills. The fact that the school district had effectively built a "private prep school supported by public funds" revealed the deep racial, ethnic, and economic inequalities that lay at the heart of the Oakland school system.[132] Skyline's attendance zone in 1960 was ten miles long (from the Hills to the Flatlands) and only two miles wide, which "effectively excluded almost every nonwhite student" in the city (see figures 5.5A and 5.5B).[133]

The exclusionary outcome was astonishing given that in 1962, Black students comprised nearly 40 percent of the Oakland public school population. The Black student population was, however, concentrated in particular schools at every level. Of the city's sixty-six schools, seventeen were more than 75 percent Black, while thirty were more than 75 percent white.[134] In West Oakland, Black students made up 95 percent of school enrollment. Black schools were more likely to be overcrowded and have students housed in portable trailers, which in addition to being unsuitable for teaching, reduced the playground area of these schools. While the teaching staff was 83 percent white at Skyline, it was more than 80 per-cent Black at McClymonds and Castlemont (the district's "Black" high schools). Black people constituted less than 20 percent of the district's nearly four thousand staff and no Black teachers were assigned to mixed and/or majority-white schools. Indeed, white teachers had the privilege of requesting and receiving transfers from majority-Black schools. As a result, Black schools were more than twice as likely to have probationary teachers as majority-white schools, and less likely to have librarians and other teaching resources.[135]

The school district was firmly in the hands of a self-perpetuating, conservative, majority-white board of education.[136] Despite a 1962 investigation by the US Commission on Civil Rights, the board was proudly indifferent to criticism and remained dedicated to maintaining an inequitable school system that continually shifted shrinking levels of public funding to majority-white schools and communities. Various contemporary accounts of the Oakland school board noted that its members prided themselves on their apolitical and professional approach to determining district policy.[137] The supposedly "apolitical space" of educational policy was based upon and sustained through a long-standing pattern of political and institutional exclusion that was self-perpetuating, as the almost entirely white school board appointed its own successors. This exclusion also meant that none of the board members had any intention of meaningfully changing Oakland's engagement with the city's growing Black and Brown communities from an approach that saw these students as a threat to the city's imagined social order. Elite bargaining and litigation had proven to be useless. Outside of the affluent Hills, in West and North Oakland and down through the Flatlands, the schools attended by children in these neighborhoods were marked by "teachers [who] were less experienced and more likely to be on temporary status, buildings [that] were shabbier [and] a higher proportion of flats students were in portable classrooms, playgrounds were small, supplies few, classes crowded."[138]

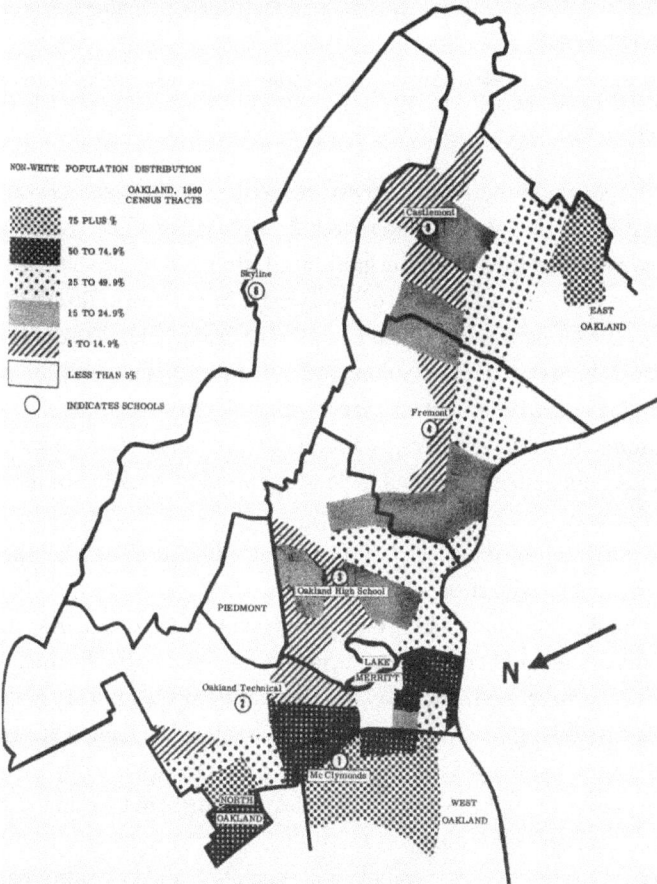

FIGURE 5.5A. Spatializing educational inequality: Schools, attendance zones, and racial imbalance

Source: Ira Michael Heyman, *Civil Rights U.S.A.: Public Schools in the North and West 1963; Oakland* (United States Commission on Civil Rights, 1963).

APPENDIX B

Table 5   Oakland

RACIAL COMPOSITION--SENIOR HIGH SCHOOLS

School	% Negro Students	% Oriental Students	% Caucasian Students
Castlemont	39.75	0.25	60.0
Fremont	10-12.0	1-2.0	86-88.0
McClymonds	97.0	0.5	2.5
Oakland	15-20.0	5.0	75-80.0
Oakland Tech	42.0	6.0	52.0
Skyline	1.0	1.0	98.0

FIGURE 5.5B. Spatializing educational inequality: Schools, attendance zones, and racial imbalance

Source: Ira Michael Heyman, Civil Rights U.S.A.: Public Schools in the North and West 1963; Oakland (United States Commission on Civil Rights, 1963).

Over the course of the 1960s, activists from dozens of Oakland's many non-white racial and ethnic groups, who reflected a wide range of ideological stances, increasingly rejected the liberal integrationism proffered by official Oakland in an attempt to break the deadly grip of this system. At one end of this challenge to Oakland's educational system would be umbrella groups like the Ad Hoc Committee for Quality Education, who along with others pressed not only for inclusive representation and greater democratic accountability from the school board, but also for more substantive moves by the district administration toward equity within the school system that went beyond the window dressing of token integration programs.

At the other end of the spectrum were groups like the Black Panthers who believed that public education was so systematically racist that a truly liberatory education for Black children had to take place outside of its control in spaces dedicated to education for liberation. This belief resulted in the establishment of East Palo Alto's Nairobi schools and the Oakland Community School (1971–82), one of the longest-running Black Power–inspired schools in the United States. In the case of Oakland, the Black Panther Party was generally not directly involved in the struggles over the public school system, leaving others to take up the struggle for just and equitable education.

Between these two ends of symbolic representation and exit from the system as symbolized by the Black Panthers lay a vast and contentious middle in which "community control" came to embody a Black Power urbanist solution to an educational system that not only failed poor Black children, but also worked as an active agent in their own community's disorganization and disempowerment.

The press for substantive "community control" over Oakland's schools would touch both ends of the spectrum, from those who argued that change in the city's schools ran directly through the superintendent's office to those who saw exit from the system as the only viable response.

In Oakland, "community control" had had a very local aspect since the early 1960s.[139] Faced with children who couldn't read before they were "pushed out" of school altogether, Black parents lobbied for greater accountability and responsiveness from principals, teachers, and administrators. Rather than enduring teachers and administrators who saw themselves as policing "socially maladjusted" and "culturally deprived" children, parents and communities agitated for staff who were willing and eager to teach where students and their communities were, and where they could be, rather than where Oakland's white power structure had deemed they should remain. Activists like Paul Cobb, working with well over one hundred community organizations, began a five-year campaign to challenge and dismantle the avowedly "apolitical" school system that continually put the concerns and needs of Black and Brown students and parents behind those of the affluent whites of the Oakland Hills.[140]

The creation of the Ad Hoc Committee for Quality Education (which included the Black Caucus, headed by Paul Cobb) was a result not just of the frustration of parents and community groups with the board of education, but also of the spirit of "community empowerment" that flowed out of the federal and foundation funds that had enabled activists to establish a range of community groups outside of the control of the city or the board. The committee reflected Oakland's long history of Black/progressive alliances with representatives from the NAACP, the Mexican American Unity Council, and the Oakland Federation of Teachers.[141]

The Ad Hoc Committee presented the board with twenty recommendations, which taken together constituted a revolutionary approach to the educational system. First and foremost, the Ad Hoc Committee put itself forward as the bargaining unit between the board and the working-class and poor people of Oakland. Second was a demand for the equalization of school equipment and other resources. Several further recommendations worked toward an educational system that did not simply "teach" but also nurtured all of its students, for example, by providing free hot lunch. Other recommendations included the "employment of Spanish-speaking and Negro counselors," the "training of school personnel in 'intergroup human relations,'" and "due process of handling of student confidential files and disciplinary actions."[142]

The demands made by the committee were in retrospect not earth-shattering, but in the context of a highly centralized and insular administration, they struck a blow against the "political" status quo. What is notable about them is that federal funding via the War on Poverty coupled with the general rhetoric around "maximum feasible participation" emboldened the committee to demand parent oversight over the educational programs funded by federal monies. The second demand struck at the very visible educational gaps between schools in the Hills and schools in the Flatlands that were attended by Black and Brown students. The committee also requested school-by-school achievement data and an accounting of the monies spent at each school in order to determine the extent to which the Oakland school district was systemically undereducating and underfunding non-white children. Finally, the committee insisted on a more permanent role in district governance by demanding that it be "recognized as a separate bargaining unit" that was not limited to "merely advice giving" but was rather given a "parity of influence."[143]

While the Ad Hoc Committee was acting as the focal point for community group coordination to battle against the board, the composition of the board itself became a focus of confrontation. Starting in 1965 board of education incumbents faced challenges to their hegemony, starting with the candidacy of Electra Price, a Black woman educator. Given that the board was elected via an at-large system, the fact that Price won "more than three-quarters of the 'ghetto' vote" proved that taking political control of the board would be long and arduous.[144] This lack of electoral success despite significant spatial majorities caused activists to realize that shaping the direction of Oakland's schools meant directly taking control of its administration and bypassing its board.

"Freedom schools" were the response to the board's continued intransigence and its failure to take these electoral and activist challenges seriously. By the fall of 1966, the rebellion in Oakland that had been ominously predicted by the media took shape in the form of a three-day school boycott by Black students, accompanied by the establishment of temporary "freedom schools" (see figures 5.6A and 5.6B). Approximately three thousand students stayed out of school and nearly one thousand attended these ad hoc freedom schools. The boycott signaled that the educational battle in Oakland was not just over resources but also over the soul of education. Activists and parents were no longer content to accept schools as merely way stations in the city's nascent school-to-prison pipeline. Instead they demanded a school system that would educate and not criminalize their children. Negotiation had led to a school system in which Black children's educational progress slipped with each year. The excitement of freedom schools and Black educational autonomy would be matched by activists like Percy Moore, who declared that West Oakland should be a city within a city and should run its own school system. Moore's call for spatial autonomy in education was radical, but it built upon the community's deepening dissatisfaction with the board of education.

BOYCOTT BABY BOYCOTT

The Ad Hoc Committee for Quality Education in Oakland was formed in March from a wide range of community groups. The committee formed in response to the publication of a booklet called "Quality Education in Oakland," which was promised as a master plan, but turned out to be a slick public relations job. Problems were minimized, claims were maximized.

The committee drew up a list of demands designed to correct the most immediate problems, yet leave room for a Master Plan.

Talks with the board went on through May and June. Even though the board came to a "consensus" on many of the demands, this "consensus" proved unrelated to action, and Ad Hoc broke off negotiations after the board's June 15th session.

In the summer, Ad Hoc ran student conferences, set up freedom schools (to help make up the deficiencies in the Oakland school system), and did research on ed-

Continued on Page Five

FIGURE 5.6A. Oakland's freedom schools: Black Power Urbanism's educational insurgency

Source: The Flatlands, November 5 to November 17, 1966. The Flatlands newspaper collection, MS 197, African American Museum and Library at Oakland.

In the face of this rebellion, the board of education's normal exclusionary and high-handed decision-making began to break down. The most visible example of this occurred during the selection of a new school superintendent, a process that had largely been controlled by the board with little or no input from community

FIGURE 5.6B. Oakland's freedom schools: Black Power Urbanism's educational insurgency

Source: *The Flatlands*, November 5 to November 17, 1966. The *Flatlands* newspaper collection, MS 197, African American Museum and Library at Oakland.

members, never mind parents or students. To Paul Cobb, Electra Price, and other Black activists who had pressed for more inclusion and a stronger say in the selection process, the fact that the board had sidestepped the consultant panel and selected highly unacceptable candidates meant that it was time for a full-scale confrontation.

"This is our Armageddon" was the rallying cry of the Black Caucus, the coordinating group of thirty-three organizations that had organized around restructuring Oakland's unequal school system. Their actions at the next board of education meeting decisively shattered the last remaining pretension that education was "not political." After denouncing the board, members of the Black Caucus announced a sit-in. The board then called in the Oakland Police Department, which used mace against the protestors and made some arrests.

Five of the protestors arrested were leaders of groups who represented significant elements of Oakland's institutional Black community, including the director of the Oakland Economic Development Council (OEDC); the president of the Oakland Federation of Teachers; the chairman of Blacks for Justice, and Cobb, chairman of the Black Caucus. Now known as the "Oakland Five," they exemplified the growing chasm between the white board and the majority-minority students and parents that it failed to represent. The fact that the board had called in the police put the school administration and board clearly on the side of the white power structure rather than the students and parents it was obligated to serve.

While the Oakland Five would be tried and most of them acquitted after a new Black superintendent had taken the position, they continued to stand as a potent symbol of the failures of the current school regime. According to one account, "in spite of the brevity of the episode and the minimal level of physical conflict, the damage to the images of the board and the Oakland public schools was done." Despite the board's efforts to counteract it, "a spectacle of violence" now hung over the superintendent selection process and the future of the district itself.[145] Perhaps due to this turmoil, although not surprisingly given past elections, the June school bond election failed.

On the heels of this failure, state auditors accused the district of misusing millions of dollars of Title I funding, diverting it to majority-white schools in the Hills and withholding it from majority-minority poor schools of the Flatlands and West Oakland where the funding was needed the most and was legally required.[146] While a "shocking revelation" to the media, this public confirmation vindicated the claims made by many Black activists.[147] In addition, the state audit found that the district had used almost one-third of the funds for administrative needs instead of addressing the critical shortages in teachers and resource specialists needed in the city's poorest schools. Reflecting what would later be called institutional racism, the report denied the existence of the systemic racism and inequality that infused the school district. Instead, it stated that while there was "no malevolence" in the misuse of the funds, neither was there "[anyone] at the policy-making level who was responsible and accountable for the implementation of the program. Not even the black compensatory education director had been able to stand up for the interests" of the district's poor Black, Brown, and Asian students.[148]

To David McCollum, the head of the Oakland branch of the NAACP, this misappropriation was an "agonizing tragedy. . . . Black people and poor people had hoped passionately that these programs would provide a breakthrough for their children." These revelations confirmed what many Black Oaklanders had long suspected about the district's institutionalized indifference. Given this clear evidence, McCollum was one of many voices who argued that there was a critical need to create a "people's system." The district's "demonstrated . . . indifference" gave those shut out of the district "no alternative than to establish a parallel school board."[149] This was not an empty declaration. Black leaders like Paul Cobb pushed for the creation of an alternative board called the Community United for Relevant Education (CURE). While the proposed board "commanded the allegiance of both the NAACP and the Black Panthers," other groups in the coalition represented the multiracial reality of 1960s Oakland.

Over the next months, activists would clash with the board over a series of proposed candidates for superintendent. Black activists were insistent that only a transformative Black superintendent could truly understand and thus change Oakland's deeply unequal public schools. The Oakland Five, Barney Hilburn, Wilson Riles, and the board would eventually focus on the candidacy of Marcus Foster.[150] Foster, then principal of Gratz High School, a majority-Black school in Philadelphia, was a rising star in the newly emerging field of "urban education." Riles, as the head of California's statewide compensatory education program (and a former member of Men of Tomorrow) had a national reputation in public education and was familiar with educators like Foster as well as Preston Wilcox and Rhody McCoy, leaders in the nascent community control movement. Foster was hired with great anticipation and approached his office with an agenda that acknowledged the demands of Black Power Urbanism while experimenting with new pedagogical and governance approaches for urban school systems.

Marcus Foster and the Possibilities of Local Control

Foster's leadership of the Oakland school system put the city's schools on a new path. With the support of the multiracial coalition that had brought him into the city, Foster pressured the board and district to shift away from a singular focus on "saving the schools" in the Hills and a general indifference toward the rest of the city. His clearest attempt at jump-starting this reorientation was the introduction of a modified decentralization plan that divided the city into three subzones.[151] This decentralization was part of his second strategic goal, which was to forge more direct links with neighborhood activists and parents concerned about the quality of their children's education. The scope of this outreach was extraordinary given the district's historic insularity and aloofness. Foster created the Master Plan Citizens Committee, made up of three hundred community members across the city's multiracial and multiethnic divide. Members included not only Blacks and whites, but also Spanish speakers, Asian Americans (including Filipinos), and Native Americans.[152] Many of these groups were small and unorganized and some had significant intragroup divisions. For example, "in the Chinese community Foster's problem stemmed from a split between newly arrived immigrant students from Hong Kong . . . and those Chinese-speaking students who came from established families in the city."[153] This wide swath of committee members were subdivided into task forces to deal with school buildings, finance, multicultural education, and community resources."[154] Unlike in New York City's controversial Ocean Hill-Brownsville experiment, Foster was determined that "community control" via outreach and inclusion would not supplant firm control by the superintendent's office.

Foster's second goal was not simply to ensure that compensatory education was supplied to students who needed it most, but also to also create a system of accountability and standards so that parents, particularly parents of color, could maintain their support of the public school system and work with the administration toward changes. Using his prior experience as a school principal in Philadelphia, Foster would develop a standards-based curriculum for the school district as a means of showing skeptical parents that schools could and would work for their children. Beyond the symbolism of his appointment and his decentralization policy, Foster's most visible impact on Oakland was changing the racial and ethnic makeup of the district's principals and teachers as well as its administrative staff.

Finally, again drawing from his Philadelphia experience, Foster paid particularly close attention to the district's fiscal health. Oakland financed its school system via separate budget votes and bond referendums. From the 1950s until Foster assumed leadership of the district, the school board's budgets had met repeated defeat at the polls. One possible source for these continual defeats was the changing complexion of the district's student body.[155] The Oakland board could not or would not make the case to Oakland's majority-white electorate that they should open their pocketbooks for a school district that increasingly did not resemble their own neighborhoods. Buoyed by Black Power Urbanism and a strong multiracial coalition, in the spring of 1973 Foster was able to lead the first successful school finance vote in decades. Yet he also recognized that Oakland could not manage to adequately fund the types of schools that its citizens needed on its own. Even as California's school equalization case, *Serrano v. Priest*, was being litigated, Foster would make the forceful case (at the head of thirty busloads of children, parents, and other activists that had journeyed to Sacramento) that the state had to step in to equalize the growing gap between Oakland and the richer and whiter suburbs that surrounded it.

Coda to Incorporation: Takeover

Marcus Foster, who embodied the quiet revolutionary potential of a more main-stream Black Power Urbanism, was murdered by the Symbionese Liberation Army (SLA) on November 6, 1973. The Oakland School District was "effec-tively paralyzed by the event and largely unable to fix a new direction for nearly two years."[156] The mostly white members of the SLA used a proposed student ID and school security proposal as justification for Foster's murder; the irony of the assassination was that Foster was battling against this latest manifesta-tion of Oakland's carceral regime, the very regime that he was hired to—and was in the process of trying to—dismantle. Foster's death weakened Oakland's momentum toward rapid school reform. After a year and half with an interim superintendent, Oakland appointed Ruth Love to the position in December 1975. According to David Kirp, Love's focus on "educational achievement and not power sharing" was "reflective of a more general change in the educational policy agendas of big cities since the early 1970s."[157] While Love recentralized the school district (in order to save money), the district made a formal commit-ment to bilingual education and continued diversifying its principal, teachers, and administrative staff.

After Foster's death, the second and perhaps most damaging blow to Oakland's urban public school system was the passage of Proposition 13 in 1979—the latest iteration of the state's "racial propositions." The proposition dramatically limited the property tax revenue that the school system relied upon. An important ele-ment of community control was the ability to employ a diverse and appropriately sized teaching force, as well as to develop and maintain up-to-date facilities and other resources. The austerity imposed by Proposition 13 was further magnified with the passage sixteen months later of Proposition 4, which placed additional limits on state and local spending. Although the impact of both propositions was initially limited, Reagan-era cuts and the state's growing reliance on increasingly volatile sales tax revenue would push Oakland and other poor urban districts down a long path of austerity.

In December 1996, the school board attempted to instantiate a new form of compensatory learning for the district's Black students in the shape of a widely ridiculed proposal to adopt an "Ebonics" initiative.[158] Pioneered by educators in Black Power spaces like East Palo Alto and Newark, Ebonics is a learning system based on African American Vernacular English (AAVE).[159] Although the Ebonics proposal was quickly withdrawn after fierce public backlash, the controversy proved to be a critical turning point in the struggle for racial equity in Oakland's public education. For some, the Ebonics debate epitomized the twenty years of political mobilization and educational reform that had animated the Black Power Urbanism of the long 1970s, in which community control over schools was not only about the political control of these systems but also the content and quality of education received by African American children. That the proposal to recognize AAVE was even part of the board discussion was testament to the political power of not only the city's Black residents, but also its growing Latino and Asian/Pacific Islander population, which in turn resulted in a majority-Black school board that led a school system with a diverse teaching staff and administration, and the first Asian American school superintendent.[160] That AAVE could even be considered also speaks to the shift in the city's teaching force. Between 1970 and 1990, Oakland went from one of the least diverse teaching staffs in California, with few Black or Spanish-speaking teachers, to one of the most diverse.

At the same time, the district's decision to advocate for Ebonics was seized upon as evidence that Oakland's public school system was "academically bankrupt." The idea of academic bankruptcy was part of a larger, growing neoliberal narrative that public schools had failed, advocated by mostly Republican "education reform" governors like Thomas Kean of New Jersey, who used this language to justify the takeover of the state's largest Black- and Brown-majority school districts, including Newark's.

The first of many salvos in the battle to advance state takeover was uttered by California's commissioner of education, Bill Honig, who stated that he "wished someone would care about [Oakland's] black children as much as they care about black administrators. . . . They just care about jobs."[161] The fiscal and political fallout from fights over state equalization funding, conservative hostility toward Oakland's majority-minority-led school district, and the seeming wrongheadedness of the Ebonics proposal provided education reformers and politicians with a casus belli that allowed them to finally engineer a state takeover of the school district in 1999. While malfeasance could never be proven, reformers nevertheless laid the failure of Oakland's schools at the feet of its teachers and administrators, arguing that if they had cared for "more than just their jobs," they would have (and should have) educated their students.

State takeover did not lead to district improvement. Instead, the system was stuck in a perpetual cycle of deficits and plagued by falling enrollments as Oakland became a state and national showcase for the charter school movement. During its time under state control, the school district accrued more debt than it had had before the takeover and employed a less diverse teaching force due to cuts in funding and the use of Teach for America instructors, a full third of whom left after a year. It also went through six superintendents in sixteen years. More importantly, spurred by state legislation and foundation support, charter schools began enrolling a growing and significant number of the district's students. The withdrawal of state control over Oakland's schools would be facilitated by the influence of former representative and then-mayor Ron Dellums—a longtime member of the city's Black and left/liberal coalition, and one of the remaining members the city's Black Power urbanist era. The end of state control in 2010 also meant the beginning of a bruising fight for local control over the city's public school system, in which Black and Brown children remained marginalized.

Defending Black Oakland

After decades of organizing and in the wake of George Floyd's killing in 2020 by the Minneapolis police, Black youth activists in Oakland achieved a signature victory: the elimination of the Oakland School Police Department (OSPD) and the reallocation of its $6 million budget to a new school safety plan that put the funding toward "student support positions such as school-based social workers, psychologists, restorative justice practitioners, or other mental or behavioral health professionals, as the budget supports, to meet the needs of students."[162] The basis of the what was called the "George Floyd Resolution" were the grim facts on the ground:

> Since the 2015–16 School Year, Black students made up 26% of the enrollment and yet made up 73% of arrests, accounting for 3 out of 4 of the arrests in our schools, and in the last four years there were over 9,000 calls for service to the police on students. . . . [S]uch a deeply embedded and institutionalized form of preemptive policing has extremely significant consequences, foreclosing opportunities toward graduation, college, and employment for Oakland's Black youth, school policing is fundamentally undermining the economic and public health of the Black community by restricting access and opportunity.[163]

As the eviction of Mrs. Daisy Allen revealed, the police—whether OPD or OSPD—occupied an outsized role in the life of Black Oaklanders, from carrying out evictions in Black neighborhoods as the city pushed through its urban renewal plans to patrolling the halls of the city's high schools, which with the exception of newly built Skyline High were in danger of turning into majority-Black/Brown spaces and were therefore seen not as sites of education but rather as inherently crimogenic spaces.

While George Floyd's death was its most proximate catalyst, the victory itself rested on decades of long-term organizing for the removal of the police from the schools, which would by extension reduce the violence of the Oakland Police

Department (OPD) and other policing agencies toward the city's Black and Brown citizens.[164] This organizing was fueled by the insistence—as seen in the Black Panther Party's Ten-Point Program—that liberation for Black people could only come with the dismantling of a police force that had long acted as if it were an occupying force.

Policing the Black Polity

The OPD had a long history of brutality and callousness toward Black and Brown Oaklanders that reached back to the early twentieth century. In the 1920s, national and local resurgence of the KKK spilled over into the ranks of the OPD, creating a legacy of organizational hostility to non-whites.[165] By the 1940s, with the large influx of Black migrants to the city due to the Great Migration, the police department increasingly served as the enforcers and defenders of the urban color line, as was the case in almost every city with a sizeable Black population.[166] Conflicts over race, class, and space only increased as World War II and the subsequent migration of both Blacks and whites to the city intertwined to decisively reshape the city's demographics and challenge its racialization of space. The OPD was one of the key elements in policing the threatened racial boundaries and in enforcing new ones.[167] In the postwar period a left-liberal alliance emerged in the wake of a series of workers' strikes, including a strike by white women retail workers in 1947. As had happened before, Oakland's conservative elites deployed the OPD to put down the strike and crush union activism. The conservative animus only grew as the left-labor coalition managed to elect their candidates to the city council.

Activists continued to highlight the prevalence of police abuse during the 1950s. In 1949, the East Bay Civil Rights Congress—a local "Popular Front holdover," pushed the California state assembly to hold hearings on police brutality in Oakland, which were "among the first such hearings in the nation."[168] Despite finding persuasive evidence of police brutality, the final report produced only "token concessions," including the hiring of a scant few Black police officers.[169] Although the progressive OVL-affiliated city council members attempted to push for further police reform, they lost power as the establishment aggressively worked to unseat them. By the early 1950s, not only had conservatives managed to retake and secure control over the council, but they had encouraged the OPD to cooperate with the Ford Foundation's Gray Areas program in the creation of a proto-carceral state designed to surveil and control Black and Brown youth.[170] This would lead to the creation of the Oakland School Police Department in 1957.

By the mid-1960s, both Black Oaklanders and the OPD itself had decisively rejected any pretense that the OPD was part of a benign urban welfare state. A "generally sympathetic" study of the OPD published in 1965 found that a "negative attitude towards Negroes was the norm among the police studies, as recognized by the chief himself. If a policemen did not subscribe to it, unless a Negro himself, he would be somewhat resented by his fellows."[171] There were in fact relatively few Black police officers to object to this prevailing racism; only twenty of the OPD's 617-person force were either Black (sixteen officers) or Mexican American (four officers).[172] The institutionalized animus was so pervasive that the OPD's chief was forced to issue a department order banning the use of a slew of racial slurs.[173] These slurs were accompanied by escalating cases of police brutality, which Bobby Seale and Huey Newton focused on as evidence of Black Oakland's embattled status. The BPP had formed to defend the ghetto from the police and the inherent violence of "urban policing."[174]

Defending the Ghetto

The BPP's audacious performance of power shook the OPD's assumption that it had carte blanche over the city's Black and Brown residents. As numerous histories of the Black Panthers have recounted, the group arose not only to create a new form of justice and community safety for Black Oakland, but to battle against the daily acts of repression and brutality against Black Oaklanders perpetrated by Oakland's almost exclusively white police force. The Panthers' 1966 Ten-Point Program statement articulated their anger with the local police as well as with the United States' unjust policing and carceral system. The BPP offered an alternative to these unjust systems, publicly bearing arms and serving as witnesses to the OPD's actions, arguing for the right to be judged by community members rather than whites who assumed guilt and criminality rather than innocence in criminal trials, and proposing mass decarceration of Black people who had been rounded up into a policing and carceral system that had a long history rooted in the country's history of slavery and Jim Crow.

The OPD's repression and violence steadily expanded as the Black Panther Party and its allies became the focus of local police agencies and other state and federal government entities. This ongoing repression would come into sharp focus when Newton and Seale adopted the tactic of community patrols created by Black activists in Los Angeles, Detroit, and elsewhere. The Newton/Seale innovation—or perhaps provocation—lay in their decision to display not just walkie-talkies and notebooks but also weapons, and to not simply shadow the police but to "directly confront the exercise of police power in black neighborhoods."[175] The Panthers' community patrols radically upended Black citizens' encounters with the police. The presence of Panthers signified immediate public accountability for police officers used to operating with impunity. These encounters also provided a venue for individual and community education as the Panthers' patrols advised those under police detention and bystanders of their individual and communal rights to freedom from brutal and arbitrary policing. The community patrols—and the cathartic pushback against police violence—attracted Oakland and other Bay Area youth to the party by the hundreds. An explicit linkage between policing and sovereignty as a solution to the problem of police violence and dispossession was forged by the April 1967 killing of Denzil Dowell, a Black teen in neighboring Richmond who not only was shot and killed by the police, but whose body was left unattended for his family to find hours later.[176]

Following Dowell's death, the Panthers were invited to join the family and community in pressuring the city to investigate the killing. Not surprisingly, local government deemed Dowell's killing a "justifiable homicide." This finding only galvanized attraction to the Panthers, who stood as forthright challengers to the political and social marginalization experienced by Black residents of Richmond. The party gained three hundred more supporters, while Dowell's brother became the leader of the Richmond chapter. The Panthers led a campaign that zeroed in on two solutions to tackling Richmond's problems: self-defense and sovereignty. In their April 1967 newspaper account of the killing, the Panthers argued that "we can end police brutality in our black community by organizing black self-defense groups that are dedicated to defending our black community from racist police oppression and brutality."[177] By June 1967, the Panthers would have progressed to the argument that only sovereignty, that is, independence for North Richmond, would solve the problem of "brutal cops" by giving the neighborhood control over their own police force and the broader power to change the "inhuman conditions that the white power structure force[d] black people in North Richmond to live under."[178]

The Panthers' coupling of the right to communal self-defense and sovereignty would largely lie unrealized as the conflict between the party and the state escalated. The Mulholland Act, which prohibited public carrying of loaded firearms, was introduced in the state assembly in April 1967 by a conservative Alameda County Republican member as a way to stop the Panthers' community defense patrols. The Panthers' occupation of the state capitol in Sacramento in May 1967 raised the level of escalation even higher, encouraging groups like the NRA that had previously been against gun control to support the legislation. The conflict between the police and the party—at least in Oakland—would become even more volatile with the October 1967 altercation between the Panthers and the

OPD, which led to Newton killing OPD officer John Frey. The possibilities for armed communal defense as a form of police abolition almost completely evaporated as the police targeted the party and its supporters in Oakland and across the United States.

From late 1967 to early 1968 there was an unprecedented level of state harassment and repression via arrests, detainments, beatings, and killings of Black Panther members and other radical groups, whether they were allies or rivals. The assassination of Martin Luther King Jr. on April 4, 1968, would bring local tensions to a head and result in a confrontation between the party and the police two days later that ended with a shootout in which Eldridge Cleaver was injured and Robert "Lil Bobby" Hutton was killed as they surrendered to the police. By this time the first iteration of the Panthers was in disarray with its most visible leaders—Newton, Seale, and Eldridge and Kathleen Cleaver—imprisoned or in exile. DeFremery Park in West Oakland, which was both an ongoing site of Black Panther organizing and a longtime node of Black Oakland "congregational" life, would be informally renamed in Hutton's honor. From 1968 onward, any overt physical resistance to Oakland's police state would be crushed. As a result, attempts to at least tame this policing regime could only come through the reformist approaches of Black Power Urbanism.

In Oakland, the Panthers' radical linkage of community control of the police and community sovereignty would get its first reformist articulation under the OEDC (itself an organizational legacy of the earlier Gray Areas initiative), which was by then city controlled. It should be noted that its new initiatives overlapped with Panther organizing around the death of Dowell and the growing friction between the OPD and the Panthers. The OEDC's proposal for a police affairs committee funded from private Ford Foundation grants as opposed to local or federal government funds elicited a near-hysterical response from the city (the mayor, the city manager, and the city council), the OPD, and ultimately state and federal legislators. Not surprisingly the city's police chief forcefully denounced the proposal, stating that the application "implied that the police need more respect for citizens." Instead, in his view, what was needed was "respect for the law and less safeguards were needed if police were to become more effective."[179] The OEDC leadership responded that the "city was in trouble if the police department did not understand the difference between enforcement of the law and the administration of justice."[180]

In a meeting to discuss the proposal, the city manager, newly hired and publicly hostile to the growing Black militancy (and who had replaced the more conciliatory Gray Areas–aligned official that had preceded him), "changed the subject of discussion to Parks and Recreation." The white-controlled city council followed up this exchange with its own forceful public rejection of the proposed police affairs committee and of the temerity of the OEDC in asserting a degree of independence, including a directive to the city manager not to disburse any of the Ford Foundation funding to the OEDC. The OEDC's subsequent struggle to gain control over the funding that had already been granted to it, albeit via city accounts, spiraled into a larger battle over community control, not just over police accountability but also the larger question of community sovereignty. In July 1967 the OEDC announced that it would "break away from the control of City Hall" and become a private nonprofit, thus making itself eligible to directly receive not only the Ford Foundation funding but also other War on Poverty funds. As its leadership stated, the OEDC (or any other organization) had to go beyond simply "providing service" to "permanently alter[ing] the relationship to the advantage of the Black community."[181]

While the OEDC would become a newly independent organization, it also dropped the idea of police reform and turned its attention toward trying gain control over the War on Poverty funding that federal policymakers were diverting to Oakland so it could serve as a showcase for "riot prevention." Indeed, direct attempts to reform the OPD—and the nature of "urban policing" in general—languished as police violence and repression toward the Panthers and their allies escalated in Oakland and nationwide. The establishment of the Law Enforcement Assistance Administration (LEAA) in 1968 would begin to constrain the paths that both radical and reformist approaches to policing could take, with the LEAA supplying funding and other kinds of organizational resources to suppress Panther activities. Ultimately the LEAA would cement order maintenance policing as the dominant mode, foreclosing the possible alternatives of community control and community policing.

Though the OEDC/WOP was forced to drop their proposal for a police review board from their immediate agenda, the issues of police reform and community control did not disappear. In addition to their ongoing attacks on the Panthers, the Oakland police continued their disturbing pattern of killing the city's Black and Brown citizens. While individuals and groups pushed for ongoing reform, each new killing would mobilize new networks of support. This was evident with the 1968 police killing of Charles "Pinky" Dominic De Baca, a Chicano (Mexican American).[182] This would serve as one of the focal points for Latino organizing, with several groups including Oakland Latinos for Justice, the Brown Berets, and the Chicano Revolutionary Party coalescing around the issue of police brutality and citizen education in the aftermath of De Baca's death. Oakland Latinos for Justice was initially one of the most visible of the groups pressing the mayor's office to charge the police officer with murder and to fire him. Again, not surprisingly, the officer was acquitted, but the radicalization of the city's Latino population had significantly accelerated.[183]

By 1968, the radicalization created by worsening behavior of the OPD had spread to the schools in conjunction with the community's attempts to wrest control of majority-Black and -Brown schools from the white, elite-controlled Oakland Unified School District (OUSD). Clashes between white and Black students and Black students and white teachers and staff became more common as the district's demographics rapidly shifted even as school governance continued to reflect the district's earlier stance that Black and Brown students were bodies to either be marginalized or pushed out of the district. At Fremont High School, located in the same area where De Baca was killed, "black militant students . . . demanded the ouster of certain white staffers, the formation of a Black student union, the hiring of Black teachers, and the inclusion of Black history in the school curriculum. The students clashed with police after an assembly with the principal to discuss their demands. As Fremont planned to reopen, Black students complained about the police presence at the school, claiming officers had called them 'n[------]' and 'had been rough with them.' . . . At a public meeting, officers said that Black students had 'harassed' them. A white mother added that she would be reluctant to send her child back to school without police protection."[184]

During the same year, in protest of "Lil Bobby" Hutton's death but also in response to continued OPD brutality, a loose coalition of individuals called for a "Black Strike for Justice," a boycott targeting the Housewives' Market, a mall-like enclave of low-cost stores and grocers whose clientele ranged from 70 to 90 percent Black. The organizers included two Black women, Sister Dolores Davis and Norma McClure, Panther members like Gayle Dickson and political activists like Paul Cobb, the WOPC, and other groups.[185] In addition to calling for the "indictment of the police" for Hutton's murder, the group issued "eleven demands for police reform and a variety of neighborhood-level checks in police authority," including "an end to police harassment and brutality, the decentralization of the Oakland Police Department, and community control of policy and administration."[186] While the strike elicited mixed support from within the Black community, it did provide a visible symbol of resistance and continued evidence of OPD's surveillance and harassment of Black activists. For example, in June Davis and McClure were pulled over by the police and arrested; they were "handcuffed, searched, hit, held in solitary confinement, and then booked for resisting arrest."[187] Their arrest would be publicized in local papers like the *Berkeley Barb* under the headline, "How 12 Cars of Fuzz Busted Two Black Oakland Housewives."[188]

The Oakland political establishment, and especially William Knowland, the conservative newspaper publisher, grew increasingly incensed at the actions of what Knowland called "Negro militants," engaged in "extortion." Another supportive *Tribune* article quoted several white store owners who expressed disbelief that police brutality was an issue as none of their predominantly Black clientele had mentioned it. Regardless of whether anyone mentioned the police brutality, one store owner said, "We can't be party to indicting Oakland policemen."[189] One of Knowland's editorials asked the (white) reader to "realize that this is an attempt to use threats and brute force to demand compliance with the views of an articulate and aggressive minority. This was a process used by both the Nazis and the Communists in destroying free institutions abroad."[190] It then urged the "average citizen" to patronize the boycotted market, stating, "This is where we stand. . . . Where do you stand?" The *Tribune* later published an ad listing "Citizens Pledged Against Coercion."[191]

Knowland's publication of a full-page ad served as a lasting symbol of his antipathy. The ad showed a white-gloved handing holding a gun and asked the reader to "think it over carefully . . . because sometime soon you may have to decide whether you want to run a business with a gun to your head or close up shop." The ad was roundly condemned, several newspaper staffers resigned including a recent Black hire, and Knowland "backed off a bit and said that no more counter boycott ads would be run."[192] The strike itself would peter out as well, although it revealed that the division between Black and white Oakland at the end of 1968 had become nearly unbridgeable, with policing being one of the central sources of mutual antipathy. For the Panthers, the strike and the ad provided an important way to signal that though the top leadership was in disarray, the party continued to mobilize at the local level. Indeed, the strike and Knowland's advertisement were prominently displayed on the second page of the Panther newspaper in 1971 as a way to justify the party's targeting of Black businesses who were reluctant to increase what they argued was coerced monetary support for the Panthers.[193]

The issue of policing, especially in the wake of continual police killings, remained a source of mobilization; however, it shared the agenda with the myriad other experiences of violence that Black Oakland resisted, from the ongoing displacement from the aftershocks of urban renewal to the severe weakening of several high-profile organizations like the OEDC and the WOPC after Nixon and Reagan targeted them for defunding. Squabbling among the Black political leadership and the ongoing disarray within the Panthers meant that policy areas were siloed, reflecting the fragmentation of Black Oakland's political structure. Not surprisingly, the OPD's long history of hostility to minorities; its insularity, which was typical of many police departments as the time; and the rise of "law and order" politics made reforming the OPD an even harder task for activists.

This insulation from accountability and tone-deafness extended to the schools and the OSPD. Even as Marcus Foster, the system's first Black superintendent, had attempted to impose more accountability and a sense of community control on the public school district, he faced increasing levels of demands from within the system. As in many "urban" school districts, parent and student fear over rising levels of violence as well as troubling levels of truancy and rising numbers of drop-outs among student of color signaled a brewing crisis. As Foster stated in despair, just as Black school administrators had finally wrested control of these institutions, they were facing a huge number of serious issues. One response to this growing fear of in-school violence and disruption was a 1973 proposal to control access to the schools. The Panthers and other radical groups saw this proposal for student identification cards as the carceral system's entering wedge. They were not incorrect, as in 1974 Congress would enact the Juvenile Justice and Delinquency Prevention Act. In the meantime, the proposal to "secure" the city's public schools would be paid for by a "$1.5 million grant from the California Council on Criminal Justice to implement the Coordinated Interagency Action Program for the Reduction of Truancy, Vandalism, and Violence in Select Urban Schools—an effort the Panthers referred to as the 'CIA.'"[194] The Symbionese Liberation Army used Foster's attempt to balance a "reformist path between the police and the Panthers" as a pretext for his assassination. As recent activist Manuel Criollo argues, the assassination "killed any momentum to stop policing in schools."[195] Indeed, in Elizabeth Hinton's words, "even as federal delinquency programs and the growing school security industry created an environment where urban schools were increasingly guarded like prisons, schools nationwide were safer in the 1970s than they were in the 1960s."[196]

The Black Panthers turned to electoral politics in 1972 and with the Seale/Brown campaign in 1973 returned police reform to visibility. In search of a broad-based electoral coalition—including both the poor and working-class Black residents of West and East Oakland and the more skeptical Black middle class, as well as the city's Latino, Asian, and progressive white residents—Seale and his campaign partner Elaine Brown put forward a moderate (for the Panthers) platform that focused on raising revenues from corporations and large landowners to fund an array of social programs such as preventative health care. But Seale also called for the development of a "senior citizen's safety program," stating that "33 percent of the crimes that are committed are committed against senior citizens in the community." Indeed, as Kenneth Gibson would later disclose, Seale's "own mother was mugged like a lot of our mothers and fathers have been mugged and robbed." However, Seale did not rely on the OPD for the solution; in fact, he promised that under his administration he would not "give the police department one more penny in the City of Oakland. They have helicopters flying around up in the sky that cost half a million dollars or more, while the senior citizens are getting mugged on the ground."[197] The solution Seale offered was community control and community repair, a safety program and jobs program for the people that would "employ 6,700 other brothers and sisters of the community to escort senior citizens, providing the radio-dispatched first aid, and what have you. That's a lot of jobs that people would have in the community."[198] The problem with crime was not the unemployed people who start "robbing and thieving . . . against their own people." Rather it was the result of the "real criminals . . . the corrupt officials infesting this system across the country." In a later speech, Seale would elaborate on the program:

> We found out that thirty-three percent of all the crimes committed in the city were against senior citizens. Wow, man, get back! So we went over to the YMCA and got a van from a brother I knew, a twelve passenger van. And then we went to Synanon and got two twelve passenger vans there, then we went to the BPP's People's Free Health Clinic and got two more vans there. And we polished those vans up and cleaned them and got us some brothers and sisters, the ones who knew karate and this kind of stuff, and we dressed them up in ties and everything and went on down to the senior citizen satellite home. We had leafletted the day before and told them that they could get personal transport and escort services. And this was on the day they cashed their social security checks at the banks. And we would have vans leaving every half hour on the half hour from the time the mailman brought their checks in the morning to three o'clock that afternoon. And I had a press conference and called on all the muggers and said that they'd better cease their wanton mugging of our senior citizens, whether they're black, white, yellow or polka dot. You'd better stop it right now because we're gonna escort these senior citizens right up to the bank window. And then take them to buy their groceries.
>
> What I'm trying to point out is that here you have a city government, abusing the people's tax money to buy more needless helicopters, and more armored equipment to "cut down on crime." When what we need is a two million dollar program, from the city budget, to get a couple hundred vans together, and to train young brothers and sisters in karate and first aid. And we want to teach them about the senior citizens, without whom we wouldn't have been here in the first place. We want to employ people to transport senior citizens, and we predicted this would stop the crimes committed against them.[199]

The Panthers' senior citizen safety program took up the multiple elements of Black Power Urbanism by creating an alternative formation of what constituted public safety and for whom. In this case safety was not found in the sky with expensive helicopters or an expansive police arsenal, but rather it was derived from the multiracial senior citizen's group that had contacted the party for assistance, and from the city's youth who would protect the community elders.

The Seale-Brown platform went even further in the direction of addressing police reform and the local, "community survival" turn taken by the party. The party's 1968 "Petition Statement for Community Control of the Police" anticipated this local turn. It called for "establishing police departments for the major communities of any city; the Black community, the predominantly white area, the Mexican American Communities, etc., etc."[200] The Black Panthers proposed a new geography of community safety for Oakland: a radical decentralization plan, in which each community police district would be administered by a full-time police commissioner, "selected by a Neighborhood Police Control Council composed of fifteen members from that community" (see figure 5.7). The council would have the power to discipline police officers, make district-wide policy changes, and most importantly recall council members who were unresponsive to the people. And finally, the plan insisted that "all police officers must live in that department they work in, and they will be hired accordingly."[201]

Seale's campaign platform touched upon some of the elements that were in the 1968 petition including a demand that Oakland's police officers be bound by residency rules. This was a response to an earlier repeal of civil service residency requirements, including cops and firefighters, by city voters. Contesting this move was critical on both fiscal and communal self-defense grounds. The Seale-Brown campaign claimed that "[70 percent] of Oakland's police and firemen live outside the city, so the bulk of their salaries—totaling around $15 million—is spent to the benefit of other cities." Residency rules, which were increasingly being proposed by majority-minority communities across the United States, would in the case of Oakland add about "$1 million annually to [the city's] budget" while forcing the police department to hire more Black, Brown, and Asian officers as white officers would presumably not move into Oakland. The lack of diversity within the OPD had been the subject of litigation since the mid-1960s and by 1977 the force was still only a quarter non-white. The proposed residency requirements had the effect of further radicalizing the majority-white police force. The police union sponsored a series of raucous protests with family members and supporters decrying these proposals. In 1974, city voters and state legislators swung their support to the police by banning residency requirements.[202]

The infighting within the Black Panthers inhibited their ability to mount a coordinated and effective campaign for police reform. This infighting was clearly

EXAMPLE ONLY
FOR OTHER CITIES IN America.

Petition # ___9000___

OAKLAND

all N.C.C.F. Members, Study throughly for

Petition for Community Control of Police

decentralization of police for Oakland & Elsewhere.

SUMMARY OF OAKLAND POLICE CONTROL AMENDMENT

This amendment to the City charter would give control of the police
to community elected neighborhood councils so that those whom the police
should serve will be able to set police policy and standards of conduct.
    The amendment provides for community control of the police by estab-
lishing separate police departments for the two major communities of Oakland:
the Black community and the predominantly white area. The departments
would be separate and autonomous. They can by mutual agreement use
common facilities. Each Department will be administered by full time
police commissions. The Commissioners are selected by a Neighborhood
Police Control Council composed of fifteen members from that community
elected by those who live there. Each department shall have five Community
Council divisions within it.
    The Councils shall have the power to discipline officers for breaches
of Department policy or violations of law. They may direct their police
Commissioner to make changes in department wide police policy by majority
vote of the five department commissioners. The Council can recall the
Commissioner appointed by it at any time it finds that he is no longer
responsive to the community. The community can recall the council members
when they are not responsive to it.
    All police officers must live in the department they work in.

MAP OF PROPOSED OAKLAND POLICE DEPARTMENTS

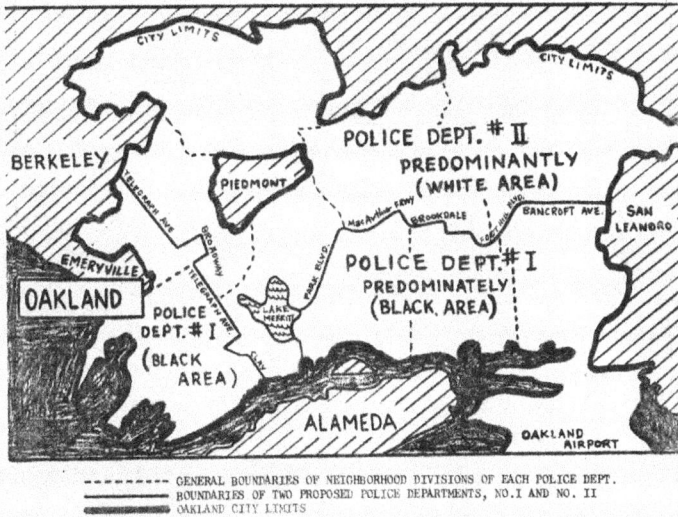

FIGURE 5.7. Community control of the police: Black Panther Party map of
Oakland

Source: Courtesy of Swann Auction Galleries.

demonstrated by the party's complicated role in the response to the shooting in
November 1973 of Tyrone Guyton, a fourteen-year-old Black youth, this time in
Emeryville, a breakaway fragment of greater Oakland.[203] The circumstances of

the shooting were sharply disputed: the police claimed that Guyton had fired a gun at pursuing officers, while crime lab tests indicated that Guyton had not discharged a gun. The grand jury convened by the Alameda County district attorney refused to indict the police. Superior Court judge Lionel Wilson immediately criticized the result, calling for the county DA to prosecute the officers via an alternative mechanism.

Once the DA rejected this call, Wilson, along with a broad mix of community leaders and groups, including the Black Panthers, began the first of a series of protest rallies and other activities to force the city as well as the US Justice Department to bring charges against the officers. The protests attracted a broad cross section of supporters. These included the Panthers, who led the creation of the Committee for Justice for Tyrone Guyton in concert with Guyton's family. Along with the Socialist Workers Party (SWP), the Panthers argued for a "moderate, single-issue" approach focused on holding the police officers accountable; they viewed the case as a way to remain a viable player in the city's next elections. The committee also attracted the support of "Black and multi-national community organizations" who saw the Guyton case a vehicle for a "broader anti-repression campaign." Keeping this fractious coalition together was Guyton's mother, Mattie Guyton Shepard. Shepard, who had never before been involved in politics, became a "forceful and moving speaker" who used her son's death to create "justice for all the future Tyrone Guytons of all races who should be able to live without fear of being gunned down by the police."[204]

Despite the increasingly bitter infighting, the committee sponsored a rally attended by 2,500 people, the city's biggest demonstration since "the Free Huey rallies in 1967 and 1968."[205] Despite this large turnout, the continued internal battles and ultimately their disconnection from the ordinary people that they purported to represent meant that the participating groups relegated Mattie Guyton Shepard's speech to the end of the rally after most of the attendees had left. While a new indictment new was issued, Guyton Shepard pursued a $2 million civil suit for wrongful death against Emeryville.[206] The case would eventually be decided in 1981 with the judge finding that the officers had "acted with callous disregard" and that the "conduct of the officers . . . was excessive, unreasonable and unjustified." Guyton Shepard would be awarded $200,000.

The period between Seale's 1973 mayoral loss and the election in 1977 of Lionel Wilson, the city's first Black mayor, saw continued killings of Black and Brown citizens by the police while the OPD engaged in a symbolic performance of police reform. The juxtaposition of actual death and symbolic reform reflected political fallout from the near collapse of the Black Panthers and the political conflict among the different political factions of Black Oakland as a result of Seale's campaign and his subsequent loss to incumbent mayor John Reading. Meanwhile the OPD, under the leadership of a new (white) police chief, embarked on a superficial course of police reform. In the aftermath of Seale's loss and the Guyton case, the OPD—with LEAA funding and partially facilitated by the national Police Foundation—engaged in a series of public relations exercises, including the production of news reports and documentaries touting the department's new "community friendly" façade.[207] One documentary argued that as "changes were implemented, blacks were hired, and blacks in the community were beginning to feel a change as older policemen were told to be less aggressive or be fired"; while another film showed the "challenges [the police] face on a daily basis and how they are trained to deal with them."[208] The reality was that the pace of this change in policing was glacial. Only 26 percent of the OPD were minority group members when Wilson was elected, and less than 10 percent of the force lived in the city.[209] Indeed, in the face of Foster's assassination and amid the mismanagement and rising crime rates of the OHA-run housing projects, the policing apparatus of the city would continue to expand with the addition of the Oakland Housing Authority Police Department in 1974.[210]

Wilson, who acknowledged the critical role of the Panthers' ongoing activism in securing his election, centered his campaign on issues of police brutality. The fragmented and insular nature of the city's political and administrative structure, and especially of the OPD, meant that it would take an extraordinary level of violence by the OPD for any structural reform to take pace. In 1979, over the course of ten months, the OPD would kill nine people, including fifteen-year-old Melvin Black.[211] At that point, Wilson finally had the political support needed to overcome the system's resistance and push through the creation of a civilian review board.[212] The OPD and the "notoriously reactionary and racist" Oakland Police Officer's Association virulently opposed the move. In response to Wilson's proposal, "450 Oakland officers, black and white, some with families" marched in protest.[213] At the same time that Wilson was pushing for the review board, he was also attempting to assert more control over the OPD. To do so he proposed a change in the department promotions process that would move more Black officers into higher-ranked roles. In addition, Wilson argued for a strong mayoralty to replace Oakland's council/city manager structure. OPD members again rallied at City Hall, "protesting . . . political interference in the department." This rally was buttressed by threats of a strike from the OPD membership. Wilson was able to get approval for the review board, although the council "split along racial lines" and rejected Wilson's other proposals.[214]

The struggle to control the OPD did not end with Wilson's election and the establishment of the review board. Within a few years the board would come under criticism as largely weak and ineffective.[215] Police brutality and deaths by police continued as both the state and federal government's War on Drugs shifted more resources to the OPD and less to the last vestiges of community policing. The spread of the drug market in Oakland—first with heroin and then with crack—led to increasingly high levels of violence that ever escalating police violence did little to quell. The 1985 death of Felix "the Cat" Wayne Mitchell Jr., whose drug organization was centered on Oakland's housing projects, only increased the level of violence. In 1993, the city's first Black police chief was appointed and in 1996, the civilian review board was reformed once again. Neither of these measures seriously challenged the entrenched organizational ethos of the OPD and its smaller siblings the OUSD and the Oakland Housing Authority Police Department.

Indeed, in the first decade of the twenty-first century the OPD became notorious for its deep levels of corruption and brutality. Yet despite the disappearance of the Panthers, their legacy lived on as the city's different communities—Black, Latino, Asian, and white progressives—continued to mobilize and protest against the OPD, the OUSD, and other policing entities, and to press for deep structural changes. The victory achieved by the elimination of the OUSD was clouded by the very deep structural resistance of the department to meaningful and durable reform. After the OPD underwent another round of reform under a new police chief, it was lauded in the press as an example of "how a dirty police force gets clean." Within two years, another article argued that in the aftermath of George Floyd and in the midst of rising rates of violent crime, "[a] powerful case [could be made] for why police reform doesn't work."[216] Both the decimated Black Panthers and the former "man of tomorrow" Mayor Lionel Wilson would agree.

Winning the Ghetto but Losing the War?

The postwar period proved to be a critical turning point for Oakland. Given the quickening pace of white out-migration and industrial relocation, white elites put forward a series of sweeping urban renewal/"Negro removal" plans. While the city's first round of plans asserted Oakland's pretension to regional dominance, later plans reflected desperate efforts to save downtown from obsolescence and creeping abandonment. Yet the more urban renewal plans were implemented, the more shattered Oakland's urban landscape became, setting off another cycle of commercial and residential decline, vacancy and abandonment, and dispossession. Urban renewal as "Negro removal" came to an end by the early 1970s as Black community activists began to successfully push back against white civic leaders and due to the grim reality that there was hardly any "there there" in historic Black Oakland. Demographic transformation also played a role given the generational decline of the Knowland-led leadership coupled with decades of white flight. Black activist–supported African Americans increasingly filled key posts in the city's unelected governing institutions like the school district, the ORA, and the Port of Oakland. In 1977, the white urban regime led by Mayor John Reading came to a formal end with the election of Lionel Wilson, although Bobby Seale's mayoral run was a clear signal of its fragility.

The BPP's mobilization of poor and working-class Black and Brown Oaklanders was built not just upon revolutionary rhetoric, but upon a recognition of the "quotidian politics of daily life."[217] These interactions with "the landlord, the storeowner, the social worker and the police" were low-level manifestations of the systems of structural dispossession and predatory inclusion that shaped the daily life of many Black Oaklanders. Black Power Urbanism produced an overarching alternative narrative that offered the potential to enact radically new possibilities. For Seale, Elaine Brown, and the other members of the Black Panther Party, Black Power Urbanism was understood as an ongoing struggle of "organizing and unifying the people around their basic desires and needs." By 1972 it was clear that Oakland's white political structure had successfully delayed, co-opted or, with the support of federal security agencies, viciously suppressed the "basic needs and desires" of poor Black Oaklanders. Ambitious but failed attempts to work within the system via federal Great Society programs and the violent suppression of the Black Panther Party had led to a new understanding among more moderate Blacks, and perhaps accommodation on the part of the BPP, that the people would have to "control those institutions that control their very lives." The 1973 mayoral campaign was a frontal assault on the belief that the people "ain't got their minds together yet."[218]

Although Seale did not win the election, the deep grassroots organizing conducted by the BPP can be credited with laying the electoral foundation for Lionel Wilson's mayoral campaign, which was managed by Elaine Brown. Though heralded as a Black "first," Wilson's 1977 election as the city's first Black mayor was bittersweet. It reflected both the promise and the limitations of Black Power Urbanism in Oakland. A former member of the Men of Tomorrow, Wilson had gotten his political start organizing against (but also negotiating with) the city's urban renewal plans in the 1960s. Yet at his core, Wilson represented the Black middle class rather than the Black working class and poor who increasingly were mobilized by and for not just the Black Panthers, but also a vision of Oakland as a city that embraced rather erased their presence.

By 1978, the BPP was almost defunct as a mass organization, while the first stages of neoliberalism and the latest iteration of the state's long-standing tradition of racial propositions was taking form in the passage of Proposition 13, a statewide cap on property taxes. The last vestiges of urban Keynesianism, which could have supported the programmatic aims of Black Power Urbanism, would abruptly disappear due to the induced conditions of austerity triggered by Proposition 13, and subsequently the Reagan administration's dismantling of federal urban programs. Though the Wilson administration and subsequent Black and white urban regimes would attempt to revive them, by the first decades of the twenty-first century the hopes and aspirations of Black Power Oakland seemed like a distant world.

Wilson faced a city whose urban fabric had been deeply damaged in order to save it, just as had happened in Black Newark. And as in Newark, Oakland's new Black leadership faced the classic problem of Black urban regimes of the 1970s: how could both the downtown and the people be saved? Unlike the case of Newark, demographics would come to work against the consolidation of a Black urban regime in Oakland. The city's African American population peaked in 1980 at 46 percent of the population. By 1980, Oakland had become a transportation node for the Bay Area, but rather than saving the city and giving it a clear identity, highways made it easier to bypass Oakland for employment and shopping opportunities in San Francisco. Urban renewal and highways had recreated Oakland's problem of "no there-ness." Nevertheless, as city officials would carefully comment in the 1980s and '90s, Oakland had an "image problem": it had become a Black city in a mostly white metropolis. Neoliberalism became the next attempt to revive what many saw as the hollow hope of Black Power Urbanism and Black cityhood. The election of former governor Pat Brown put a decisive end to the prospect of a Black urban regime focused on justice, equity, and the right to stay, and instead encouraged Black and Brown Oaklanders to leave. By 2020, Moms 4 Housing and the Black Lives Matter movement would begin a wave of activism that sought to reclaim a place for Black Oakland in the twenty-first century.

EAST PALO ALTO
Building a Nairobi

> **The birth of this City is a labor of love,**
> **It was formed in the womb of our pride**
> **as we learned our work together.**
>
> —"East Palo Alto, Incorporated—July 1, 1983," *The East Palo Alto Progress*,
> July–August 1983

In 2019, Sand Hill Property Company announced the purchase of East Palo Alto's Four Corners site for $42 million. The empty six-acre site situated at the center of the small community was no ordinary place: it was the location of the Nairobi Shopping Center. Reflecting the Black Power Urbanism sweeping through Oakland, Newark, East Orange, and many Black spaces across the United States, the small suburban shopping strip had been renovated and rebranded in 1970 with high hopes (see figure 6.1). The Nairobi Shopping Center was an attempt by East Palo Alto's majority-Black community to instantiate a distinctive and vibrant Black sense of place for the community. The phrase "Uhuru Na Umoja" ("freedom and unity" in Swahili) was used to describe this attempt at community that was built behind a segregated "concrete curtain" of highways, disinvestment, and exclusion.[1] For a few years after its opening, the center acted as a hub for Black East Palo Alto, offering spaces for small retailers and restaurants, a new cooperative grocery store (for a community that was by then a "food desert"), cultural groups, nonprofits, and local government satellite offices including the community's first permanent branch of the county library. Nairobi—as a collection of buildings, and as an idea—was a visible testament to the ability of local Black activists and politicians to achieve a new East Palo Alto (EPA) controlled by and for Black residents.

Despite the hopes it engendered, Nairobi would enter into a state of decline within a few years of its opening due to the frailty of both the Nixonian Black capitalism and the suburban interracialism upon which the center was founded,

Robert Hoover, founder and director of Nairobi College (above l.), talks about future plans with Don Smothers, who is president of the college, in front of the school's administrative offices located in an East Palo Alto shopping center. At right, Robert Clemons teaches a math class and later gives individual instruction to a student. College has 300 students and seven instructors.

FIGURE 6.1. "Uhuru Na Umoja": Nairobi shopping center

Source: Palo Alto Historical Society.

as well as the first wave of austerity budgets that led to the slow demise of the community groups and nonprofits that had emerged out of federal Great Society and Model Cities funding. Nairobi Center's closure coincided with the state's expansive War on Drugs: it was identified as a hot spot whose demolition would clear the neighborhood of drug dealers and their largely out-of-town buyers. Given the logic of punitive clearance and banishment common to the War on Drugs, instead of rebuilding the shopping center as a means to restore community peace and safety, it was bulldozed by the city in 1987. The site lay empty, passing through multiple owners until Sand Hill made its 2019 purchase.[2]

Though the site remained vacant, the project of "Nairobi"—embodied or not—remained vibrant in the spatial imaginary of Black East Palo Alto.[3] The question of what should happen in this space and who should control its destiny was a subject of contentious political debate as well as more sedate city planning documents. The unfolding of decades of discussion, fears, and theorizations about gentrification and displacement would be reflected in Sand Hill's proposed master plan for the property. In its proposal for a "vibrant, mixed-use downtown," Sand Hill agreed to abide by five core principles: (1) "Respect what came before us," (2) "Create a vibrant, mixed-use 'Main Street,'" (3) "Create places to live and gather," (4) "Improve mobility and access," and (5) "Create jobs and local revenue." How well Sand Hill would adhere to these core principles over the course of the next few years is perhaps a moot point.

Following the 2008 Great Recession, Sand Hill emerged as owner of the city's largest stock of relatively affordable apartment buildings and the company signaled its intent to "upgrade" the units for rental to the city's growing numbers of young tech workers. Many of these workers were employed by the tech company then known as Facebook, located on the city's northern boundary (see figure 6.2).

The tech boom spurred a massive wave of gentrification and displacement of the city's working-class residents, especially those who were Black, Latino, or Pacific Islander. The city's school district reported that between 2000 and 2025 its enrollment had declined by 76 percent.[4] East Palo Alto was no longer a community of families, rather it was community that catered to the well-educated and well-connected (and childless) workers of Silicon Valley. For these new residents, the evocation of "Nairobi" and the Black freedom struggle allowed for what the geographer Brandi Summers has called the aesthetics of Blackness, which would

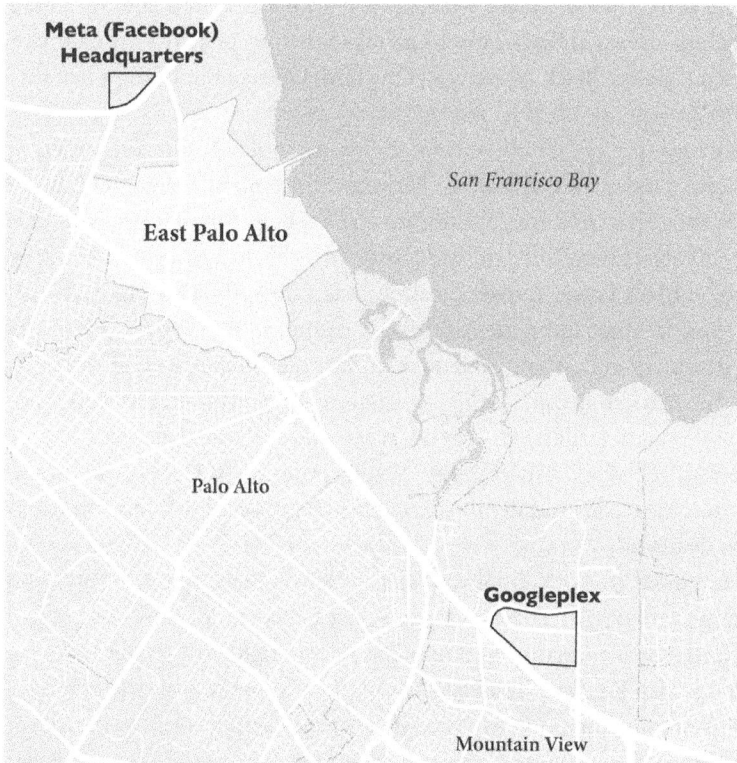

FIGURE 6.2.   East Palo Alto and the landscape of technology

Source: "East Palo Alto—in Between Facebook and Google," cartography by Jake Coolidge, basemap data © OpenStreetMap Contributors, 2012.

grant the new East Palo Alto of Sand Hill and Facebook an imprimatur of progressivism, authenticity, and "cool" necessary to create a "vibrant, mixed-use community" backed by a billion-dollar budget.[5]

Nairobi Shopping Center was one of the most visible symbols of a 1968 campaign led by Black youth to change East Palo Alto's name to Nairobi.[6] For these young people, a decade's worth of failed or limited success against discrimination and segregation would result in an assertion of independence, leading them to proclaim that "no longer will the beautiful Black people of [East Palo Alto] allow the community to be considered a mere suburb of 'honkeyville.'"[7] While the campaign was enthusiastically supported in some parts of this small suburban community, local, national, and international observers looked upon the renaming with some bemusement.[8] East Palo Alto—by then locally identified as a suburban ghetto—seemed an improbable place for a Black Power gesture that would make international waves. Yet the quest to change the name of East Palo Alto to Nairobi reflected not just the unique circumstances of a particular city, but the contested nature of suburban racial formations and the varied and conflicting visions of Black Power Urbanism that swept across the nation's Black spaces during the Black Power era of the mid-1960s to the 1980s, when the Reagan revolution unleashed its war on (Black) cities.

The meaning of Nairobi and its resonance in day-to-day life varied across age, class, gender, and education. For some, the embrace of Nairobi, like Black Power, showed an ambivalence toward and a touch of impatience with the inefficacy of racial liberalism as it stood battered by challenges of the late 1960s. For emergent Black Power activists, Nairobi was a clear signal to whites and also an invitation to other more skeptical Black community members that it was not only necessary but also possible to articulate their identity as "an African people."[9] For Black moderates—the vast majority of the community and especially its middle-class leadership—the idea of "Nairobi" could be used to buttress notions of suburban respectability. Nixon's program of Black capitalism would link these two sides and demonstrate both the possibilities and weaknesses of a new "Nairobi."

The campaign for Nairobi as a self-conscious Black space is not surprising given the varied paths taken by Black Power Urbanism nationwide, but particularly the path taken in the Bay Area's Black communities of greater Oakland, San Francisco, San Jose, and East Palo Alto. East Palo Alto was the site of three Black Power summits from 1967 to 1970. Many of the leading voices in the movement were part of these gatherings, including Stokely Carmichael, Angela Davis, Ron Karenga, and Amiri Baraka. For some Black activists, the idea of "Nairobi" was a fulcrum upon which rested the possibilities of the "Black city" as a force both within their communities and in their interactions with white American politics and society. Local activists and residents began multifaceted efforts to put EPA's Black Power Urbanism into concrete form. In the wake of the renaming campaign, Nairobi became a geographic identity used by local residents and businesses like Nairobi Shopping Center, Nairobi Day School, and Nairobi College.[10] For a brief moment, Nairobi—in the words of one local activist, would be "a show place of the nation for black people."[11]

Black Power Urbanism unfolded in the unique socio-spatial landscape of East Palo Alto and within Silicon Valley's suburban landscape. As in other places, Black Power Urbanism in East Palo rested on three pillars: housing, education, and policing. However, due to EPA's distinctive status as an unstable and contested space, these pillars are expressed in four separate but intertwined areas: (1) the struggle for political autonomy and self-determination, (2) community control over the education of Black children, (3) local control over policing and public safety, and (4) community economic development. EPA's first building block of political self-determination was the formation of the East Palo Alto Municipal Council (EPAMC) in 1965 out of the collision between the uneasy and unstable commitment to racial liberalism/liberal integrationism of the city and county and the emergence of Black Power Urbanism. However, it was the much longer struggle over education for Black children that in many ways shaped East Palo Alto's formative identity as a Black space. Policing and public safety were likewise important issues in EPA, as residents first sought safety from the county police whom residents saw as an "occupying army" and also searched for safety in their homes and streets. The city's limited ability to effectively mount community control of the police and hold them to account would worsen as the city's social-spatial marginalization led East Palo Alto to become an intersection of the peninsula's drug trade by the early 1980s, infamously earning it the title of "murder capital of the nation."[12] The Clinton-era War on Drugs, the massive expansion of California's carceral complex, and the rise in aggressive, militarized policing would lead to the hollowing out of a generation of young Black and Brown residents of EPA, as they were sent into what Ruth Wilson Gilmore calls the "golden gulag" of California.[13]

Given the institutional and fiscal weakness of EPA within California's postwar suburban political economy, local activists—first white, and then Black, grappled for a solution. In the late 1960s and 1970s the quest for political independence briefly coincided with community economic development efforts that spanned both Johnson's Great Society policies and Nixon's Black capitalism and New Federalism initiatives. Nixon's Black capitalism initiatives would bring together Black residents wishing to create the physical embodiment of a new Nairobi with the establishment of Black-owned businesses and the development of Nairobi Shopping Center.

While the Nairobi vote in 1968 signaled an optimism regarding the power of Black space, the political and fiscal crises of the 1970s—from the winding down of intergovernmental aid to the passage of Proposition 13 in 1978 and the Reagan administration's ending of the final vestiges of urban Keynesian—signaled the start of East Palo Alto's transition to a "distressed" or "Black suburb." In 1983, East Palo Alto's long-term struggle to achieve political and cultural independence would finally reach fruition almost twenty years after it was initially proposed. However, independence could not save the city from its even more segregated schools, its crumbling infrastructure and environmental pollution, and its growing problems with crime. Although East Palo Alto took a historic step in voting for incorporation in 1983, it should be noted that history did not end at that point. By 2000, the city had lost well over half of its Black population and sold its small downtown of "Whiskey Gulch" to a developer in a bid to increase its tax revenues. The developer in turn would erect an office building and a luxury hotel that turned its back toward EPA in its focus on serving the now-booming tech industry on the other side of the concrete curtain.

Unstable Foundations

The struggle to make EPA into Nairobi rested on historically unstable and heavily contested socio-spatial ground. EPA was a spatially and environmentally marginalized community. Located on the San Francisco Bay marshlands, it was a space initially inhabited by the indigenous Ohlone peoples. By the late nineteenth and early twentieth centuries, it was a place of agricultural utopian experiments, light industry, small truck farmers, and small Japanese American nursery growers (who would be sent to internment camps in 1941).

Space, race, and class would play a significant role in the shaping of East Palo Alto from the beginning of the postwar era onward, as the area's agricultural property became attractive to residential real estate developers. As in Oakland, the suburban communities of the San Francisco peninsula were shaped by topography. Affluent communities were situated inland, on high ground, while working-class areas were relegated to the marshy shoreland of the bay. The area's attractiveness to development also rested on more recent events: the displacement caused by the socio-spatial engineering induced by the policy of interning Japanese Americans during World War II and of dispossessing Japanese American truck farmers and florists.[14] This "affordable" land—cleared via dispossession, with lowered values due to environmental issues, and secured by redlining and racial covenants—was targeted by real estate developers whose primary market would be the blue-collar whites who fueled the first wave of the state's mass suburbanization. Due to its marginalization, East Palo Alto became a "blue-collar heaven" for the white workers needed for a nascent Silicon Valley and a place for affordable housing for Stanford University students and staff. EPA would grow as the small historic Black communities of Silicon Valley such as Palo Alto and Redwood City were pushed across the highway. Meanwhile these older residents were be joined by new migrants coming directly from Louisiana and Texas, or due to the growing "Negro removal" urban renewal regimes gaining strength in San Francisco and Oakland.

Starting in 1947, developers built the community's first of four new housing developments.[15] Often built on flood-prone lands and with inadequate sewer and roads, this cheap housing became the core of the peninsula's white blue-collar suburb.[16] However, preexisting populations of non-whites—Japanese Americans as well as African Americans—coupled with relatively loose zoning laws and weak local governmental mechanisms, made whites unable to completely block the entry of non-whites into these new developments. Despite their jurisdictional weakness, whites quickly formed homeowners' groups and neighborhood associations like the Palo Alto Gardens Association to enforce their segregated developments. For example, in 1954, when the Baileys, a Black family, moved into an all-white neighborhood, the family was met with violence and death threats, while the leader of the neighborhood group declared that "the people [of the community] were not yet ready for the end of segregation."[17] Efforts to push Black families out these neighborhoods were resisted by an interracial coalition that included the fairly new local chapter of the NAACP and the Fair Play Council, which had been created in 1945 to help Japanese Americans "relocated after the war."[18] In response to the success of this interracial coalition and the quiet "back door purchases" Black buyers were using to access housing, local white real estate agents engaged in blockbusting, triggering a wave of panic selling.[19] It was mainly African Americans who bought these homes and at inflated values. Often Black buyers had no choice but to purchase at an inflated price given the racially divided dual housing market in the United States. Indeed, a 1958 study conducted by the local NAACP chapter found that nineteen out of twenty local realtors conducted business on "racially discriminatory terms."[20]

Despite this discrimination, Black migration continued. For African Americans, East Palo Alto quickly became an attractive place to settle especially given the pervasive and legal housing discrimination in the Bay Area. Access to relatively new and affordable suburban housing stock led to chain migration as friends and families spread the word in the Bay Area and beyond. One source of settlement came from Black autoworkers working in the large General Motors (GM) plant in Fremont who were actively dissuaded from settling near the plant.[21] The last leg of the Great Migration also played a role in this settlement, as migrants from Texas and Louisiana found East Palo Alto's still-semirural atmosphere similar to the places they had left back in the South. A small middle-class Black population linked to Stanford University or emerging local electronics and defense firms, who were unable or unwilling to live in majority-white neighborhoods elsewhere on the peninsula, made up another group of residents. Though some of the town's new Black residents were willingly pulled in by the lure of suburban life (even though constrained by housing discrimination), others may have been reluctant settlers. In one account, it was alleged that staff from San Francisco's powerful redevelopment agency—which had targeted African Americans for removal from the city—"'offered free bus rides' to East Palo Alto and relocation assistance to Black San Franciscans displaced by urban renewal."[22] As the work of Mary Patillo-McCoy and others has documented, like other African American enclaves in the United States' hyper-segregated metropolises, East Palo Alto had a surprisingly high level of class diversity, with poor, working-class, and middle-class African Americans living in close proximity to each other.[23] This class diversity played a role in shaping East Palo Alto's history, as each group had varied conceptions of what kind of place East Palo Alto ought to be, ranging from a segregated suburban space to a defiantly conscious Black Power space.

Bloody Bayshore and the Creation of Racialized Space

While race and class contributed to East Palo Alto's postwar identity, the community's spatialization as a distinctly racialized place was a result of the expansion of Bayshore Highway during the late 1950s. The four-lane highway was initially built in the mid-1920s. It was straddled by a commercial area that abutted each side, which was easily crossed by cars and pedestrians. The commercial area of East Palo Alto closest to Palo Alto was known as "Whiskey Gulch" due to a large concentration of liquor stores, restaurants, and other service establishments. To residents of more affluent areas, East Palo Alto was disreputable and marginal, a "slumming" area for university students and local residents. Although there was some resistance to the highway, the few residents and businesses of East Palo Alto quickly adapted with the development of a more intensive commercial corridor largely defined by auto rather than pedestrian usage. By the late 1950s the imperatives of the interstate highway system would destroy the uneasy accommodation that East Palo Alto had made with the freeway that had largely come to define its western boundary.[24]

As in Oakland and San Francisco to the north and Newark and East Orange to the east, state highway planners, with the cooperation of local county officials, planned for highway construction and improvements directly through what were defined as "blighted" areas. Identification of these locations was key to the construction of highways through any populated area.[25] In 1962, Highway 101 (the Bayshore Freeway) was opened. This modern highway was unlike the previous locally centered freeway that had allowed for interaction through and between East Palo Alto and its neighbors. Instead the new highway decisively separated East Palo Alto (located to the east of the highway) from Palo Alto (located to the west), as the purpose of the highway was to lessen the numerous accidents and fatalities that gave that stretch of road the nickname "bloody Bayshore" while also facilitating passage for commuters between San Francisco and communities on the peninsula.

The construction of Highway 101 meant that the spatial and racial ambiguity of East Palo Alto was removed, which in turn shaped the future of residential and educational integration. One consequence of Highway 101's construction was that it precipitated a further round of white out-migration from a distinctive geographic space that was now more easily seen as separate from the historically more upscale Palo Alto or even middle-class Menlo Park. Three waves of realtor-instigated panic selling or "blockbusting" occurred between 1961 and 1963.

Property values, which had always differed between the three areas Palo Alto, Menlo Park, and East Palo Alto, began a sharp divergence as the concrete barrier of the Bayshore drew into sharp relief the "Black spaces" of Menlo Park and East Palo Alto, leading to their consolidation into an area now known as East Palo Alto. Though some of East Palo Alto's properties had racial covenants attached to them, which restricted buyers from selling to non-whites, East Palo Alto's longer history of marginalization meant that much of its non-Black population was transient, as were the Stanford graduate students and lower-income white residents who occupied its large stock of garden apartments. Redlining meant that these newly Black areas had less access to conventional mortgages. Black East Palo Alto, although it had a higher than average rate of homeownership, also featured a housing stock controlled by absentee landlords rather than through homeownership. The concrete curtain of housing discrimination meant that while whites could leave, Blacks could not.

Increased Black settlement provoked white hostility as some white residents found themselves and their children's schools on the wrong side of a newly visible housing and educational color line. Other whites (especially those that remained) were more welcoming of integration. This welcome was reflective of the postwar suburban interracialism that had emerged in a few pockets of the American

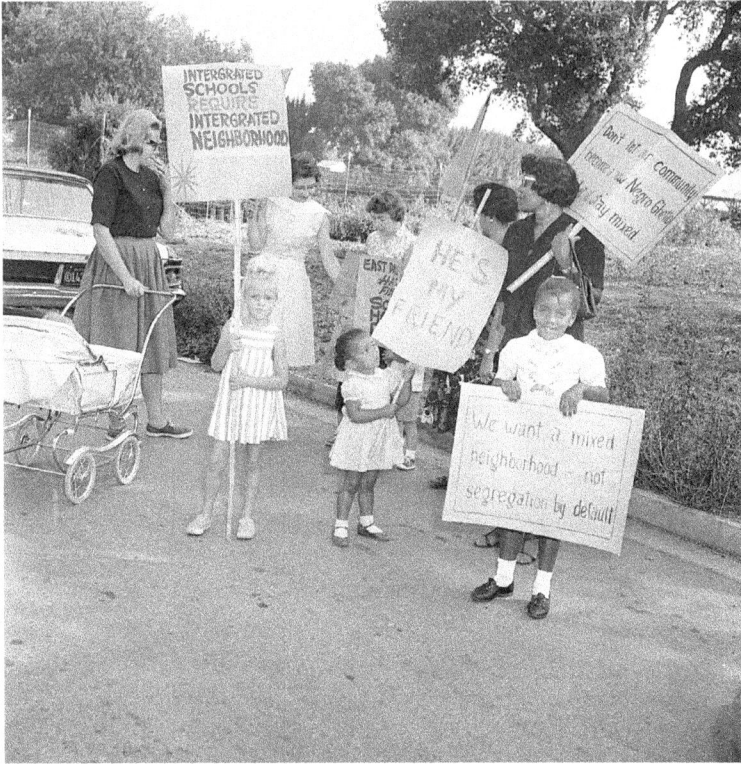

FIGURE 6.3. Before Nairobi: We want integrated neighborhoods, 1963.

Source: "Integration March—East Palo Alto," University of California, Berkeley, Bancroft Library.

metropolis. Locally, much of this suburban interracialism came out of churches and women's clubs located in neighboring Menlo Park, Palo Alto, and other afflu-ent areas. An interracial group of women protested early blockbusting, recognizing that segregation would harm their children's education but also damage their belief in decency and fair play for all children and their families (see figure 6.3).

Education and the Concrete Curtain

Education would ultimately challenge this suburban interracialism. Although East Palo Alto boosters had been pushing for a high school since 1946, as the area's population swelled and as the number of Black students increased, con-cerns arose about where these students would go as the numbers now exceeded the "acceptable" levels of integration that area high schools (and residents) had tolerated.[26] For example, at Atherton High School the Black student population went from "a handful" in 1951 to about 285 in 1955.[27] Like at other putatively "integrated" school systems in the north and west, the toleration for integration dramatically waned as the number of Black students increased beyond a token number.[28] Black residents were acutely aware of this dynamic. In 1952, the South San Mateo County NAACP raised funds to file a suit against the Sequoia District for its de facto segregation policies.[29] After attempts to find other sites for a new high school outside of East Palo Alto failed and as threats from communities to withdraw from the district increased, the board of education was forced to take action. The board would open Ravenswood High in 1958 on the east side of 101, within the boundaries of the now increasingly minority East Palo Alto. Race and class also shaped the decision of where to place a high school in East Palo Alto. The district chose to situate the high school not on a piece of currently undeveloped land (owned by a prominent local white family), but rather on condemned land that included twelve residences and twenty acres formerly owned by Japanese American flower growers.[30]

While the initial attendance boundaries of Ravenswood High indicated that the school population would be majority white, the boundary lines issued by the board post-construction effectively contained all of East Palo Alto's Black students in one school. Not coincidentally, packing Black students into this new school effectively resegregated adjacent schools. Menlo-Atherton's Black student population had dropped to 225 by 1958.[31] The creation of the new Ravenswood High School boundary lines was initially advertised quietly, perhaps indicating that the all-white school board did not want a rancorous public debate about racial integration to take place. However, despite this effort an anonymous letter alerted the local NAACP chapter to these proposed changes. When the NAACP and other East Palo Alto residents questioned district officials about the drawing of the high school's attendance boundaries, the school superintendent and other officials denied that "racial and economic factors" had played a role in determining them. Instead, the board relied on "five well established criteria: distance from homes to schools, estimated school population, minimum bus transportation, the advisability of keeping elementary school populations together, and the avoidance of major traffic arteries within a school district."[32]

A largely Black parents committee was quickly established in response to these moves to entrench formal spatial segregation. The parents committee argued that the proposed changes would lead to a "separation of youth [that] would breed race prejudice, deny students a sufficiently broad social experience, and would hasten the development of a residential ghetto east of Bayshore."[33] The response of the parents committee echoed the continual assertions of many pro-integration parents and activists about the multiple and damaging effects of attendance boundary changes that effectively segregated within school districts.[34]

Both Black parents and the white power structure understood that the creation of Ravenswood High was a case of social-spatial engineering, which would shift East Palo Alto from an area that was still somewhat racially integrated to an effectively segregated community. White families had continued to live in East Palo Alto despite its growing racial diversity because of the area's low-cost housing (which in turn was created by a decrease housing values due to high levels of racial diversity). Under the prior boundaries, their children could attend the high-quality Menlo-Atherton High School. Now that their homes were considered part of the East Palo Alto/Ravenswood High School catchment, their children would not only be educated in a "Black" high school, but also, according to the inexorable logic of the racial marketplace of suburban space, their property values would decline even more, reflecting their location on the Black side of the color line. Indeed, in their protests to the school board, white parents were straightforward in their concerns: "Many people who are financially able to move will leave the Willows area if the proposed boundary change is made. Even property owners who have no youngsters involved in the situation are concerned about their property values in the event the real estate market is flooded with homes for sale in a given area."[35]

While whites felt that they had no choice but to leave East Palo Alto, the durability of redlining, ongoing racial discrimination, and the growing backlash to California's 1963 fair housing law meant that Black residents, especially the poor and working class, were still blocked from leaving East Palo Alto to gain access to better-resourced schools. In addition to the frustration of being unable to move, there was also a growing disenchantment with liberal integrationism—of chasing after school resources rather than obtaining them in their communities. These feelings were a small but growing element of Black parents' reaction to the school board's actions. As Gertrude Wilks would later argue: "We used to follow the whites. . . . They would move out and we would go right after them. They moved and we moved. But we're going to stay here and make something of this place."[36]

In the face of criticism by both Black and white parents, the school board offered a compromise. Students who resided in the Belle Haven section would continue to be able to enroll in Menlo-Atherton High, thus keeping "intact" access to one integrated high school. Meanwhile, because the Belle Haven students were considered an excess burden, white students from the western part of Menlo Park were allowed to shift to the still all-white Woodside High School. Though some in the community accepted this compromise, the NAACP noted that East Palo Alto and its children would be damaged by this decision, arguing that "the token handful of Negro students in a big high school may very well become an unassimilated lump in a sea of white kids." The decision "leaves East Palo Alto school just as it was before, with virtually no white students from upper income families. Whether we gained anything at all is questionable."[37]

Suburban interracialism would first touch upon housing and the turmoil and hostility caused by blockbusting as well as widespread housing discrimination. It would ultimately collapse under demands for integrated education by Blacks and the prerogatives of segregated education by whites. As residential segregation hardened and integration became a moot point, Black Power Urbanism would supplant this suburban interracial coalition as Black Palo Alto began to focus on self-government, education, and community economic development. Like many Black communities in the Northern freedom struggle, the battle over access to quality education would be one of the binding elements in creating Black Palo Alto's identity.

A Government for Nairobi

East Palo Alto's status as an unincorporated area meant that it could not address the multiple issues that faced the community: key markers of suburban life like quality libraries and parks were absent or woefully underfunded relative to the community's needs, while the lack of residents' control over development meant that infrastructure issues such as persistent flooding due to lack of adequate drainage and flood control planning were not dealt with. Compounding this state of affairs was a sense of isolation and neglect by the county government due to the fact that the area was also overlaid by multiple special districts whose unelected leadership controlled vital services like water and sanitation, but who were opaque and unaccountable to residents. Even more alarming was a long-standing history of neighboring cities annexing East Palo Alto's land and ongoing efforts by white residents adjacent to Menlo Park and Palo Alto to have their neighborhoods annexed rather than staying within East Palo Alto. Both of these efforts raised the prospect of EPA losing portions of its property tax revenue and land for future development before it achieved cityhood.

Cityhood was seen by many middle-class residents as the means to solve East Palo Alto's problems, especially in the wake of extraordinary postwar growth. By 1957 an interracial coalition had begun to form around the issue.[38] Emery Curtis, the president of the Menlo Park-East Palo Alto NAACP, spoke for some middle-class Black East Palo Altoans when he said that incorporation would allow for a "larger voice in government" and lead to the "instill[ing] of a greater pride in the community."[39] The perennial issues of East Palo Alto also dominated: fears about racial balance and political influence, concerns over which group (homeowners, renters, landlords, commercial owners) had adequate representation, and fiscal anxiety. On top of these representation and infrastructure issues was the fear that without cityhood and a chance to chart its own course, East Palo Alto would be plagued by "perceptions of unemployment, transiency and crime," thus undoing the "blue-collar heaven" of whites and the "place of their own" of Black residents.[40] This 1957 push for incorporation was widely supported but failed due to the structure of annexation law, which required not only the majority of voters to approve but also the majority of landowners. The largest landowners, including apartment-building owners and industrial firms, believed annexation would pave the way for higher taxes and greater code enforcement.[41] This failed attempt at incorporation reflected East Palo Alto's liminal state: most of it was not valuable enough to be annexed by other cities, but it was also not valuable enough (in terms of tax revenue) to stand on its own.

East Palo Alto's designation as a "suburban ghetto" did not rest on the quality and type of its housing stock.[42] EPA was racialized as a "ghetto" space largely due to its growing Black population and the economic inequality between it and its majority-white neighbors. Although the growth of East Palo Alto's Black population was rapid, it rested on some preexisting foundations. Prior to the growth of the community, the center of South Bay Black life lay in and around San Jose, where a small NAACP chapter existed, as well as churches and lodge associations serving the area's small Black population. The growth of East Palo Alto coupled with the expansion of the Civil Right Movement led to the breaking up of the larger San Jose NAACP chapter so that a new NAACP chapter could be formed for the East Palo Alto/Menlo Park area. This chapter would lead the early battles for integrated housing and education. This foundation of earlier activism and organizational growth led to some symbolic gains. For example, an African American, Dr. Andrew Willis White, had been elected to the school board in 1961.

Despite this election, Black students and parents saw the school district as largely unaccountable and unresponsive to their needs. The struggle for quality integrated education brought new arrivals into local politics, particularly a group of women including Gertrude Wilks and Barbara Mouton, who would help shape East Palo Alto politics over the next four decades. Even as they organized for the future education of East Palo Alto's children, their ongoing battles with the white-controlled and geographically removed school board (both at elementary and high-school level) underscored the lack of control the town's Black residents had over not just education, but also issues like local infrastructure spending, affordable housing, and policing. Given East Palo Alto's rapid emergence as the center of Black life in the peninsula, many of its more middle-class Black residents increasingly saw the political powerlessness of the community as untenable.

By the early 1960s, political activism had led to some Black representation on the elementary school board and to the formation of the "Alto Park Council."[43] This body was purely advisory and by the mid-1960s was still controlled by white residents. The council would be a dissenting voice in the battle to secure War on Poverty funding for East Palo Alto, as its leadership did not want the community to be labeled a "poverty area," even though the community had already been racially coded by adjacent communities thanks to residential and school policies. Indeed, a 1963 community plan argued that self-government was needed as "without a sense of physical and social identity, East Palo Alto could easily slip into a pattern of irreversible deterioration. Permanent residents should be able to feel that the kind of environment they have sought will be preserved. New residential developments should be geared to long-term occupancy, not to high turnover. It is reasonable to assume that people who feel that they have a stake in the community will take more interest in local affairs."[44]

East Palo Alto's path toward community and political empowerment, like Oakland's—but less so in the case of Newark and East Orange—was fueled by the rhetoric as well as the funding unleashed by Johnson's War on Poverty programs and most importantly the requirement of "maximum feasible participation." Johnson's Great Society programs did two things. First, they offered East Palo Alto a source of funds to address its social and infrastructural needs. Second, the Great Society's community participation requirements gave community activists and later ambitious local politicians a lever to pry some political power and autonomy from the county board, which had largely ignored or marginalized East Palo Alto's issues.

However, for the possibilities of the War on Poverty to be realized, Black East Palo Alto would not only have to organize, but also take their protest directly to the county to make the needs of their marginal space visible to those in formal positions of power. This organizing began in the early 1960s as new residents confronted the suburban color line of housing and education. Soon a loose group of local organizers and activists—the "Floating Crap Game"—began monthly meetings.[45] When the county announced their participation in the War on Poverty, members of this group quickly mobilized themselves into a new group called Committee of the Poor. The committee included recent working-class migrants like Gertrude Wilks, who was one of the leaders in the fight against segregated and unequal education in the community, as well as more middle-class residents like Harry Bremond.

The committee began by organizing against the county's framework for its participation in the program. First, they lambasted the county's top-down approach, which used existing county programs and administrators to deliver what were supposed to be innovative new programs based on the input of local people in the county's high-poverty enclaves. Second, they criticized the fact that the programs themselves were delivered by organizations from outside of the committee, again violating the sprit as well as the letter of the law in terms of "maximum feasible participation." The Committee of the Poor would struggle over the next year and half, with the regional federal Office of Economic Opportunity (OEO) periodically stepping in, over who and what the War on Poverty was for. As Harry Bremond would declare to the county board of supervisors, "the people are not willing to accept another colonial welfare program."[46]

The invocation of East Palo Alto as a "colonial space" reflected the wave of Black Power Urbanism that was sweeping across the country. For a time, East Palo Alto served as an important though overlooked transmission node in the rise of the

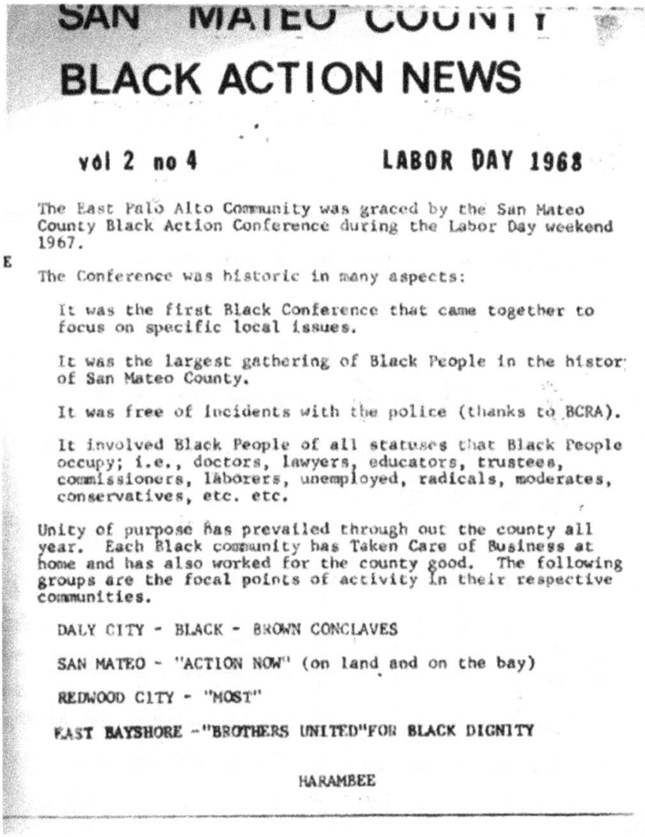

SAN MATEO COUNTY

BLACK ACTION NEWS

vol 2 no 4 LABOR DAY 1968

The East Palo Alto Community was graced by the San Mateo County Black Action Conference during the Labor Day weekend 1967.

The Conference was historic in many aspects:

It was the first Black Conference that came together to focus on specific local issues.

It was the largest gathering of Black People in the histor[y] of San Mateo County.

It was free of incidents with the police (thanks to BCRA).

It involved Black People of all statuses that Black People occupy; i.e., doctors, lawyers, educators, trustees, commissioners, laborers, unemployed, radicals, moderates, conservatives, etc. etc.

Unity of purpose has prevailed through out the county all year. Each Black community has Taken Care of Business at home and has also worked for the county good. The following groups are the focal points of activity in their respective communities.

DALY CITY - BLACK - BROWN CONCLAVES

SAN MATEO - "ACTION NOW" (on land and on the bay)

REDWOOD CITY - "MOST"

EAST BAYSHORE -"BROTHERS UNITED"FOR BLACK DIGNITY

HARAMBEE

FIGURE 6.4. Black Power politics in East Palo Alto

Source: *San Mateo County Black Action News*, vol. 2, no. 4. Barbara Mouton Collection, Courtesy East Palo Alto Community Archive, East Palo Alto, California.

Bay Area Black Power movement, from Oakland's Black Panthers to San Francisco State's Black Studies movement and San Jose State's Black athlete movement, the latter of which inspired the Black Power salutes of Tommy X and Carlos Smith at the 1968 Olympics. Closer to East Palo Alto was the San Mateo County Black Action Conference (SMCBAC, "smack back"), which linked East Palo Alto with other Brown and Black communities in the county and across the Bay Area (see figure 6.4).

Over the course of three years (1967–69), a series of Black Power conferences would be held in East Palo Alto. The first conference, held on Labor Day, drew around 1,500 attendees, while the second conference held the following year featured luminaries of the Black Power movement such as Amiri Baraka, Ron Karenga, Eldridge Cleaver, Huey Newton, and Stokely Carmichael. The visit from Carmichael would prove to be particularly influential as his presentation pushed many of the more militant activists to drop their still-lingering commitment to liberal integrationism in favor of full-throated support for community control and autonomy. As a result of its location within the transnational Black Power network, East Palo Alto for a moment articulated an alternative vision of its identity as a proudly self-assured "Nairobi" with a local Afrocentric school and junior college and small-scale economic developments that tried to realize the Black Power ethos (see figure 6.5). At the same time, activists in the city struggled

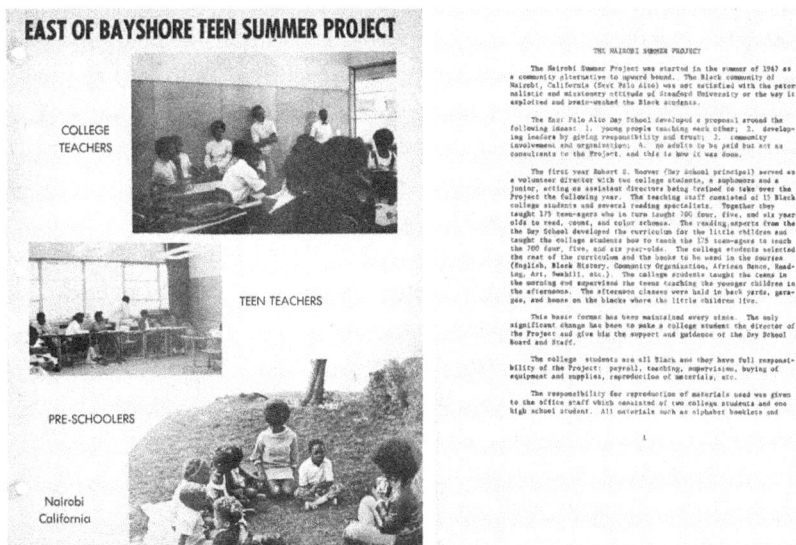

FIGURE 6.5.   "Our kids can learn!" Instantiating Black Power Urbanism and education

Source: "East of Bayshore Teen Summer Project—Nairobi Summer Project," August 1, 1969. Barbara Mouton Collection, Courtesy East Palo Alto Community Archive, East Palo Alto, California.

with the ambivalences and limitations of ideas of self-determination as well as with demands from some within the movement that participants "close ranks" and forgo interracial cooperation.

While the struggle for formal political incorporation was one that high-lighted and privileged members of EPA's Black middle class, political power—whether in the shape of a city council or a local program or institution in the hands of "the people"—was the concern of a significant proportion of EPA's Black residents who were poor or working class. As one Black high school student put it, activism came in many shapes and forms: "There would be the Day School, or the Community House was having something, we were picketing, we were canvassing for the new Co-op, we were getting people out to vote. We were asking people if they wanted to change East Palo Alto's name to Nairobi; we were knocking on doors."[47]

East Palo Alto Municipal Council: Undoing the Colony

The formation of East Palo Alto as a Black political space with specific govern-mental functions and policies was historic given that most "Black spaces" and their accompanying political and institutional structures were the result of racial succession. Black power in these latter types of spaces meant the pouring of new wine into increasingly fragile wine bottles—as the newly empowered Black lead-ers of East Orange, Newark, and later Oakland would discover. In the case of East Palo Alto, the availability of federal funding, first through Great Society programs and then Nixon's early New Federalism, allowed community activists to push forward a vision of self-determination on a number of different fronts.

Despite the formation of an advisory council, there still remained no formal representation at all on the county board of supervisors, which controlled all spending and policy priorities for unincorporated East Palo Alto. The city's unin-corporated status would vex activists and residents for over three decades. On one side of this issue were residents, first white and later Black, who argued that as an unincorporated space the community did not have effective control over zoning or policy delivery. This meant that prime developable areas of the city were continually being annexed by adjacent communities, resulting in a weak-ened tax base and its attractiveness as a site for the county's "locally unwanted land uses" like chemical plants, or increasingly, "the poor." The community's landlords—of both apartment buildings and houses—primary stood on the other side of the issue. They foresaw rising property taxes as there was not enough commercial development to fund a fully incorporated town. Against this backdrop was rising Black organizing among East Palo Alto's new community activists over whether the community should incorporate.

This split between whites and Blacks was accompanied by divisions within the Black community over the best path toward political autonomy between "moderates," who favored a more tempered approach to the county in terms of gaining local control, and militants who favored immediate independence. The moderates formed their own organization, the Committee for Equal Representation, while the more militant group organized as the Committee for Self Government.[48] In 1966, the Committee for Self Government formally requested funds for a community organizer and a feasibility study for the incorporation of East Palo Alto. This request was accompanied by two hundred East Palo Alto community members appearing at a county board meeting. Reflecting the intertwined linkages between the East Palo Alto leadership and Stanford, the feasibility study championed by Bremond, along with Edward Becks and Robert Hoover, was led by Professor Thelton Henderson, head of the East Palo Alto Legal Aid Society (funded by the OEO), who was also affiliated with Stanford's legal aid clinic.

Black activists' repeated demands for autonomy from the county met with limited success. During the War on Poverty's early years the county had remained resistant to moving program development and delivery to organizations based in East Palo Alto or in the county's other high-poverty areas. In the face of this obstinacy, local activists regularly brought scores of residents to county board meetings to loudly protest the county's unwillingness to engage with the OEO guidelines of meaningful participation. By May 1967, changes in the War on Poverty, including a decline in funding coupled with near constant prodding and protest by local activists, convinced the county to cede some measure of control to the community. Though the ceding of control was couched as merely a technical response to the requirements of filing an application for the new Model Cities Program, the establishment of a local council rested on an earlier history of activism and opposition than the county was willing to publicly admit. In fact, the move to support more autonomy for the community was in response to an attempt by the majority-white "west of the highway" community to be annexed to Menlo Park. The county's Local Agency Formation Commission (LAFCO) noted that the proposal "opened up a political Pandora's box."[49]

With the pressure mounting from all sides, the county announced that a new five-member East Palo Alto Municipal Council (EPAMC) would act "in lieu of an official city government, [and] advise the supervisors on county and federal programming."[50] The move by the county diverted the Community Action Council (CAC) from its pressure on the county. The creation of a new quasi-electoral body also proved to be prescient given the wave of urban rebellions that swept the nation during the summer of 1967. Indeed, the county manager would claim that the creation of the EPAMC was necessary intervention in order to avert East Palo Alto from "descending to the depth reached in 1965 by another predominantly Black suburb—Watts."[51]

The creation of the EPAMC was touted by both the new Black officeholders such as Herbert Rhodes and by observers as "revolutionary" and the "only one of its kind."[52] According to Rhodes, the new chair of the EPAMC, the objectives of the organization were to ensure greater responsibility and communication with East Palo Alto's residents and to provide an "opportunity for redress" when government entities, such as the police, acted against them. To achieve these objectives, Rhodes argued that the city had to be run not only on the basis of technical competence but also on "soul competence" as well. "Soul competence," Rhodes asserted, was not necessarily tied to racial categories. Rather, this kind of competence came from "an understanding of the people [they] try to serve." Though focused on "soul" services, the EPAMC was not intended to become a "political ghetto."[53] The council would use its quasi-formal status as a means to press for representation in other county bodies as well as to press for the establishment of the increasingly popular option of community advisory boards.

Despite this hopeful and at times fiery rhetoric, the municipal council had extremely limited powers. Although it had more funding and standing than its predecessor, the Alto Park Council, its powers were still limited in regard to the county. What power it did have was in negotiating with the federal government. However, as the War on Poverty and later Nixon's New Federalism wound down, the municipal council's lack of substantive local power was steadily revealed. As a result, the issue of incorporation remained contentious during municipal elections throughout the 1970s. The formation of the EPAMC was problematic as it had no formal powers. Indeed, it could be argued that it deflected Black anger away from the white-controlled county board of supervisors and toward a Black-dominated council. Nonetheless, the municipal council became a forum in which the different factions of Black East Palo Alto could come together, with each side struggling to frame a future for the de facto town, up to and including eventual formal incorporation.

The initial elections to the board proved that interest in and commitment to local government was extraordinarily high. Thirteen candidates ran to fill the five council seats. The candidates represented both the moderate and more militant factions of the Black community. Voter turnout was around 32 percent of all registered voters, an impressively high rate for a local election.[54] Despite the council's limited powers, it took the lead on transitioning East Palo Alto into a community in which more services were delivered by and for those who lived there. With the aid of a part-time urban planner, the municipal council was able to secure federal funding to create a comprehensive development plan for the city and to address the frequent flooding of homes due to the inadequate storm drainage system.[55] Other amenities that had been lacking in the community like a library and a community health center were also facilitated by the presence of the municipal council.

"We Want Integrated Housing"

"Pray for me, darling. . . . I don't know what I'll do if I lose my house" was Oneida Branch's plea to a reporter who was covering the impact of the subprime mortgage crisis on East Palo Alto.[56] Mother Branch, as she was known to the EPA community, had distributed "clothing, food, hope and prayers" to EPA's needy for over fifty years. In 2004, she, like thousands of other, often elderly Black women homeowners, was targeted by mortgage brokers who offered supposedly low-cost loans at seemingly favorable terms. Branch was a particularly attractive target. She had bought her EPA house in 1958 for $18,500; by 2004 it was worth more than $500,000. Branch took out a reverse mortgage, which was then followed by a solicitation to refinance it into a new subprime loan. The loan would be used to pay off old debts and living expenses and provide a small amount of cash ($21,000). By the end of the "teaser" period, the monthly loan amount was almost 90 percent of the household income (which included the income of her adult son). The ultimate holder of Branch's subprime mortgage was Countrywide, which was eventually named as the most egregious of the mortgage companies that had targeted Black and Latino communities. Branch was not alone: East Palo Alto was one of the Bay Area's subprime foreclosure hot spots. Ultimately, the wave of foreclosures would be the final factor in pushing out many of EAP's longtime Black residents. The lack of access to mortgage loans for Black applicants, as in Oakland, and the now stratospherically high cost of housing in the Silicon Valley meant that the children and grandchildren of EPA's Black pioneers could never move back to the city that their forebears had birthed.[57]

The story of the near loss of Branch's house was reflective of a longer history of unjust and unequal housing access and dispossession in East Palo Alto. By the mid-1960s, predatory exclusion—in the shape of redlining, discrimination, and "blockbusting," had created the conditions for a majority-Black suburb like EPA to come into being. At the same time, California's racial propositions also thwarted the ability of residents to build publicly owned and/or supported housing when federal support for such housing was at its height. The racial proposition that blocked the possibility of publicly supported housing in East Palo Alto and most other small and medium-sized California cities was Article 34 of the state's constitution, which declared that "no low rent housing project shall . . . be developed, constructed, or acquired in any manner by any state public body until, a majority of the qualified electors of the city . . . or county . . . in which it is proposed to develop, construct or acquire the same, voting upon such issue, approve such project by voting in favor thereof at an election."[58] The effect of this act on public housing in California was disastrous. According to the *Los Angeles Times*,

> By 1969, voters across the state had turned down nearly half the public housing that had been proposed in Article 34 elections—15,000 units— and many housing agencies didn't hold elections, fearing that their plans would be rejected. A federal Department of Housing and Urban Development report at the time found that California had the nation's largest population of poor people but ranked 22nd in the amount of housing available for them. The report blamed Article 34.[59]

One of the main reasons that large cities like Oakland and Los Angeles were able to build thousands of public housing units was that the cities had already made commitments to build these units prior to the passage of Article 34 (in the case of Oakland). Also, public housing units were routinely bundled into larger urban renewal schemes that powerful big-city renewal agencies in cooperation with urban elites could push through. For most smaller cities, public housing became a nonstarter, while for unincorporated places like East Palo Alto, construction was not even within the realm of possibility as they lacked jurisdictional authority to apply for and subsequently build it. In EPA, this lack of jurisdictional authority extended even to the county government's unwillingness to connect residents with rental-based assistance programs like Section 23 (Section 8's precursor), which had proven to be politically popular in Oakland and Los Angeles. Like other Silicon Valley local governments, San Mateo County's participation in housing assistance programs was a small fraction of the county's actual need, and as local EPA activists had learned, the county supervisors were quite happy with that status.[60]

The housing assistance that did arrive for EPA's residents occurred through the first stage of the "predatory inclusion" schemes that ultimately put Mother Branch's house in jeopardy. In addition to the passage of the federal Fair Housing Act, the separate Housing Act of 1968 contained two programs—Section 235 and Section 236—designed to promote homeownership of the poor and working class and to aid economic and racial desegregation of the suburbs in particular. The

Section 235 program subsidized interest payments for homebuyers by paying mortgage interest above 1 percent (over a predetermined price cap), while the Section 236 reduced interest rates for developers (nonprofit, cooperative, and private) of multiunit housing. Under this program, developers were required to offer a certain number of units to low-income tenants, whose rental payments were capped at 25 percent of their income.

The goals of the Housing Act were ambitious, and to some observers "wildly optimistic."[61] The plan was to create 26 million units through new construction between 1969 and 1978; 6 million of those units were to be built with federal assistance and 20 million units without. By some metrics, the Section 235 and Section 236 programs were successful. Units built under these sections represented the majority of subsidized housing in the United States between 1967 and 1974, and a large segment of total housing. Between 1967 and 1970, subsidized housing starts rose from 6.7 to 29.3 percent of all housing starts.[62] However, the overall "success" of the Section 235 program came about by shifting federal aid away from local housing authorities and indirectly providing it to the private sector.[63] This shift in funding, while motivated by a desire to move inner-city residents out of the city, was also related to the collapse of support for "traditional" high-rise public housing. The disaster of high-rise housing complexes like Pruitt-Igoe had made members of Congress resistant to any government-funded or government-built housing.

As Keeanga-Yamahtta Taylor shows, the Section 235 program proved to be disastrous for prospective Black homeowners (especially poor Black women) and for what were then euphemistically called "transitional" neighborhoods. The program seemed designed to fail—at least for its Black and Brown buyers—as the program's structure made default and foreclosures profitable for the real estate agents, appraisers, builders, mortgage brokers, and banks who speculated and sold often shoddy and mostly overpriced housing to unsuspecting buyers. The legislative provision of mortgages for new housing did not necessarily translate into integrated living: the Section 235 mortgages issued in suburban areas displayed a distinctive racial and spatial pattern. Almost all Section 235 mortgages obtained by whites were in new suburban areas. By contrast, African Americans and other racialized groups obtained mortgages in suburban "transitional" areas that real estate speculators and developers had targeted due to their lack of zoning regulations or low civic capacity.[64] This was the case in East Palo Alto. Predatory exclusion, including persistent discrimination and de facto redlining, meant that most Black homebuyers could not obtain conventional mortgages (indeed, this condition continues to persist). Predatory inclusion made homeownership a tantalizing possibility, and to unsophisticated eyes perhaps of low risk for aspiring Black homeowners seeking middle-class suburban respectability.

After the program's collapse in 1974, congressional inquiries abounded. One Senate hearing deliberating the Abandonment Disaster Demonstration Relief Act of 1975 focused on the impact of Section 235 on majority-Black and -Latino communities. East Palo Alto and Compton (adjacent to Los Angeles) were singled out as places where the collapse of Section 235 programs had led to high numbers of HUD foreclosures and subsequently to rising levels of "blight" induced by housing vacancy, as the HUD-owned houses lay empty and deteriorating in the recessionary housing market of the mid-1970s.

The effect of the Section 235 disaster, like the subprime disaster thirty years later, felt more severe in smaller communities. In her testimony to Congress, Mayor Doris Davis noted that although Compton had a population "a fraction of the size" of the city of Los Angeles, on a per capita basis it had the "second highest number of boarded-up units and the highest number of abandoned properties . . . in the entire state of California."[65] This was a result of the repossession of over four hundred HUD/VA properties as well as an "undeterminable number of conventional repossessions totaling between 700 and 1,000 units." The end result of this dispossession and abandonment was a community caught in a spiral of dispossession and destabilization, in which the federal government emerged as the city's "largest slum landlord."[66]

While not on the scale of Compton or Oakland, the HUD foreclosures in EPA alarmed local Black activists who saw them as an early sign that the hold of the Black community and particularly of aspiring homeowners on East Palo Alto was still tenuous. The number of absentee landlords went up as investors bought foreclosed homes. Not coincidentally, the rates of overcrowding also went up as more families struggled to remain in an area that was increasingly unaffordable but had high levels of job growth, and that featured pervasive housing discrimination against Black residents.[67]

Some activists saw the answer to fear of displacement and dispossession as a renewed push for formal city status; others believed that a new model of organizing for the right to remain and live in East Palo Alto needed to be developed. Community land trusts, that is, local nonprofit organizations that "provide affordable housing in perpetuity by owning land and leasing it to those who live in houses built on that land" were one such solution proposed by Bob Hoover and others.[68] However, like many of the initiatives put forward by these activists, there was little take-up beyond the city's small progressive community. Meanwhile lack of knowledge, mistrust, and/or hostility from Black middle-class homeowners/voters as well as pressure from the absentee landlords who dominated EPA's local political and philanthropic scene meant that the idea of community land trusts to maintain the "right to the city" remained an unrealized dream.[69] The idea of linking housing stability to the right to remain would have another hearing in the early 1980s.

The high inflation of the 1970s coupled with the passage of Proposition 13 in 1978 meant a financial windfall for landlords, increasing costs for tenants, and a real fear that East Palo Alto would be fiscally abandoned due to the looming austerity budgets triggered by Proposition 13. In the wake of these developments, there was a renewed if not fervent zeal to push for formal incorporation in order to reduce the city's vulnerability to the whims of an unresponsive county board of supervisors.[70] The fight for formal cityhood was intertwined with the proposed passage of a local rent-control law.[71] Taken together these causes managed to unite the disparate communities that made up East Palo Alto, namely the Black working-class households doubled up in rental homes east of the highway, apart-ment dwellers (Latino households, Stanford students, and other white-collar residents), and progressives. Against this coalition were the absentee landlords and remaining Black homeowners. For the latter, cityhood raised the prospect of higher taxes, which many felt threatened their tenuous toehold into the middle class. For the absentee landlords—who activists argued were bankrolling the anti-incorporation campaign—cityhood (and rent control) not only raised the prospect of higher taxes and less profit but also more regulation and oversight, especially of the deteriorating conditions of their properties.

Cityhood and rent control would win, but by then Black East Palo Alto would be experiencing another wave of foreclosures spurred on by the savings and loan crisis, and yet another cycle of dispossession and speculation would engulf the city. Cityhood made possible the first visible response to worsening housing con-ditions and the affordability crisis enveloping the city through construction of the city's first affordable housing development. The process triggered an acrimoni-ous battle between Black EPA officials and an emergent Latino political class who each argued that "their" communities were being shortchanged in the allocation of the units in this development.[72] The scale of nonprofit-backed housing was miniscule compared to the need for it created by the 2008 wave of foreclosures that swept over the city.[73] Most homeowners of color as well as renters would be caught up in this this tsunami of risk and dispossession. Nearly a decade later, many of EPA's former homeowners and renters were living in RVs in order to keep their children in local schools and access the booming social media econ-omy of the 2010s.[74] Others were not so lucky and moved to the extreme edges of the East Bay, Stockton, or Sacramento. Some would leave California entirely, reversing their grandparents' Great Migration and moving to Black meccas like Atlanta. Black Power Urbanism, at least in the realm of housing, had found no concrete forms and left no material traces in East Palo Alto.

Education: It's a Black Thing

The September 1971 issue of *Ebony* magazine (the publication that had by far the broadest reach in showcasing Black Power Urbanism to a mainstream Black audience) featured an article titled "Learning Is an All-Black Thing: California Community Creates Its Own School System." The article showcased the efforts made by Gertrude Wilks and Bob Hoover to create a network of "independent Black institutions" that promised to offer real education for the Black children and youth of East Palo Alto, who had not been helped by the decade-long struggle for liberal integrationism at both the elementary and high-school level.[75]

Although many Black residents argued that the formal political citizenship attendant upon East Palo Alto's cityhood would help address the educational crisis facing their children, activists like Wilks argued that the needs of their children could not wait for political freedom to be wrested from the white power structure. Instead, activists like Wilks and Hoover would engage in "pioneering a brand new way for Black folks."[76] For Hoover, the founder of East Palo Alto's Nairobi College, the primary goal of the city's educational experiment was to "train leaders for the Black community. We need to offer them something useful." Indeed, to Wilks, the cost of the current alienation and educational malpractice was akin to placing Black children in a prison. Without freedom, "you can become a slave. . . . And then you're lost."[77]

A model for Black Power Urbanism emerged from the political activism and improvisation of Black women like Gertrude Wilks, who with other Black parents and activists not only articulated a sharp critique of the existing system but also posed alternative models of Black education. This improvisation was critical as East Palo Alto confronted layered systems of institutional and political inequality that were embedded within the suburban context of marginalization, fragmentation, and erasure in which East Palo Alto's Black citizens found themselves.

For example, although Black residents had won the 1958 battle to locate a high school within East Palo Alto's boundaries with a racially diverse attendance zone, as parents discovered to their dismay the quality of the education offered was subpar and their children were allowed to graduate high school with abysmal literacy. Despite the early activism of parents who insisted on integrated education, the high school district repeatedly finessed attendance boundaries and policies to allow white students to exit East Palo Alto's high school while keeping Black students at that location. Housing discrimination only strengthened both this racial exit and racial containment. In less than a decade, the high school was well on its way to becoming a de facto segregated school.

At the primary (K-8) level, the possibility for integration was forestalled from the beginning as East Palo Alto's students were corralled into their own district—Ravenswood—which mostly aligned with the area's unincorporated but increasingly racialized spatial boundaries. The almost immediate proximity of Palo Alto's high-performing, well-resourced, and almost entirely white schools on the other side of the "concrete curtain" of the Bayshore Freeway made the frayed quality of education offered at Ravenswood—whether at the elementary or high school level—increasingly apparent and an untenable situation to Black parents and residents. While some parents and community activists looked to the courts and the local NAACP and CORE chapters to help them in their struggle with the school district, other parents embraced Black Power Urbanism. Parents like Gertrude Wilks realized that their children were not only not being educated according to mainstream standards, but their children were also being miseducated, given the tenets of Black Power Urbanism.

The conditions that might result in the loss of a generation of students were revealed as the mixed results of ad hoc ways of addressing the failings of Ravenswood High became more clear. In addition to protest, Wilks, with other Black parents and with the help of white allies, created the "sneak-out" program in 1966. Approximately one hundred Black students would live with white families during the week in order to attend nearby, high-quality high schools like Palo Alto High. This program was fraught with problems. Although the "sneak-out" program was eventually given tacit approval by some white school administrators and teachers, the issue remained that schools were officially unwilling to admit more than a handful of Ravenswood students. More fundamentally the "sneak-out" program was not a long-term or just solution for the Black students remaining at Ravenswood High. Finally, the daily harassment that "sneak-out" students faced from teachers, staff, and even students over their presence in these majority-white schools took a huge mental and emotional toll on these students. Wilks recounted visiting a visibly distressed Black high schooler at her host family home and vowing "to do something about giving a Black some security, [and] proving that we as Black people could build an institution that was as good as anybody's right here in our own community."[78]

Against this backdrop, Wilks and her fellow activists shifted toward thinking about not only the academic and emotional difficulties of the relatively few "sneak-out" students, but also the quality of the education received by the vast majority of East Palo Alto students who could not or would not "sneak-out." Their answer was to create a "Saturday school" that would supplement East Palo Alto's now visibly troubled school system. Although organizers expected a "handful" of high school students to show up, over two hundred "mostly elementary" age children appeared. To accommodate the demand, the organizers quickly expanded the Saturday school to Wednesdays as well.[79]

With this visible demand for a new alternative, Wilks, along with local activists like Bob Hoover and local college students, opened Nairobi Day School in 1966, followed by Nairobi High School in 1968.[80] Nairobi College—though not discussed here—was also part of this new educational improvisation.[81] The schools were staffed by volunteers from the East Palo Alto community and by Stanford students. While improvisation and need had led to the formation of the day school and high school, Black Power gave a mission to these schools that other schools would follow. A meeting held by East Palo Alto activists over the ongoing integration struggle provoked a visiting Stokely Carmichael to say, "I don't understand. . . . Why would you be working this hard to send your children's minds to be educated by people who have oppressed you for four hundred years"?[82]

For Wilks, the mission was close to home, because EPA's Black "children were moving out of the eighth grade, illiterate, into the mortification process of an unteaching public high school" or "catching hell" at the integrated high schools they were attending via the "sneak-out" program.[83] Both schools were small: Nairobi Day School had an initial enrollment of fifty students, while Nairobi High had only thirty students. Although small, the high school performed an especially important role given the troubled racial atmosphere in the Sequoia district high schools, especially for the former "sneak-out" participants. For Black high schoolers who were "being harassed by teachers, administration, white students and everybody else," Nairobi provided a respite from these hostile educational spaces.[84] With the schools occupying four "cottages" scattered around East Palo Alto and the siting of Nairobi College in Nairobi Village, an actual spatialization of Black Power Urbanism seemed imminent.

The premise of the Nairobi schools was revolutionary. As Black scholar Barbara Mouton argued, the schools' pedagogical approach was "focused entirely on the premise that Black children could learn and it attempted to extend and build on the values found in Black homes." This approach upended the long-standing approach of liberal integrationism wherein at "schools for Blacks, other minorities and low-income groups [white educators] nearly always try to act as agents of intervention. . . . They label home-parent values [of Blacks] as bad and school-teacher values as good."[85] Wilks was quick to point out the day school's success: "Nairobi Schools, after documenting student achievement over a period of years, began offering families in 1972, an iron-clad guarantee."[86]

Although these independent Black institutions were created with the enthusiastic support of parent volunteers and college students, the Nairobi schools faced increasing difficulties as the first flush of Black Power Urbanism waned.

The day school and the high school were initially entirely funded by tuition, donations, and "chicken dinners or sweet potato pies."[87] By the late 1970s the independence of Nairobi schools and especially Nairobi College was contingent on access to financial support both within—and problematically for activists—outside of the Black community.[88] In addition to private donations, the Nairobi educational institutions benefited from the remaining Great Society programs still in operation, including "Equal Opportunity Grants, National Defense Loans, work-study programs, Talent Search and Student Special Service."[89] The demise of some of these programs and budget cutbacks during the late Carter and then Reagan administrations would lead to financial difficulties. Just as East Palo Alto was taking its decisive steps toward formal political incorporation, Nairobi College would close in 1981, followed by the closure of the day school in 1984.

Although the establishment of the Nairobi schools created a space for Black educational self-determination, the small size of the schools meant that the vast majority of East Palo's Alto Black students as well as a small but growing (both numerically and politically) Latino population remained in the public school system. Activists, parents, and increasingly students pressed for meaningful, integrated education at Ravenswood High and throughout the high schools in the district, while working toward equity, inclusion, and cultural attentiveness within the walls of Ravenswood High itself.[90]

"Fiery People": Black Youth Revolt

Looking back at 1968, Schery Mitchell, a former Ravenswood High School student, remembered that Black students at the school that fall were a "fiery people" who were "do or die" in creating a new Nairobi.[91] Like their peers across the United States, Black Ravenswood students took up the banner of Black Power Urbanism. On the first day of school that September, a group of students began the first of many demonstrations, strikes, and sit-ins. Their first demands were revolutionary and reflected this "do or die" attitude toward a school administration that they saw as indifferent to the academic, social, and cultural aspirations of its now majority-Black student body. A later report summarized these initial demands as a broad call for "improved classes, ethnic studies, teacher transfers, and a new minority principal."[92] By the end of the first week of classes, after a series of sit-ins and rallies attended by hundreds of students, the school's white principal resigned and was replaced by a Black principal. The outgoing white principal and the local California Teachers Association (CTA) chapter placed the blame for the school's poor track record of Black student engagement and achievement on the Black community, deeming the search for new kinds of educational practice as fruitless and a diversion from the structural inequalities faced by students as well as by the district. The latter argument was less than plausible given that parents and community activists had been battling the district to end its quiet commitment to de facto segregation.

Ravenswood's status as a majority-Black school offered students a chance to take part in the sweeping Black Power movement that was spreading across the United States. Taking their cue from these movements, but also reflecting their lived experiences as marginalized by both race and space, Black students at Ravenswood pushed for a curriculum that reflected their interests and concerns. The list of demands they presented demonstrated this push for a new Black Power urbanist pedagogy. Some of the demands—such as daily after-school study halls and tutoring, the "abolition of remedial classes and worksheets," and a change in the school's overemphasis on pushing Black students into shop, homemaking, and other vocational courses—were seemingly "without reference to Black issues per se." However, these classroom practices were the means by which Black student's educational needs were disregarded or subverted. Students were also explicit in their demands for Black Power urbanist pedagogy, which included a call for more Black teachers, counselors, and staff (while removing white staff deemed to be hostile or insufficiently attentive to the needs of Black students) and more classes and resources devoted to the cultural and social education and development of students such as Black history and culture courses (including a course in Swahili).[93]

While Black students pushed for a school in tune with Black Power Urbanism, parent activists from East Palo Alto continued to apply pressure on the district to breach the segregated school district lines and to upgrade Ravenswood High School as well. None of the alternatives considered by the district were politically palatable as residential segregation had not only created and indeed hardened white and Black spaces, but had also divided spaces by class. Various school consolidation schemes either placed all of the burden of busing on Blacks or even more problematically, given white political hegemony, on the affluent whites of Atherton and Palo Alto whose homes (and students) lay closest to East Palo Alto.

In 1969, three pro-integration candidates won seats on the school board.[94] In addition to pledging to address the issues at Ravenswood High, the new board members pushed for the district to achieve racial balance in its schools by September 1971. The district also faced pressure from a variety of state and federal government agencies. Pressure from the state came from the 1968 California State Board of Education Report, which decried de facto segregated education, while pressure from the federal Office of Civil Rights (OCR) arose from an investigation of the Sequoia District as one of eighty-four districts outside of the South that were charged with violating the Civil Rights Act of 1964.[95] The push to resolve Ravenswood's problems also had some teeth, courtesy of federal desegregation cases such as *Swann v. Mecklinberg*, which took direct aim at so-called de facto segregation. By 1970, the pro-integration board members and parents had more leverage to press for change since the OCR had made the determination that the district had violated the Civil Rights Act of 1964. The federal government gave the district until September 1970 to fully desegregate. The board subsequently proposed desegregation of all schools with the goal of each school having no more than a 25-percent minority population.

Under federal pressure, the school board created an open enrollment plan that would allow students in the district to cross the "concrete curtain." This plan would fail, as most students opted to leave Ravenswood and only one student applied to transfer in.[96] District officials then looked for a solution that would avert a "forced desegregation" of the district's other schools, which would trigger further hostility and political pushback from white parents. School officials were also particularly concerned about a threatened walkout by the majority-white Sequoia District Teachers Association if teachers were forced to move schools. The teachers' justification for the threatened walkout was blunt: "Ravenswood [was] an undesirable place to teach."[97]

After the failure of the open enrollment plan, the high school district considered a number of alternatives to address the issue including a "racial balance plan" and a "mandatory desegregation" plan.[98] Tremendous backlash toward busing was by then emerging with politicians both in California and nationwide, including the White House, fomenting resistance. Busing also increasingly came under fire from many Black parents and activists, and as seen in the Black Power Conventions proceedings, was antithetical to Black Power urbanist ideas as well. As Gertrude Wilks would ask, instead of following whites, why could Blacks not "stay here and make something of this place?"[99]

In the face of these pressures, the Sequoia board decided on a third path of quasi-voluntary enrollment by making Ravenswood High a "model school"—a magnet school with a redesigned curriculum that would hopefully attract white high school students. Creating an attractive school in order to induce voluntary white attendance seemed to Sequoia and other school districts the best way to achieve a semblance of desegregation and avoid the raw acrimony of what was now being called "forced busing." Although a bold step, the board's hand was also forced by pressure from community activists who used the lever of federal intervention and the embarrassment of the "sneak-out program" to highlight the racial segregation that had become obvious to many. In spring 1971 two new school board members were elected, each of whom had run on an anti-busing platform, and who in turn replaced the two pro-busing and pro-integration board members. The two new members shifted the board to an anti-busing majority and in July 1971 the board repealed the mandatory busing program and rescinded student placements to schools outside of their attendance zone. In return for effectively giving up on the earlier desegregation plan, the board pledged to consider "viable" alternatives. Given that the board had spent much of the 1960s considering and rejecting numerous possibilities, it did not seem likely that a new alternative would appear.

Two Schools, One Building

The "new" Ravenswood opened in 1971 with mixed forecasts over whether school performance would improve and whether there would be a sense of student cohesion due the mixing of two very different groups. Many of the 415 white students who transferred in were attracted by what was touted as a new, innovative curriculum; others followed popular teachers who had volunteered to join the "new" Ravenswood.[100] By contrast, that same year, Asian American students (Japanese, Filipino, and Samoan), as well as 810 Black students "transfer[red] out of Ravenswood when offered the opportunity."[101]

Black parents and students did not fully embrace the magnet school concept. Some Black parents were vocal about their support for "traditional" modes of pedagogy and saw the experimental classes and permissive teachers as a way of subverting their educational aspirations for their students, leaving already vulnerable students behind and not pushing ambitious students enough. For Black students, the discomfort rested on their belief that the magnet school plan would turn Ravenswood back into a majority-white space with an accompanying student culture that was alienating and unwelcome to Black students. As one student argued,

> Our black beautiful school is going to turn into one of the biggest hippie fields in the district. . . . I don't want to walk down the halls . . . and say "Hi guy." I want to say "what's happening brother!" I don't want to listen to Simon and Garfunkel at my senior prom . . . I want to dig the Temps. And I don't want to be doing the frug either. I want to be digging on the Cold Duck if it's still in.[102]

In an editorial in the school newspaper, another student argued that desegregation would lead to individual and communal harm. Echoing Gertrude Wilks, who asked why Black East Palo Altoans always had to chase after white residents (and resources), the student argued that when we wanted to go to his white schools, he said "hell no?" Then we started to being halfway proud and black, only to have [whites] take it away . . . The new school, the desegregation means phasing out of the black community; black people, black students will lose. We as black students, will be going through so many changes that we won't have a chance to be educated to survive in our own community.[103]

There was another side to the new Ravenswood. Many white students found that being in a progressive educational environment was ideal to meet the emotional and intellectual needs that were overlooked in the district's traditional high schools. For others, being in an integrated school helped them feel that they were participants in an important social struggle and experiment. Still other whites (new teachers and students), while generally open to the experience, saw Black students as threatening, unfriendly, and "resentful."[104] The mixed motives of the white students, including support for diverse learning experiences, could not bridge the large chasm between white students who arrived at Ravenswood by choice and the Black students who struggled to create meaning and purpose behind their concrete curtain. Ravenswood was two schools in one building (see figure 6.6).

Despite the high hopes of the board and some educators based on these enrollments, the initial surge of interest did not turn Ravenswood High School around. Between 1973 and 1974, enrollment dropped from 956 to 823 students. The school also remained a majority-minority school, with African American students making up 59 percent of the student body.

While Ravenswood High's declining enrollment can be attributed to cultural clashes and concerns about the quality of education at the school, it can also be traced to another demographic shift occurring in the early 1970s: the first wave of the "baby bust" that hit California and many other places in the United States as the baby boomers aged out of the K-12 system, leaving a much smaller cohort of children. The district thus faced the problem of needing to close some schools due to excess capacity. Closing Ravenswood and later San Carlos High School and distributing their students among the remaining high schools was an easy choice. The closure of Ravenswood in 1976 instantly desegregated the school district while also addressing the district's capacity issues, although the community lost the ability to effectively unify East Palo Alto's residents around the issue of equity and access to a quality high school education.

The closing of Ravenswood had a long-term negative effect on the East Palo Alto students who now had no choice but to be sent to white-majority schools through a "one-way busing program."[105] Parents and local activists charged that East Palo Alto students were marginalized at these schools, often tracked out of

FIGURE 6.6.   Ravenswood High School: Two schools, one building

Source: Greg Gavin et al., eds., *Ravenswood* (Pressed for Time Press, 1976), www.gregorygavin.com/documents/ravenswood.pdf.

college prep courses, and disproportionately disciplined. Not surprisingly given this institutional hostility, dropout rates for Black students soared. Yet because these students were scattered among the remaining high schools, no institutional actor could or would track this dismal performance. Certainly the district did not, as it had solved the issue of segregation by creating a system that ultimately drove the average Black student away from higher education or even from inclusion in the rapidly expanding high-tech industries of Silicon Valley. It would be left to activists like Bob Hoover to start community outreach groups for the young people pushed out of school or into the spreading War on Drugs and the increasing number who were enmeshed in California's unfolding golden gulag. The trajectory of the now-closed high school site echoed what Elizabeth Hinton argues was the shift from the War on Poverty to the War on Crime, as "police departments began to establish themselves in the spaces that had been vacated by War on Poverty programs"; part of now-closed Ravenswood High would become a sheriff's office substation, while the rest of the site slowly deteriorated.[106] After the police moved to better offices, the site became known as a hot spot for criminal activity until its demolition in 1995 to make way for a shopping center, Gateway 101.[107]

Though Gertrude Wilks and other parents had fought to stem white flight and keep East Palo Alto's elementary schools integrated, by the late 1960s EPA had a largely Black and Brown student body. This change in student demographics was not accompanied by a change in teachers or staff. Parents complained that the largely white teaching staff was not only uninterested in teaching, but also hostile toward Black children and parents. The shortfalls of the teaching staff were accompanied by the poor state of the district's finances as East Palo Alto, given that it was an unincorporated place with a weak retail and commercial base, had little in the way of property taxes. Despite these drawbacks, Black East Palo Altoans made continual attempts to gain more influence and ultimately control over the school district, which served younger children from kindergarten through eighth grade.

Climbing Toward Community Control

The dramatic demographic shift in East Palo Alto's population was accompanied from almost the very beginning by sharp disagreements about the nature and future of education in the town. In 1961, the Black physician Andrew White was elected to the Ravenswood School Board. White had moved to the area in the late 1950s and had immediately become involved in educational issues. In 1967, Bob Hoover and Satella Cabot, two longtime community activists, were also elected to the board. The balance of power on the five-person board shifted and the board was now not only majority-Black but it also represented members who lived east of the highway, unlike the other two members who lived on the west side of Bayshore.[108] The election finally allowed Hoover and his fellow board members to directly confront the school administration and its lack of commitment to children of color. Among the initiatives the board members pushed was a rethinking of the schools' haphazard approach to teaching reading. They found that very few teachers in the system had actually been trained to teach reading and that the teaching of reading varied by classroom, by grade, and by school. The reform efforts as well as community organizing resulted in the Ravenswood District embracing more aspects of community control.

In 1974, Hoover led an effort to create and implement attendance area school boards (or school site councils, as they were also known), similar to and inspired by New York City's experience. The goal of these school site council initiatives was to "give the schools to the parents and also to allocate a budget for each one of the schools and the parents would have the parent board [and it] would have the authority to make decisions on spending at that school on hiring the principal and dealing with curriculum and all those kinds of things." While in the process of designing this program, the board appointed the district's first Black superintendent, Warren Hayman.[109] Although Hayman had moved up through the system and was politically and organizationally linked to some of the members of the board, he was less than supportive of the school site councils, which were eventually shelved. The other initiative that Hayman opposed, along with some members of the board, was a move to use the $4.5 million school budget as a means to stimulate local economic growth, which to Hoover "meant hiring people, having contracts for services, whatever we could do," and in a related vein, establishing residency requirements.[110] While none of these initiatives had a permanent effect, they did signal that the ongoing struggle for a quality education took place both within and outside of formal political structures and organizations.

Despite this shift in the student body and the slow movement of Black East Palo Altoans into positions of power within the school district, including its board, the dream of integrated education did not immediately end, but rather it continued along the now more conventional path of litigation. The movement toward a more integrated elementary school system was similar to the suburban civil rights politics of the 1950s and 1960s in the sense that interracial women's civic groups led the way toward creating a dialogue and then action for the integration of suburban schools. In 1970, white women in neighboring communities began to take action in response to the activism of Black women and the education they provided. Their first step was to hold a conference at the local Palo Alto Presbyterian Church titled, "How Can We Act as Responsible White Women?"[111] Following that conference, the women took a small, concrete step by creating of a two-week integrated summer camp named "Fun and Friendship." Although sponsored by the Portola Valley School District and the Ravenswood District, the camp was run by volunteer mothers and students. Transgressing the dividing lines between the communities, one week's session was held in East Palo Alto while the other week was held elsewhere. The next step came the following year (1971) when a campaign largely led by Black and white women created the Mid-Peninsula Task Force for Integrated Education. As a first step toward integrating Ravenswood with the surrounding communities, the group proposed a primary education center (K–2) to bring together different parts of town. After a number of setbacks and with little to show for the task force's efforts, some of the parents who had been involved with the struggle over integrating the elementary schools joined with local white allies to challenge the jurisdictional lines that created and reinforced de facto school segregation.[112]

In the wake of the *Milliken v. Bradley* (1974) and the *Serrano. v. Priest* decisions, it would be difficult to challenge this so-called de facto segregation. Milliken left suburban school district lines virtually untouchable while the Serrano decision seemed to begin the long and undoubtedly contested process of equalizing education funding, which for some precluded the need to push for integration as long as equalization offered a form of political cover. While Serrano may have offered political cover, it is likely that it also later fomented a wave of white suburban frontlash. Equalization of school funding aimed at the heart of California's "home-voters," who tended to see the reallocation of property taxes to "undeserving" (and increasingly majority-minority) school districts as an act that breached the social contract of the white suburban spatial imaginary.[113] This breach of contract was one of the triggers for the passage of Proposition 13. This constitutional amendment capping local property taxes would have catastrophic effects on low-income, majority-minority school districts.

Margaret Tinsley, an African American woman from East Palo Alto, was selected to be the lead plaintiff for the case against the school system: "She was Black, articulate, unafraid, the mother of two girls in Ravenswood, and along with her husband Bill who was similarly gifted, was willing to the spokesperson at public meetings and with the press."[114] Tinsley's background also made her case compelling. She had been born in Palo Alto's small African American community and had been educated through high school in Palo Alto schools. Racial discrimination and "steering" pushed her and her husband across the highway into East Palo Alto.[115] Like many parents, she found the Ravenswood schools to be deeply troubled by the late 1960s: "I thought that the schools were fine 'til grade three," she said, "but after that I felt that they weren't doing a good job."[116]

The case that activists brought, *Tinsley v. Palo Alto Unified School District*, was complex, as the suit was filed not only against the State of California and the state board of education, but also nine neighboring school districts.[117] Ravenswood joined the other districts in opposing the suit, all of whom directed their legal counsel to "fight [Tinsley] to the last ounce of their blood and the last of the districts."[118] The unified opposition of all of the districts was not a surprise, as the Tinsley case challenged the heart of the racial suburban contract, which was that administrative lines could and would be used to enforce racial segregation and the prerogatives of white home-voters. The case dragged on for years while California's political tradition of countering civil rights advances via "racial propositions" powered by white backlash erupted once again. Meanwhile, Proposition 1 was adopted in November 1979 in reaction to the desegregation battles in California cities such as Los Angeles and cases like Tinsley that were winding their way through the court system. The proposition amended the state constitution to "provide that Californians no longer had greater rights, but only the *same* rights as afforded by the equal protection clause of the Fifth and Fourteenth Amendments to the United States Constitution." In short, this meant that "forced busing and pupil assignment would be court ordered only as a remedy of de jure but not de facto segregation."[119] Thus, although East Palo Alto's segregated schools were created by quiet actions and complicit administrative decisions made by private actors like banks, mortgage brokers, real estate agents, and white homeowner-voters, as well as by county and local politicians, including school district officials, the court affirmed that the silences and elisions of suburban racial formations would continue to be unassailable.

The Tinsley case was finally settled in 1983 after more legal wrangling over the constitutionality of Proposition 1 (it was ultimately allowed to stand) and the scope of the case in the aftermath of its passage. As a result of Proposition 1, the school district's implacable opposition, and the exhaustion of the volunteers who had lent time rather than money, the solution had little impact. Rather than breach school district lines to allow East Palo Alto's students to attend integrated and better-resourced schools, the Tinsley settlement created a small transfer program.[120] The program came with a number of strings attached and strict conditions that limited the number of students who could transfer and the grades they came from.[121] Each child would have district funds following them to their new school. Given that no students would transfer to East Palo Alto's schools, Tinsley was a limited one-way transfer of Black and Brown students to other districts. Thus Ravenswood, a Title I district, was sending its meager resources out of the district to districts that were indescribably wealthy in terms of resources and had no actual need for the funds, in addition to being actively hostile toward the students and the program.

The Tinsley case made no difference to the everyday experience of the hundreds of students that remained in East Palo Alto's schools. The dream of creating a world of integrated schools imagined by Black and white women in the optimistic days of the late 1950s and even through the 1970s was largely gone. Increasingly those who were able to take advantage of the Tinsley decision were the remaining middle-class parents and by the early twenty-first century recent gentrifiers of color, who could successfully advocate with the district to get their child a "Tinsley spot."

East Palo Alto's experiments in Black education, while small in numerical size relative to those in large urban districts like Oakland and Newark, were impressive in their scope. They ran the gamut from experiments that focused on the public school system and the administrative and jurisdictional barriers that blocked Black students from accessing majority-white schools (and their accompanying resources) to internal experiments that attempted to create quality *integrated* schools, as well as schools that centered on Black students' needs within the spatial boundaries of East Palo Alto. Still other experiments, as profiled in *Ebony* magazine, were the independent Black institutions of Nairobi Day School and Nairobi College. These experiments overlapped each other in terms of their timing and the activists and educators who were involved. Victory in the battle over access to quality education remained very much in doubt, whether it was at the primary or high-school level. Past decisions over jurisdictions had left East Palo students in a fragmented and marginal educational zone. The "concrete curtain" of the Bayshore Freeway and the county line separated many of EPA's children from the high-quality schools of nearby Palo Alto. The first decade of the twenty-first century saw East Palo Alto emerge with a new model of public education. Disappeared along with the majority of the city's Black population was a sense of Black, let alone community, self-determination around education. With local funding lagging and additional funding largely contingent on state control and policy directives, the Ravenswood School District was transformed by the opening of multiple charter schools, including, for the first time in decades, a new high school: Eastside College Preparatory (ECP) in 1996.

Community Safety and Policing the Margins

The relationship between East Palo Alto and the police was shaped not only by race, ethnicity, and class, but also by space. As the home of "Whiskey Gulch," East Palo Alto was a space to which the respectable and white residents of Palo Alto and other communities could travel in order to procure alcohol, visit bars, and engage in other sources of entertainment. Within Whisky Gulch different groups, including a small gay and lesbian community, established bars, lounges, baths, and other spaces.[122] Overseeing this marginalized space was the San Mateo County Sheriff's Department, which saw itself as upholding homeowner-voter values. In the aftermath of a 1956 police raid on a gay bar that led to ninety arrests, one sheriff proclaimed that the "purpose of the arrest was to let it be known that we are not going to tolerate gathering of homosexuals in this county."[123]

While this lack of tolerance, intertwined with active surveillance and harsh policing methods, was extended to the LGBT community, it was absolutely centered on the Black and Latino communities in and around East Palo Alto. From the 1950s onward, Black community leaders constantly noted both the ongoing daily harassment of residents and the department's indifference toward combating crime. The all-white San Mateo Sheriff's Department had an antagonistic and dismissive attitude toward the community and its younger residents. By the early 1960s some Black community leaders were arguing that political incorporation would lead to the creation of a locally controlled police force and thus better control over and accountability from the police. Indeed, Some Black community members complained that the department had a "shoot first, ask questions later" pattern of behavior.[124]

As East Palo Alto became a majority-Black community and as more of its residents were embroiled in the Black Power movement sweeping the Bay Area, the relationship between Black East Palo Alto and the county sheriff's department became even more contentious, especially in the aftermath of police confrontations in nearby Menlo Park in 1966 and EPA's own rebellion in July 1967. In majority-white Menlo Park, these contestations led to an era of early police reform and demilitarization under a charismatic white police chief.[125] East Palo Alto's path toward police accountability and control lay through the prism of Black Power Urbanism. The clashes between Black youths and the police resulted in the creation of a local Black-led group, the Black Community Relations Council (BCRS), whose goal was to reduce tensions between the city's Black youths and the sheriff's department.[126] The BCRS used federal funding to support youth groups and to create a youth patrol in an attempt to "cool down" tensions a "month or two before any predicted outbreak of racial violence." One study found that EPA's youth patrol and those established in other cities were successful in reducing tensions due to young people's "sense of duty to their neighborhoods."[127]

As the threat of rioting receded, the funding for these types of community engagement initiatives dried up, and the study's authors lamented a lost opportunity to expand these patrols to combat neighborhood crime. While the BCRS was funded by federal monies, it had its own agenda. The longer-term goal of the group (possibly in affiliation with or connected to EPA's Black Panthers) was to create a shadow police force that would be more accountable and sensitive to the needs of East Palo Alto residents. Though the group's proposal to do so was quickly and publicly rebutted by the county sheriff, the sheriff's hostile response to the proposal to change how the department dealt with minority communities revealed that the lack of representation both in the composition of the force and in the shaping of departmental policy could lead to potentially even more dangerous problems.[128]

The establishment of the East Palo Alto Municipal Council and the availability of money, first through the federal Model Cities Program, and later through LEAA funding, provided the material basis for East Palo Alto's initial policing infrastructure. This structure would be tenuously controlled by community residents and a still relatively powerless EPAMC. New funding allowed for a county sheriff's lieutenant to be permanently stationed within East Palo Alto who essentially functioned as its de facto police chief.[129] In addition to the lieutenant, the new force included "12 deputies, a community relations worker and following the adoption of the 1969–70 budget, two sergeants, four detectives and one female community relations deputy."[130]

In addition, federal funds allowed the city to create a training program so that new Black police officers could be trained and hired by the county, an important first step for a force that did not have any Black police officers. Funding also helped with creation of the Community Youth Responsibility Program, which offered juvenile offenders an opportunity to appear before a "five-member Community panel that includes two members under 18 years of age." The panel was allowed to "'sentence' [the offender] to useful community work as restitution for his offense."[131] A less positive development, especially given the emergence of the carceral state during the 1980s and 1990s, was that the program was funded via the federal Omnibus Safe Streets Act of 1968 and by the California Youth Authority (CYA); the latter has been seen as one of the historic drivers of mass incarceration in the state.[132]

The establishment of the EPAMC provided a path toward community control over policing and allowed Black Palo Alto to offer "redress to its citizens."[133] However, the creation of this community safety and policing infrastructure did little to protect EPA's Black residents. In 1972, another fatal encounter between the county sheriff's department and a Black teenager occurred when the police shot fifteen-year-old Gregory White in the back and refused to allow his parents to go to him he lay dying in a neighbor's yard.[134] White's shooting garnered immediate condemnation from the Black Panthers, who offered support to the family while featuring the case in an article titled "Murder in Your Own Backyard" (see figure 6.7).

The sheriff's department denied any wrongdoing and a county supervisor justified the killing with incendiary "law and order" comments. Willia Gray, the then-chair of EPAMC, pushed back, leading a broad-based call for an independent investigation of the shooting. After a delay of several months, the county grand jury absolved the sheriff's department of any wrongdoing.[135] The reaction from EPA residents was mixed. While some EPAMC members were measured in their response to the decision, Gray called for the deputy sheriff who killed White to be fired and indicted and for the sheriff to be fired as well for his "blatant disregard and obstruction of justice: and his utter disrespect for the black community."[136]

The difference between Gray's condemnation of the sheriff's department and the rest of the council's more muted response perhaps lay in the crisis of

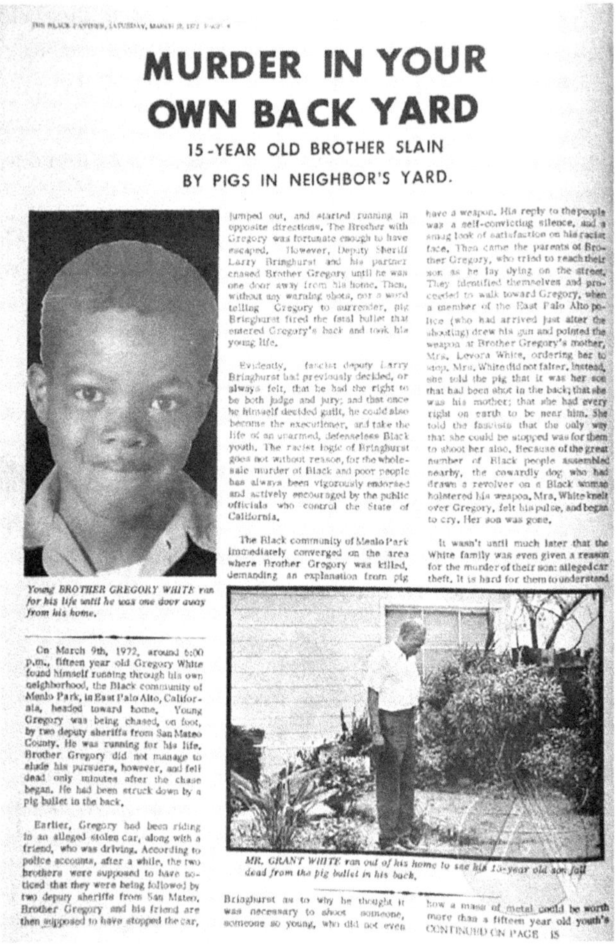

THE BLACK PANTHER, SATURDAY, MARCH 18, 1972 PAGE 4

MURDER IN YOUR OWN BACK YARD

15-YEAR OLD BROTHER SLAIN
BY PIGS IN NEIGHBOR'S YARD.

Young BROTHER GREGORY WHITE ran for his life until he was one door away from his home.

On March 9th, 1972, around 6:00 p.m., fifteen year old Gregory White found himself running through his own neighborhood, the Black community of Menlo Park, in East Palo Alto, California, headed toward home. Young Gregory was being chased, on foot, by two deputy sheriffs from San Mateo County. He was running for his life. Brother Gregory did not manage to elude his pursuers, however, and fell dead only minutes after the chase began. He had been struck down by a pig bullet in the back.

Earlier, Gregory had been riding in an alleged stolen car, along with a friend, who was driving. According to police accounts, after a while, the two brothers were supposed to have noticed that they were being followed by two deputy sheriffs from San Mateo. Brother Gregory and his friend are then supposed to have stopped the car,

jumped out, and started running in opposite directions. The Brother with Gregory was fortunate enough to have escaped. However, Deputy Sheriff Larry Bringhurst and his partner chased Brother Gregory until he was one door away from his home. Then, without any warning shots, nor a word telling Gregory to surrender, pig Bringhurst fired the fatal bullet that entered Gregory's back and took his young life.

Evidently, fascist deputy Larry Bringhurst had previously decided, or always felt, that he had the right to be both judge and jury; and that once he himself decided guilt, he could also become the executioner, and take the life of an unarmed, defenseless Black youth. The racist logic of Bringhurst goes not without reason, for the wholesale murder of Black and poor people has always been vigorously endorsed and actively encouraged by the public officials who control the State of California.

The Black community of Menlo Park immediately converged on the area where Brother Gregory was killed, demanding an explanation from pig

have a weapon. His reply to the people was a self-convicting silence, and a smug look of satisfaction on his racist face. Then came the parents of Brother Gregory, who tried to reach their son as he lay dying on the street. They identified themselves and proceeded to walk toward Gregory, when a member of the East Palo Alto police (who had arrived just after the shooting) drew his gun and pointed the weapon at Brother Gregory's mother, Mrs. Levora White, ordering her to stop. Mrs. White did not falter. Instead, she told the pig that it was her son that had been shot in the back; that she was his mother; that she had every right on earth to be near him. She told the fascists that the only way that she could be stopped was for them to shoot her also. Because of the great number of Black people assembled nearby, the cowardly dog who had drawn a revolver on a Black woman holstered his weapon. Mrs. White knelt over Gregory, felt his pulse, and began to cry. Her son was gone.

It wasn't until much later that the White family was even given a reason for the murder of their son: alleged car theft. It is hard for them to understand

MR. GRANT WHITE ran out of his home to see his 15-year old son fall dead from the pig bullet in his back.

Bringhurst as to why he thought it was necessary to shoot someone, someone so young, who did not even

how a mass of metal could be worth more than a fifteen year old youth's
CONTINUED ON PAGE 18

FIGURE 6.7. Murder in our backyard: Police killing of Gregory White, March 1972

Source: The Black Panther, March 18, 1972, 4.

community safety confronting East Palo Alto. Like many (sub)urban Black communities, the heroin epidemic had crashed into EPA, shattering the belief of many residents that they had secured a peaceful—albeit small—slice of suburban life. The rapid spread of heroin addiction, as well as the petty thefts, robberies, and other disorder that came in its wake, prompted EPA to declare its "own war on crime." Echoing the penal populism of Harlem and Washington, DC, EPA political leaders as well as longtime community activists were angered and frustrated by this wave of crime and in response embraced a law-and-order politics that reflected what Michael Fortner calls the "Black silent majority."[137] For some, the escalation of crime and the rise in perceptions of fear ran counter to the aspirations of Black Power Urbanism. Although probably hyperbole on the part of the *San Francisco Examiner*, its account of the "Ghetto's [i.e., EPA's] Own War on Crime" invoked militant Black Power tropes: "Don't depend on whitey to protect life and property. You have to do it yourself."[138] EPA officials proposed the creation of an additional "community protection" agency to supplement the small sheriff's substation. In December 1971, a new group was announced: "Black and White Women Against Crime."[139]

EPA's "war on crime" pointed toward the heart of the emerging penal populism of "straight blacks" and more militant left/Black Power supporters that would upend the fragile consensus around Black Power and policing that had stated first, that community control and Black representation would help Black communities, and second, that an idealized Black community—united in purpose—existed beyond the rhetoric of Black Power. For "straight blacks," the heroin-fueled crime wave was a struggle for the "many" in the face of a "destructive few."[140] Indeed, one community leader argued that "if those 'few' do not respond to our pleas for mercy for this community and its people, a plea for all we hold common and all we hope for as a people, we will move to eliminate by any means at our disposal these 'few' and the activities from our community."[141]

This endorsement of Black militancy was coupled with an aside that San Mateo County government was growing "impatient" with EPA and suggesting that EPA's incorporation should occur sooner rather than later, so that it could "assume full responsibility for government in the ghetto." San Francisco's Black newspaper, the *Sun-Reporter*, echoed the idea that EPA needed to assert more community control as a means to tame the crime wave. However, reflecting its roots as a Black-owned newspaper, it argued that the "drug menace" was also the result of an unequal policing regime under which police patrol and protect white areas, but allow drugs and violence to spread unchecked in Black areas. Acknowledging the paper's own placement within the Bay Area's Black elite circles, the article noted with some irony that "militants' suggestions that Blacks 'should be given power to police Black communities' was finally being taken seriously by 'the straights.'"[142]

Other analyses were blunt in assessing the racialized impact of heroin and policing. One analysis argued that the "crime war" bill that operated on the premise of more punitive policing would not work, as the root causes of the crime wave were not community apathy but rather the flood of guns and drugs spreading through communities like East Palo Alto. Instead, some argued that more grassroots efforts to protect community safety should be tried, such as those that lay in the hands of community leaders like Wilks and Hoover.[143] Wilks strongly supported the idea of neighborhood patrols, a three-year program that divided the city into districts patrolled by semi-paid volunteers, which would be paid for out of the Nixon crime bill. The program also included the creation of a youth justice panel that would judge local youth accused of minor crimes, who if found guilty would be sentenced to community "work chores."[144] Young people could be held accountable without ensnaring them in the state's carceral complex. This aligned with Hoover's own activism: he would create several youth intervention and incarceration recovery groups for the Black and Brown youths that were ensnared in the state's growing "golden gulag."

Criticism of EPA's "war on crime" also came from leftist quarters, with one critic arguing that EPA's Black middle-class "nationalists" were uncritically joining the "hysteria against crime" and engaging in a "reformist diversion" of the "struggle away from the basic crimes" of unemployment and poverty.[145] Wilks and others pushed back against these critiques, arguing that the crime wave in EPA was rooted in the "inhuman conditions" that faced the community, ranging from growing poverty and overcrowded and expensive housing for single mothers and seniors to the ongoing crisis of EPA's schools, where busing was creating a generation of angry alienated teenagers and making it "impossible to build a community when you strip it of its young every day."[146] With the closure of Ravenswood in 1975, Black youth had no educational or civic place of their own, while their ejection/expulsion from other high schools escalated. East Palo Alto's dream of Black Power Urbanism faltered. When crack cocaine hit the West Coast in 1982, East Palo Alto would become the epicenter of the peninsula's drug trade.

Incorporation did not check the burgeoning waves of violence unleashed by the crack epidemic, nor did it dislodge EPA's place as a site for its sale and distribution. The next two decades would see the small police force fielded by the new city gradually become overshadowed by the growing drug enforcement agencies that would take the lead in pursuing the War on Drugs. Although there were periodic efforts during the 1980s to include residents in confronting the problems of the drug trade such as neighborhood watches and community cleanup efforts, the vast majority of funding and people-hours went into facilitating raids and arrests.[147] Despite this periodic assistance, which often came with many strings, the city's police force remained relatively small, continually losing officers due to budget cuts. In 1988 the department faced its most serious crisis: the death of a police officer in the line of duty.[148] The officer's death triggered a massive attempt by government officials to finally end the "scourge" of drugs in East Palo Alto.

In 1989, the Nairobi Shopping Center—mostly empty and inhabited by drug dealers and homeless people—would be razed. City officials claimed that its demolition would "give us the city we so richly deserve—a city that is clean, safe, comfortable and well-maintained."[149] Demolishing Nairobi did not bring about a different future, nor did any one of the many crackdowns on the drug trade; as one resident observed, "it was a like a nightmare that wouldn't end."[150]

A dozen people were shot in January 1992, leading to one death, and a police emergency was declared.[151] A multiagency, regional task force—the RED (Regional Enforcement Detail) team was formed in response. Palo Alto and Menlo Park "donated" six officers and the county sheriff's department contributed eighteen officers. More ominously for Black residents, the California Highway Patrol posted twelve officers who were charged with increasing "routine traffic stops," which heightened the risks of "driving while Black."[152] On top of this heavy police presence, neighboring communities, fearing that the violence of EPA would jump across the concrete curtain of the Bayshore Highway, agreed to give funds, personnel, or equipment to East Palo Alto.[153]

By the late 1990s, efforts by community groups gained greater ground as these groups pushed for more reform and accountability for the East Palo Alto police force and greater coordination with local residents.[154] In the early twenty-first century the gradual reduction in crime and the abating of the crack epidemic would finally give East Palo Alto residents some breathing room and a greater sense of safety. But by then a whole generation of the city's youth were involved in the state's carceral system and fundamentally shut out of the Silicon Valley booming tech economy.

Umoja—Building a New Community

In many ways, Nairobi would be built upon the unstable foundations of the Black nationalism that lay at the heart of much of Black Power Urbanism, which Nixon's Black capitalism adroitly tapped into.[155] Black capitalism was fortuitous for East Palo Alto and cities across the nation in that it provided rhetoric as well as some funding to reduce the tensions between Black Power activists (including many who veered toward Black nationalism) and Black moderates who saw in Nixon an echo of respectability politics. The provision of SBA funding to the city and the accompanying press coverage allowed the selected "everyman" to voice an alternative to the untenable threat of Black Power as embodied by the Black Panther organization and other radical Black groups. For example, a *New York Times* article covering the plans for the building of a "Negro Mall" featured James Wilmore, who owned a barber shop, among the new business owners.[156] Wilmore proclaimed his support for Nairobi Village on the basis that "the white community respects one who stands on his own feet." Another *Times* interviewee, William B. Moore, a Korean

War veteran and owner of the Umoja Construction Company, stated that he and his "fellow Negroes should try to solve problems themselves."[157]

The development of Nairobi Village Shopping Center began with multiple motives. For some small store operators, the establishment of the shopping center allowed their nascent business to be identified with a focal point of community pride (Nairobi) as well as the commercial appeal of the hot new fashion that proclaimed, "Black is beautiful." For others, the shopping center aligned with the Black capitalism being pushed by the Nixon administration. For some Black Power supporters and many of the Black pluralism advocates, the establishment of Nairobi Village would be a concrete symbol of the ways in which community pride and solidarity could be transformed into political and economic resources. There was some opposition to Nairobi—albeit of the rhetorical kind. For some Black-Power thinkers, Black capitalism melded with Black Power was a trap that would result in demobilization and continued powerlessness (see figure 6.8). For some committed integrationists, Nairobi and its assertion of autonomy was a retreat from their embrace of and belief in militant integrationism; it was a step backward from the slow racial progress that they had achieved working through the mechanisms of suburban interracialism. Nairobi Village would also carry the hopes of liberal and moderate whites that Black capitalism would head off the dangerous and foolhardy aspects of Black Power and its associated violent images.

Support for Nairobi's Black capitalism also neatly dovetailed with the area's earlier traditions of suburban interracialism. One report of Nairobi's founding cited the role of Rev. Harold Varner, "Negro Associate pastor of the First Lutheran Church of Palo Alto," who was "instrumental in forming the Black Business Coalition" through his church's "Action Coalition." The Action Coalition defined itself as the "the first and only white organization that has attempted to unite the Black business interests into a cohesive group for the economic development of the Black community" as a means of "helping the Negroes develop a sound economic base."[158]

The development of Nairobi Village reflected the multiple ideological and philosophical currents swirling around in EPA. For Black Power supporters, Nairobi was first and foremost a symbol of Black autonomy. Yet this invocation of Black autonomy also fit comfortably though imperfectly with older notions of Black nationalism and respectability politics. For Black moderates like Kemp Miller, who had worked his way up from a janitor's position to an engineering position at Hewlett-Packard, the development of Nairobi Village meant the opportunity for Black residents to develop dignity—not only in their own eyes but in the eyes of whites. Miller was not alone: when interviewed, Black small business owners like James Wilmore or William Moore all asserted that Black people needed to reclaim "dignity" as the first means of meeting whites as equals.

In this sense they invoked a folk type of Black Power; where Hamilton and Carmichael stressed coming together as the first means of achieving Black solidarity, the folk understanding of Black Power as filtered through Black capitalism stressed the achievement of economic parity with whites, and thus dignity, as a precursor to further political and social change.

This emphasis on respect and autonomy was exactly what the Nixon administration had hoped for when it rolled out its Black capitalism policy. Created with the input of Daniel Patrick Moynihan and others, the program was the Nixon administration's attempt to craft a racial political strategy that would signal its growing resistance to Black radicalism while also appearing far more moderate than George Wallace, thus picking up suburban white votes. A twist on the emerging "Southern strategy" unfolded: a strategy that emphasized Black responsibility, but also Black culpability for its almost inevitable failure.[159] While Black capitalism may have been designed to succeed only in rhetorical terms, its initial phase and funding allowed Black moderates and white suburban interracialists to come together. This relationship was not easily separated from white paternalism. Wallace Stegner, then a professor at Stanford, would describe Counterpart, a local interracial group founded by Miller, as a "model of Blacks and whites working together as a team."[160] In Stegner's account of the groups: "The Blacks have the problems; the whites, so far, the money, and the political power. Instead of accepting white philanthropy, often misguided and always humiliating, Counterpart [the organization] uses teams under the joint direction of a Black man and a white man—the counterparts—to try to solve problems *that are always defined by the Blacks*."[161] Undergirding this need for mutual cooperation was a perceived need for "dignity" that only Black capitalism could provide. According to Kemp Miller: "This is why we have tried to help Black-owned business and why we want to have a Black-run industrial park. If you develop an economic enterprise, it has the ability to expand and to generate new money." He predicted that it would not only generate new money, it would also ensure independence when the "spigot" of funding induced by political pressure ran dry.[162]

Kemp Miller's employer, the Hewlett-Packard Corporation, in one of its lesser-known roles, built the foundation for East Palo Alto's future as a center of tech philanthropy. In a July 1971 employee newsletter, Bill Hewlett discussed the efforts the company was engaging in "toward solving the critical minority problems that face this country."[163] In addition to monetary support for projects like Nairobi Village (though not referred to by its full Afrocentric name), Hewlett listed the company's personal involvement or "investment" in the Palo Alto area. This ranged for "loan[ing] HP individuals on a fulltime basis to Counterpart, to the National Alliance of Businessmen, and to the OICW [Opportunities Industrial Center West]. The present head of the Mid-Peninsula Urban Coalition was loaned to the Coalition on a full time basis prior to his permanent appointment to that position."[164] Hewlett-Packard also quietly provided nearly three-quarters of the $450,000 that Nairobi Village and other local businesses received. In addition to acting as a conduit for Hewlett-Packard funds for the shopping center, Counterpart also claimed credit for attracting East Palo Alto's first bank, which was located across the street from the shopping center, and planned on "assist[ing] with the development of a federally funded health care center and a $2.3 million, 50,000 square feet, civic center" that would save East Palo Alto residents from having to go to Redwood City for services.[165]

All of these disparate groups would unite behind the Black Business Coalition, which was formed December 1, 1968, under the leadership of Harold Rhodes, chairman of the "all-Negro Community Council" (that is, the EPAMC), as well as other local Black leaders—self-appointed, anointed, or otherwise. The purpose of the Black Business Coalition would be to "promote the development and expansion of Negro Businesses."[166] The site of this new Black Power foundation would be the University Village Shopping Center. While the complex was envisioned as the first step in the emergence of East Palo Alto as a Black Power city, the site and its business model faced challenges. Built in 1957 on the east side of the Bayshore Freeway, the complex lost traffic and business from affluent west side shoppers when the new and expanded highway opened. Due to its inability to attract business, the shopping center changed hands several times until it was bought by the eclectic group of Nairobi investors.

Although the Black Business Coalition viewed itself as the lead organization in getting Nairobi Village off the ground, the real power lay in the network of white-dominated groups that controlled access to minority business funding. The key and most visible element in Nairobi financing was the involvement of Arcata Investment Company.[167] Rejecting the often slow and nearly impenetrable loan process that had been offered to minority business in earlier years, Arcata pursued a "bold approach" by using the "simple method of putting money into the hands of minority businessmen [and] toss[ing] out the rule book on find[ing] and financ[ing] them."[168]

Nairobi's opening received considerable press—for Black moderates and white supporters, it symbolized a neat synthesis of Black Power and traditional notions of uplift and progress. Thus, although the complex's sign read "Uhuru Na Umoja" (freedom and unity), the slogan also meant progress and moderation.[169] The reports on the complex's opening were nearly triumphal: "The pride of East Palo Alto's 30,000 Blacks is the Nairobi Shopping Center. Of the dozen stores in the center, half were financed by Arcata." There was some dissent from the Black Panther Party who believed that inclusion of the center in the Nairobi movement was naïve and a distraction from the harder work of Black liberation.[170] The businesses that opened in the Nairobi plaza were far from the grand industrial concerns often envisioned by the enthusiastic proponents of Black capitalism. Instead they reflected the traditional pattern of small Black establishments such as barber shops, beauty salons, and "soul food" restaurants. The operators of these small businesses included some of the city's younger leaders, like "Chuck Stevens, 27, president of the Black Business Coalition and operator of the Chuck Stevens For Men Clothing Store." Other business included the "Nairobi House of Music," and the "Nairobi Village Cleaners."[171]

Despite the high hopes for the shopping center, Black capitalism was fundamentally flawed. Of the fifty or so businesses that Arcata had funded, a 1971 report

FIGURE 6.8.   Black Panther politics in East Palo Alto

Source: "A Structure for Survival: East Palo Alto Branch Black Panther Party, Opens with Community Survival Day," The Black Panther, vol. 8, no. 7, September 23, 1972, 4.

found that "46 [were] still in operation, two in trouble, and four gone under." These businesses included a "'soul food restaurant,' a commuter bus service, beauty and barber shops, a magazine, nightclubs, bookstores and a delivery service." Arcata, "once regarded by the Nixon administration as a successful model of its minority capitalism program," turned out to be a failure, and the collapse of these business and Nairobi was "viewed by some officials of the Department of Commerce as a potential threat to the success of the entire program."[172]

By 1977, the Nairobi Shopping Center had been mostly abandoned after a fire partially destroyed the complex. Locally it acquired a reputation as a place collapsing under vandalism and neglect and a known gathering spot for the drug trade and homeless people. By 1989, the now almost vacant Nairobi was bulldozed by the city over the objections of its last owner, whose mother had operated a liquor store in the complex.[173] The declaration of the center as a public nuisance was a sad reversal of the high hopes that had surrounded its development. An article from the *San Jose Mercury News* commented that the center's deteriorated presence "mocked the struggle" of East Palo Alto to "achieve some measure of civic pride and development."[174] The paper later wondered "why anyone would want to preserve those buildings in their current condition." At the time of its demolition, a San Mateo county sheriff in attendance would remark: "I just wanted to make sure the demolition is really going to happen. I'm a little nostalgic about it. This was the most exciting place on East Palo Alto when we were here."[175]

From A Black Power Space to a Black City

Black Power Urbanism would remain on East Palo Alto's agenda up thorough and beyond its final and successful push for municipal incorporation in 1983. By that point, Nairobi was in retreat as the full impact of California's "taxpayers revolt," also known as Proposition 13, took effect. As one county supervisor noted in 1978:

> We started out of the 70s with the thought that we could solve all the human problems and we started all kinds of programs, there being plenty of money, especially from the state and the feds. . . . [A]ll the special interest groups got money. . . . We spent more and more money and got farther and farther away from the traditional role of local government in offering such basic services as police and fire, libraries, parks and roads.[176]

The irony of this statement is vast, in that East Palo Alto had not been given many of these basic services as an unincorporated, unrepresented, and heavily minority part of the county. With the elimination of state and federal money, the citizenship demands of Black East Palo Alto were dismissed as merely those of "special interests." The cuts imposed by the county board, who were "no lon-ger going to subsidize" the community, included "the dismantling of everything" from the library to the probation officer, according to Gertrude Wilks.[177] These cuts were vociferously resisted by community activists and only strengthened their case for formal incorporation as a means to protect the city from the county balancing its budget at East Palo Alto's expense. Reagan's defunding of the cities and local governments during his first year in office only heightened the city's crisis. Again according to Wilks, the cuts were devastating: "It didn't take long to know that a change had come . . . because they began to dismantle all the . . . social programs . . . in the country, and it was felt really strong in communities here because of most of the [remaining] programs were subsidized by some fed-eral programs."[178]

Support for East Palo Alto's attempt to create a Black Power suburb that was a just and emancipatory space for its residents foundered as the political and fiscal shocks of the 1970s unfolded. These transformations strengthened arguments for incorporation of the city as a means to finally secure the rights of suburban citi-zenship. Incorporation, however, would not solve all of the city's problems, as the expansion of the Silicon Valley tech industry and increased real estate development pushed an already marginalized East Palo Alto into a new racialized spatial econ-omy that increasingly left behind its residents and the community's property val-ues. The absence of durable preexisting local structures and the timing and extent of EPA's postwar growth meant that the emergence of East Palo Alto as a "Black space" was the result of a racial architecture of containment created by the social, political, and administrative lines of housing and education discrimination, which in turn were buttressed by a literal "concrete curtain" of highway construction.

By the turn of the twenty-first century, this architecture of containment would be turned inside out as ongoing processes of displacement and dispos-session made the area into a new frontier space for the expansion of Silicon Val-ley, the rise of the glocalization of real finance, and (sub)urban development. The demolition of Nairobi Plaza was just the first of these new transformations, as the new city (along with most cities in California) faced tremendous pres-sure to develop additional revenue streams in response to the fiscal austerity induced by Proposition 13.[179]

In 1983, the city council (all of whom were African Americans) embarked on two ambitious, albeit highly contested redevelopment projects: Gateway 101 and University Circle.[180] Gateway 101 focused on the private development of a 146-acre site that included the demolition of long-closed Ravenswood High School; the acquisition of additional properties through eminent domain; and the displace-ment of 126 households.[181] The redevelopment plan also included the building of 217 units of affordable housing and the promise to fulfill a "first hire" policy for local residents. The development opened in 1998, and by 2009 the assessed value had grown to $341 million. As of 2025, Gateway 101 had become EPA's "largest revenue generator with more than $2.2 million in annual sales tax" and employing "more than 800 workers," with "approximately 40 percent representing EPA residents."[182] Jones Mortuary, a funeral home that mostly served the city's Black and Brown community, was allowed to remain; however, given the decline in the city's Black population, its future is in doubt.[183] The second redevelopment project, University Circle, would entail a fundamental alteration to the city's spatial fabric. The project involved demolishing Whiskey Gulch, the city's historic retail core, which was home to restaurants, small businesses, and local non-profits that served the city's Black, Latino, and Pacific Islander populations.[184] After many delays and protests from community members who argued that the city was overly concessionary to the various developers or to neighboring cities, University Circle finally opened. The complex included "three class-A office towers totaling 450,000 square feet of office space, 15,000 square feet of retail space, with underground and surface parking in a landscaped master planned development."[185] While the complex sported "Brazilian granite and Italian limestone exteriors and large, dramatic water fountains in a courtyard setting," the buildings presented a collective blank back wall to their EPA neighbors, while their windows looked across the Bayshore Highway to Palo Alto and the rest of Silicon Valley.[186]

Black Power Urbanism, a belief that activists and residents could build spaces that supported and nourished communities of color, was redefined in purely monetary terms. The city no longer had a downtown of its own; indeed, the city noted that "due to limited commercial space elsewhere, few businesses were able to secure retail space in the city."[187] In the new logic of suburban competition, University Circle was, however, a victory for the city: a space that was assessed in 1988 at $7.3 million had an assessed value of $422 million in 2009. As Michael Kahan notes, the demolition of Whiskey Gulch "illustrates how state power and global capitalism produce 'abstract' space—[Henri] Lefebvre's term for a space valued for money, a space of prohibition, a space 'founded on the vast network of banks, business centres, and major productive entities, but also on motorways, airports, and information lattices."[188] This space, however, was not for the people who had struggled to bring the city into life.

Yet, under the pressure of hyper-development, East Palo Alto's Black Power urbanist past would be used by remaining local activists to wring slight concessions from developers, such as Sand Hill Property's plans for redeveloping the former Nairobi Plaza site, even as the developers themselves would use East Palo Alto's Black Power past as a new kind of Black spatial aesthetics that aligned with the vaguely progressive ethos of the early social media/tech industry.[189]

Conclusion

THE RISE AND FALL OF BLACK POWER GOVERNANCE

Ain't no stoppin' us now
We're on the move

—McFadden & Whitehead, "Ain't No Stoppin' Us Now"

"Oakland: That Other Great City by the Bay" was the celebratory title of an October 1980 article in *Ebony* magazine—mainstream Black America's most popular publication.[1] The 1977 election of Lionel Wilson, the city's first African American mayor, spurred the publication of an extensive overview of the city. Alongside a flattering portrait of the sixty-year-old Wilson (a "vigorous tennis-playing former judge"), the article highlighted the city's new Black political and cultural elite. Wilson's Black appointees included the director of economic development, the city clerk, and the director of parks and recreation. Ruth Love's position as superintendent of the OUSD was a partial triumph over the fragmented jurisdictional landscape that had stymied earlier progressive and liberal political organizing. Love—who had succeeded the assassinated Marcus Foster—was the city's second Black school superintendent, and was lauded for her recent success in boosting academic achievement in a majority-Black school system. Black people held the top management positions on the board of port commissioners and within BART (Bay Area Rapid Transit).

The rise of this political class rested on decades of organizing by Black Oaklanders and more recently on the 1973 political campaigns of Bobby Seale (for mayor) and Elaine Brown (for city council), both members of the Black Panthers. In support of these campaigns, the BPP engaged in massive outreach to and energetic mobilization of previously disengaged working-class and poor Black Oaklanders. This engagement took place as part of the Panthers' community survival programs, which included its direct action of distributing groceries to over one hundred thousand recipients (which famously included a "chicken in every bag"), as well as voter outreach and political education efforts.[2] This kind of community mobilization "to interject 'black populism'" into city politics was necessary as Oakland—unlike Newark—lacked a party infrastructure that could continuously connect the average citizen with local political structures.[3] As Donna Murch notes in her history of Oakland, "In order to participate in these mass gatherings, people had to show their voter registration cards. If they did not have one, volunteers helped them register. This ingenious form of organizing served multiple purposes. In addition to swelling the rolls with thousands of new black voters, the survival conferences made the link between the Party's survival programs and their new electoral agenda explicit."[4]

Oakland's 1973 mayoral race did not display unity or uniformity within the city's Black community. In a separate "showdown in Oakland," Otho Green, a member of the Afro-American Association who in the early 1960s had worked with a number of other Black activists to open up the city's closed political system and displace the older entrenched Black elite, decided to compete against Seale.[5] By the early 1970s, Green's vision of Black empowerment (and the vision of other members of the association, as well) had been recoded as a mild form of militant integrationism. Green, not Seale, was the choice of the Democratic political establishment, which included many members of city's Black middle class.[6] Although Green lost, Seale and Brown (and by extension the party) were forced to bridge intra-class divisions in order to develop a broad coalition with a range of other left/liberal groups in order to defeat Mayor Reading. This mobilization and coalition-building was so successful that it pushed Seale into a run-off (which he lost) with the incumbent mayor, John Reading. Oakland's closed political system was fundamentally shaken. As Seale would say to his supporters on election night: "You yourselves, all of you precinct workers . . . All the work you've done today has blown their minds . . . They're going to know, the Republican administration, that Watergate system, is gonna know that from here on in we ain't backin' up!"[7] Indeed, the election was a "people's victory. The people in our community and the city of Oakland. They like people to make concession speeches. I don't make concessions, 'cos I will not concede . . . the rights of human beings."[8]

Though both Seale and Brown lost their elections, the massive mobilization they had unleashed increased the certainty that Oakland's next mayor would be Black. This certainty was magnified with the death of Senator William Knowland Jr. in 1974, which marked the end of the Knowland family's influence over the city's political life. The weakening of the Knowland-backed elite meant that within Seale's defeat lay a huge symbolic win for the new Black political class (though with the exception of Brown, not a class derived from the Panthers). Oakland's fragmented institutional landscape could be pried open far enough that a limited form of Black Power Urbanism could take hold. Rather than institutional transformation or the creation of "new forms," electoral pressure from Black activists and community groups would instead coalesce around an agenda to diversify the personnel within these institutions—both at the top and within the rank-and-file—as a means to reshape their focus, though not their function. This was a far different result than the one the Panthers had envisioned in their calls for a wholesale restructuring of the police, of housing, and of education.

The appointment of "Black faces in high places" such as John Williams, director of the Oakland Redevelopment Agency, and Marcus Foster, OUSD superintendent, could be seen as the Knowland regime's efforts to co-opt and deflect more radical governance by activists like Paul Cobb or Elaine Brown. Indeed, their appointments fit within Oakland's long-standing political culture and institutional configurations, which favored siloed bureaucracies helmed by leaders picked by the city's ruling coalition. However, these appointments, especially Foster's, could also be seen as instantiations of Black Power Urbanism, as Black activists and white liberals pushed vigorously for both appointments in the face of white conservative resistance. Foster's push for a massive reorientation of the OUSD away from its quasi-institutionalized focus on the affluent (and majority-white) residents of the Hills raised the promise of Black Power Urbanism. Foster forced the OUSD to confront and repair the damage wrought by the district's institutionalized racism toward the Black and Brown children of the Flatlands. Policing and public safety were the exception to this pattern of targeted transformation. Though Mayor Wilson made his push for structural reform of the police department a key element of his campaign and administration, the police department remained determinedly outside of Black political influence during and long after Wilson's administration.

The Oakland *Tribune*, voice of the city's conservative elite, determinedly attacked even the mildest of liberal initiatives, opposed unions, and stood firmly behind the large corporations that dominated the city's economy.[9] The paper was deeply supportive of white small-business owners and landlords and was implacably opposed to Black activism. An example of this hostility occurred in 1969 when its owner William Knowland ran a provocative advertorial of a white-gloved hand symbolically pointing a gun toward Black protests of police brutality. In 1977 Gannett newspapers acquired the paper, triggering a fundamental transformation: no longer would it be the overt mouthpiece of a local ruling clique. Indeed, in a clear break with the past, two years later Gannett appointed Robert Maynard as the chief editor; Maynard would be the first Black editor of a major white-owned newspaper. In addition to this milestone, other cultural changes occurred. For the first time, three of the city's (white) elite cultural institutions—the symphony, the ballet, and the museum—had respectively a Black conductor, manager, and curator.

Oakland was "probably the best city for Blacks in America" according to Thomas Barkley, the then-president of the board of port commissioners, and like Wilson, one of the original members of the 1950s-era Men of Tomorrow. Barkley's buoyant opinion and the *Ebony* article were a fitting complement to the optimistic 1979 disco anthem "Ain't No Stoppin' Us Now," which during this period reached the top of charts at local radio station KDIA, a fixture of local Black media since 1945.[10] Black Oakland was a city on the move, with nothing "stopping it now."

Yet despite this optimistic take, what some critics had feared about Black Power's potential path—that it would be subject to not just repression but more importantly co-optation—was also evident.[11] With Wilson's ascension, Oakland's top leadership positions were held either by either people who were involved in the Men of Tomorrow network, members of the Afro-American Association, or members of Oakland's new post–civil rights middle class. Though relegated to the last pages of the article, critical voices such as the journalist Brenda Payton and longtime activist Paul Cobb were included. These critics pushed back against the notion that the many groups that constituted Black Oakland—especially the Black lumpenproletariat that had been the ideological and organizational focus of the Black Panthers—had substantively benefited from this change in political faces. Other political actors were missing or sidelined in this process of regime change. For example, by the time of Wilson's election, the Black Panther Party was a shadow of itself due to a decade or more of the federal government's COIN-TELPRO (Counterintelligence Program).[12] In 1982, the party was formally dissolved in a dispute between BPP cofounder Huey Newton and Ericka Huggins, the director of the Oakland Community School, a direct instantiation of the Black Panther Party's community survival strategy.[13]

Conditions on the ground also challenged this sunny narrative. Some of the many challenges facing the city included high levels of Black unemployment (near 40 percent among young Black men, as alleged by Cobb) resulting from the departure of the city's remaining heavy industry and an ongoing low-income/affordable housing crisis exacerbated by high levels of abandoned and vacant houses due to the Section 235 mortgage debacle. A surge in police-related killings of Black and Latino boys and men resulted in few or no consequences for the officers involved. This lack of accountability left many Black and Brown Oaklanders infuriated, especially given the city's now decades-long history of police violence. In light of these problems, Payton, who had extensively covered the police killings in her reporting, argued that there was "no real Black power" in the city.[14]

Payton charged that instead of instituting actual substantive change, Wilson and by extension the city's Black political and social elite, as well as its rising Black middle class, were "classic example[s] of people who were active and rallied for change, and then were given *something* and were satisfied."[15] Paul Cobb went even further in this critique, likening Oakland's Black empowerment to a merely symbolic, Potemkin-like "plantation," whose fiscal foundation (including his own organization) rested on an unstable mix of private foundation and public state and federal funding that replaced or supplemented the faltering budgets of these Black spaces.[16] Decades of past and current waves of white flight, commercial disinvestment, and deindustrialization weakened local budgets even as the desire and need for interventions grew. Proposition 13, enacted in 1978, was seen by many political observers as a "racial proposition" designed to fiscally undercut the newly empowered Black and Brown spaces.[17] In the end, Cobb's critique of the uneasy authority and durability (both markers of political development) of Oakland's Black Power Urbanism (and by extension that of other Black cities) proved to be prophetic. A month after this article was published President Ronald Reagan was elected and Black Power Urbanism would come to a quick and decisive end with the rollout of Reaganomics.[18]

Ebony's profile of Oakland is remarkable in that the story of this moment—between the near past of the devastation of urban renewal, the sorrow of urban rebellions and the exhilaration Black Power insurgencies, and the then-present of "chocolate cities" that were "on the move"—could be told of any number of Black cities. In this moment stood Oakland and Newark, East Palo Alto and East Orange, as well as all of the cities large and small that had embraced the notion that Black Power (Urbanism) could reshape their cities into just places. The guarded optimism of this article could be felt not only in the four cities that were covered in this book, but across Black spaces where many sensed that something fundamental had changed about the relationship between race, space, and power.

Toward a New History of Black Cities

Black Power Urbanism is what changed cities. Emerging in the early 1960s and subsiding by 1980, it was a political order that sought to challenge the existing urban order and redefine the role of Black Americans in shaping metropolitan spaces. Black Power Urbanism emphasized the interconnectedness if not centrality of space and race, both real and imagined, in influencing the experiences of Black as well as other communities of color within the city. It was a reimagining of Black urban life that centered the agency of Black and other minoritized people of color in America's cities. Black Power Urbanism sought to redefine how Black life could and should be lived in urban environments. This involved not just recognizing the harms of the postwar urban renewal order, but also repairing these harms by challenging existing norms and structures and by advocating for changes in policies and practices that limited the opportunities and well-being of Black communities. In its most aspirational sense, Black Power Urbanism envisioned and advocated for the creation of "just cities" where Black communities could not only survive but thrive. Black Power Urbanism was a distinctive political order characterized by a cohesive collection of ideas, interests, and organizations—or what I call ideas, imaginings, and instantiations—that revolved around a particular vision of Black urban life, emphasizing the importance of race and space in shaping urban governance.

A Black Power archive undergirds much of the book's analysis.[19] By drawing on a wide variety of sources—speeches, texts, studies, music, performances—the book reflects the myriad ways in which Black Power Urbanism cohered in terms of ideas, interests, institutions, and instantiations. Sources include a vast "gray literature" that ranges from government reports, urban renewal plans, maps, and testimony located in the dusty corners of local libraries, to the flyers and letters in the stacks of boxes that fill the homes of neighborhood activists. The Black Power archive can be seen in the ephemera of everyday Black life captured in the anecdotes of crossing guards sharing stories about the buses that carried Black domestics to white suburban neighborhoods. It can be seen in conversations both past and present with students, parents, and teachers who shared their struggles to save majority-Black educational spaces that were deemed failures instead of being recognized, as Eve Ewing argues, as places of home, family, and safety; as "site[s] of a history and a pillar of Black pride in a racist [metropolis]."[20] A Black Power archive unfolded in sometimes silent and imagined conversations with closed storefront churches, vacant houses and apartment buildings, and sometimes empty lots willing to open up to a stranger taking pictures of spaces that had played a part in the rise and fall of Black Power Urbanism.

More concretely, the Black Power archive in this book rests on artifacts like the Black Power Manifesto, issued at the 1967 National Conference on Black Power. The Black Power Manifesto serves as a clear early articulation of the goals of this new potential order to act as a "third force" in the shaping the post–urban renewal metropolis but also the American state. The Black Power archive highlights three key elements of the ordering of Black Power Urbanism. First was the strategy to induce what Black Power theorists called "unity without uniformity." Hamilton and Ture called this strategy "closing ranks."[21] Second was the need to develop new, concrete forms that would disrupt current patterns—from beliefs about political efficacy to the built environment, from education to policing—and replace them with new instantiations that reflected a more just and emancipatory city for all. Third, the ultimate goal of Black Power Urbanism as outlined in the Black archive was to shift Black communities from a position of disadvantage and disempowerment to one of empowerment and agency. Black cities could and should "be on the move."

Black Power Urbanism took place within a concatenation of three long-term historical institutional structures and processes. The first process is that of urban regime development, broadly defined as a temporally specific formation and layering of ideational, political, institutional, and socio-spatial arrangements and understandings. The process of urban regime development can be seen in the "rules of the game." Some of the "rules," or rather regime structures, included whether a city/metropolis was governed along machine or reform lines, whether representatives were elected at-large or by district, whether mayors were strong or weak, and whether there was direct political control of the city agencies. These "rules of the game" are the result of processes of political development that shaped Black Power Urbanism across space, place, and time. The second long-term process was Black urban political development, here defined as the historical as well as ongoing efforts of Black communities to secure political power, advocate for their rights, and address systemic issues affecting their communities. Emerging at the interstice of institutions and Black political development was the third factor that shaped the rise of Black Power Urbanism, that is, Black Power–infused political insurgencies. Black Power insurgencies were both ideational—"Black Consciousness" influenced political and cultural mobilizations and helped to shape the "search for new forms"—and were connected to actions carried out by a coalition of activists at the local, state, and federal levels who attempted to put these ideas into action.

As the cases of Newark, East Orange, Oakland, and Palo Alto show, the banner of Black Power Urbanism enabled everyday Black people to pursue individual and collective visions of freedom, justice, and dignity. Or as the Black Panthers would boldly state, enabled claims to "Land, Bread, Housing, Education, Clothing, Justice and Peace."[22] More prosaically but no less critically, Black Power Urbanism meant reframing the classic formulations of urban politics of "who gets what" and challenging the "how" of urban politics. Black Power urbanists questioned the ordinary urban administrations in these emergent Black urban spaces about what kinds of services were delivered, in what kinds of ways, for what ends, and for whom. Chuck Stone, one of the earliest theorist-activists of the Black Power movement, argued that true political empowerment entails "control [of] the black community, proportionately control [of] the decision-making apparatus of a white racist government and guarantee[ing] black survival. This can only be done by acquiring political power. There is no other recourse. Political power is government control or the ability to decide who shall control."[23] Even as these questions were asked and new answers formulated, Black Power Urbanism faced an existential question that emerged at nearly the same time the first Black mayors/Black urbanist regimes ascended to office: what if Black Power Urbanism was too little, too late? What if Black cities were, in fact, "hollow prizes"?[24] Indeed, some critics opined that "'the Negro problem' was the 'most decisive of the social problems that we think of when we consider the urban crisis.'"[25] Black bodies and the "urban crisis" were thus conjoined into a recognizable political and institutional configuration, the Black-governed city, a city in trouble.

In the face of this rising skepticism of Black governance, street-level organizing and ongoing contestations against unjust cities continued. Much of this organizing rested on the labor of Black women like Gertrude Wilks of East Palo Alto, who along with others established Nairobi Day School; or women like Mattie Guyton Shepherd, whose thirteen-year-old son, Tyrone Guyton, was killed by the Emeryville police in 1973. These women, their families, friends, and neighbors had all witnessed the harmful ways in which indifferent if not hostile education, housing, and policing structures affected their families. Even in these supposedly "hollow cities," community control of schools, housing, and police held the potential for better futures. And indeed, given the dire conditions, what did these activists and their communities have to lose?

These local activists were not alone. A range of professionals, academics, and elected officials who emerged out of the new civil rights state would come together to develop a top-down Black urban agenda.[26] While this agenda-setting was a manifestation of Black Power as a "third force" in American politics, it was also—as some Black Power intellectuals had feared—a bid to incorporate Black actors into the American political establishment as junior partners, not central agents. Some of this development was the result of the New Federalism of the Nixon and Ford administrations, which brought Great Society–funded, neighborhood-centered possibilities to a halt, replacing them with a patchwork of new ideas and institutions like Community Development Block Grants (CDBG) for community development, the Law Enforcement Assistance Administration (LEAA) to support law enforcement, and housing vouchers and revenue-sharing programs. These programs served as a bridge between Nixon's policy of benign neglect and the full collapse of urban policy during the Reagan years.

A wave of newly elected Black mayors offered a counterpoint to 1970s-era New Federalism and the retreat from the Black freedom struggle/Civil Rights Movement (however attenuated by that point). As the music group Parliament would proclaim in their song "Chocolate City," the election of Cleveland's Carl Stokes (1967), Gary's Richard Hatcher (1967), and Newark's Kenneth Gibson

(1970) would soon be followed during the 1970s by the election of Black mayors across American cities and towns.[27] Black mayors would soon become the face of both urban and Black America, as exemplified by Kenneth Gibson's image and the headline "The Black Mayors," on the cover page of *Newsweek* magazine's August 3, 1970 issue.[28] In an era marked by the rise of associations of government officials that became part of the state and local response to Nixon's New Federalism, Black mayors would also organize. For example, Black mayors created the National Black Caucus of Locally Elected Officials within the nation's preeminent local government organization, the US Conference of Mayors (established in 1932 as part of the New Deal Keynesian order). The Southern Conference of Black Mayors (SCBM) was organized in 1974 and their numbers rapidly increased. In 1977 the National Conference of Black Mayors (NCBM) was born out of a merger of the SCBM and the non-Southern Black mayors who had generally been members of the US Conference of Mayors.[29]

The fragility of Black Power Urbanism could be seen in cases where its ethos competed with individual ambition, such as in the power struggle within the US Conference of Mayors, an organization that had historically and decidedly not been geared toward centering Black urban citizens.[30] In 1974, Kenneth Gibson and Richard Hatcher competed against each other and a third mayor (a Republican) in a bid to become the organization's next president.[31] Although other members of the Black caucus feared that the split between Hatcher and Gibson would pave the way for the third candidate to win, Gibson ultimately prevailed.[32] His successful election was seen by some other caucus members as shortsighted. Gibson's ambition was not in keeping with the Black Power ethos that he had displayed in Gary two years earlier, and it was certainly a snub to Richard Hatcher, who had hosted the 1972 Black Power Conference when no other city would agree to.[33] Doris A. Davis, mayor of Compton, California, "said she was upset by the Newark Mayor's actions. . . . [she said,] 'I am so mad, I can't find words to express, it. . . . I think he has been shortsighted and has gone for the short-term political benefits rather than thinking of the long-range impact on blacks and minorities, and his image among them.'"[34]

The presumed solidarity of Black Power Urbanism was not as deep nor as long-lasting as its supporters had hoped. Indeed, critics of "bourgeois politics" like Chuck Stone had predicted that without the strong ideological frame of a disciplined party apparatus, short-term jockeying for positions within the existing political struggle would almost always prevail.[35] The lack of unity and shortsightedness among Black mayors was a troubling portent of what was to come.

From today's perspective, these everyday activists, their neighborhoods, and their cities had everything to lose—and many of them did lose everything. A present-day reading of *Ebony*'s article on the hopeful future of Black Power

Urbanism in Oakland (and elsewhere) elicits a certain measure of melancholy. We *know* what will happen in these cities, though there is some disagreement about the sequence. If, as Peniel Joseph argues, there is a narrative based on an "archaeology of failure" for Black cities, this narrative assumes that these cities were so fundamentally doomed that nothing, not even Black (Power) activism, could save them from large impersonal forces such as white flight, commercial disinvestment, and deindustrialization.[36]

The election of Jimmy Carter did not reverse the decline of Black Power Urbanism. Much of the Black political class was hesitant about endorsing Jimmy Carter during the early days of the 1976 presidential primary. Some of the strongest adherents of the Black Power movement hesitated to support Carter from the considered belief that white politicians should earn Black votes, and that Black voters needed to vote strategically and cohesively in order to maximize "the balance of power" that Black communities held in certain key voting districts.[37] Another source of reluctance stemmed from the fact that Carter not only positioned himself against the (Republican) establishment, but also seemed to agree with rising white conservatism, especially among those white voters that four years later would be relabeled as "Reagan Democrats." Carter made no effort to reach out to Black groups while awkwardly espousing beliefs that neighborhoods had a right to "ethnic purity."[38] In the end, Carter won over 92 percent of the Black vote without promising much in return. Black voters had little choice between a somewhat conservative white Southern Democrat and Gerald Ford, a Watergate-tainted incumbent.

Carter displayed his reluctance to overtly seek out Black support with a tepid and belated acknowledgment of the Black vote during his election in a telephone call to the National Black Caucus of Local Elected Officials meeting being held in Denver, Colorado. In his "lukewarm" message Carter acknowledged that Black voters had been "instrumental in helping me to become elected to the highest office in our land."[39] In the following year Carter reversed course with a major speech, "Message to the Black Community: The Present Administration and Its Domestic Achievements and Goals," delivered at the 1977 National Urban League Annual Conference, which was published in full in the *Black Scholar* and covered in the national press.[40] Carter's preliminary remarks acknowledged his "good friend" Vernon Jordan Jr., who was transitioning from a civil rights leader to a rising Democratic party insider. Carter also touted the array of "Black faces in high places" appointed to high-level positions, including Patricia Harris, the secretary of HUD.

In this speech Carter laid out his administration's urban agenda, which turned out to be a rather generic one emphasizing public service jobs (many targeted to poor, hard-core unemployed and youths), revenue-sharing, and Black capitalism via an expanded minority purchasing program. While this proposed agenda was accompanied by the promise of millions of dollars of increased funding, it only partially reversed the deep cuts imposed by the Nixon/Ford administrations. In addition, Carter's proposals did not display the creativity of the Great Society programs, especially the possibilities of a renewed commitment to community control. Instead, presaging the neoliberal urbanism that was to come, Carter proposed an expansion of the still-experimental housing vouchers program for families while making a somewhat larger commitment to housing for the worthy poor of the elderly and disabled via the Section 202 program. Even more alarming was that Carter called for welfare reform, arguing that

> jobs will be the thrust behind this reform program for those who are able to work, and self-respect and adequate living conditions for those who are not able to work. Our goal is for all those who want to work to be able to find work so that they can be independent . . . and so they can be proud and they can be self-sufficient. And I would like to point out that an emphasis on jobs and work for those who are able is not discriminatory, it is not moving backwards, and it is not a deprivation of basic rights. What we want is for people who are able not to be permanently dependent on Government, but able to stand on their own feet, support their own family and have a constructive attitude toward our society.[41]

To be fair, Carter linked welfare reform to a "guaranteed job by Government if necessary." Yet given the increasing punitiveness of welfare reform proposals that had preceded and then followed the Carter administration, the jobs guarantee was perhaps window dressing. Seeking to shore up its rocky relationship with Black voters, the administration developed a new partnership with selected Black interest groups like the NCBM, the National Urban League, and the Congressional Black Caucus through contracts with HUD and the Department of Labor (DOL).[42] Carter's urban agenda looked suspiciously like co-optation. By 1980, Patricia Harris was gone from HUD, replaced by Moon Landrieu, the (white) former mayor of New Orleans who "changed the direction of HUD and started a new policy process, 'Development Choices for the Eighties.' This emphasized development opportunities for the real estate sector and evidenced little concern for urban distress. It was operated directly out of the Secretary's office and consisted of a consultative process via a council of state and local officials and private developers."[43] Like his deregulatory moves in trucking and airlines, Carter's post-Harris urban policy was the unacknowledged forebear of Reagan's nascent neoliberal order.[44]

If Carter's ambivalence toward cities and the malaise of the 1970s was not enough, the 1980s and 1990s came calling with concentrated poverty and the rise of the urban underclass, the crack epidemic, the War on Drugs, mass incarceration, and finally the collapse of the inner city. This narrative of essentialized failure, drawn from a darker well of American history, rested on the fear of Black governance, which was last seen during the backlash to the First Reconstruction during the late nineteenth century. Nearly one hundred years later, in the late 1970s and early 1980s, the Second Reconstruction would come to an end. In 1980 Ronald Reagan, a month after "not respond[ing] to a speaking invitation from the NAACP," gave a "state's rights" speech in Philadelphia, Mississippi, the town where three civil rights workers (James Chaney, Andrew Goodman, and Michael Schwerner) were killed by Ku Klux Klan members in 1964.[45] In 1984, Reagan's message about a new era was punctuated by another speech, this time in Macon, Georgia, proclaiming that "the South would rise again."[46]

Reagan accompanied his calls for a post–Second Reconstruction age with a new anti-urban policy agenda as Washington abandoned the cities.[47] From 1980 to 1990, the Reagan administration imposed a "cut of 46 percent or some $26 billion in constant 1990 dollars" to "grants programs that benefited cities."[48] These cuts would bring a decisive end to any lingering traces of Black Power Urbanism at the national level. Meanwhile, decisions about school integration, minority set-asides, affirmative action, and voting rights would gradually curb and then erode the civil rights state.[49] The essentialized failure of Black cities and their irrelevance to the Republican triumphal political calculus was exemplified in Reagan's genial greeting of "Hello, Mr. Mayor!" to Samuel Pierce, then-secretary of HUD and the only Black member of the Reagan cabinet.[50] HUD itself would be seriously weakened during Pierce's tenure, not only by massive cuts in funding but also by allegations of corruption and mismanagement.[51]

The fear of Black governance meant that missteps and failures, no matter how large or small, were all proffered as evidence of Black failure. At the same time, commentators ascribed a certain haplessness as well as malevolence to these Black communities. Some of them were explicit, arguing that the "real urban crisis" was found not simply in the economic forces of deindustrialization and suburbanization that were battering most American cities, but rather in the populations that were left behind or still arriving who could not or would not make a go at being responsible and productive urban citizens. Future neoconservative Irving Kristol stated in 1967 that "what we call the urban crisis is mostly just a euphemism for problems *created* by the steady influx of Southern Negroes into Northern and Western cities."[52] Other commentators, couching their critique in the objective and neutral language of the social sciences, shook their heads at the continued migration of Black people to cities even though it was obvious in their data that deindustrialization had already started to occur in the 1960s. Still others ascribed life in the vertical slums, created as the Kerner Commission noted by white society, as the result of a culture of poverty or the result of dysfunctional Black families.[53] As the journalist Ta-Nehisi Coates would argue in his 2014 case for reparations, "the ghetto was public policy."[54] This debate of course has been raised and argued for decades. During the late 1980s, however, the "urban underclass" emerged as a causally neater explanation for the failure of Black cities and the seemingly durable inequalities that cohered around race and space.[55]

With the rise of the urban underclass, a reason—not institutional racism, not Reaganism, and not "fear of a Black planet"—could be deployed as an explanation for all that was seen to be wrong with cities.[56] In the wake of this powerful political and sociological construct, Black Power Urbanism receded, forgotten into the background. Who (in the "white society" of the Kerner Commission) could imagine that the single welfare mother living in a filthy, crumbling high-rise project with her "children having children" or her children joining the drug trade for flashy consumer goods had once upon a time been a political actor? Who could imagine seeing teachers and students envisioning their school buildings as places of liberation and community, rather than places where metal detectors, shabby facilities, and mutual contempt marked daily life within "urban schools"? Who could imagine a police force that was accountable to the people, instead a police force that did not stand—heavily armed with military-grade weapons, SWAT teams, and no-knock warrants—between the mayhem and violence of the "inner city" drug trade and the allegedly few respectable citizens of those communities, and between the dealers and the suburban residents who drove to the busy drug corners of Newark, Oakland, East Orange, and East Palo Alto on the very highways that had devastated these Black communities while facilitating white flight and disinvestment?

Of course, Black and poor people continued to organize for just cities, and Black mayors continued to be elected and, in some cases, reelected, but their activism and governance were continually overshadowed by this dominant narrative of essentialized failure. Theorists like James Boggs continued to puzzle through what Black Power Urbanism meant "in terms of our actual daily lives at work, in our communities and our neighborhoods, in our classroom, our offices, on the streets, in our families."[57] Though couched in the language of constraint and not failure, political scientists like William E. Nelson Jr. argued that "Black mayors [and their activist constituents] face problems that are fundamentally different. . . . They must contend with constraints on their capacity for leadership not common to big city mayors generally. . . . They are, on the one hand, pressured by expectations of high performance, but on the other, handicapped in their ability to live up to these expectations by social, economic, and political factors that rob them of the resources and power they need to be successful in their roles."[58]

For cities where Black Power rested on a precarious demographic or institutional basis, one possible political alternative to failure or constraint was to pursue a deracialization strategy. Mayor Tom Bradley of Los Angeles, elected in a city where only 18 percent of the population was Black, argued that "some politicians say that talks about the conditions in our cities is not good politics because such a position exposes them to the criticism that they are only concerned about blacks. That argument won't work. This year, we are going to de-racialize the issues."[59] Such a strategy, Bradley argued, could widen political coalitions by "enlist[ing] the support of labor, the progressive leadership and the ecumenical leadership of this country."[60]

By the turn of the twenty-first century, a neoliberal urban order had emerged that rested on engineered austerity, mass incarceration, dispossession and gentrification, and the privatization of public goods like education and affordable housing.[61] In some places, including Newark and Oakland, Black Power Urbanism was replaced with Black urban regimes forced to triage the needs of the poor in order to assuage the demands of local growth machines and then increasingly, global capital. In suburbs like East Orange and East Palo Alto, officials desperately attempted to compete within the suburban political economy for affluent residents and ratables by doubling down on an imagined middle-class uniformity (and unanimity).

Along the way to the instantiation of this new order, the Black spaces inhabited by the so-called urban underclass (or simply poor Black people) were cleared of this population; they were cleared of New Deal relics like the Stella Wright Houses and the concrete formations of Black Power Urbanism and the Great Society like Nairobi Shopping Center and communities like Kuzuri-Kijiji.[62] Black spaces saw the erasure of new ways of doing things, of imagining and instantiating new forms like decentralized school boards and parent governance, youth justice councils, neighborhood-based drug treatment programs, community centers, arts programs, and so on. These instantiations were replaced with a new carceral infrastructure to support a school-to-prison pipeline as the new Jim Crow of mass incarceration.[63] The elements of Black Power Urbanism—the ideas, imaginings, interests, and instantiations that cohered to envision the creation of just emancipatory cities for all—lay seemingly forgotten.

Yet Black Power Urbanism had an unexpected revival once a "color-blind" neoliberal order that promised to raise all boats was revealed to have been a false and incredibly damaging promise. The Great Recession of 2008, which rested in part on the collapse of the subprime mortgage bubble, showed the enduring reality of predatory inclusion.[64] The collapse revealed a financial system that exploited Black and Brown communities, and in some cases, targeted vulnerable Black elders—all in a brazen bid to strip these individuals and their communities of their few remaining assets. Once again, echoing HUD's Section 235 mortgage program, Black communities were destroyed for cash.[65] While the 2008 election of Barack Obama was articulated by some as the dawning of a new post-racial era, the rise of the Tea Party and the killing of Trayvon Martin (and so many others) suggested otherwise. The movement for Black Lives and the uprising in Ferguson rearticulated for a new generation the fact that that race and space mattered.

From this recognition, a new Black Power Urbanist spatial imaginary was born, which draws upon myths, dreams, and in some cases the concrete manifestations of Black Power and more specifically Black Power Urbanism.[66] The Black Power urbanist spatial imaginary has empowered grassroots groups like Oakland's Moms 4 Housing who—in occupying a vacant house held by real estate speculators—drew explicitly on the Black Panthers' Ten-Point Program to push for the recognition that housing is a human right. East Palo Alto's Nairobi era has offered an alternative repertoire for Black, Latino, and Pacific Islander residents in their resistance to the expansion of tech companies and the resulting gentrification and dispossession in their communities. In an echo of the rent strikes and tenant organizing by women activists living in Stella Wright homes, renters in East Orange have created a Greater East Orange Tenants Organization to protect the right to remain in the city as gentrification (spurred in part by Black political leaders) threatens to push them out.[67] The spirit of Newark's African Free School can be seen in the ways in which Newark's parents and students have mobilized to save neighborhood schools and wrest back local control of the city schools after two decades under control of the state.[68] This book with its excavation of the promise of Black Power Urbanism is offered as a usable past to support these movements to create new and just cities of the future for all who stand at the margins.

Acknowledgments

Like raising children, the process of writing and publishing a book is both joyful and harrowing. As the first full draft of the manuscript was being completed, a long-awaited sabbatical collided with a pandemic, and I suddenly had a very full house. Time stopped, and my family, friends, and the communities I wrote about emerged afterward, some shaken but still moving and others, including dear relatives and friends, gone.

The work of every scholar including myself rests on our communities—both those that we actively engage with and those that have come before us. I have presented research from this book in a variety of academic spaces, including at Columbia University, the City University of New York, Johns Hopkins University, the University of Oregon, Northwestern University, and the University of Washington. I have benefited from stimulating and invaluable conversations at academic conferences, including those for the American Political Science Association, the Urban Affairs Association, the Social Science History Association, and the Toronto Political Development Workshop. In addition to attending these meetings, I have been honored to present this work to community groups in both California and New Jersey. Indeed, this book rests on dozens of conversations that I conducted with residents, activists, local officials, and community leaders of the four cities that I explore in this book. Several people, including Michael Levin, Tara Marlowe, John Atlas, and the late Mayor Robert Bowser, were particularly invaluable in connecting me to their networks and uncovering lost or neglected stories. I would also like to thank the many archivists who helped me track down everything from community meeting minutes to flyers, planning documents, and maps. I do not think I have enough words to thank the librarians and archivists at Columbia University, Barnard College, the East Orange Public Library, the Newark Public Library, Rutgers University, the Montclair Public Library, the New York Public Library, the East Palo Alto Library, the East Palo Alto Community Archive, Stanford University, and the University of California, Berkeley. The writing of local history, especially suburban history, could not exist without people at these institutions carving time and space out of their busy days and sometimes cramped quarters to save the stories of everyday people and communities.

My professional colleagues—my community of scholars and friends—have been invaluable as I have wrestled with trying to forge a usable past. In particularly, I would like to thank James DeFilippis, Richardson Dilworth, Michael Fortner, Megan Ming Francis, Christina Greer, Christine Harrington, Daniel Kato, Desmond King, Robert Lieberman, John Mollenkopf, Domingo Morel, Kathe Newman, Michael Leo Owens, Akira Drake Rodriguez, Hilary Silver, Lester Spence, Chloe Thurston, Timothy Weaver, and so many others for their feedback on the many moving parts of this book. The fantastic Michael McGandy was my primary editor at Cornell University Press for most of the time that I was researching and writing this book; after his departure, Jim Lance very capably took over helping me get to the final stages. I thank them both. I also thank the two reviewers who asked tough questions about the manuscript, ultimately pushing me to rethink parts of it and develop a stronger work as a result. My many thanks.

This work received extraordinary institutional support, first from my longtime academic home of Barnard College, where undergraduate research assistants as well as resources from the Claire Tow Scholar-Practitioner Award enabled me to develop the initial framing of the book and fund my research visits to California. At New York University, my most recent academic home, my work has benefited from the distinguished group of scholars in my department who have forged a challenging and enriching intellectual environment. The book's very final stages coincided with my time as the John G. Winant Visiting Professor of American Government at the University of Oxford and the Rothermere American Institute, where staff have provided a congenial work environment.

I am thankful for and forever indebted to the support of family and friends who witnessed the very long journey that was the writing of this book, including thank you to my mother, sister, brothers, aunts and uncles, cousins, and many, many in-laws, nieces, and nephews. Words simply cannot express my love and gratitude for Daniel, who has always been my champion and rock. To my beloved eldest sister Sharon who died from COVID-19 in July 2020, I remain heartbroken.

Unlike my previous books, my three young adult children (MM, AM, and LM) would now like to be anonymous; I thank them for the joy that they have brought to the world. And I am thankful to AM who—when faced with a parent's angst and writer's block—rolled their eyes and then asked, "This is a book about Black people? About cities? OK, dark concrete," and came up with the brilliant title for this book. This is for them; they got this.

Notes

PREFACE

1. Matt O'Brien, "Black Panther Birthplace Flipped and Sold as Trendy Oakland Showpiece," March 22, 2012, https://www.mercurynews.com/2012/03/22/black-panther-birthplace-flipped-and-sold-as-trendy-oakland-showpiece/.

2. Black Panther Party, "The Ten Point Program: What We Want" (October 15, 1966), in *War Against the Panthers: A Study of Repression in America* by Huey P. Newton (Harlem River Press, 1998).

3. On the racial and gendered targeting of subprime loans, see Elvin Wyly et al., "New Racial Meanings of Housing in America," *American Quarterly* 64, no. 3 (2012): 571–604, http://www.jstor.org/stable/23273535.

4. "The Foreclosure Crisis in Oakland, CA: Before and After (Observations from the American Community Survey)," December 13, 2016, https://www.ocf.berkeley.edu/~jyelen/2016/12/13/the-foreclosure-crisis-in-oakland-before-and-after/.

5. Eli Moore et al., *Roots, Race, and Place: A History of Racially Exclusionary Housing in the San Francisco Bay Area* (Haas Institute for a Fair and Inclusive Society, University of California Berkeley, October 2, 2019), 20–21, https://belonging.berkeley.edu/rootsraceplace.

6. Fusion Staff, "America's Top Banks Gave Oakland's Black Borrowers Just Four Home Loans in 2013: Four," *Splinter*, February 25, 2016, https://splinternews.com/americas-top-banks-gave-oaklands-black-borrowers-just-f-1793854984. See also Sasha Werblin and Zach Murray, "Locked Out of the Market: Poor Access to Home Loans for Californians of Color," The Greenlining Institute, February 2016.

7. O'Brien, "Black Panther Birthplace."

8. O'Brien, "Black Panther Birthplace."

9. Data on population change drawn from "Bay Area Census," Metropolitan Transportation Commission and the Association of Bay Area Governments, accessed May 3, 2025, https://census.bayareametro.gov/cities-counties.

10. See "Bay Area Census."

11. Black Panther Party, "The Ten Point Program."

12. The formulation of Black Power Urbanism used here rests on the following germinal works: Brian D. Goldstein, "'The Search for New Forms': Black Power and the Making of the Postmodern City," *Journal of American History* 103, no. 2 (2016): 375–99, https://doi.org/10.1093/jahist/jaw181; and Brian D. Goldstein, *The Roots of Urban Renaissance: Gentrification and the Struggle over Harlem* (Harvard University Press, 2017). See also Daniel Matlin, "'A New Reality of Harlem': Imagining the African American Urban Future During the 1960s," *Journal of American Studies* 52, no. 4 (2018): 991–1024, https://doi.org/10.1017/S0021875817000949; and Matthew J. Countryman, "'From Protest to Politics': Community Control and Black Independent Politics in Philadelphia, 1965–1984," *Journal of Urban History* 32, no. 6 (2006): 813–61, https://doi.org/10.1177/0096144206289034.

13. On the "right to the city," see Henri Lefebvre, "The Right to the City" (1966), in *Writings on Cities*, trans. Eleonore Kofman and Elizabeth Lebas (Wiley-Blackwell, 1996), 158; and David Harvey, "The Right to the City," *New Left Review* 53 (2008): 23–40.

14. On "just cities," see Susan S. Fainstein, "The Just City," *International Journal of Urban Sciences* 18, no. 1 (2013): 1–18, https://doi.org/10.1080/12265934.2013.834643; and

Peter Marcuse et al., eds., *Searching for the Just City: Debates in Urban Theory and Practice* (Routledge, 2009). On the intersections of race and the just city, see Toni L. Griffin et al., eds., *The Just City Essays: 26 Visions for Urban Equity, Inclusion, and Opportunity* (J. Max Bond Center on Design for the Just City, Next City, and the Nature of Cities, 2015), PDF, EPUB, https://nextcity.org/ebooks/the-just-city-essays.

15. George Lipsitz, *How Racism Takes Place* (Temple University Press, 2011).

16. See Adam Sheingate, "Institutional Dynamics and American Political Development," *Annual Review of Political Science* 17, no. 1 (2014): 461–77, https://doi.org/10.1146/annurev-polisci-040113-161139; and on urban political development, see, for example, Richardson Dilworth, ed., *The City in American Political Development* (Routledge, 2009).

17. "Black Power Manifesto and Resolutions," National Conference on Black Power, Newark, NJ, July 20–23, 1967, RiseUpNewark, https://riseupnewark.com/wp-content/uploads/2020/10/Black-Power-Manifesto-and-Resolutions-compressed.pdf.

18. This articulation of Black Power Urbanism as a political order rests heavily on Desmond S. King and Rogers M. Smith's work on racial political orders (see "Racial Orders in American Political Development," *American Political Science Review* 99, no. 1 (2005): 75–92 (esp. 75), https://doi.org/10.1017/S0003055405051506. For "new forms," see Kwame Ture and Charles V. Hamilton, *Black Power: The Politics of Liberation in America* (Vintage, 1992).

19. See Ture and Hamilton, *Black Power*, 165–71.

20. See Leonard Cole, *Blacks in Power: A Comparative Study of Black and White Elected Officials* (Princeton University Press, 2017), xiii.

21. See Robert Self, *American Babylon: Race and the Struggle for Postwar Oakland* (Princeton University Press, 2003).

22. Daniel HoSang, *Racial Propositions: Ballot Initiatives and the Making of Postwar California* (University of California Press, 2010).

1. BLACK CITIES

1. See Jeffery C. Mays, "Boarded-Up and Foreclosed, Houses Await Action by Newark and Partners," *New York Times*, May 14, 2009. On the racial and gendered targeting of subprime loans, see Elvin Wyly et al., "New Racial Meanings of Housing in America," *American Quarterly* 64, no. 3 (2012): 571–604, http://www.jstor.org/stable/23273535.

2. The testimony "assert[ed] municipalities' authority to address the consequences of the Wall Street-induced foreclosure crisis and fight the blight created by underwater PLS loans." Christopher Niedt and Stephen McFarland, *Our Homes, Our Newark: Foreclosures, Toxic Mortgages, and Blight in the City of Newark* (National Center for Suburban Studies, Hofstra University, 2015), 6, https://www.hofstra.edu/pdf/academics/css/ncss-our-homes-our-newark-final-report.pdf.

3. David Dayen, "Newark's Terrible New Foreclosure Fix Idea," *The New Republic*, May 8, 2013.

4. Testimony of Grace Alexander at the Newark City Council committee hearing on July 9, 2013, in Niedt and McFarland, *Our Homes, Our Newark*, 11.

5. See Komozi Woodard, *A Nation Within a Nation: Amiri Baraka (LeRoi Jones) and Black Power Politics* (University of North Carolina Press, 1999), 145.

6. Alexandra Hill, "Baraka Signs Affordable Housing Ordinance into Law," WBGO News, October 12, 2017, https://www.wbgo.org/news/2017-10-12/baraka-signs-affordable-housing-ordinance-into-law.

7. Parliament, "Chocolate City," produced by George Clinton, track 1 on *Chocolate City*, Casablanca Records, recorded April 8, 1975, https://mother.pfunkarchive.com/motherpage/lyrics_parliament/lyr-cc.html#lyr-s-cc.

8. See James Boggs and Grace Lee Boggs, "The City Is the Black Man's Land," *Monthly Review* 17, no. 11 (April 1966), https://doi.org/10.14452/MR-017-11-1966-04_4.

9. Parliament, "Chocolate City."

10. For important examples of this comparison, see J. Phillip Thompson III, *Double Trouble: Black Mayors, Black Communities, and the Call for a Deep Democracy* (Oxford University Press, 2005); and John Mollenkopf, "New York: The Great Anomaly," *PS* 19, no. 3 (1986): 591–97.

11. Work on American political development (APD) and historical institutionalism (HI) is quite robust. For overviews of APD, see Adam Sheingate, "Institutional Dynamics and American Political Development," *Annual Review of Political Science* 17, no. 1 (2014): 461–77, https://doi.org/10.1146/annurev-polisci-040113-161139; and Karen Orren and Stephen Skowronek, *The Search for American Political Development* (Cambridge University Press, 2004). For HI, see Sven Steinmo et al., eds., *Structuring Politics: Historical Institutionalism in Comparative Analysis* (Cambridge University Press, 1992).

12. See Robert C. Lieberman, "Ideas, Institutions, and Political Order: Explaining Political Change," *American Political Science Review* 96, no. 4 (2002): 702; Sheingate, "Institutional Dynamics," 464; Orren and Skowronek, *Search for American Political Development*, 14, 123.

13. Orren and Skowronek, *Search for American Political Development*, 123.

14. See Paul Pierson, "Not Just What, but *When*: Timing and Sequence in Political Processes," *Studies in American Political Development* 14, no. 1 (2000): 72–92.

15. Definition from Grace Skogstad, "Historical Institutionalism in Public Policy," in *Encyclopedia of Public Policy*, ed. M. van Gerven et al. (Springer, 2023), https://doi.org/10.1007/978-3-030-90434-0_21-1.

16. See Karen Orren and Stephen Skowronek, "Institutions and Intercurrence: Theory Building in the Fullness of Time," *Nomos* 38 (1996): 117.

17. For intercurrence, see Orren and Skowronek, *Search for American Political Development*, 113–18, esp. 118. See also Paul Pierson, "When Effect Becomes Cause: Policy Feedback and Political Change," *World Politics* 45, no. 4 (1993): 595–628.

18. For discussion of urban political spaces, see Neil Brenner, "Is There a Politics of 'Urban' Development? Reflections on the US Case," in *The City in American Political Development*, ed. Richardson Dilworth (Routledge, 2009).

19. For urban regime theory, see Clarence Stone, *Regime Politics: Governing Atlanta, 1946–1988* (University Press of Kansas, 1989); Amy Bridges, *Morning Glories: Municipal Reform in the Southwest* (Princeton University Press, 1997); and Jessica Trounstine, *Political Monopolies in American Cities: The Rise and Fall of Bosses and Reformers* (University of Chicago Press, 2008).

20. In addition to Richardson Dilworth, ed., *The City in American Political Development* (Routledge, 2009), see also Jack Lucas, "Urban Governance and the American Political Development Approach," *Urban Affairs Review* 53, no. 2 (2015): 338–61; Joel Rast, "Why History (Still) Matters: Time and Temporality in Urban Political Analysis," *Urban Affairs Review* 48, no. 1 (2011): 3–36; Rast, "Urban Regime Theory and the Problem of Change," *Urban Affairs Review* 51, no. 1 (2014): 138–49; and Timothy P. R. Weaver, "Charting Change in the City: Urban Political Orders and Urban Political Development," *Urban Affairs Review* 58, no. 2 (2021): 319–55. On Black politics, see Martin Kilson, "From Civil Rights to Party Politics: The Black Political Transition," *Current History* 67, no. 399 (1974): 193–99.

21. For embeddedness of US cities in broader political orders, see Tom Ogorzalek, *Cities on the Hill: How Urban Institutions Transformed National Politics* (Oxford University Press, 2018); Christopher Klemek, *The Transatlantic Collapse of Urban Renewal: Postwar Urbanism from New York to Berlin* (University of Chicago Press, 2011); and Timothy Weaver, *Blazing the Neoliberal Trail: Urban Political Development in the United States and the United Kingdom* (University of Pennsylvania Press, 2016).

22. In addition to N. D. B. Connolly, *A World More Concrete: Real Estate and the Remaking of Jim Crow South Florida* (University of Chicago Press, 2014), see David M. P. Freund, *Colored Property: State Policy and White Racial Politics in Suburban America*

(University of Chicago Press, 2007); Colin Gordon, *Mapping Decline: St. Louis and the Fate of the American City* (University of Pennsylvania Press, 2008); Arnold R. Hirsch, *Making the Second Ghetto: Race and Housing in Chicago, 1940–1960* (University of Chicago Press, 1998); Kenneth T. Jackson, *Crabgrass Frontier: The Suburbanization of the United States* (Oxford University Press, 1985); and Thomas J. Sugrue, *Sweet Land of Liberty: The Forgotten Struggle for Civil Rights in the North* (Random House, 2008).

23. Earl Lewis defines Black urban "congregation" as resting on an "ethos of empowerment and self-determination, often in pointed contrast with the vulnerabilities and dependencies" of southern small-town and rural life. Lewis, *In Their Own Interests: Race, Class, and Power in Twentieth-Century Norfolk, Virginia* (University of California Press, 1991), 5.

24. Marcus Anthony Hunter et al., "Black Placemaking: Celebration, Play, and Poetry," *Theory, Culture & Society* 33 (2016): 31–56.

25. On the color line, see W. E. B. Du Bois, *The Souls of Black Folk* (Oxford University Press, 2007), 5. For the impact of World War II and democratization on Black expectations, see Kevin Mumford, *Newark: A History of Race, Rights, and Riots in America* (New York University Press, 2007).

26. This quote and following, Woodard, *A Nation Within a Nation*, 198, 199.

27. For quote, see "George Richardson Discusses Demonstrations Against Police Brutality in Newark, 1963," uploaded August 25, 2016, Henry Hampton Collection, Washington University Libraries, Vimeo, 54 sec., https://vimeo.com/180204102.

28. On the "Black Power archive," see N. D. B. Connolly, "A Black Power Method," *Public Books*, June 15, 2016, https://www.publicbooks.org/a-black-power-method/. See also Kwame Ture and Charles V. Hamilton, *Black Power: The Politics of Liberation in America* (Vintage, 1992).

29. See Rhonda Y. Williams, *Concrete Demands: The Search for Black Power in the 20th Century* (Routledge, 2015), 4.

30. On "communities of possibilities," see Nikhil Pal Singh, *Black Is a Country: Race and the Unfinished Struggle for Democracy* (Harvard University Press, 2005).

31. See Brenner, "Is There a Politics of 'Urban' Development?," 121.

32. Brenner, "Is There a Politics of 'Urban' Development?," 121.

33. The use of "pillars" was inspired by Eve Ewing's notion of "paired institutions." Ewing, *Ghosts in the Schoolyard: Racism and School Closings on Chicago's South Side* (University of Chicago Press, 2018).

34. On the inevitability of co-optation, see Tom Adam Davies, *Mainstreaming Black Power* (University of California Press, 2017); and Devin Fergus, *Liberalism, Black Power, and the Making of American Politics, 1965–1980* (University of Georgia Press, 2009).

35. For overviews of Oakland history, see Donna Murch, *Living for the City: Migration, Education, and the Rise of the Black Panther Party in Oakland, California* (University of North Carolina Press, 2010); Chris Rhomberg, *No There There: Race, Class, and Political Community in Oakland* (University of California Press, 2004); and Robert O. Self, *American Babylon: Race and the Struggle for Postwar Oakland* (Princeton University Press, 2003).

36. For overviews of Newark history, see Robert Curvin, *Inside Newark: Decline, Rebellion, and the Search for Transformation* (Rutgers University Press, 2014); Andra Gillespie, *The New Black Politician: Cory Booker, Newark, and Post-Racial America* (New York University Press, 2012); Mark Krasovic, *The Newark Frontier: Community Action in the Great Society* (University of Chicago Press, 2016); Mumford, *Newark*; Julia Rabig, *The Fixers: Devolution, Development, and Civil Society in Newark, 1960–1990* (University of Chicago Press, 2016); Brad R. Tuttle, *How Newark Became Newark: The Rise, Fall, and Rebirth of an American City* (Rivergate Books, 2009); Woodard, *A Nation Within a Nation*.

37. See Martin Shefter, *Political Crisis/Fiscal Crisis: The Collapse and Revival of New York City* (Columbia University Press, 1985).

38. See Robert Curvin, "The Persistent Minority: The Black Political Experience in Newark" (PhD diss., Princeton University, 1975); and Stanley Winters, "Charter Change and Civic Reform in Newark, 1953–1954," *New Jersey History* 118 (2000): 35–65.

39. See Howard Kaplan, *Urban Renewal Politics: Slum Clearance in Newark* (Columbia University Press, 1963).

40. On the history of "political reform" in Oakland and the rise and fall of the KKK, see Rhomberg, *No There There*, 50–72.

41. On the idea of "root shock," see Mindy Thompson Fullilove, *Root Shock: How Tearing Up City Neighborhoods Hurts America, and What We Can Do About It* (One World, 2004), 14, 122–23; and Marc Fried, "Grieving for a Lost Home: Psychological Costs of Relocation," in *Urban Renewal: The Record and the Controversy*, ed. James Q. Wilson (MIT Press, 1966), 359–60.

42. On the role of "place," in addition to Mollenkopf, "New York," see Peter Dreier et al., *Place Matters: Metropolitics for the Twenty-First Century* (University Press of Kansas, 2014); and J. Eric Oliver, *Local Elections and the Politics of Small-Scale Democracy* (Princeton University Press, 2012).

43. Jackson, *Crabgrass Frontier*; Freund, *Colored Property*; and Gordon, *Mapping Decline*.

44. Manfred B. Steger and Ravi K. Roy, "First-Wave Neoliberalism in the 1980s: Reaganomics and Thatcherism," in *Neoliberalism: A Very Short Introduction*, 1st ed. (Oxford University Press, 2010).

45. Orren and Skowronek, *Search for American Political Development*, 117. See also David Collier and Gerardo L. Munck, "Building Blocks and Methodological Challenges: A Framework for Studying Critical Junctures," *Qualitative and Multi-Method Research* 15, no. 1 (Spring 2017): 2–9.

46. On the post–World War II "spatial fix," in addition to Klemek, *Transatlantic Collapse*, see also David, "The Right to the City," *New Left Review* 53 (2008): 23–40.

47. The literature on the racial impacts of urban renewal and highway construction (aka "Negro removal") is vast. See Connolly, *A World More Concrete*; Klemek, *Transatlantic Collapse*. See also Deborah N. Archer, "'White Men's Roads Through Black Men's Homes': Advancing Racial Equity Through Highway Reconstruction," *Vanderbilt Law Review* 73, no. 5 (2020): 1259–1330; Charles E. Connerly, *"The Most Segregated City in America": City Planning and Civil Rights in Birmingham, 1920–1980* (University of Virginia Press, 2005); Roger Biles, *The Fate of Cities: Urban America and the Federal Government, 1945–2000* (University Press of Kansas, 2011); and Jon C. Teaford, *The Rough Road to Renaissance: Urban Revitalization in America, 1940–1985* (Johns Hopkins University Press, 1990).

48. Robert Dahl, *Who Governs? Democracy and Power in an American City* (Yale University Press, 1962).

49. See Digital Scholarship Lab, "Renewing Inequality," *American Panorama*, ed. Robert K. Nelson and Edward L. Ayers, accessed June 14, 2023, https://dsl.richmond.edu/panorama/renewal/#view=0/0/1&viz=cartogram&text=sources.

50. See Sugrue, *Sweet Land of Liberty*, 354.

51. On the segregated state, see Desmond King, *Separate and Unequal: Black Americans and the US Federal Government* (Oxford University Press, 1995); Richard Rothstein, *The Color of Law: A Forgotten History of How Our Government Segregated America* (Liveright Publishing, 2018).

52. Ta-Nehisi Coates, "The Ghetto Is Public Policy," *The Atlantic*, March 19, 2013, https://www.theatlantic.com/national/archive/2013/03/the-ghetto-is-public-policy/274147/.

53. See Kevin M. Kruse, *White Flight: Atlanta and the Making of Modern Conservatism* (Princeton University Press, 2005); Matthew D. Lassiter, *The Silent Majority: Suburban*

Politics in the Sunbelt South (Princeton University Press, 2006); and Lisa McGirr, *Suburban Warriors: The Origins of the New American Right?* (Princeton University Press, 2001). On broader trends in American politics, see Joseph E. Lowndes, *From the New Deal to the New Right: Race and the Southern Origins of Modern Conservatism* (Yale University Press, 2009); and Byron Shafer and Richard Johnston, *The End of Southern Exceptionalism: Class, Race, and Partisan Change in the Postwar South* (Harvard University Press, 2009). On the cultural construction of suburbanization and whiteness, see Lizabeth Cohen, *A Consumer's Republic: The Politics of Mass Consumption in Postwar America* (Vintage, 2004); and Becky M. Nicolaides, *My Blue Heaven: Life and Politics in the Working-Class Suburbs of Los Angeles, 1920–1965* (University of Chicago Press, 2002).

54. Elizabeth Hinton, *From the War on Poverty to the War on Crime: The Making of Mass Incarceration in America* (Harvard University Press, 2016), 26.

55. On the war on cities, see Demetrios Caraley, "Washington Abandons the Cities," *Political Science Quarterly* 107, no. 1 (1992): 1–30, https://doi.org/10.2307/2152132. On the war on crime and the war on drugs, see Heather Ann Thompson, "Why Mass Incarceration Matters: Rethinking Crisis, Decline, and Transformation in Postwar American History," *Journal of American History* 97, no. 3 (2010): 703–34. See also Hinton, *War on Poverty*.

56. On the material and philosophical destruction of the New Deal city, see Edward G. Goetz, *New Deal Ruins: Race, Economic Justice, and Public Housing Policy* (Cornell University Press, 2013); and Lawrence J. Vale, *Purging the Poorest: Public Housing and the Design Politics of Twice-Cleared Communities* (University of Chicago Press, 2013). On the "rolling back"/"rolling out" nature of urban neoliberalism, see Jamie Peck and Adam Tickell, "Neoliberalizing Space," *Antipode* 34, no. 3 (2002): 380–404, https://doi.org/10.1111/1467-8330.00247.

57. For the color line, see Du Bois, *The Souls of Black Folk*, 5.

58. See Lester K. Spence, "Race and the Neoliberal City," paper presented at the Arrighi Center for Global Studies' Sawyer Seminar on Capitalism in the Twenty-First Century, March 28, 2014.

59. Charles W. Mills, *The Racial Contract* (Cornell University Press, 1997), 41–42.

60. On urban "congregation," see Lewis, *In Their Own Interests*.

61. Katherine McKittrick "On Plantations, Prisons, and a Black Sense of Place," *Social & Cultural Geography* 12, no. 8 (2011): 947–63, https://doi.org/10.1080/14649365.2011.624280.

62. See Michael Javen Fortner, "Urban Autonomy and Effective Citizenship," in *Urban Citizenship and American Democracy*, ed. Amy Bridges and Michael Javen Fortner (State University of New York Press, 2016), 23–64.

63. Clarissa Rile Hayward, *How Americans Make Race: Stories, Institutions, Spaces* (Cambridge University Press, 2013); George Lipsitz, *How Racism Takes Place* (Temple University Press, 2011); David Harvey, *Social Justice and the City* (Johns Hopkins University Press, 1973).

64. See Hayward, *How Americans Make Race*, 140.

65. See David Harvey, "From Space to Place and Back Again: Reflections on the Condition of Postmodernity," in *Mapping the Futures: Local Cultures, Global Change*, ed. Jon Bird et al. (Routledge, 1993).

66. For discussion of "thick injustice," see Clarissa Rile Hayward and Todd Swanstrom, eds., *Justice and the American Metropolis* (University of Minnesota Press, 2011).

67. See Marcus Anthony Hunter's *Black Citymakers: How the Philadelphia Negro Changed Urban America* (Oxford University Press, 2013), for a recent work that reinterprets Black Philadelphia through the lens of spatial theory.

68. See Alice O'Connor, *Poverty Knowledge: Social Science, Social Policy, and the Poor in Twentieth-Century U. S. History* (Princeton University Press, 2002); see also recent work that interrogates the Chicago School approach: Rashad Shabazz, *Spatializing Blackness: Architectures of Confinement and Black Masculinity in Chicago* (University of Illinois Press, 2015); and Saidiya V. Hartman, *Wayward Lives, Beautiful Experiments: Intimate Histories of Social Upheaval*, 1st ed. (Norton, 2019).

69. St. Clair Drake and Horace R. Cayton, *Black Metropolis: A Study of Negro Life in a Northern City*, rev. ed. (University of Chicago Press, 1993).

70. Robert Clifton Weaver, *The Negro Ghetto* (Russell & Russell, 1948), v.

71. In addition to Weaver on the rise of racial covenants, see Christopher Silver, "The Racial Origins of Zoning in American Cities," in *Urban Planning and the African American Community: In the Shadows*, ed. June Manning Thomas and Marsha Ritzdorf (Sage Publications, 1997); and Gordon, *Mapping Decline*.

72. For discussion of Euclidean zoning, see Andrew Cappel, "A Walk Along Willow: Patterns of Land Use Coordination in Pre-Zoning New Haven (1870–1926)," *Yale Law Journal* 101, no. 3 (1991): 617–42; for its effects, see Douglas S. Massey and Nancy A. Denton, *American Apartheid: Segregation and the Making of the Underclass* (Harvard University Press, 1993).

73. In addition to Rothstein, *Color of Law* and Freund, *Colored Property*, see Michael Jones-Correa, "The Origins and Diffusion of Racial Restrictive Covenants," *Political Science Quarterly* 115, no. 4 (2000), 541–68, https://doi.org/10.2307/2657609. See also Keeanga-Yamahtta Taylor, *Race for Profit: How Banks and the Real Estate Industry Undermined Black Homeownership* (University of North Carolina Press, 2019).

74. Mark Benton, "'Saving' the City: Harland Bartholomew and Administrative Evil in St. Louis," *Public Integrity* 20, no. 2 (2018): 194–206, https://doi.org/10.1080/109999 22.2017.1306902; Joseph Heathcott, "'The Whole City Is Our Laboratory': Harland Bartholomew and the Production of Urban Knowledge," *Journal of Planning History* 4, no. 4 (2005): 322–55, https://doi.org/10.1177/1538513205282131.

75. Benton, citing Guy B. Adams and Danny L. Balfour (*Unmasking Administrative Evil* [Routledge, 2014], https://doi.org/10.4324/9781315716640) defines administrative evil "as occurring when people 'engage in acts of evil unaware that they are in fact doing anything at all wrong,' with evil defined as 'the actions of human beings that unjustly or needlessly inflict pain and suffering and death on other human beings.'" Benton, "'Saving the City,'" 195–96.

76. See Clement Price, "The Afro-American Community of Newark, 1917–1947: A Social History" (PhD diss., Rutgers University, 1975); and Arish Gupta, "Black Church Near Rutgers—Newark Is Recognized as Historic Site of Underground Railroad," *The Daily Targum*, April 26, 2022, https://dailytargum.com/article/2022/04/black-church-near-rutgers-newark-is-recognized-as-historic-site-of.

77. See Robert C. Smith, *We Have No Leaders: African Americans in the Post-Civil Rights Era* (State University of New York Press, 1996); and Michelle R. Boyd, *Jim Crow Nostalgia: Reconstructing Race in Bronzeville* (University of Minnesota Press, 2008).

78. Clement Price, "The Beleaguered City as Promised Land: Blacks in Newark, 1917–1947," in *A New Jersey Anthology*, ed. Maxine N. Lurie (Rutgers University Press, 2002).

79. See N. Barnett Dodson, "Race Progress in New Jersey: Washington's Tour in the State Benefits General Public," *Afro-American* (Baltimore), October 17, 1914.

80. See August Meier and Elliott M. Rudwick, "Early Boycotts of Segregated Schools: The East Orange, New Jersey, Experience, 1899–1906," *History of Education Quarterly* 7, no. 1 (1967): 22–35; Marian Wright Thompson, "The Education of Negroes in New Jersey" (PhD diss., Teachers College, Columbia University, 1941); and Sugrue, *Sweet Land of Liberty*, 163–99.

81. "N. J. Town Called Model Interracial City," *Chicago Daily Defender*, August 20, 1962.

82. On the early history of Oakland, see Gretchen Lemke-Santangelo, *Abiding Courage: African American Migrant Women and the East Bay Community* (University of North Carolina Press, 1996).

83. For discussion of this early twentieth-century racialized landscape, see Marta Gutman, *A City for Children: Women, Architecture, and the Charitable Landscapes of Oakland, 1850–1950* (University of Chicago Press, 2014).

84. On the impact of World War II on Oakland's Black political development, see Marilynn S. Johnson, *The Second Gold Rush: Oakland and the East Bay in World War II* (University of California Press, 1994); and Robert O. Self, "'Negro Leadership and Negro Money': African American Political Organizing in Oakland Before the Panthers," in *Freedom North: Black Freedom Struggles Outside of the South, 1940–1980*, ed. Jeanne Theoharis and Komozi Woodard (Palgrave Macmillan, 2003).

85. See Murch, *Living for the City*.

86. For brief discussion of Japanese American residents of East Palo Alto, see "Japanese-American Internment: Palo Alto's Deported Patriots," Palo Alto History, accessed April 14, 2025, https://www.paloaltohistory.org/japanese-american-internment.php; and Kim-Mai Cutler, "East of Palo Alto's Eden: Race and the Formation of Silicon Valley," TechCrunch, January 10, 2015, techcrunch.com/2015/01/10/east-of-palo-altos-eden/?renderMode=ie11.

87. Nicolaides, *My Blue Heaven*.

88. "A Conversation with James Baldwin," June 24, 1963, American Archive of Public Broadcasting (GBH and the Library of Congress), http://americanarchive.org/catalog/cpb-aacip-15-0v89g5gf5r.

89. In addition to Connolly, *A World More Concrete*, see Preston H. Smith, *Racial Democracy and the Black Metropolis: Housing Policy in Postwar Chicago* (University of Minnesota Press, 2012).

90. Mary Lou Finley et al., eds., *The Chicago Freedom Movement: Martin Luther King Jr. and Civil Rights Activism in the North* (University Press of Kentucky, 2016); Thomas J. Sugrue, "Affirmative Action from Below: Civil Rights, the Building Trades, and the Politics of Racial Equality in the Urban North, 1945–1969," *Journal of American History* 91, no. 1 (2004): 145–73.

91. In addition to Woodard's *Nation Within a Nation*, see Komozi Woodard and Jeanne Theoharis's *Groundwork: Local Black Freedom Movements in America* (New York University Press, 2005); also Brian D. Goldstein, *The Roots of Urban Renaissance* (Harvard University Press, 2017).

92. Boggs and Boggs, "The City Is the Black Man's Land," 39.

93. Boggs and Boggs, "The City Is the Black Man's Land," 39.

94. Boggs and Boggs, "The City Is the Black Man's Land," 36.

95. The Organization for Black Power was created by members of the Revolutionary Action Movement (RAM). Control over the organization would be assumed by Grace Lee Boggs and James Boggs. "Civil Rights and Black Power Advocacy," Deconstructing the Model Minority at the University of Michigan, accessed April 14, 2025, https://aapi.umhistorylabs.lsa.umich.edu/s/aapi_michigan/page/civil-rights.

96. Woodard, *A Nation Within a Nation*, 145.

97. See Jeanne Theoharis, "Introductions," in *Freedom North: Black Freedom Struggles Outside of the South, 1940–1980*, ed. Jeanne Theoharis and Komozi Woodard (Palgrave Macmillan, 2003); Self, "Negro Leadership."

98. See Woodard, *Nation Within a Nation*; for "ghetto walls," see Manuel Castells, *The City and the Grassroots: A Cross-Cultural Theory of Urban Social Movements* (University of California Press, 1983), 54.

99. See Connerly, *"The Most Segregated City."*

100. On the Black cities as a "hollow prize," see H. Paul Friesema, "Black Control of Central Cities: The Hollow Prize," *Journal of the American Institute of Planners* 35, no. 2 (1969): 75–79, https://doi.org/10.1080/01944366908977576; also Neil Kraus and Todd Swanstrom, "Minority Mayors and the Hollow-Prize Problem," *PS: Political Science and Politics* 34, no. 1 (2001): 99–105.

101. Adolph L. Reed, *Stirrings in the Jug: Black Politics in the Post-Segregation Era* (University of Minnesota Press, 1999). On Black-majority or Black-governed cities as inherently "unheavenly" and/or "ungovernable" cities, see Edward C. Banfield, *The Unheavenly City: The Nature and Future of Our Urban Crisis* (Little, Brown, 1970); and Douglas Yates, *The Ungovernable City: The Politics of Urban Problems and Policy Making* (MIT Press, 1977).

102. For formulation of Black Power critiques as an "archaeology of failure," see James Taylor, "The Politics of the Black Power Movement," *Annual Review of Political Science* 24 (2021): 443–70. The critiques of the critiques of Black Power are also vast in number. See, for example, Smith's *We Have No Leaders* and Cedric Johnson's *Revolutionaries to Race Leaders: Black Power and the Making of African American Politics* (University of Minnesota Press, 2007).

2. BLACK POWER URBANISM

1. Darren Tobia, "NJPAC Could Demolish Newark 'Black Power' Building for Loading Bays and Parking," *Jersey Digs*, June 6, 2022, https://jerseydigs.com/historic-black-power-building-newark-demolition/; and Tobia, "NJPAC Agrees to Save 'Black Power' Building in Newark Historic District," *Jersey Digs*, September 21, 2022, https://jerseydigs.com/njpac-save-black-power-building-newark/.

2. Adam Clayton Powell Jr., "My Black Position Paper," in *The Black Power Revolt: A Collection of Essays*, ed. Floyd B. Barbour (Porter Sargent, 1968); see also Art Pollock, "'My Life's Philosophy': Adam Clayton Powell's 'Black Position Paper,'" *Journal of Black Studies* 4, no. 4 (1974): 457–62.

3. Nathan Wright, "Why Black Power? An Interview with Dr. Nathan Wright," interview by David Holstrom, *Christian Science Monitor*, September 18, 1967.

4. See Komozi Woodard, *A Nation Within a Nation: Amiri Baraka (LeRoi Jones) and Black Power Politics* (University of North Carolina Press, 1999), 144.

5. Elizabeth Strom, "Let's Put on a Show! Performing Arts and Urban Revitalization in Newark, New Jersey," *Journal of Urban Affairs* 21, no. 4 (January 1999): 423–35.

6. Darren Tobia, "Artist Paula Scher Responds to NJPAC's Plans to Destroy Her Famous Mural," *Jersey Digs*, June 24, 2022, https://jerseydigs.com/paula-scher-mural-njpac-newark/.

7. Tobia, "NJPAC Could Demolish."

8. Tobia, "NJPAC Could Demolish."

9. Lauren C. O'Brien, "The Resurrection of a Ghost City: The Fight to Preserve Newark's African Burial Ground," *The Public Historian* 44, no. 4 (2022): 104–25.

10. An article covering the controversy noted that "NJPAC had promised to preserve the building next to the Cathedral House as well. The former Ballantine Brewery, an art deco industrial building, caught fire after years of neglect and was considered too unsafe to preserve. Such loopholes are often exploited." See Tobia, "Artist Paula Scher."

11. Strom, "Let's Put on a Show!"

12. The literature on the Black Power movement is extensive. For a discussion of focus on charismatic leaders, see Peniel E. Joseph, "Rethinking the Black Power Era," *Journal of Southern History* 75, no. 3 (2009): 707–16; and Joseph, *Waiting 'til the Midnight Hour: A Narrative History of Black Power in America* (Henry Holt, 2006). For a political science

perspective, see James Lance Taylor, "The Politics of the Black Power Movement," *Annual Review of Political Science* 24 (2021): 443–70. Other works include Scot Brown, *Fighting for US: Maulana Karenga, the US Organization, and Black Cultural Nationalism* (New York University Press, 2003); Judson L. Jeffries, *Comrades: A Local History of the Black Panther Party* (Indiana University Press, 2007); Cedric Johnson, *Revolutionaries to Race Leaders: Black Power and the Making of African American Politics* (University of Minnesota Press, 2007); Peniel E. Joseph, *The Black Power Movement: Rethinking the Civil Rights–Black Power Era* (Routledge, 2006); Leonard Moore, *The Defeat of Black Power: Civil Rights and the National Black Political Convention of 1972* (Louisiana State University Press, 2018); Nikhil P. Singh, *Black Is a Country: Race and the Unfinished Struggle for Democracy* (Harvard University Press, 2004); Robert C. Smith, *We Have No Leaders: African Americans in the Post–Civil Rights Era* (State University of New York Press, 1996); Robyn C. Spencer, *The Revolution Has Come: Black Power, Gender, and the Black Panther Party in Oakland* (Duke University Press, 2016).

13. "Powell to Call Parley to Define Black Power," *Washington Post*, July 28, 1966.

14. See Johnson, *Revolutionaries to Race Leaders*, 58. The speech itself was entered into the Congressional Record multiple times under the title "My Black Position Paper." See Powell in Barbour, *The Black Power Revolt*, 257–59. See also Pollock, "'My Life's Philosophy,'" 457–62.

15. Powell, "My Black Position Paper," 258.

16. Powell, "My Black Position Paper," 258–60.

17. Powell's congressional career is complex, especially from 1964. He has been the subject of several biographies. See Charles Hamilton, *Adam Clayton Powell, Jr.: The Political Biography of an American Dilemma* (Atheneum, 1991); and Wil Haygood, *King of the Cats: The Life and Times of Adam Clayton Powell, Jr.* (Houghton Mifflin, 1993).

18. See Cedric Johnson, who notes that "though Powell's adamance and messianic rhetorical delivery lent an air of militancy to his position paper, his conceptualization of Black Power as institutional access was rather conventional." Johnson, *Revolutionaries to Race Leaders*, 58.

19. Baraka quoted in Johnson, *Revolutionaries to Race Leaders*, 72.

20. See Woodard, *A Nation Within a Nation*, 128.

21. For discussion of Powell's personal life, see Lea E. Williams, "Adam Clayton Powell Jr.: The Uses and Abuses of Charismatic Power," in *Servants of the People: The 1960s Legacy of African American Leadership* (Palgrave Macmillan, 1996).

22. See Nathan Wright Jr., "Invitation to Black Power Conference Planning Committee," Rise Up Newark, February 15, 1967, https://riseupnewark.com/wp-content/uploads/2016/09/Invitation-to-Planning-Committee-for-National-Conference-on-Black-Power-February-15-1967.pdf. See also Chuck Stone, "The National Conference on Black Power," in Barbour, *The Black Revolt*.

23. Other conference planners included Omar A. Ahmed, Maulana Karenga, Isaiah Robinson, and Chuck Stone. See Johnson, *Revolutionaries to Race Leaders*, 59–65.

24. On analyzing Black political development as racial or political orders, see Desmond S. King and Rogers M. Smith, "Racial Orders in American Political Development," *American Political Science Review* 99, no. 1 (2005): 75–92. Harold Cruse also suggested a political developmental approach to Black urban political development. See Taylor, "Politics of the Black Power Movement," 459.

25. See Daryl Michael Scott, *Contempt and Pity: Social Policy and the Image of the Damaged Black Psyche, 1880–1996* (University of North Carolina Press, 1997).

26. On the co-optation of the Black Power movement, see Tom Adam Davies, *Mainstreaming Black Power* (University of California Press, 2017); Devin Fergus, *Liberalism, Black Power, and the Making of American Politics, 1965–1980* (University of Georgia Press,

2009); and Manning Marable, *Black American Politics: From the Washington Marches to Jesse Jackson* (Verso, 1985).

27. James Boggs, "Black Power: A Scientific Concept Whose Time Has Come," in *Racism and the Class Struggle: Further Pages from a Black Worker's Notebook* (Monthly Review Press, 1970), 51–62. Reprinted in *e-flux Journal* 79 (February 2017), https://www.e-flux.com/journal/79/94443/black-power-a-scientific-concept-whose-time-has-come/.

28. Boggs, "Black Power."

29. See Harold Cruse, who claimed that modern scholars did not recognize migration's central role in Black history. "Part 1—Black and White: Outlines of the Next Stage," *Black World* 20, no. 1 (January 1971): 19–41, 66–71; part 2, no. 3 (March 1971): 4–31; part 3, no. 5 (May 1971): 9–40.

30. For critiques, see Marable, *Black American Politics*; and Harold Cruse's commentary in "Black and White—Part 1."

31. Bayard Rustin, "'Black Power' and Coalition Politics," *Commentary* 42 (September 1966): 35–40. This essay builds upon Rustin's more celebrated essay, "From Protest to Politics: The Future of the Civil Rights Movement," *Commentary* 39 (February 1965): 25–31. Rustin would follow his critiques of Black Power with another essay, "The Failure of Black Separatism," *Harper's* 240 (January 1970): 25–34.

32. Grace Lee Boggs and James Boggs, "The City Is the Black Man's Land," *Monthly Review* 17, no. 11 (1966): 35–46. See also James Turner, "Black in the Cities: Land and Self-Determination," *Black Scholar* 1, no. 6 (1970): 9–13.

33. Stokely Carmichael, "Black Power" (October 29, 1966), Voices of Democracy: The U.S. Oratory Project, accessed April 15, 2025, https://voicesofdemocracy.umd.edu/carmichael-black-power-speech-text/.

34. Sam Roberts, "Charles V. Hamilton, an Apostle of 'Black Power,' Dies at 94," *New York Times*, February 18, 2024.

35. See Kwame Ture and Charles V. Hamilton, *Black Power: The Politics of Liberation in America* (Vintage, 1992).

36. Ture and Hamilton, *Black Power*, 46–47.

37. In addition to Taylor, "Politics of the Black Power Movement," see, for example, Johnson, *Revolutionaries to Race Leaders*, 119–28.

38. David Harvey's essay, "The Right to the City" (*New Left Review* 53 [2008]: 23–40) is an example of the recasting and deracialization of the programmatic elements of Black Power Urbanism that flattens Black rebellion into "neighborhood" activism.

39. Woodard argues that these modern conventions stand in the historical lineage created by the first Black convention movement of the nineteenth century as well as the Negro congresses held during the 1930s (Woodard, *A Nation Within a Nation*, 1–45).

40. See N. D. B. Connolly "A Black Power Method," *Public Books*, June 15, 2016, https://www.publicbooks.org/a-black-power-method/.

41. See Lisa Veroni-Paccher, "Black Power 1968: 'To Stumble Is Not to Fall, but to Go Forward Faster,'" *L'Ordinaire des Amériques* 217 (2014), https://doi.org/10.4000/orda.1624. Veroni-Paccher argues that "few authors . . . attempted to give [Black Power] meaning." Instead scholars tend to "focus . . . on the National Black Political Conventions (NBPC), and the Gary one in particular, as a series of events that either marked the end of the movement or led to a political dead-end in the conservative era of American politics."

42. Sam Durant, ed., *Black Panther: The Revolutionary Art of Emory Douglas* (Rizzoli, 2007).

43. On the history of ARCH, see Brian Goldstein, "'The Search for New Forms': Black Power and the Making of the Postmodern City," *Journal of American History* 103, no. 2 (2016): 375–99, https://doi.org/10.1093/jahist/jaw181. For discussion of The New Thing Center and its founder Topper Carew, see Michael Kernan, "That Summer 'Thing,'"

Washington Post, August 19, 1984, https://www.washingtonpost.com/archive/lifestyle/style/1984/08/19/that-summer-thing/42428f46-58b1-4044-a48e-a1016dd164f4/; and also "Interview with Topper Carew," *Harvard Educational Review* 39, no. 4 (December): 98–115.

44. See James A. Tyner, "'Defend the Ghetto': Space and Urban Politics of the Black Panther Party," *Annals of the Association of American Geographers* 96, no. 1 (2006): 105–18.

45. See Martha Biondi, *The Black Revolution on Campus* (University of California Press, 2012); and Noliwe Rooks, *White Money/Black Power: The Surprising History of African American Studies and the Crisis of Race in Higher Education* (Beacon Press, 2006); Russell Rickford, *We Are an African People: Independent Education, Black Power, and the Radical Imagination* (Oxford University Press, 2016).

46. On the emergence of Black Power in Detroit, see Matthew Birkhold, "Theory and Practice: Organic Intellectuals and Revolutionary Ideas in Detroit's Black Power Movement" (PhD diss., Binghamton University, 2016); Grace Lee Boggs, *Living for Change: An Autobiography* (University of Minnesota Press, 1998); and Angela Dillard, *Faith in the City: Preaching Radical Social Change in Detroit* (University of Michigan Press, 2009). The following website provides a clear overview: "Resurgence of Black Nationalism," Rise Up Detroit, accessed April 15, 2025, https://riseupdetroit.org/chapters/chapter-3/part-1/resurgence-of-black-nationalism/.

47. A number of conferences occurred from 1970 to 1972. In addition to conferences convened by various branches of the Congress of African People (CAP), other conferences included the Black Leadership Unity Conference (Washington, DC, 1971), the Black Political Conference (Brooklyn, July 1971), and the Northlake Summit (Northlake, Illinois, 1971) (Woodard, *A Nation Within a Nation*, 1–30. Also see M. Keith Claybrook Jr., "Maulana Karenga, Operational Unity, and the Black Power Movement," *Black Perspectives*, African American Intellectual History Society, accessed April 15, 2025, https://www.aaihs.org/maulana-karenga-operational-unity-and-the-black-power-movement/.

48. See *Regional Conference on Black Power* (Bermuda, 1969); *Black Power Conference Reports* (Action Library, Afram Associates, 1970); and also Quito Swan, "*Blueprint for Freedom*: Bermuda's Black Power Conference of 1969," in *Black Power in Bermuda: The Struggle for Decolonization* (Palgrave Macmillan, 2009).

49. Chuck Stone listed the workshop topics and their respective coordinators as follows: "(1) The City and Black People—Lee Montgomery and Oswald Sykes; (2) Black Power Through Black Politics—Chuck Stone and Dan Watts; (3) Black Power in World Perspective: Nationalism and Internationalism—Ron Karenga; (4) Black Power Through Economic Development—Robert Browne; (5) The Black Home—Nathan Hare; (6) Black Power and American Religion—Reverend C. Lincoln McGhee; (7) New Roles for Black Youth—Cleveland Sellers; (8) Black Artists, Crafts, and Communication—Ossie Davis and Carol Green; (9) Black Professionals and Black Power—Hoyt Fuller and Gerald McWorter; (10) Developmental Implications of Black Power—Dr. James Comer; (11) Black Power and Social Change—John Davis and Lou Gothard; (12) Fraternal, Civic, and Social Groups—Fay Bellamy; (13) Cooperation and Alliances—James Farmer and Vivian Braxton; and (14) New Trends for Youth—William Strickland." From Stone, "The National Conference," 193.

50. "Newark Black Convention Set for June," *Black Newark: The Voice of Newark's Inner City* 1, no. 1 (April 1968): 1.

51. Tyner, "'Defend the Ghetto,'" 105–18.

52. See David Hilliard, ed., *The Black Panther Party: Service to the People Programs* (University of New Mexico Press, 2008).

53. See David Hilliard, "Community Survival Programs," in Hilliard, *The Black Panther Party*; and also "Community Survival Programs," *A Huey P. Newton Story*, PBS, 2002, https://www.pbs.org/hueypnewton/actions/actions_survival.html.

54. Archives of the Episcopal Church, "The Church Awakens: African American Struggles for Justice," 2017, https://www.episcopalarchives.org/church-awakens/; James Forman, *The Making of Black Revolutionaries* (University of Washington Press, 2000); and "Jim Forman Delivers Black Manifesto at Riverside Church," SNCC Digital Gateway, SNCC Legacy Project and Duke University, May 1969, https://snccdigital.org/events/jim-forman-delivers-black-manifesto-at-riverside-church/.

55. Black Panther Party, "The Ten-Point Program" (October 1966), in Hilliard, *The Black Panther Party*, appendix A.

56. See Hilliard, "Community Survival Programs," 79.

57. Ruth Wilson Gilmore, *Golden Gulag: Prisons, Surplus, Crisis, and Opposition in Globalizing California* (University of California Press, 2007).

58. Boggs, "City Is the Black Man's Land," 36–38.

59. See David Goldberg and Trevor Griffey, eds., *Black Power at Work: Community Control, Affirmative Action, and the Construction Industry* (Cornell University Press, 2010); and Laura Warren Hill and Julia Rabig, eds., *The Business of Black Power: Community Development, Capitalism, and Corporate Responsibility in Postwar America* (Boydell & Brewer, 2012).

60. See Premilla Nadasen, *Welfare Warriors: The Welfare Rights Movement in the United States* (Routledge, 2005). In addition, see Rhonda Williams, *The Politics of Public Housing: Black Women's Struggles Against Urban Inequality* (Oxford University Press, 2004); and Williams, *Concrete Demands: The Search for Black Power in the 20th Century* (Routledge, 2015). See also Annelise Orleck, *Storming Caesar's Palace: How Black Mothers Fought Their Own War on Poverty* (Beacon Press, 2005).

61. See Black Panther Party, "The Black Panther Party Program" (March 29, 1972), in Hilliard, *The Black Panther Party*, appendix B.

62. Black Panther Party, "The Black Panther Party Program" (March 29, 1972).

63. Eana Meng, "Use of Acupuncture by 1970s Revolutionaries of Color: The South Bronx 'Toolkit Care' Concept," *American Journal of Public Health* 111, no. 5 (2021): 896–906.

64. See Hilliard, "Community Survival Programs," 44.

65. See Goldstein, "'The Search for New Forms,'" 375–99; Daniel Matlin, "'A New Reality of Harlem': Imagining the African American Urban Future During the 1960s," *Journal of American Studies* 52, no. 4 (2018): 991–1024.

66. *Black Power Conference Reports* (1970), 24.

67. Christopher Strain, "Soul City, North Carolina: Black Power, Utopia, and the African American Dream," *The Journal of African American History* 89, no. 1 (2004): 57–74; Thomas Healy, *Soul City: Race, Equality, and the Lost Dream of an American Utopia* (Metropolitan Books, 2021).

68. See A Veteran of Newark's Blight Wars of the 1950s and 1960s, "'Fighting the Blight': Or Urban Resistance to Authoritarian Social Change," in *From Riot to Recovery: Newark After Ten Years*, ed. Stanley Winters (University Press of America, 1979).

69. Veteran, "Fighting the Blight," 54.

70. See Boggs, "City Is the Black Man's Land," 36; Turner, "Blacks in the Cities," 10.

71. See "Activist Bertha Gilkey," Neighborhood Women, YouTube, posted January 15, 2025, 13 min., 32 sec., accessed May 5, 2025, https://www.youtube.com/watch?v=j5_0ij3S00M; see also Jason Deparle, "Cultivating Their Own Gardens, *New York Times*, January 5, 1992.

72. Black Panther Party, "The Black Panther Party Program" (March 29, 1972).

73. The Community Reinvestment Act was enacted in 1977 to provide better credit access to low-income communities. See Rebecca K. Marchiel, *After Redlining: The Urban Reinvestment Movement in the Era of Financial Deregulation* (University of Chicago Press, 2020).

74. On the Ocean Hill-Brownsville community control experiment, see Heather Lewis, *New York City Public Schools from Brownsville to Bloomberg: Community Control and Its Legacy* (New York: Teachers College Press, 2013); and Jerald Podair, *The Strike That Changed New York: Blacks, Whites, and the Ocean Hill-Brownsville Crisis* (Yale University Press, 2002).

75. See Rhody McCoy, "Why Have an Ocean Hill-Brownsville," in *What Black Educators Are Saying*, ed. Nathan Wright (Hawthorn Books, 1970); Preston R. Wilcox, "The Community Centered School," in *The Schoolhouse in the City*, ed. Alvin Tiffler (Praeger, 1968); Whitney Young, "Minorities and Community Control," *Journal of Negro Education* 38, no. 3 (1969): 285–90.

76. See August Meier and Elliott M. Rudwick, "Early Boycotts of Segregated Schools: The East Orange, New Jersey, Experience, 1899–1906," *History of Education Quarterly* 7, no. 1 (1967): 22–35.

77. See Eve Ewing, *Ghosts in the Schoolyard: Racism and School Closings on Chicago's South Side* (University of Chicago Press, 2018).

78. See Vincent J. Cannato, *The Ungovernable City: John Lindsay and His Struggle to Save New York* (Basic Books, 2002), 273; but also Marta Gutman, "Intermediate School 201: Race, Space, and Modern Architecture in Harlem," in *Educating Harlem: A Century of Schooling and Resistance in a Black Community*, ed. Ansley T. Erickson and Ernest Morrell (Columbia University Press, 2019).

79. In addition to McCoy, "Why Have an Ocean Hill-Brownsville"; see also Podair, *The Strike That Changed New York*.

80. See Black Panther Party, "The Black Panther Party Program" (March 29, 1972) and the initial demand in "The Ten-Point Program" (October 1966).

3. NEWARK

1. Lilo H. Stanton, "University Hospital Newark Faces New Scrutiny Following Infant Deaths," *NJ Spotlight News*, November 28, 2018, https://www.njspotlightnews.org/2018/11/18-11-27-university-hospital-newark-faces-new-scrutiny-following-infant-deaths/.

2. "Agreements Reached Between Community and Government Negotiators Regarding New Jersey College of Medicine of Dentistry and Related Matters (as Amended)," April 30, 1968, https://riseupnewark.com/wp-content/uploads/2016/09/Agreements-Reached-Between-Community-and-Government-Negotiators-Regarding-UMDNJ-and-Related-Matters-As-Amended-April-30-1968-ilovepdf-compressed.pdf. See also Luther J. Carter, "Newark: Negroes Demand and GET Voice in Medical School Plans," *Science* 160, no. 3825, April 19, 1968, 290–92, https://doi.org/10.1126/science.160.3825.290; Junius Williams, *Unfinished Agenda: Urban Politics in the Era of Black Power* (North Atlantic Books, 2014).

3. City of Newark, "Mayor Baraka Calls for Over Haul of University Hospital," November 27, 2018, https://www.newarknj.gov/news/mayor-baraka-calls-for-over-haul-of-university-hospital; Sam Sutton, "State Monitor: Poor Management Weakened Services, Care at University Hospital," *Politico.com*, December 10, 2018, https://www.politico.com/states/new-jersey/story/2018/12/09/state-monitor-poor-management-weakened-services-care-at-university-hospital-734898.

4. City of Newark, "Mayor Baraka."

5. City of Newark, "Mayor Baraka."

6. See Anthony Vecchione, "Report University Hospital Needs 'Transformational Leader,'" NJBIZ, December 10, 2018, https://njbiz.com/report-university-hospital-needs-transformational-leader/; and HPAE, "Position Paper: Fulfilling the Historic Charge of University Hospital in Newark and Sustaining the Opportunity for Public Health for Future Generations of New Jerseyans," Newark, 2018, https://www.hpae.org/wp-content/uploads/2022/06/HPAE_PositionPaper_05.pdf.

7. Urban renewal and dispossession looms large in almost every monograph on twentieth-century Newark. This chapter draws heavily on Howard Kaplan, *Urban Renewal Politics: Slum Clearance in Newark* (Columbia University Press, 1963). See also Robert Curvin, *Inside Newark: Decline, Rebellion, and the Search for Transformation* (Rutgers University Press, 2014); and Curvin, "The Persistent Minority: The Black Political Experience in Newark" (PhD diss., Princeton University, 1975); Andra Gillespie, *The New Black Politician: Cory Booker, Newark, and Post-Racial America* (New York University Press, 2012); Mark Krasovic, *The Newark Frontier: Community Action in the Great Society* (University of Chicago Press, 2016); Kevin Mumford, *Newark: A History of Race, Rights, and Riots in America* (New York University Press, 2007); Julia Rabig, *The Fixers: Devolution, Development, and Civil Society in Newark, 1960–1990* (University of Chicago Press, 2016); Brad R. Tuttle, *How Newark Became Newark: The Rise, Fall, and Rebirth of an American City* (Rivergate Books, 2009); Komozi Woodard, *A Nation Within a Nation: Amiri Baraka (LeRoi Jones) and Black Power Politics* (University of North Carolina Press, 1999).

8. See "Agreements Reached." On the lead poisoning crisis, see Gwendolyn G. Grant, "Childhood Lead Poisoning: Newark, New Jersey's Preventable Disease; An Exploratory Study" (master's thesis, Newark State College, 1971).

9. On "hollow prize," see H. Paul Friesema, "Black Control of Central Cities: The Hollow Prize," *Journal of the American Institute of Planners* 35, no. 2 (1969): 75–79, https://doi.org/10.1080/01944366908977576; and also Neil Kraus and Todd Swanstrom, "Minority Mayors and the Hollow-Prize Problem," *PS: Political Science and Politics* 34, no. 1 (2001): 99–105, https://www.jstor.org/stable/1350317.

10. University Hospital, "A Letter to the Newark Community: The Future of University Hospital," October 2020, https://www.uhnj.org/UH-Vision.pdf.

11. The role of women in CFUN, especially that of Amina Baraka, is discussed in Woodard, *A Nation Within a Nation*, 122–26. Kidd's role in Newark's welfare rights movement can be seen in the documentary *With No One to Help Us* (1967) and in correspondence ("Consumers Buyers Club" [Marion Kidd], Newark, NJ, 1971–72, Guida West Papers, Sophia Smith Collection, SSC-MS-00555, Smith College Special Collections, Northampton, Massachusetts). For a broader discussion of Black women and the Black Power movement, see Ashley D. Farmer's *Remaking Black Power: How Black Women Transformed an Era* (University of North Carolina Press, 2017).

12. For an invaluable and critical framing of the role of Baraka and the idea of "New-Ark," see Woodard, *A Nation Within a Nation*" and Curvin, *Inside Newark*; Jerry G. Watts, *Amiri Baraka: The Politics and Art of a Black Intellectual* (New York University Press, 2001).

13. Congress enacted HOPE VI (Housing Opportunities for People Everywhere) in 1992 to "replace severely distressed public housing projects, occupied exclusively by poor families, with redesigned mixed-income housing and provides housing vouchers to enable some of the original residents to rent apartments in the private market." See Susan J. Popkin et al., *A Decade of HOPE VI: Research Findings and Policy Challenges* (Urban Institute, May 2004), 1, https://www.urban.org/research/publication/decade-hope-vi?ID=411002.

See also Lawrence J. Vale, *Purging the Poorest: Public Housing and the Design Politics of Twice-Cleared Communities* (University of Chicago Press, 2013). On Newark's demolition of its public housing projects, see Alfonso A. Narvaez, "Newark Rips Down Its Projects," *New York Times*, November 28, 1987.

14. On the Ocean Hill-Brownsville community control experiment, see Heather Lewis, *New York City Public Schools from Brownsville to Bloomberg: Community Control and Its Legacy* (Teachers College Press, 2013); and Jerald Podair, *The Strike That Changed New York: Blacks, Whites, and the Ocean Hill-Brownsville Crisis* (Yale University Press, 2002).

15. For discussion of the African Free School and other independent Black schools established during this era, see Russell Rickford, *We Are an African People: Independent Education, Black Power, and the Radical Imagination* (Oxford University Press, 2016). For a brief history of Chad School, see "History of Chad," Chad School Foundation, 2023, https://chadschoolfoundation.org/history-of-chad-schools.

16. On the recent history of Newark's public schools, see Wilbur C. Rich, *Black Mayors and School Politics: The Failure of Reform in Detroit, Gary, and Newark* (Garland, 1996); and Dale Russakoff, *The Prize: Who's in Charge of America's Schools?* (Houghton Mifflin Harcourt, 2016).

17. See Kate Zernike, "Cami Anderson, Picked by Christie, Is Out as Newark Schools Superintendent," *New York Times*, June 22, 2015; Dan Ivers, "Baraka Joins Anti-Cerf Protest, Calls Critics of School Control Deal 'Crackpots,'" NJ.com, July 8, 2015; David W. Chen, "After More Than 20 Years, Newark to Regain Control of Its Schools," *New York Times*, September 12, 2017; "Mayor Baraka Discusses Why Newark Should Have an Elected School Board," City of Newark, November 3, 2018, https://www.newarknj.gov/news/mayor-baraka-discusses-why-newark-should-have-elected-school-board.

18. For discussion of historic Black Newark, see Clement Price, "The Afro-American Community of Newark, 1917–1947: A Social History" (PhD diss., Rutgers University, 1975). In addition to the historic Black churches of Saint James African Methodist Episcopal Church (1842) and Saint Philips Episcopal Church (1848), Bethany Baptist Church was established in 1871. The latter church would be home to the Black leadership that emerged in the wake of the first wave of the Great Migration (see Curvin, *Inside Newark*, 18–19).

19. Until 1930, slightly more Black people lived outside of Newark in the suburban towns of East Orange and Montclair, where they created their own "domestic service suburbs." For discussion of the domestic service suburbs, see Andrew Wiese, "The Other Suburbanites: African American Suburbanization in the North before 1950," *Journal of American History* 85, no. 4 (March 1999): 1495–1524.

20. During this early period of community consolidation, a Black leadership class emerged that was made up of educators like James Baxter, principal of the Colored School; clergy; small business owners; and the small number of men and women who held Jim Crow–era prestige jobs as clerks and messengers in white firms and as federal employees such as mail carriers. See Price, "The Afro-American Community," 74–100; also William Ashby, "Reflections on the Life of Negroes in Newark," address delivered to the Frontier's Club on February 16, 1972, William M. Ashby Papers, Newark Public Library.

21. For history of Dr. John A. Kenney, in addition to Price, "The Afro-American Community," see Glenn G. Geisheimer, "Newark Care Facilities: Old Newark," 1998, http://newarkcarefacilities.com/kenney.php.

22. Ashby was a member of the small interracial social welfare movement that emerged in Newark during World War I. He aimed to facilitate the assimilation of Southern Black migrants into urban industrial life. See Price, "The Afro-American Community," 74–99.

23. See Curvin, "The Persistent Minority"; also Curvin, *Inside Newark*, 40–44; and Price, "Afro-American Community."

24. On the role of organized crime in Newark politics and in Black Newark, see Curvin, *Inside Newark*, 40–44; and Price, "Afro-American Community."

25. Newark's informal groups, nightlife, and other community gatherings are discussed in Price, "Afro-American Community," 67–69. On "undercommons," see Stefano Harney and Fred Moten, *The Undercommons: Fugitive Planning and Black Study* (Minor Compositions, 2013).

26. On role of policing and the police in creating and maintaining segregation, especially of nightlife, see Khalil Gibran Muhammad, *The Condemnation of Blackness: Race, Crime, and the Making of Modern Urban America* (Harvard University Press, 2010); and Rashad Shabazz, *Spatializing Blackness: Architectures of Confinement and Black Masculinity in Chicago* (University of Illinois Press, 2015).

27. Price, "Afro-American Community," 50.

28. Price, "Afro-American Community," 50.

29. See Krasovic, *The Newark Frontier*, 38; Price, "Afro-American Community," 50.

30. The commissioners' fiefdoms covered the following departments: Public Affairs, Revenue and Finance, Public Safety, Streets and Public Improvements, and Parks and Public Property. See Price, "Afro-American Community," 156.

31. Price, "Afro-American Community," 158–59.

32. On the impact of wartime mobilization and the "Double-V for Victory" campaign on Blacks Newark, see Kevin Mumford, "Double V in New Jersey: African American Civic Culture and Rising Consciousness Against Jim Crow, 1938–1966," *New Jersey History* 119, no. 3 (2001): 33–55.

33. For an overview of conditions in Newark's Black neighborhoods, see Chester Rapkin, *Group Relations in Newark, 1957: Problems, Prospects and a Program for Research* (Urban Research, 1957). See also Robert Curvin, "Black Ghetto Politics in Newark After World War II," in *Cities of the Garden State: Essays in the Urban and Suburban History of New Jersey*, ed. Joel Schwartz and Daniel Prosser (Kendall/Hunt, 1977).

34. "Housing Survey of the Third Ward," unpublished study by the Newark Department of Health, 1938, cited in Price, "Afro-American Community," 70.

35. Price, "Afro-American Community," 70.

36. Price, "Afro-American Community," 70.

37. On the illicit economy, see Price, "Afro-American Community," 68–69, 73.

38. Price, "Afro-American Community," 70, 72.

39. For discussion of Newark charter reform in the early 1950s and the role of good government groups as well as financial support from the city's leading corporations, see Stanley Winters, "Charter Change and Civic Reform in Newark, 1953–1954," *New Jersey History* 118 (2000): 35–65; "Voters to End Rule by Commission: Charter Group Cites Major Advantages Mayor-Council Rule Would Bring to City," *New Jersey Afro-American*, August 15, 1953. See also Curvin, *Inside Newark*, 48–53; Krasovic, *The Newark Frontier*, 38–39.

40. Krasovic, *The Newark Frontier*, 39.

41. Infighting and alleged political payoffs meant that Roger Yancey, an African American handpicked by the reform coalition to become the city's first Black council member, would be replaced by Irvine Turner, an African American who was an up-and-coming member of the city's Democratic machine. Woodard argues that Turner had run as a "progressive anti-McCarthy candidate criticizing the H-bomb" and was swept into office by a Black/labor alliance (Woodard, *A Nation Within a Nation*, 37). The subsequent collapse of the communist left and the New Jersey Negro Labor Council led to Turner's absorption into the Newark political machine. See also Curvin, *Inside Newark*, 53–59; and Krasovic, *The Newark Frontier*, 38–40.

42. See Central Planning Board, *A Preliminary Report on the Scope of the City Plan, No. 1 of a Series* (The Board, 1944); and Central Planning Board and Harland Bartholomew

and Associates, *A Preliminary Report on Past, Present and Probable Future Population for Newark, New Jersey* (The Board, 1944).

43. See Tuttle, *How Newark Became Newark*, 125, quoting Central Planning Board, "A Preliminary Report on the Scope of the City Plan."

44. Tuttle, *How Newark Became Newark*, 124–25.

45. See "Newark Gets Plan for City Changes: 3-Year Project Would Involve Slum Clearance—Costs Would Be $250,000,000," *New York Times*, April 3, 1947.

46. Steven Strunsky, "National Park Service Adds Site of Black Church in Newark to Underground Railroad Network," NJ.com, February 15, 2023, https://www.nj.com/education/2022/06/national-park-service-adds-site-of-black-church-in-newark-to-underground-railroad-network.html.

47. The "white noose" of the suburban areas to the west of Newark presented a formidable barrier to Blacks leaving the city. See Yutaka Sasaki, "'But Not Next Door': Housing Discrimination and the Emergence of the 'Second Ghetto' in Newark, New Jersey After World War II," *The Japanese Journal of American Studies* 5 (1993–94): 113–35; Jonathan M. Rich, "Municipal Boundaries in a Discriminatory Housing Market: An Example of Racial Leapfrogging," *Urban Studies* 21, no. 1 (February 1984): 31–40; and Kenneth T. Jackson, *Crabgrass Frontier: The Suburbanization of the United States* (Oxford University Press, 1985).

48. Kaplan, *Urban Renewal Politics*, 66–67.

49. Central Planning Board, *A Preliminary Report*.

50. Krasovic, *The Newark Frontier*, 22–25.

51. Krasovic, *The Newark Frontier*, 41.

52. Krasovic, *The Newark Frontier*, 57.

53. "George Richardson Describes the Emergence of Black Independent Politics in Newark," Vimeo, 3 min., 15 sec., posted September 18, 2016, https://vimeo.com/183243581. See also Max Pizarro, "The Roots of Newark: Richardson and Sarcone Meet Again Almost 50 Years After Historic State Senate Race," *Observer*, February 8, 2010, https://observer.com/2010/02/the-roots-of-newark-richardson-and-sarcone-meet-again-almost-50-years-after-historic-state-senate-race/.

54. Richardson quoted in Pizarro, "The Roots of Newark."

55. Pizarro, "The Roots of Newark."

56. For an overview, see Krasovic, *The Newark Frontier*, 15–63. On "maximum feasible participation" and its critique, see Lillian B. Rubin, "Maximum Feasible Participation: The Origins, Implications, and Present Status," *The Annals of the American Academy of Political and Social Science* 385, no. 1 (1969): 14–29; Daniel P. Moynihan, *Maximum Feasible Misunderstanding: Community Action in the War on Poverty* (Free Press, 1969); and J. David Greenstone and Paul E. Peterson, *Race and Authority in Urban Politics: Community Participation in the War on Poverty* (Russell Sage Foundation, 1973).

57. Krasovic, *The Newark Frontier*, 57.

58. See Cyril DeGrasse Tyson, *2 Years Before the Riot!: Newark, New Jersey and the United Community Corporation, 1964–1966* (Jay Street Publishers, 2004); and Williams, *Unfinished Agenda*, for another firsthand account of the Addonzio campaign.

59. See also Jennifer Frost, *An Interracial Movement of the Poor: Community Organizing and the New Left in the 1960s* (New York University Press, 2001).

60. Woodard lists many of them: "Simba Wachunga (Young Lions), NewArk Student Federation, cultural and artistic groups like Spirit House, Hekalu Mwalimu, Spirit House Movers and Players, two newspapers (Black NewArk Voice and Unity and Struggle), a journal of jazz criticism (Cricket), Jihad Publications, the Black NewArk radio show and television programs, several independent and autonomous African Free schools; and a

host of cooperative stores, shops and other business developments, including a housing complex" (Woodard, *A Nation Within a Nation*, 2).

61. For discussion of the Modern Black convention movement, see Woodard, *A Nation Within a Nation*, xiii–xiv, 1–3.

62. In addition to Kaplan, *Urban Renewal Politics*, this section draws on Martin Anderson, *The Federal Bulldozer: A Critical Analysis of Urban Renewal, 1949–1962* (MIT Press, 1964); Arnold R. Hirsch, *Making the Second Ghetto: Race and Housing in Chicago, 1940–1960* (University of Chicago Press, 1998); Christopher Klemek, *The Transatlantic Collapse of Urban Renewal: Postwar Urbanism from New York to Berlin* (University of Chicago Press, 2011); and Preston H. Smith, *Racial Democracy and the Black Metropolis: Housing Policy in Postwar Chicago* (University of Minnesota Press, 2012).

63. Tuttle, *How Newark Became Newark*, 123–24.

64. Kaplan, *Urban Renewal Politics*, 11; Tuttle, *How Newark Became Newark*, 115–16.

65. Kaplan, *Urban Renewal Politics*, 12.

66. As early as 1939, news accounts related the deep involvement of the city's organized crime groups in securing NHA contracts. See Harry L. Margulies, "Public Housing in Newark: The Struggle to Survive," in *From Riot to Recovery: Newark After Ten Years*, ed. Stanley Winters (University Press of America, 1979), 232–33; and Curvin, *Inside Newark*, 40–44.

67. Steven Strunsky, "National Park Service Adds Site of Black Church in Newark to Underground Railroad Network," NJ.com, February 15, 2023, https://www.nj.com/education/2022/06/national-park-service-adds-site-of-black-church-in-newark-to-underground-railroad-network.html.

68. See Sasaki, "'But Not Next Door.'"

69. See Kaplan, *Urban Renewal Politics*; Tuttle, *How Newark Became Newark*; and Mumford, *Newark*.

70. See Curvin, *Inside Newark*, 52–60.

71. Kaplan, *Urban Renewal Politics*, 154.

72. For this quotation and next, see Kaplan, *Urban Renewal*, 16.

73. See George Sternlieb and Robert W. Burchell, *Residential Abandonment: The Tenement Landlord Revisited* (Center for Urban Policy Research, Rutgers University, 1973). On the long-term effect of Newark's urban renewal and dispossession, see Mindy Thompson Fullilove, *Root Shock: How Tearing Up City Neighborhoods Hurts America, and What We Can Do About It* (One World, 2004), 11–17.

74. See Sternlieb and Burchell, *Residential Abandonment*, 193.

75. The relationship between tax delinquency and building abandonment is discussed in Sternlieb and Burchell, *Residential Abandonment*, 193–94.

76. In addition to Fullilove, *Rootshock*, see William J. Collins and Robert A. Margo, "The Economic Aftermath of the 1960s Riots in American Cities: Evidence from Property Values," *Journal of Economic History* 67, no. 4 (2007): 849–83. For a critical view, see Jonathan J. Bean, "'Burn, Baby, Burn': Small Business in the Urban Riots of the 1960s," *The Independent Review* 5, no. 2 (2000): 165–88.

77. Alex Poinsett, "Countdown in Housing," *Ebony Magazine*, September 1972, 62.

78. Governor's Select Commission on Civil Disorder, *Report for Action* (State of New Jersey, 1968), 55.

79. "Platform of the Black and Puerto Rican Convention," Rise Up Newark, 1969, https://riseupnewark.com/wp-content/uploads/2016/09/Platform-of-the-Black-and-Puerto-Rican-Convention-Including-Additions-ilovepdf-compressed.pdf. See also, "Ken Gibson Campaign Brochure," Rise Up Newark, 1970, https://riseupnewark.com/wp-content/uploads/2016/09/Ken-Gibson-Campaign-Brochure-1970-ilovepdf-compressed.pdf.

80. Woodard, *A Nation Within a Nation*, 224, 226–27.

81. Woodard, *A Nation Within a Nation*, 228–29.

82. Woodard, *A Nation Within a Nation*, 229.

83. See "Ken Gibson Campaign Brochure."

84. A comprehensive overview of the Stella Wright strike is provided by Rabig, *The Fixers*, 142–70. See also National Urban Coalition, *The Stella Wright Rent Strike and the Greater Newark Urban Coalition* (The National Urban Coalition, 1975), https://riseupnewark.com/wp-content/uploads/2017/03/The-Stella-Wright-Rent-Strike-and-the-Greater-Newark-Urban-Coalition.pdf; Harris David, "The Settlement of the Newark Public Housing Rent Strike: The Tenants Take Control," *Clearinghouse Review* 10, no. 2 (June 1976): 103–10; Laura Maslow-Armand, "The Newark Tenant Rent Strike: Public Housing Policy and Black Municipal Governance," *Patterns of Prejudice* 20, no. 4 (1986): 17–30. For a pro-NHA perspective, see Margulies, "Public Housing in Newark."

85. On earlier moments of housing activism by Black Newarkers, see Price, "Afro-American Community," 70.

86. See "Map of Generalized Environments," Rise Up Newark, n.d. [1960s], http://riseupnewark.com/chapters/chapter-3/part-1/housing/.

87. On early 1960s tenant organizing, see John Baranski, "Something to Help Themselves: Tenant Organizing in San Francisco's Public Housing, 1965–1975," *Journal of Urban History* 33, no. 3 (2007): 418–42; Michael Karp, "The St. Louis Rent Strike of 1969: Transforming Black Activism and American Low-Income Housing," *Journal of Urban History* 40, no. 4 (2014): 648–70; Joel Schwartz, "Tenant Power in the Liberal City 1943–1971," in *The Tenant Movement in New York City, 1904–1984*, ed. Ronald Lawson (Rutgers University Press, 1986); and Michael Lipsky, "Rent Strikes in New York City: Protest Politics and the Power of the Poor" (PhD diss., Princeton University, 1967).

88. See Lipsky, "Rent Strikes."

89. See Mumford, *Newark*, 203–4; Krasovic, *The Newark Frontier*, 70–74.

90. Rhonda Williams, *The Politics of Public Housing: Black Women's Struggles Against Urban Inequality* (Oxford University Press, 2004), 201.

91. Williams, *The Politics of Public Housing*, 155–228.

92. See also Annelise Orleck, *Storming Caesar's Palace: How Black Mothers Fought Their Own War on Poverty* (Beacon Press, 2005).

93. On public housing tenant activism, in addition to Williams, *The Politics of Public Housing*; see Baranski, "Something to Help Themselves"; and Karp "The St. Louis Rent Strike."

94. On the destruction of the Pruitt-Igoe myth, see *The Pruitt-Igoe Myth*, directed by Chad Freidrichs, 79 min., First Run Features, 2011. See also Edward G. Goetz, *New Deal Ruins: Race, Economic Justice, and Public Housing Policy* (Cornell University Press, 2013).

95. See Kaplan, *Urban Renewal Politics*; and for a more critical overview, United States Commission on Civil Rights, *Public Housing in Newark's Central Ward: A Report by the New Jersey State Advisory Committee to the United States Commission on Civil Rights*, HathiTrust, April 1968, https://babel.hathitrust.org/cgi/pt?id=uc1.31822027490077&seq=1.

96. See National Urban Coalition, *The Stella Wright Rent Strike*.

97. Cost-saving features that once were lauded at Saint Louis's infamous Pruitt-Igoe housing project like skip-stop elevators were now criticized for contributing to the Scudder's lack of livability. For a discussion of efforts to reduce project costs and so-called amenities in the 1950s, see R. Allen Hays, *The Federal Government and Urban Housing* (State University of New York Press, 2012).

98. See Fullilove, *Root Shock*, 11–17; and also Mindy Thompson Fullilove, "Root Shock: The Consequences of African American Dispossession," *Journal of Urban Health* 78, no. 1 (2001): 72–80.

99. Map of nexus area from Tom Hayden, *Rebellion in Newark: Official Violence and Ghetto Response* (Vintage, 1967), 11.

100. See National Urban Coalition, *The Stella Wright Rent Strike*.

101. See New Jersey Public Broadcasting Authority, *Towers of Frustration*, videorecording, 28 min., Public Television Library, 1971.

102. See Maslow-Armand, "The Newark Tenant Rent Strike," 22.

103. Joan Cook, "Federal Aid and Tenant Gains Bring a New Era to Stella Wright Homes," *New York Times*, July 28, 1975.

104. Kaplan, *Urban Renewal Politics*, 42–43.

105. Laura Maslow-Armand, "The Newark Tenant Rent Strike: Public Housing Policy and Black Muncipal Governance," *Patterns of Prejudice* 20, no. 4 (1986): 23.

106. See Maslow-Armand, "The Newark Tenant Rent Strike," 23.

107. For discussion of the Brooke Amendment, see Alex F. Schwartz, *Housing Policy in the United States* (Routledge, 2014), 177.

108. Accounts of the rent strike are drawn from Harris David and J. Michael Callan, "Newark's Public Housing Rent Strike," *Clearinghouse Review* 7 (1974): 581–87; as well as Rabig, *The Fixers*; National Urban Coalition, *The Stella Wright Rent Strike*; David, "The Settlement"; Maslow-Armand, "The Newark Tenant Rent Strike."

109. David, "The Settlement."

110. Maslow-Armand, "The Newark Tenant Rent Strike," 27.

111. For discussion of the "end of public housing," see Hays, *The Federal Government*.

112. "Stella Wright: Housing Crisis," *New York Times*, April 8, 1973; Joan Cook, "Judges Slashes Rent by 80% in Strike at Newark Project," *New York Times*, November 28, 1973.

113. Housing Authority of the City of Newark v. Aikens, No. 2919132, N. J. Dist. Ct., Essex County (November 29, 1973).

114. On "community fixers" and Heninburg's preeminent role, see Rabig, *The Fixers*, 1–3.

115. See Kenneth K. Baar, "Rent Control in the 1970's: The Case of the New Jersey Tenants' Movement," *Hastings Law Journal* 28, no. 3 (1977): 631–83. Maslow-Armand argues that eventually this tenant activism ended up benefiting predominantly white middle-class suburban tenants rather than poor Newarkers (Maslow-Armand, "The Newark Tenant Rent Strike," 25).

116. Cook, "Federal Aid."

117. Indeed, Rabig argues that this approach "departed from most anti-poverty initiatives and black nationalist platforms that focused on the male wage earner." Rabig, *The Fixers*, 220.

118. See Stella Wright Tenant Association, *The New Stella Wright Handbook* (n.d.), https://riseupnewark.com/wp-content/uploads/2017/04/The-New-Stella-Wright-Handbook-1975.pdf.

119. J. S. Fuerst, "Tenant Management in Low-Rent Public Housing," *Social Service Review* 62, no. 2 (1988): 337–45; Robert Kolodny, *What Happens When Tenants Manage Their Own Public Housing* (NAHRO, August 1983); Daniel J. Monti, "The Organizational Strengths and Weaknesses of Resident-Managed Public Housing Sites in the United States," *Journal of Urban Affairs* 11, no. 1 (1989): 39–52.

120. See *The Pruitt-Igoe Myth*. See also Goetz's *New Deal Ruins*.

121. Maslow-Armand, "The Newark Tenant Rent Strike," 19.

122. Andre Shashaty, "U.S. Cuts Back and Shifts Course on Housing Aid," *New York Times*, October 18, 1981.

123. As Michael Leo Owens and others have shown, the demolition of high-rise public housing also had the support of middle-class Blacks. See Michael Owens et al., "'Let's Get Ready to Crumble': Black Municipal Leadership and Public Housing

Transformation in the United States," *Urban Affairs Review* 57, no. 5 (2020), https://doi.org/10.1177/1078087419901299.

124. See Newark Coalition for Low Income Housing et al. v. Newark Redevelopment and Housing Authority, 524 F. Supp. 2d 559, 2007 U. S. Dist. Lexis 92553. Rabig notes that "Harris David [of Legal Services of New Jersey], who had advised striking tenants two decades earlier, represented the coalition" (Rabig, *The Fixers*, 169).

125. See Rachelle Garbarine, "Newark Slowly Replacing Its Bleak Public Housing," *New York Times*, July 30, 1995; Guy Gugliotta, "Newark Housing Authority Raises Its HUD Rating As It Razes High-Rises," *Washington Post*, September 2, 1995.

126. Kelly Robinson, *Executive Summary, Stella Wright Homes Hope VI Project: Evaluation Interim Report Prepared for the Housing Authority of the City of Newark (2000)* in "Transforming Today's Vision into Tomorrow's Reality: HOPE VI Steering Committee Meeting," June 23, 2004, Newark City Documents, Charles F. Cummings New Jersey Information Center, Newark Public Library.

127. Jennifer Del Medico, "City Razes Three of Seven Stella Wright High Rises," *Star-Ledger*, April 28, 2002; Christine V. Baird, "Last Newark High-Rise Project Is Demolished," *Star-Ledger*, May 12, 2002.

128. Clifford J. Levy, "4 High-Rises Torn Down by Newark," *New York Times*, March 7, 1994, https://www.nytimes.com/1994/03/07/nyregion/4-high-rises-torn-down-by-newark.html.

129. Ronald Smothers, "A Step to End Newark's Chapter in High-Rise Public Housing Projects," *New York Times*, September 2, 1999, https://www.nytimes.com/1999/09/02/nyregion/a-step-to-end-newark-s-chapter-in-high-rise-public-housing-projects.html.

130. This quote and next from "Schools in Newark to Display the Flag of Black Liberation," *New York Times*, December 2, 1971.

131. "Schools in Newark."

132. See "Schools in Newark."

133. For demographic data on Newark public schools, see Kathryn Yatrakis, "Electoral Demands and Political Benefits: Minority as Majority; A Case Study of Two Mayoral Elections in Newark, New Jersey, 1970, 1974" (PhD diss., Columbia University, 1981). For a discussion of the history of "Black" education in Newark, see Jean Anyon, *Ghetto Schooling: A Political Economy of Urban Educational Reform* (Teachers College Press, 1997); for more recent history, see Rich, *Black Mayors and School Politics*, and Russakoff, *The Prize*.

134. Tuttle, *How Newark Became Newark*, 140.

135. "Education," Rise Up Newark, April 8, 2025, http://riseupnewark.com/chapters/chapter-3/part-1/education/.

136. "Education."

137. See NAACP, "A Report on Newark Public Schools Prepared by the Education Committee of the Newark Branch, NAACP," Rise Up Newark, November, 1961, https://riseupnewark.com/chapters/chapter-3/part-1/education/. See also Sidney Reitman, "Request to the Board of Education President of the Urban League of Essex County for a New Vice-Principal Promotional Examination (Draft Memorandum)," Rise Up Newark, [1960?], posted September 2016, https://riseupnewark.com/wp-content/uploads/2016/09/Memo-from-Urban-League-to-Newark-Agencies-Request-to-Board-of-Ed-for-New-Vice-Principal-Promotion-Exam-August.pdf.

138. See Anyon, *Ghetto Schooling*, 91, 110–13; and also NAACP, "A Report on the Newark Public Schools."

139. See Anyon, *Ghetto Schooling*, 112.

140. For discussion of this transition, see W. M. Phillips Jr., "Educational Policy, Community Participation, and Race," *Journal of Negro Education* 44, no. 3 (Summer 1975): 257–67, 263.

141. Phillips, "Educational Policy," 263.

142. Phillips, "Educational Policy," 264.

143. "Platform of the Black and Puerto Rican Convention" (ratified November 15, 1969), Junius Williams Collection, Rise Up Newark, accessed April 9, 2025, https://riseupnewark.com/chapters/chapter-3/part-3/the-black-and-puerto-rican-convention/.

144. Eugene Campbell would become the Newark public schools superintendent in 1984. Two consultants to the session, C. Herbert Oliver and Lester Campbell, were controversial figures. In 1967, Oliver was the chairman of New York City's "experiment in decentralization and community control" and would later have a Newark public school named after him (see Sam Roberts, "Rev. C. Herbert Oliver, Civil Rights Activist, Dies at 96," *New York Times*, updated December 13, 2021, https://www.nytimes.com/2021/12/11/us/rev-c-herbert-oliver-dead.html). In December 1968, Lester Campbell would become infamous for reading a "virulently anti-Semitic poem on a radio show hosted by Julius Lester, [which] further cemented belief that the Ocean-Hill Brownville" controversy was "fundamentally about anti-Semitism." See Margalit Fox, "Julius Lester, Chronicler of Black America, Is Dead at 78," *New York Times*, January 19, 2018.

145. Quotes in this paragraph and next are from "Platform of the Black and Puerto Rican Convention."

146. See "Platform of the Black and Puerto Rican Convention."

147. This could have been in reaction to the city's carceral-adjacent approaches to students and to youth discipline in the name of combating "juvenile delinquency," which expanded under Newark's Ford Foundation–funded Gray Areas program; see Krasovic, *The Newark Frontier*, 18–19.

148. "Platform of the Black and Puerto Rican Convention"

149. For a discussion of political tensions within the NPS, see Joseph M. Conforti, "Racial Conflict in Central Cities: The Newark Teachers' Strikes," *Society* 12, no. 1 (1974): 22–33; and William M. Phillips Jr. and Joseph Conforti, *Social Conflict: Teacher's Strikes in Newark, 1964–1971* (New Jersey State Department of Education, October 1972), https://files.eric.ed.gov/fulltext/ED073519.pdf. According to Phillips and Conforti, the NPS board decided that the "appointment of principals will henceforth be based upon minimal state requirements which are 5 years teaching experience within Newark, or 10 years' teaching experience outside Newark for appointment to a principal position; and 3 years' experience in Newark for appointment to a vice principal position." Phillips and Conforti, *Social Conflict*, 18. For further discussion of Newark's teachers' strikes and a detailed timeline of events, in addition to Phillips and Conforti, see also Steve Golin, *The Newark Teacher Strikes: Hopes on the Line* (Rutgers University Press, 2002); and Lois Weiner, "Class, Gender, and Race in the Newark Teacher Strikes," *New Politics* 9, no. 2 (2003): 101–7.

150. Phillips and Conforti, *Social Conflict*, 19.

151. The teachers claimed that "the Board's action violate[d] the agreement signed with NTA in 1967," which stated that "the position of principal, vice-principal, head teacher, department chairman, and counselor shall be filled in order of numerical ranking from the approved list, which rankings shall be determined by written and oral examinations." See Conforti, "Racial Conflict," 21.

152. See Helen P. Means, "The Cry for Black Community Control of Education in the Black Communities of Newark," unpublished paper, Newark State College, December 16, 1969, https://riseupnewark.com/wp-content/uploads/2020/10/The-Cry-for-Black-Community-Control-of-Education-in-Black-Communities-of-Newark-by-Helen-Means-1969.pdf.

153. For Black activists' critiques of the teachers unions, see Golin, *The Newark Teacher Strikes*, 108–15.

154. For discussion of the rise in state oversight and district takeovers in New Jersey, see Domingo Morel, *Takeover: Race, Education, and American Democracy* (Oxford University Press, 2018).

155. For discussion of rise of "indigenous nonprofessionals" or teaching paraprofessionals, see Nick Juravich, "Making a 'Paraprofessional Movement' in New York City," The Gotham Center for New York City History, August 3, 2016, https://www.gotham-center.org/blog/making-a-paraprofessional-movement-in-new-york-city. For Newark, see Conforti, "Racial Conflict"; and Scientific Resources Incorporated, "A Proposal from the Newark Board of Education to the Ford Foundation," paper presented at the conference Training the Non-Professional, March 15–17, 1967, Washington, DC, https://eric.ed.gov/?id=ED023627.

156. See Juravich, "Making a 'Paraprofessional Movement.'"

157. According to Conforti, "Sidney Rosenfeld, Executive Director of NTU, propose[d] to the Board that funds be obtained from the United Community Corporation, Newark's umbrella anti-poverty agency, to train teachers' aides for the Newark school system" (Conforti, "Racial Conflict," 4).

158. See Phillips and Conforti, *Social Conflict*, 13.

159. Phillips and Conforti, *Social Conflict*, 12.

160. Phillips and Conforti, *Social Conflict*, 27.

161. Phillips and Conforti, *Social Conflict*, 51.

162. The collapse of Kawaida Towers and the hostile relationship between Baraka and Gibson contributed to retaliation by Notte and the NHA, which led to the demolition of several CFUN buildings, including Spirit House. The African Free School's preschool program was forced to close, although the elementary school program survived. See Woodard, *Nation Within a Nation*; and Rickford, *We Are an African People*. For a history of Chad School, see "History of Chad," Chad School Foundation, 2023, http://chadschoolfoundation.org/history-of-chad-schools.

163. Another semiautonomous educational space created during this period was "School Within a School," located at South Side High (aka Malcolm X. Shabazz High School). The school program featured rigorous academics with a required entrance exam and an eleven-month school year. "District History," Newark Board of Education, accessed January 25, 2023, https://www.nps.k12.nj.us/info/district-history/.

164. The school was created using funding from the US Department of Labor, the New Jersey State Department of Educational Research, and the New Jersey State Department of Community Services, with supplemental funding from the Newark Board of Education. See American Institutes for Research, *Model Programs, Childhood Education: Springfield Avenue Community School, Newark, New Jersey* (National Center for Educational Communication, 1970), https://files.eric.ed.gov/fulltext/ED045784.pdf.

165. For additional discussion of Springfield,; American Institutes for Research et al., *Springfield Avenue Community School, Newark, New Jersey: A School Whose Curricular Emphasis Is on the Black "Life-Style"* (US Department of Health, Education, and Welfare, Office of Education, Office of Economic Opportunity, 1970); Leslie Rich, "Newark's Parent Powered School; Springfield Avenue Community School," *American Education* 7 (December 1971): 35–38; Tim Parsons, "The Community School Movement," *Community Issues* 2, no. 6 (December 1970): 3–79; and Charles Burack, "An Assessment of the Influence of Community Schools on the Attitudes and Involvement of Urban Parents" (PhD diss., University of Massachusetts Amherst, 1977). For a discussion of "takeover," see Carole Layne Willis, "The Educational Aspirations of Parents Who Send Their Children to a Community Controlled School: A Case Study of Newark's Springfield Avenue Community School" (PhD diss., University of Wisconsin, 1976).

166. Rich, "Newark's Parent Powered School," 38.

167. Charles Strum, "Helping Children Beat the Odds Against Them: Harriet Tubman School in Newark Thrives, but Only by Working Outside the System," *New York Times*, June 18, 1993.

168. Rich, *Black Mayors*, 105.

169. Rich, *Black Mayors*, 105.

170. Rich, *Black Mayors*, 105.

171. Deborah Yaffe, *Other People's Children: The Battle for Justice and Equality in New Jersey's Schools* (Rutgers University Press, 2007).

172. Anyon, *Ghetto Schooling*, 126.

173. Wilbur Rich, in *Black Mayors*, for example, argues that the referendum for an elected school board was "engineered by a strongly union-backed group of citizens" (120).

174. Rich, *Black Mayors*, 110.

175. Rich, *Black Mayors*, 114–15.

176. An example of the NPS's role in creating patronage jobs was the 1987 indictment of a board of education member for "selling administrative jobs" (Rich, *Black Mayors*, 120).

177. See Morel, *Takeover*, 105–6.

178. On urban education systems as sources of lucrative benefits and jobs, see Rich, *Black Mayors*, 144–45; and Russakoff, *The Prize*.

179. Rich, *Black Mayors*, 145.

180. "Only Colored Man on City Police Force," *Newark Sunday Call*, August 22, 1909. Additional information on Coleman from "History of the Black Experience in Newark," Newark Library Main Collection, Newark Public Library, accessed April 9, 2025, https://archive.org/details/MGNwkWardsandSections001/mode/2up.

181. See "Only Colored Man."

182. See "From Rebellion to Review Board: Fighting for Police Accountability in Newark," Paul Robeson Galleries exhibition, March 8, 2017–March 31, 2017, https://paulrobesongalleries.expressnewark.org/exhibition/from-rebellion-to-review-board-fighting-for-police-accountability-in-newark/.

183. See Tuttle, *How Newark Became Newark*, 155. For discussion of Black activism and police reform in mid-twentieth-century Newark, see Troy M. Pearsall, "Police Relations with the African-American Community in Newark, 1957–1967," in *Newark: The Durable City*, ed. Stanley Winters (New Jersey Institute of Technology, 1990); and Imani Radney, "Reasonable, Warranted and Consonant": Police Violence and Police Sovereignty in 1960s Newark," *Journal of Urban History* 51, no. 2 (2025): 341–60.

184. For a broader discussion of pre-1960s policing in Newark, see Rapkin, *Group Relations*; Curvin, "The Persistent Minority"; Price, "The Afro-American Community"; and W. Marvin Dulaney, *Black Police in America* (Indiana University Press, 1996).

185. See Mayor's Commission on Group Relations, *Newark: A City in Transition*, vol. 3, *Survey and Recommendations* (City of Newark, June 1959), 35–36.

186. Mayor's Commission on Group Relations, *Newark,* 36.

187. For discussion of the police-community relations model in action, see Karl E. Johnson, "Police-Black Community Relations in Postwar Philadelphia: Race and Criminalization in Urban Social Spaces, 1945–1960," *Journal of African American History* 89, no. 2 (2004): 118–34.

188. See Commission on Group Relations, *Newark: A City in Transition*, 47.

189. See Dulaney, *Black Police in America*, 71; and Tuttle, *How Newark Became Newark*, 154–57.

190. Dulaney, *Black Police in America*, 71.

191. Mayor Hugh Addonzio quoted in Curvin, *Inside Newark*, 85.

192. See Alexander Elkins, "Battle of the Corner: Urban Policing and Rioting in the United States, 1943–1971" (PhD diss., Temple University, 2017); and Robert Machover and Norm Fruchter, *We Got To Live Here*, 16mm film, 20 min., 1965.

193. See "Newark Divided on Police Tactics: Proposed Civilian Review Becomes Major Issue," *New York Times*, August 8, 1965, 60.

194. See *Newark Police-Community Relations Training Program*, 1965, NCJRS Virtual Library, Office of Justice Programs, U.S. Department of Justice, accessed April 9, 2025, https://www.ojp.gov/pdffiles1/Digitization/132NCJRS.pdf.

195. Tuttle, *How Newark Became Newark*, 156.

196. On the political and legal motivations for New Jersey state government takeovers of public school systems, see Morel's *Takeover*, 11–14.

197. Tuttle, *How Newark Became Newark*, 158–59.

198. Tuttle, *How Newark Became Newark*, 156.

199. See Rick Rojas and Khorri Atkinson, "Five Days of Unrest That Shaped, and Haunted, Newark," *New York Times*, July 11, 2017. For further discussion, see Hayden, *Rebellion in Newark*; and Ronald Porambo, *No Cause For Indictment: An Autopsy of Newark* (Holt, Rinehart and Winston, 1971).

200. For quote, see Dulaney, *Black Police in America*, 83.

201. The Governor's Select Commission on Civil Disorder (New Jersey's post-rebellion report) made several recommendations for reforming law enforcement, including a suggestion that Newark create a "five-man Board of Police Commissioners, made up of outstanding citizens representing the total Newark community . . . to receive and review all citizen complaints in police misconduct." See Governor's Select Commission, 164. See also Walter H. Waggoner, "Newark Mayor Bars Police Review Board," *New York Times*, March 1, 1968.

202. "Black Power Manifesto and Resolutions," National Conference on Black Power, Newark, NJ, July 20–23, 1967, 7–8, Rise Up Newark, https://riseupnewark.com/wp-content/uploads/2020/10/Black-Power-Manifesto-and-Resolutions-compressed.pdf.

203. "Black Power Manifesto," 18.

204. From "Law Enforcement," in "Platform of the Black and Puerto Rican Convention," Rise Up Newark, 1969, https://riseupnewark.com/wp-content/uploads/2016/09/Platform-of-the-Black-and-Puerto-Rican-Convention-Including-Additions-ilovepdf-compressed.pdf, n.p. (approx. p. 9).

205. See "Law Enforcement," in "Platform of the Black and Puerto Rican Convention."

206. See Dulaney, *Black Police in America*, 85.

207. Krasovic provides a clear overview of the emergence of Anthony Imperiale and his leadership of the North Ward Citizens' Committee: "With about 200 dues-paying members [the committee] became a vocal advocate of police officers' 'civil rights' and white grievance in the name of 'law and order.' Imperiale, who frequently attacked 'Martin Luther Coon,' leveraged his post-riot fame to win a special election to city council." See Krasovic, *The Newark Frontier*, 210–22.

208. Tuttle, *How Newark Became Newark*, 197.

209. See "The People Mount a National Campaign . . . Stop Killer Cops," *Unity and Struggle* 3, no. 11 (October 1974): 6, 9; and *Stop Killer Cops: Struggle Against Police Brutality; Your Child May Be Next!* (Congress of Afrikan People [1976]), https://www.marxists.org/history/erol/ncm-1a/cap-cops.htm.

210. The committee proposed an "autonomous board with 'jurisdiction over all complaints received from the citizens of Newark alleging police misconduct, police corruption, the use of unnecessary or excessive force, abuse of authority, discourteous or insulting language or ethnic discrimination.'" From "Civilian Complaint Review Board," in *Stop Killer Cops*.

211. See *Stop Killer Cops.*

212. See *Stop Killer Cops.*

213. See *Stop Killer Cops.*

214. For the Black Power Urbanism/post–civil rights pivot in Newark policing, see Dorothy Guyot, "Coping with Crime in Newark," Governmental Responses to Crime Project, Northwestern University Center for Urban Studies, rev. ed., October 1993, https://archive.org/details/MGNWKPOLICE166. For broader discussion of post–civil rights policing and welfare-state policy, see Elizabeth Hinton, *From the War on Poverty to the War on Crime: The Making of Mass Incarceration in America* (Harvard University Press, 2016).

215. See Guyot, "Coping with Crime," and Curvin, *Inside Newark,* for discussion of the rolling out of "fear city" and the adoption of reform policing.

216. See George L. Kelling, *The Newark Foot Patrol Experiment* (Police Foundation, 1981), https://www.policinginstitute.org/wp-content/uploads/2015/07/144273499-The-Newark-Foot-Patrol-Experiment.pdf. For critique, see Bernard E. Harcourt, *Illusion of Order: The False Promise of Broken Windows Policing* (Harvard University Press, 2001).

217. Guyot, "Coping with Crime," 227.

218. See Evelyn Nieves, "Newark Police Shootings Revive Calls for a Civilian Review Board," *New York Times,* September 11, 1992, http://www.nytimes.com/1992/09/11/nyregion/newark-police-shootings-revive-calls-for-a-civilian-review-board.html; B. Carter, "Newark Activists Demand Election of Civilian Board to Review Police," *Star-Ledger,* September 11, 1992; D. S. Onley, "James Endorses Civilian Board to Monitor Cops," *Star-Ledger,* July 2, 1997, 45.

219. See Andrew Jacobs, "White Police Chief Could Upset a Balance in Newark," *New York Times,* August 15, 2007, http://www.nytimes.com/2007/08/15/nyregion/15police.html; J. C. Mays, "Newark to Revisit Review Board—Hearing Will Explore Oversight Measure," *Star-Ledger,* January 17, 2008, 25; J. Queally, "Timetable Unclear for Newark Cop Review Panel—Booker, Police Director Offer a Mixed Message," *Star-Ledger,* March 31, 2013, 21; Nick Corasaniti and Stephanie Saul, "'Newark's Original Sin' and the Criminal Justice Education of Cory Booker," *New York Times,* March 27, 2019, https://www.nytimes.com/2019/03/27/us/politics/cory-booker-2020-criminal-justice.html.

220. Corasaniti and Saul, "'Newark's Original Sin.'" See also Sam Sutton, "Newark Mayor: Dismantling Police a 'Bourgeois Liberal' Solution for a Much Deeper Problem," *Politico.com,* June 11, 2020, https://www.politico.com/states/new-jersey/story/2020/06/11/newark-mayor-dismantling-police-a-bourgeois-liberal-solution-for-a-much-deeper-problem-1292674.

221. See Stephen Danley and Julia Sass Rubin, "What Enables Communities to Resist Neoliberal Education Reforms? Lessons from Newark and Camden, New Jersey," *Journal of Urban Affairs* 42 no. 4 (2020): 663–84, https://doi.org/10.1080/07352166.2019.1578174.

4. EAST ORANGE

1. "East Orange, New Jersey: Setting the Standard for Urban Excellence," *Business View Magazine,* June 9, 2016, https://businessviewmagazine.com/east-orange-new-jersey/.

2. Sheila Rule, "Middle Class Is a State of Mind, Not Money," *New York Times,* June 24, 1979.

3. Rule, "Middle Class."

4. For a history of Black suburban politics, see Andrew Wiese, *Places of Their Own: African American Suburbanization in the Twentieth Century* (University of Chicago Press, 2004). For a more contemporary account, see Marvin E. Porch, *The Philadelphia Main Line Negro: A Social, Economic, and Educational Survey* (pub. by author, 1938). For critique of the notion of "domestic service suburbs," see Leslie E. Wilson, "Dark Spaces: An Account of Afro-American Suburbanization, 1890–1950" (PhD diss., City University of

New York, 1992). See also Thomas J. Sugrue, *Sweet Land of Liberty: The Forgotten Struggle for Civil Rights in the North* (Random House, 2008).

5. For a discussion of the white suburban spatial imaginary, see George Lipsitz, *How Racism Takes Place* (Temple University Press, 2011). For discussion of consumer citizenship and suburbanization, see Lizabeth Cohen, *A Consumer's Republic: The Politics of Mass Consumption in Postwar America* (Vintage, 2004); Alison Isenberg, *Downtown America: A History of the Place and the People Who Made It* (University of Chicago Press, 2004); Kenneth T. Jackson, *Crabgrass Frontier: The Suburbanization of the United States* (Oxford University Press, 1985); Jon C. Teaford, *The Twentieth-Century American City* (Johns Hopkins University Press, 1993).

6. "Teacher Reads Negro Poetry, Dismissed, Reinstated," *Jet Magazine*, December 1, 1966, 19.

7. "Teacher Reads Negro Poetry."

8. "Teacher Reads Negro Poetry."

9. The following quotations are from "N. J. Town Called Model Interracial City," *Chicago Daily Defender*, August 20, 1962.

10. "First Negro Named to East Orange, N.J. School Board," *Atlanta Daily World*, February 8, 1961.

11. "N. J. Town."

12. On respectability politics, see Evelyn Brooks Higginbotham, *Righteous Discontent: The Women's Movement in the Black Baptist Church, 1880–1920* (Harvard University Press, 1993); and Kevin Gaines, *Uplifting the Race: Black Leadership, Politics, and Culture in the Twentieth Century* (University of North Carolina Press, 1996). On Black suburban identity formation, see Bruce D. Haynes, *Red Lines, Black Spaces: The Politics of Race and Space in a Black Middle-Class Suburb* (Yale University Press, 2008); Valerie C. Johnson, *Power in the Suburbs: The Myth or Reality of African-American Suburban Political Incorporation* (State University of New York Press, 2012); and Gregory Smithsimon, "In the Suburbs We Mean Business: Race, Class, Space, and Local Government in an African-American Middle-Class Suburb," *Urban Research & Practice* 5, no. 1 (2012): 26–43.

13. See Michael Ebner, "Re-Reading Suburban America: Urban Population Deconcentration, 1810–1890," *American Quarterly* 37, no. 3 (1985): 368–81; and Joel Schwartz, "Suburban Progressivism in the 1890s: The Policy of Containment in Orange, East Orange, and Montclair," in *Cities of the Garden State: Essays in the Urban and Suburban History of New Jersey*, ed. Joel Schwartz and Daniel Prosser (Kendall/Hunt Publishing, 1977).

14. See City Plan Commission, *City Plan for East Orange, Essex County, New Jersey* (Technical Advisory Corporation, 1922).

15. See Schwartz, "Suburban Progressivism."

16. James Q. Wilson defines "amateur democrats" as a "new class of individuals who feel "rewarded by having satisfied a felt obligation to 'participate'" and whose "satisfaction is greater the higher the value the amateur can attach to the ends which the outcomes of politics serve" (James Q. Wilson, "The Amateur Democrat in American Politics," *Parliamentary Affairs* 16, no. 1 [1962]: 73–86, 75). See also Robert C. Wood, *Suburbia: Its People and Their Politics* (Houghton Mifflin, 1959); and Amy Bridges, *Morning Glories: Municipal Reform in the Southwest* (Princeton University Press, 1997).

17. See City Plan Commission, *City Plan for East Orange*. The boards were: Board of Health (Health Department), Local Assistance Board (Welfare Department), Board of Police Commissions (Police Department), Board of Fire Commissioners (Fire Department), Board of Recreation Commissioners (Recreation Department), Shade Tree Commission, Board of Water Commissioners (Water Department), Board of Education, Trustees of the Free Public Library.

18. City Plan Commission, *City Plan for East Orange*.

19. Indeed, one of the key zoning cases in the United States, Village of Euclid v. Ambler Realty Co. (272 U.S. 365 [1926]) centered on control over the building of apartment buildings. See also Andrew Cappel, "A Walk Along Willow: Patterns of Land Use Coordination in Pre-Zoning New Haven (1870–1926)," *Yale Law Journal* 101, no. 3 (1991): 617–42.

20. City Plan Commission, *City Plan for East Orange*. The plan also stated: "However, the rapidly growing Italian district in the southern part of East Orange is tending to develop unduly congested conditions. These will be partially checked by the light and area provisions of the recently adopted Zoning Ordinance and by the domestic animals, housing, nuisance, and plumbing and drainage provisions of the new Sanitary Code of the city" (*City Plan*, 17).

21. By 1900, many Black residents, especially women, worked in domestic service for the town's white residents, giving rise to the city's categorization as a "domestic suburb." See Wiese, *Places of Their Own*; Porch, *The Philadelphia Main Line Negro*. On the "domestic service suburb," see Wilson, "Dark Spaces."

22. See "Social Settlement Work: How Mr. and Mrs. W. P. Burrell Are Shaping Young Lives," *Baltimore Afro-American*, September, 26, 1914. The City of Orange and Montclair each secured a "colored YMCA," while Montclair also had a colored YWCA. This YWCA helped Southern women migrants become acclimated to life in the North, offering classes and a boarding house for women. See Patricia Hampson Eget, "Challenging Containment: African Americans and Racial Politics in Montclair, New Jersey, 1920–1940," *New Jersey History* 126, no. 1 (2011): 1–17.

23. See N. Barnett Dodson, "Race Progress in New Jersey: Washington's Tour in the State Benefits General Public," *Baltimore Afro-American*, October 17, 1914.

24. On Black electoral realignment, see Keneshia N. Grant, *The Great Migration and the Democratic Party: Black Voters and the Realignment of American Politics in the 20th Century* (Temple University Press, 2020).

25. See Marcus Cooke, "Hargrave, Bates and Burrell Are Candidates," *Baltimore Afro-American*, February 27, 1932; "Burrell's Friends Confident He'll Go to the Assembly," *Baltimore Afro-American*, November 5, 1932; "Burrell Wins N. J. Legislature as Republican," *Baltimore Afro-American*, November 19, 1932.

26. See "Burrell Labor Bill Passes in Jersey House," *Baltimore Afro-American*, June 3, 1933. On the Trenton Six, see "NAACP to Take Part in 'Trenton 6' Retrial," *Baltimore Afro-American*, January 14, 1950; and "Yesterday in Afro-American History," *Jet Magazine*, November 26, 1970.

27. Eget, "Challenging Containment," 16.

28. William M. Stringer, "Progressive East Orange Lays Claim to the Title of 'Ultimate in Suburbs,'" *Christian Science Monitor*, October 23, 1940.

29. *The Master Plan for East Orange, New Jersey* (City Planning Board, 1950).

30. See Mark A. Stuart and Jesse Boutillier, *A Centennial History of East Orange* (East Orange Centennial Committee, 1964), 27.

31. On the pace of business relocations, see Stuart and Boutillier, *A Centennial History*, 33.

32. See "Table 26: East Orange Number of Insurance Offices by Type, 1955, 1960," and "Table 27: East Orange, Number of Offices and Professional Buildings, 1950–1962," in *Special Study on the Proposed Brick Church Urban Renewal Area* by Jules Pomerantz, prepared for the Housing Authority of East Orange (Author, September 1963).

33. Melvin B. Johnson, "Claim 'Blighted Area' Laws Will Establish Negro Ghettoes," *New York Amsterdam News*, March 9, 1946.

34. See Marian Wynn Perry, Memorandum to files from Marian Wynn Perry, subject: East Orange housing situation, January 4, 1946, NAACP Papers, part 5: Campaign Against Residential Segregation, 1914–1965, Housing (January 1, 1945–December 31,

1947), ProQuest History Vault: *Slum Clearance and Urban Renewal in East Orange, New Jersey* (University Publications of America, 2014) (hereafter NAACP Papers, *Slum Clearance*). See also "Segregation Best Proof of Discrimination, Judge Holds," *Baltimore Afro-American*, January 22, 1949; "No Segregation in New Jersey Housing Project," *Pittsburgh Courier*, January 22, 1949.

35. See "5,000 Protest Plan for Ghetto," *Baltimore Afro-American*, December 22, 1945; and "Jersey Housing Plan Attacked," *Baltimore Afro-American*, December 14, 1946.

36. Samuel Williams, "Release," Branch of the Oranges, NAACP (Orange, NJ, November 17, 1945), NAACP Papers, *Slum Clearance*.

37. See "Jersey Housing Plan Attacked" and "Everett B. Simmons to Marian Wyn Parry," October 30, 1946, NAACP Papers, *Slum Clearance*.

38. Joint Municipal Planning Boards, *An East-West Freeway for Essex County* (Joint Municipal Planning Boards in Essex County, New Jersey, 1947).

39. See Cohen, *A Consumer's Republic*.

40. See Raymond A. Mohl, "Urban Expressways and the Racial Restructuring of Postwar American Cities," *Jahrbuch für Wirtschaftsgeschichte* 42, no. 2 (2001): 89–104; Robert M. Fogelson, *Downtown: Its Rise and Fall, 1880–1950* (Yale University Press, 2001).

41. See "Elevated Freeway Opposed in Jersey," *New York Times*, August 10, 1958; and Milton Honig, "Depressed Road Backed in Essex," *New York Times*, April 1, 1959.

42. On highway revolts, see Raymond A. Mohl, "Stop the Road: Freeway Revolts in American Cities," *Journal of Urban History* 30, no. 5 (2004): 674–706. For the situation in East Orange, see Honig, "Depressed Road"; see also Milton Honig, "Jersey Officials Seek Road Plans," *New York Times*, March 30, 1961; "Freeway Parley Slated in Jersey," *New York Times*, July 24, 1960; "Depressed Freeway Is Backed by Case," *New York Times*, August 14, 1960; "Interchage Fight Settled in Jersey," *New York Times*, March 31, 1962.

43. See Stuart and Boutillier, *Centennial History*, 31.

44. Stuart and Boutillier, *Centennial History*, 33.

45. "Statement of Hon. James W. Kelly, Jr., Mayor of the City of East Orange, N.J.," U.S. Congress, Senate, Special Committee on Aging: Hearings Before the Subcommittee on Involuntary Relocation of the Elderly of the Special Committee on Aging Relocation of Elderly People, 87th Cong., 2nd sess., October 26, 1962, 127–31.

46. See Joint Municipal Planning Boards, *An East-West Freeway*.

47. Jackson, *Crabgrass Frontier*; Cohen, *A Consumer's Republic*.

48. "Renewal Studied for East Orange: 9 Million Plan Is Aimed at Counteracting Blighting Effects of Freeway," *New York Times*, August 24, 1961.

49. East Orange (N. J.) Housing Authority, "Doddtown Urban Renewal Project N.J.R-36"; "Application for Recertification of the Workable Program for Urban Renewal of City of East Orange, New Jersey, 1959–1960, James W. Kelly Jr., Mayor," 1959, East Orange Library Local History Collection; East Orange (N. J.) Citizens' Advisory Committee and Housing Authority, *Progress Report and Development Guide: 1960–1961 East Orange Urban Renewal Program* (East Orange, NJ, 1961), East Orange Library Local History Collection.

50. See League of Women Voters of Montclair-Glenridge, N. J., "Know Your Town: Montclair, N. J.," 1968, 57.

51. "Statement of Hon. James W. Kelly, 128–29.

52. See *Master Plan*, 54.

53. By 1964, there were two Black people on the city council—Thomas Cook (D) and Edward T. Bowser Sr. (R). See "Councilmen Serve in 11 Communities," *Baltimore Afro-American*, June 27, 1964.

54. See "N. J. Town."

55. The Hughes report (also known as the Lilley Commission) is formally titled *Report for Action* and authored by the Governor's Select Commission on Civil Disorder (State of New Jersey, 1968), 104, 111.

56. See "Did Newark Cops Stage E. O. Raid?," *Baltimore Afro-American*, July 22, 1967.

57. See N. M. Gerstenzang, "Muir's Closing Shop After 93 Years," *New York Times*, July 28, 1974; Andy Newman, "In the 30's, When East Orange Was Gold," *New York Times*, May 7, 1995.

58. Even more significant—and drawn from the literature on the racial "tipping point"—20 percent of those over sixty-five were more than eighty years of age. Older, predominantly white residents had not been replaced by younger white residents. Instead, over time these residents were being replaced by younger Black families. In 1960, the average number of persons in white households was 2.52, while the average number in non-white households was 3.58. See Pomerantz, *Special Study*, 18–21.

59. See "Affluent East Orange?," M-SO Message Board—Local History: Maplewood and South Orange, Saturday, September 9, 2006, 11:50 p.m, accessed April 15, 2025, https://jamieross.com/discus/messages/3517/28515.html?1157860228.

60. Amy Foerster has a comprehensive and insightful discussion of East Orange's Model City Program in "'Progress and Perfectability': Urban Policy, Model Cities, and Community Control in the Shadow of Newark," *City & Community* 18, no. 3 (2019): 815–36, esp. 19.

61. This section draws from Foerster, "'Progress and Perfectability'" and East Orange's grant application: "Application to the Department of Housing and Urban Development for a Grant to Plan a Comprehensive City Demonstration Program," City of East Orange, April 26, 1967, East Orange Public Library, Local History Collection; HUD East Orange Model Cities Proposals (1 of 2), 1972, Harrison A. Williams Jr. Papers, MC 2, box 167, folder 14, New Brunswick Special Collections, Rutgers University, Special Collections; HUD: East Orange Model Cities Proposals (2 of 2), 1972, Harrison A. Williams Jr. Papers, MC 2, box 167, folder 15, New Brunswick Special Collections, Rutgers University, Special Collections; Rita T. Di Trolio and New Jersey Division of State and Regional Planning, *New Jersey's Model Cities* (Trenton, 1969).

62. Foerster, "'Progress and Perfectability,'" 919.

63. Foerster cites a report commissioned for the Model Cities Program by Ghettonomics (Foerster, "'Progress and Perfectability,'" 924).

64. On role of Upsala College faculty and students, see Foerster, "'Progress and Perfectability,'" 922–31.

65. Foerster "'Progress and Perfectability,'" 922–24.

66. In 1966 the church decided to design and erect a new building in a new location "after learning that a new major highway threatened Calvary's Main Street location." See Calvary Baptist Church, *130th Anniversary, 1887–2017*, October 29, 2017, https://issuu.com/mldcomm/docs/calvary_baptist_church_130th_journa.

67. See "Blacks Opening a Housing Co-Op," *New York Times*, October 13, 1973; and "Blacks Open Housing Complex in East Orange, New Jersey," *Jet Magazine*, November 1, 1973.

68. See "Blacks Opening a Housing Co-Op."

69. Alix Bryant, "A Conversation with Robert Bowser, Mayor of East Orange NJ," interviewed April 27, 2009, posted March 14, 2011, *Fellsbridge 249 Runnymede Road*, https://fellsbridge249runnymederoad.blogspot.com/2011/06/conversation-with-alan-bowser-mayor-of.html. Robert was Edward T. Bowser Jr.'s brother. For Jefferies, see "East Orange Mourns the Passing of Business Owner and Civic Icon Jesse Jeffries Jr.," *TAPinto East Orange/Orange*, January 21, 2016, https://www.tapinto.net/towns/east-orange-slash-orange/sections/obituaries/articles/east-orange-mourns-the-passing-of-business-owner.

70. "Blacks Opening a Housing Co-Op."

71. Bowser would later travel to Ghana to work on community development projects. See "Edward Theodore Bowser Jr. (1924–1995)," *US Modernist*, accessed April 14, 2025, https://usmodernist.org/bowser.htm.

72. For a discussion of Black capitalism, see Mehrsa Baradaran, *The Color of Money: Black Banks and the Racial Wealth Gap* (Harvard University Press, 2017); Devin Fergus, *Liberalism, Black Power, and the Making of American Politics, 1965–1980* (University of Georgia Press, 2009), and Dean J. Kotlowski, *Nixon's Civil Rights: Politics, Principle, and Policy* (Harvard University Press, 2002). On the rise of Black-owned construction firms and their intersection with Black capitalism, see David A. Goldberg and Trevor Griffey, eds., *Black Power at Work: Community Control, Affirmative Action, and the Construction Industry* (Cornell University Press, 2010). For Black capitalism, see Laura Warren Hill and Julia Rabig, eds., *The Business of Black Power: Community Development, Capitalism, and Corporate Responsibility in Postwar America* (Boydell & Brewer, 2012).

73. See "Blacks Opening a Housing Co-Op,"

74. See Darren Tobia, "This Black Architect from East Orange Studied Under Le Corbusier, but the Future of His Project Is Uncertain, *The Four Oranges*, March 9, 2024, https://thefouroranges.com/this-black-architect-from-east-orange-studied-under-le-corbusier-but-the-future-of-his-project-is-uncertain/.

75. For a discussion of Black parent activism before the civil rights era, see August Meier and Elliott M. Rudwick, "Early Boycotts of Segregated Schools: The East Orange, New Jersey, Experience, 1899–1906," *History of Education Quarterly* 7, no. 1 (1967): 22–35; Marian Wright Thompson, "The Education of Negroes in New Jersey" (PhD diss., Teachers College, Columbia University, 1941); and Sugrue, *Sweet Land of Liberty*, 163–99.

76. See Andrew R. Highsmith and Ansley T. Erickson, "Segregation as Splitting, Segregation as Joining: Schools, Housing, and the Many Modes of Jim Crow," *American Journal of Education* 121, no. 4 (2015): 563–95.

77. See *Master Plan*, 73–86. According to the city, "In the theoretically perfect school system, no elementary school pupil will walk more than half a mile from home to school. This service area of approximately one square mile usually means that the school's enrollment will be between 700 and 900 pupils, which is an economical and desirable size. The elementary school should be centrally located in a reasonably homogeneous neighborhood, bounded by major streets on its outer edges and protected from traffic in the interior so that none of its pupils is subjected to unusual traffic hazards." *Master Plan*, 74.

78. See *Master Plan*, 81.

79. For data, see Ernest Chan-Nui, "Study of the Reported Attitudes of the 1965–1966 Teaching Staff of the East Orange, New Jersey Public School System Toward Some Selected Educational Aspects of the Proposed East Orange Education Plaza" (EdD diss., Teachers College, Columbia University, 1967), 12–14.

80. "N. J. Has First Negro Principal," *New York Amsterdam News*, August 4, 1962; and see Jeff S., "Kentopp School," Stockton School, September 11, 2011, http://stocktonschool.blogspot.com/2011/09/kentopp-school.html.

81. See Chan-Nui, "Study of the Reported Attitudes," 10–25.

82. "East Orange Plan: All Schools to Be in One Place," *New York Times*, November 12, 1964; "The Week in Education; High Stakes; Angry Teachers," *New York Times*, November 15, 1964, https://www.nytimes.com/1964/11/15/archives/the-week-in-education-high-stakes-angry-teachers.html; and brochure reprinted in Board of Education, "The East Orange Education Plaza," *Equity & Excellence in Education* 3, no. 1 (1965): 33–35.

83. Seitzer became superintendent after Henry Kentopp stepped down, having served thirty-six years in the position.

84. The city's plans gained favorable attention from both the Black and white press. Many of their articles drew upon language contained in the brochure released by the East Orange Board of Education, "The East Orange Education Plaza." See also "NJ City Considers One-School Mix Plan," *Baltimore Afro-American*, November 21, 1964; "Board Proposes All City Students Attend One Education Complex," *New Pittsburgh Courier*,

November 21,1964; Monroe W. Karmin, "Integrating Classes: Federal Officials Now Favor End to Tradition of Neighborhood School," *Wall Street Journal*, August 12, 1966. For further discussion, see Ansley T. Erickson, "Desegregation's Architects: Education Parks and the Spatial Ideology of Schooling," *History of Education Quarterly* 56, no. 4 (2016): 560–89, https://doi.org/10.1111/hoeq.12211.

85. "NJ City Considers."

86. "NJ City Considers."

87. "NJ City Considers."

88. See Erickson, "Desegregation's Architects"; see also Matthew Brillinger, "Educational Park Planning in Berkeley, California, 1965–1968" (master's thesis, Université d'Ottawa/University of Ottawa, 2016). For educational plaza plans in Columbus, Ohio, see Patrick Potyondy, "Reimaging Urban Education: Civil Rights, Educational Parks, and the Limits of Reform," in *Reimagining Education Reform and Innovation*, ed. Matthew Lynch (Peter Lang, 2014), 27–54. A contemporary account is Alvin Toffler, ed., *The Schoolhouse in the City* (Frederick A. Praeger, 1968); also Max Wolff and Benjamin Rudakoff, *Educational Park Development in the United States, 1969: A Survey of Current Development Plans with a List of Reports and References on the Educational Park* (Center for Urban Education, 1970).

89. See June Shagaloff, "A Review of Public School Desegregation in the North and West," *Journal of Educational Sociology* 36, no. 6 (1963): 292–96; and "Public School Desegregation—North and West," *The Crisis*, February 1963, 92–95. See also Zoë Burkholder, *An African American Dilemma: A History of School Integration and Civil Rights in the North* (Oxford University Press, 2021); and Sugrue, *Sweet Land of Liberty*, 190–99.

90. See Taylor v. Board of Education of New Rochelle, 191 F. Supp. 181 (S.D. N.Y., 1961), afftd, 294 F2d 36 (C.A. 2, 1961).

91. See Booker v. Board of Education of City of Plainfield (45 N.J. 161 [1965]), 212 A.2d 1.

92. Brillinger argues that Howe was a "central figure" in the "debate about educational parks . . . not because he was the loudest or most enthusiastic backer of educational parks, but because he was the most powerful, and so the most threatening to park opponents" (Brillinger, "Educational Park Planning," 69–70). See also Leonard Buder, "Education: School Parks—The Pro and Con," *New York Times*, June 20, 1965; and Buder, "Now, 'Educational Parks,'" *New York Times*, June 26,1966. Opponents argued that "segregated schools were much less problematic than federal involvement in education" (Brillinger, "Educational Park Planning," 69–70). Howe was the US commissioner of education from 1966 to 1968 and a "driving force in the Great Society campaign to abolish segregation under the 1964 Civil Rights Act. Among segregationist Southern legislators, who fought to keep the matter local, his sobriquet was U.S. commissioner of integration" (Wolfgang Saxon, "Harold Howe II, 84, Fighter Against Segregated Schools," *New York Times*, December 3, 2002, https://www.nytimes.com/2002/12/03/us/harold-howe-ii-84-fighter-against-segregated-schools.html).

93. See John H. Fischer, "School Parks for Equal Opportunities," *Journal of Negro Education* 37, no. 3 (Summer 1968): 301–9; and LeRoy Allen, "Replications of the Educational Park Concept for the Disadvantaged," *Journal of Negro Education* 40, no. 3 (Summer 1971): 225–32.

94. See, for example, "The NAACP Case Against the Great High Schools," *New Pittsburgh Courier*, April 26, 1969, 7.

95. See Chan-Nui, "Study of the Reported Attitudes," 12.

96. See Erickson, "Desegregation's Architects," 570–71.

97. "East Orange Plan."

98. Allen, "Replications," 2.

99. "The Week in Education."

100. Brillinger discusses how planners in Berkeley perceived East Orange's plans; they noted that East Orange by 1966 had "rather detailed architectural drawings and have published an attractive brochure" (Brillinger, "Educational Park Planning," 87).

101. Brillinger, "Educational Park Planning," 88n59.

102. Brillinger, "Educational Park Planning," 90.

103. Indeed, Brillinger argues that a "final lesson the BUSD gleaned from its meetings with eastern educational park planners," especially districts like East Orange, was that "federal funding—specifically, funding supplied under Title III of ESEA—was important to the success of an educational park project." See Brillinger, "Educational Park Planning," 91.

104. Leonard Cole, *Blacks in Power: A Comparative Study of Black and White Elected Officials* (Princeton University Press, 2017), 180.

105. Like Mayor William Hart, Jackson played a role in the development of associations of Black local officials. In 1971 Jackson was the founding leader of the National Alliance of Black School Superintendents, which in 1973 became the National Association of Black School Educators (NABSE). See Hugh J. Scott, "National Alliance of Black School Educators (NABSE)," in *Encyclopedia of African-American Education*, ed. Faustine C. Jones-Wilson et al. (Greenwood Publishing, 1996).

106. See Saxon, "Harold Howe II."

107. See Ezola B. Adams, "A Descriptive Study of the Intermediate School in East Orange, New Jersey, with Emphasis on the Development of a Positive Self Image" (master's thesis, Newark State College, 1969); and also Stu Chapman, "Planners Approve Middle School Site," *The Home News* (New Brunswick, NJ), March 4, 1971.

108. Cole, *Blacks in Power*, 178.

109. See Cole, *Blacks in Power*, 179. Hart argued that a recently vacated office building would provide a suitable and less expensive site for the complex. It is not clear why he believed this site would be better (indeed a later study found that the cost to convert it to educational use would be prohibitive). Perhaps the site was proposed as a result of Hart's heavy involvement with the ethically challenged Essex County Democratic Party machinery.

110. Cole, *Blacks in Power*, 179–81.

111. Cole, *Blacks in Power*, 180. Cole argues that concerns about expenditures were real given that East Orange had one of the highest tax rates in the state (Cole, *Blacks in Power*, 180).

112. Cole, *Blacks in Power*, 180.

113. Cole, *Blacks in Power*, 180.

114. Cole, *Blacks in Power*, 181.

115. The Uniplan firm was based in New Jersey and led by the architect Jules Gregory. See James A. Murphy, "School Planning by the People: How It Was Done in East Orange, NY," *The Education Digest* 37, no. 9 (May 1972): 15–17; see also David Lewis, "Listening and Hearing," *Journal of Architectural Education* 33, no. 1 (1979): 27–29, https://doi.org/10.2307/1424461.

116. On the EFL, see Amy S. Weisser, "'Little Red Schoolhouse, What Now?' Two Centuries of American Public School Architecture," *Journal of Planning History* 5, no. 3 (2006): 196–217.

117. See Brian D. Goldstein, "'The Search for New Forms': Black Power and the Making of the Postmodern City," *Journal of American History* 103, no. 2 (2016): 375–99, https://doi.org/10.1093/jahist/jaw181; and for discussion of the history of Black-led community architecture, see Craig Wilkins, "The Soul Practitioner," in *Activist Architecture: The*

Philosophy and Practice of the Community Design Center, ed. Dan Pitera et al. (Detroit Collaborative Design Center, April 2015).

118. Murphy, "School Planning," 17.

119. Murphy, "School Planning," 16.

120. David Lewis, "User Participation in Planning and Design," in *Building for School and Community* (Organization for Economic Cooperation and Development, 1978), 3:187–91.

121. Murphy, "School Planning," 16.

122. Lewis, "User Participation," 188.

123. Uniplan's design emphasized breaking a large student body into smaller houses that are "connected by a 'street' with a variety of configurations and spatial events along the way. All levels of the roof are designed for use as play areas for students and as a park for the community" (Murphy, "School Planning," 17).

124. Murphy, "School Planning," 17.

125. See Roosevelt Weaver, "The Preparation and Planning for the Opening of a New Middle School in East Orange, New Jersey" (EdD diss., Harvard University, 1975).

126. For the architectural award, see "East Orange Middle School," *Architecture New Jersey* 6, no. 2 (1972): 14–17.

127. Teachers in Newark and the nearby suburbs of Irvington and West Orange were also engaged in labor actions. See Robert Hanley, "East Orange Teachers Continue Walkout as Negotiations Fail," *New York Times*, March 12, 1973, 67; and Don Prial, "Newark Teachers and School Board See a New Era of Peace," *New York Times*, March 4, 1973.

128. See "Did Newark Cops Stage E. O. Raid?" The small role East Orange residents played in the Newark rebellion is noted in the Hughes report, 16, 104, and 111. For a history of the Black Community Defense and Development Organization, see "History of the Congress of Afrikan People," *Unity and Struggle* 5, no. 6 (June 1976): 1–12.

129. For discussion of the Newark police officer, see Kerner Commission, *Report of the National Advisory Commission on Civil Disorders* (US Government Printing Office, 1968), 68.

130. See Alfonso A. Narvaez, "U.S. Names 12 Cities in Jersey in Job Bias," *New York Times*, October 5, 1977; and "Rights Group Seeking Changes in East Orange Police Structure," *New York Times*, December 19, 1975.

131. See Foerster, "'Progress and Perfectability,'" 921.

132. For the specifics of East Orange, see Foerster, "'Progress and Perfectability,'" 925. On the turn from model cities to mass incarceration, see Elizabeth Hinton, *From the War on Poverty to the War on Crime: The Making of Mass Incarceration in America* (Harvard University Press, 2016). More broadly, see also James Forman Jr., *Locking Up Our Own: Crime and Punishment in Black America* (Farrar, Straus and Giroux, 2017); and Michael Javen Fortner, *The Black Silent Majority: The Rockefeller Drug Laws and the Politics of Punishment* (Harvard University Press, 2015).

133. On this police reform effort, see Michael Stern, "11 at City U. Turn Law Enforcement Theory into Fact," *New York Times*, May 25, 1970.

134. See Stern, "11 at City U."

135. See Stern, "11 at City U."

136. Pat Gleeson, "Hopes Rise for East Orange," *New York Times*, December 18, 1977.

137. Gleeson, "Hopes Rise."

138. Sandra Gardner, " New Jersey Journal," *New York Times*, March 28, 1982.

139. Michael Norman, "In East Orange, Mayor Leads a 'War' on Slums,'" *New York Times*, August 13, 1982.

140. Mayor Lester Taylor, "State of the City," 2016, transcript in author's possession.

141. See W. Marvin Dulaney, *Black Police in America* (Indiana University Press, 1996), 74.

142. Dulaney, *Black Police*, 74.

143. Heather Mac Donald, "The NYPD Diaspora: Former New York Cops Bring Cutting-Edge, Effective Policing to Beleaguered Communities," *City Journal*, Summer 2008, https://www.city-journal.org/html/nypd-diaspora-13097.html.

144. "Broken windows" policing measures was a policing strategy adopted in the 1980s that focused on monitoring and aggressively enforcing quality-of-life violations as well as other types of crime through enhanced surveillance, especially via computer-aided geographical information systems that track where crime occurs. Compstat is one such system. See Bernard E. Harcourt, *Illusion of Order: The False Promise of Broken Windows Policing* (Harvard University Press, 2001).

145. "Police patrols take place in what are called 'affidavit buildings.' Landlords or building management sign an affidavit with the police department that gives officers access—either with keys or access codes—to patrol indoor common areas. A sweep can take anywhere from five to 15 minutes for a routine check to longer if officers arrest trespassers or encounter other criminal activity." Eunice Lee, "East Orange Residents Appreciate Cops, but Want Security Staff Back," *Star-Ledger*, January 15, 2012, https://www.nj.com/news/2012/01/east_orange_residents_apprecia.html.

146. Richard Khavkine, "East Orange Police Chief Announces Retirement After Council Declines to Re-Hire Police Director," *Star-Ledger*, January 16, 2011, https://www.nj.com/news/local/2011/01/east_orange_police_chief_annou.html.

147. Taylor, "State of the City."

148. N. M. Gerstenzang, "East Orange Mall Sought," *New York Times*, November 9, 1975; Welton Smith, "Merchants Fight Plan for a Mall in E. Orange," *New York Times*, March 17, 1974. On the rise of pedestrian malls, see Kent A. Robertson, "The Status of the Pedestrian Mall in American Downtowns," *Urban Affairs Review* 26, no. 2 (1990): 250–73.

149. See brochure by the Department of Economic Development, *Central Evergreen Arcade: New Jersey's Premiere In-Town Shopping Experience*, n.d., East Orange Public Library, Local History Archive.

150. See Kevin Coyne, "Avenue That Used to Be Awaits a Rebirth, *New York Times*, November 4, 2007; and Halley Bondy, "East Orange to Invest $1.5 Million in Sprucing Up Business District," *Star-Ledger* (Newark), April 13, 2009.

151. Melody Petersen, "Figuring Out How to Put a Town's Financial House Back in Order," *New York Times*, September 22, 1996, https://www.nytimes.com/1996/09/22/nyregion/figuring-out-how-to-put-a-town-s-financial-house-in-order.html;   Ronald Smothers, "State Auditors to Examine Books of Distressed City," *New York Times*, July 15, 1999, https://www.nytimes.com/1999/07/15/nyregion/state-auditors-to-examine-books-of-distressed-city.html; "State Takes Over East Orange Finances After 2d Year of Debt," *New York Times*, September 30, 1999, https://www.nytimes.com/1999/09/30/nyregion/state-takes-over-east-orange-finances-after-2d-year-of-debt.html.

152. Julie Leupold, "Making the Tough Choices," *Real Estate New Jersey* 5, no. 7 (July–August 2004): 12.

153. Leupold, "Making the Tough Choices."

154. Antoinette Martin, "A Focus on 'Work Force' Housing," *New York Times*, September 10, 2010.

155. Leupold, "Making the Tough Choices."

156. See Kathe Newman, "The New Economy and the City: Foreclosures in Essex County New Jersey," in *Subprime Cities: The Political Economy of Mortgage Markets*, ed. Manuel B. Aalbers (Wiley-Blackwell, 2012).

157. Antoinette Martin, "Dissecting the 'Heart of Orange,'" *New York Times*, April 17, 2009.

158. Minutes of the 384th Board Meeting of the New Jersey Housing and Mortgage Finance Agency, May 15, 2013, https://nj.gov/dca/hmfa/about/boardinfo/minutes/2013_minutes/130515.pdf.

159. Antoinette Martin, "In East Orange, Seeds for Redevelopment are Planted," *New York Times*, March 26, 2010.

160. See Domingo Morel, *Takeover: Race, Education, and American Democracy* (Oxford University Press, 2018), for discussion of state takeovers of urban school districts in New Jersey.

161. Antoinette Martin, "Just What a City Ordered," *New York Times*, August 20, 2006, https://www.nytimes.com/2006/08/20/realestate/20njzo.html; see also "Woodlands at Upsala: Springdale and Prospect Avenues, East Orange, NJ," The Alpert Group, accessed April 15, 2025, https://www.thealpertgroup.com/properties/woodlands-at-upsala/.

162. Taylor, "State of the City."

5. OAKLAND

1. On social and economic losses caused by internment of Bay Area Japanese Americans, see Eli Moore et al., *Roots, Race, and Place: A History of Racially Exclusionary Housing in the San Francisco Bay Area* (Haas Institute for a Fair and Inclusive Society, University of California Berkeley, October 2, 2019), 20–21, https://belonging.berkeley.edu/sites/default/files/haasinstitute_rootsraceplace_oct2019_publish.pdf.

2. Katie Ferrari, "The House on Magnolia Street: Even Before Moms 4 Housing Was Evicted from 2928 Magnolia, Racism and Capitalism Shaped the Home's History," *Curbed San Francisco*, April 29, 2020.

3. This quotation and following from Moms 4 Housing, accessed January 25, 2023, https://moms4housing.org/.

4. For a definition of "predatory inclusion," see Keeanga-Yamahtta Taylor, *Race for Profit: How Banks and the Real Estate Industry Undermined Black Homeownership* (University of North Carolina Press, 2019), 5.

5. Moms 4 Housing is profiled in Sarah Holder and Brentin Mock, "A Group of Mothers, a Vacant Home, and a Win for Fair Housing," Bloomberg CityLab, January 28, 2020, https://www.bloomberg.com/news/articles/2020-01-28/the-oakland-moms-who-launched-a-housing-movement; Melissa Colorado, "Mothers Who Took Over Abandoned Oakland Home Say They'll Stay Put Despite Eviction Notice," NBC Bay Area, aired December 6, 2019, https://www.nbcbayarea.com/news/local/mothers-who-took-over-abandoned-oakland-home-say-theyll-stay-put-despite-eviction-notice/2190757/; E. Tammy Kim, "Moms 4 Housing: Redefining the Right to a Home in Oakland," *New York Review of Books*, March 9, 2020; Michael Bott and Sean Myers, "Examining Wedgewood: A Look at the Home-Flipping Giant in Battle with Homeless Mothers," NBC Bay Area, aired January 6, 2020, https://www.nbcbayarea.com/investigations/examining-wedgewood-a-look-at-the-home-flipping-giant-in-battlewith-homeless-mothers/2208119/.

6. Holder and Mock, "A Group of Mothers."

7. See James A. Tyner, "'Defend the Ghetto': Space and Urban Politics of the Black Panther Party," *Annals of the Association of American Geographers* 96, no. 1 (2006): 105–18.

8. On police abolitionism, see Derecka Purnell, "What Does Police Abolition Mean?," *Boston Review*, August 23, 2017, https://www.bostonreview.net/articles/derecka-purnell-how-will-we-be-safe-police/. See also David J. Knight and Vesla M. Weaver, "Black Political Mobilization and the US Carceral State: How Tracing Community Struggles for Safety Changes the Policing Narrative," *Annual Review of Criminology* 8, no. 1 (2025): 25–52.

9. For discussion of this racialized landscape, see Marta Gutman, *A City for Children: Women, Architecture, and the Charitable Landscapes of Oakland, 1850–1950* (University of Chicago Press, 2014). The discussion in this chapter covering the nineteenth- and early twentieth-century history of Black Oakland and the broader Bay Area is drawn from the following works: Marilynn S. Johnson, *Second Gold Rush: Oakland and the East Bay in World War II* (University of California Press, 1994); Gretchen Lemke-Santangelo, *Abiding Courage: African American Migrant Women and the East Bay Community* (University of North Carolina Press, 1996); Shirley Ann Wilson Moore, *To Place Our Deeds: The African American Community in Richmond, California, 1910–1963* (University of California Press, 2000). For postwar Oakland, see Frédérick Douzet, *The Color of Power: Racial Coalitions and Political Power in Oakland* (University of Virginia Press, 2012); Donna Murch, *Living for the City: Migration, Education, and the Rise of the Black Panther Party in Oakland, California* (University of North Carolina Press, 2010); Robert Stanley Oden, *From Blacks to Brown and Beyond: The Struggle for Progressive Politics in Oakland, California, 1966–2011* (Cognella, 2012); Mary Praetzillis and Adrian Praetzillis, "'Black Is Beautiful': From Porters to Panthers in West Oakland," in *Putting the "There" There: Historical Archaeologies of West Oakland*, ed. Mary Praetzillis and Adrian Praetzillis (Anthropological Studies Center, Sonoma State University, 2004), 279–304; Chris Rhomberg, *No There There: Race, Class, and Political Community in Oakland* (University of California Press, 2004); Joseph A. Rodriguez, "From Personal Politics to Party Politics: The Development of Black Leadership in Oakland, California, 1900–1950" (master's thesis, University of California Santa Cruz, 1983); Robert Self, *American Babylon: Race and the Struggle for Postwar Oakland* (Princeton University Press, 2003); Jennifer Soliman, "The Rise and Fall of Seventh Street in Oakland," FoundSF: The San Francisco Digital History Archive, 2015, https://www.foundsf.org/index.php?title=The_Rise_and_Fall_of_Seventh_Street_in_Oakland; Robyn C. Spencer, *The Revolution Has Come: Black Power, Gender, and the Black Panther Party in Oakland* (Duke University Press, 2016).

10. Description of East Bay cities from W. J. D. Thompson, "Summary of Statistics of Colored Population of the East Bay Cities" in *East Bay Colored Business Directory* (California Voice Press, 1930), xii.

11. The institutional core of Black Oakland was Beth Eden. Established in 1889, the church moved into a permanent space in 1901, east of Adeline Street. See Gutman's *A City for Children*, 304; and Gutman, "'Race Work' in West Oakland," Anthropological Studies Center, Sonoma State University, June 5, 2003. The prewar organizational landscape is discussed in Rodriguez, "From Personal Politics," 5–23; and gleaned from Charles F. Tilghman Jr., *Colored Directory of the Leading Cities of Northern California* (Tilghman Publishing, 1917).

12. Organizational information from Tilghman, *Colored Directory*, and Thompson, *East Bay Colored Directory*. History of Liberty Hall from Rebecca Woodham, "Liberty Hall (Marcus Garvey Building)," *Clio*, April 11, 2017, https://theclio.com/entry/36447. Founded in 1920, Local 188 was the largest chapter of the UNIA in northern California and would purchase a building, known as Liberty Hall, in 1925.

13. Mrs. Hettie B. Tilghman (a member of one of the city's leading Black families) led the establishment and expansion of Oakland's chapter of the National Association of Colored Women and the Northern Federation of California Colored Women's Club (NFCCWC). See Gutman, "The Tilghman Family and 'Race Work in West Oakland,'" in Praetzellis and Praetzellis, *Putting the "There" There*, 282–87.

14. While these groups developed structures by and for the Black community, they at times also worked with organizations led by white women, thus developing a long-standing pattern of interracialism among the city's Black and white civic elites. See Gutman, *A City for Children*, 304nn48–49; see also Patricia Hampson Eget, "Envisioning Progressive

Communities: Race, Gender, and the Politics of Liberalism; Berkeley, California and Montclair, New Jersey, 1920–1970" (PhD diss., Rutgers University, 2011).

15. As was the case in many early twentieth-century cities, despite playing in front of integrated audiences, Bay Area Black musicians and performers belonged to segregated unions. See W. R. Collins, "The Train Stopped Where the Music Began: The Fertile Black and Tan Venues of West Oakland's Seventh Street and Beyond," in Praetzellis and Praetzellis, *Putting the "There" There*.

16. See Rhomberg, *No There There*, 83.

17. Soliman, "The Rise and Fall of Seventh Street," 3.

18. Discussion here rests heavily on Johnson, *Second Gold Rush*. In addition to Rhomberg's *No There There*, other works that cover this transitional period (1945–65) include Edward Carey Hayes, *Power Structure and Urban Policy: Who Rules in Oakland?* (McGraw-Hill, 1972); Murch, *Living for the City*; and Self, *American Babylon*.

19. On the rise and influence of the KKK in Oakland, see Rhomberg, *No There There*, 50–72.

20. Soliman, "The Rise and Fall of Seventh Street," 4. On the policy implications of the recovery of "lost spaces," see Michelle R. Boyd, *Jim Crow Nostalgia: Reconstructing Race in Bronzeville* (University of Minnesota Press, 2008).

21. Early twentieth-century planning documents include: Werner Hegemann's *Report on a City Plan for the Municipalities of Oakland and Berkeley* (Municipal Governments of Oakland and Berkeley, 1915); Harland Bartholomew and Associates, *A Proposed Plan for a System of Major Traffic Highways* (Major Highway and Traffic Committee of One Hundred, 1927), https://archive.org/details/major-traffic-highways-oakland/mode/2up. See also, "Four Plans That Shaped Downtown Oakland's First 100 Years," *The Urbanist*, no. 540, February 2015, https://www.spur.org/publications/urbanist-article/2015-02-03/four-plans-shaped-downtown-oaklands-first-100-years.

22. See Gutman, *A City for Children*, 343–48. See also Works Progress Administration, *1936 Real Property Survey*, vol. 1, *Analyses and Summary of Data*, WPA project number 2309 (Oakland City Planning Commission, November 1937); John G. Marr, *One Year of Planning in Oakland, 1938* (Oakland City Planning Commission, 1939).

23. WPA, *1936 Real Property Survey*, 55.

24. For Oakland HOLC map, see figure P.1.

25. On segregation of housing for war workers, see Marilynn S. Johnson's "Urban Arsenals: War Housing and Social Change in Richmond and Oakland, California, 1941–1945," *Pacific Historical Review* 60, no. 3 (1991): 283–308; and Johnson, *Second Gold Rush*, 87–112.

26. Self, *American Babylon*, 27–34.

27. Oakland's attempt to transform the city into an "industrial garden" and the effect of this attempt on Black displacement is discussed in Self, *American Babylon*, 25–34, 136–39.

28. Two early studies on Black homeownership in Oakland are Jacob M. Regal, *Oakland's Partnership for Change* (Oakland Department of Human Resources, 1967); and Charles Daniels, *An Investigation of the Influence of Racial Segregation on Housing Prices in the Oakland, California Housing Market* (Stanford University Food Research Institute, 1972). One study found that there were few conventional mortgages in majority-Black areas and that it was "not uncommon in West Oakland for homeowners to have a third mortgage [or junior mortgages] at flagrantly exorbitant rates of interest, conditions which in themselves, account, in large measure, for keeping the poor in poverty." See Hayes, *Power Structure*, esp. 64–67.

29. On white blue-collar suburbs, see Becky M. Nicolaides, *My Blue Heaven: Life and Politics in the Working-Class Suburbs of Los Angeles, 1920–1965* (University of Chicago Press, 2002).

30. For numbers of white out-migration, see Self, *American Babylon*, 166.

31. See Daniel HoSang, *Racial Propositions: Ballot Initiatives and the Making of Postwar California* (University of California Press, 2010); and William A. Fischel, *The Homevoter Hypothesis: How Home Values Influence Local Government Taxation, School Finance, and Land-Use Policies* (Harvard University Press, 2005).

32. On the rise of this labor militancy and the city's general strike, see Rhomberg, *No There There*, 104–10; and Self, *American Babylon*, 34–60.

33. Rhomberg, *No There There*, 111–12.

34. For discussion of Oakland's lack of representation, see Hayes, *Power Structure*, 11–17, 27–36.

35. On the structured exclusion of the city's electoral/administrative bodies, see Hayes, *Power Structure*, 3–35; Jeffrey L. Pressman, "Preconditions of Mayoral Leadership," *American Political Science Review* 66, no. 2 (June 1972): 511–12; and David L. Kirp, "Race, Schooling, and Interest Politics: The Oakland Story," *American Journal of Education* 87, no. 4 (1979): 359.

36. On "morning glory" reform cities and limited democracy, see Amy Bridges, *Morning Glories: Municipal Reform in the Southwest* (Princeton University Press, 1997); and Jessica Trounstine, *Political Monopolies in American Cities: The Rise and Fall of Bosses and Reformers* (University of Chicago Press, 2008).

37. For discussion on the dominance of the Knowland family and other downtown business elites, see Rhomberg, *No There There*, 74–79.

38. See "*Urban Redevelopment in Oakland: A Part of the Master Plan* (City Planning Commission, 1949).

39. Photo of Cypress Freeway, 1950, from the Oakland Tribune Collection, Oakland, CA, in "EcoJustice: From the Bottoms Up," Daily Kos, Monday, September 14, 2009, https://www.dailykos.com/story/2009/09/15/776343/-EcoJustice-From-the-Bottoms-Up.

40. For discussion of the General Neighborhood Renewal Plan (GNRP), see Hayes, Power Structure, 101–17. Hayes notes that "between 1959 and 1965 vacancies in the downtown area rose to a phenomenal 21 percent, while in the five years between 1958 and 1963 a total of 80 businesses went bankrupt or simply left town" (109). On the exit of white middle-class women shoppers from downtown businesses, see Alison Isenberg, *Downtown America: A History of the Place and the People Who Made It* (University of Chicago Press, 2004).

41. For a definition of urban renewal "treatment," see E. Bruce Wedge, "The Concept 'Urban Renewal,'" *The Phylon Quarterly* 19, no. 1 (1958): 55–60; and more generally Martin Anderson, *The Federal Bulldozer: A Critical Analysis of Urban Renewal, 1949–1962* (MIT Press, 1964).

42. Ed Salzman, "Acorn's Amazing Progress: Redevelopment Way Ahead of Schedule," *Oakland Tribune*, January 6, 1964.

43. For the term "containment" and the use of police to "anchor" downtown, see Hayes, *Power Structure*, 87. The term is also used in Floyd Hunter, *Housing Discrimination in Oakland, California: A Study Prepared for the Oakland Mayor's Committee on Full Opportunity and the Council of Social Planning, Alameda County* (Berkeley, CA, 1964).

44. Hayes, *Power Structure*, 148.

45. See Judith May, "Struggle for Authority: A Comparison of Four Social Change Programs in Oakland, California" (PhD diss., University of California Berkeley, 1973), 69.

46. The Black residents argued that the city, in effect, "deprive[d] them of homeownership [as well as other residential options] because they have limited access to other residential areas." See Self, *American Babylon*, 147–49.

47. "Councilman Opens Row on Housing," *Oakland Tribune*, November 25, 1959.

48. On the destruction of the Black charitable landscape and the varied fates of organizations and structures, see Gutman, *A City for Children*, 324–25.

49. Gutman, *A City for Children*, 324–25.

50. For the scope of the destruction, in addition to Gutman's discussion, see Hayes, *Power Structure*, 116.

51. Hayes, *Power Structure*, 78.

52. Hayes notes that it was "extremely difficult for the Negroes of West Oakland to get good financing terms for house repairs. As a result, there is a tendency for this area to go into an accelerated economic decline due to capital starvation, while the Lake Merritt and hillside areas continue a normal rate of economic growth" (*Power Structure*, 61–62).

53. On the multiracial/multiethnic world of postwar Oakland where Chicano, Asian American, and Native American interests were also struggling to be heard, see Juan C. Herrera, "Unsettling the Geography of Oakland's War on Poverty: Mexican American Political Organizations and the Decoupling of Poverty and Blackness," *Du Bois Review* 9, no. 2 (2012): 375–93.

54. On the role of the Men of Tomorrow, in addition to Rodriguez, "Personal Politics," see Robert O. Self, "'Negro Leadership and Negro Money': African American Political Organizing in Oakland Before the Panthers," in *Freedom North: Black Freedom Struggles Outside of the South, 1940–1980*, ed. Jeanne Theoharis and Komozi Woodard (Palgrave Macmillan, 2003); Teron McGrew, "The History of Residential Segregation in the United States, Title VIII, and the Homeownership Remedy," *American Journal of Economics and Sociology* 77, no. 3–4 (2018): 1013–48.

55. Other founding members of Men of Tomorrow included Donald McCollum, the longtime head of the NAACP; Allen Broussard, lawyer and future associate justice of the California Supreme Court; Carlton B. Goodlett, the owner of the *California Voice* and other northern California Black newspapers; Willie Brown, a rising young lawyer and future mayor of San Francisco; Kenneth Smith of the Bay Area Urban League; George Vaughn, lawyer and president of Trans-Bay Federal Savings and Loan Association; Clinton White of the Oakland NAACP; and Eveio Grillo of East Bay Democratic Club. According to Smith, virtually all of the Men of Tomorrow's forty or fifty active members were Democrats. For a discussion of Men of Tomorrow, see Norvel L. Smith et al., "A Life in Education and Community Service: Oral History Transcript" (Bancroft Library Regional History Office, University of California Berkeley, 2004).

56. Norvel Smith described Hilburn as "an older man—really not very energetic near the end of his career." See Smith et al., "A Life in Education."

57. Smith et al., "A Life in Education."

58. Indeed, in the case of Wilson, Rumford and Brown become central actors in the state's Civil Rights Movement.

59. See Smith et al., "A Life in Education."

60. See Murch, *Living for the City*, 62. In addition, see William Brown, "Class Aspects of Residential Development and Choice in the Oakland Black Community" (PhD diss., University of California Berkeley, 1970); and Will D. Tate, "The New Black Urban Elites" (PhD diss., University of California Berkeley, 1974).

61. On the role of Black middle-class professionals and the management of Black working-class youth, see Murch, *Living for the City*, 59–63. On Oakland's Gray Areas project, see Jacob M. Regal, *Oakland's Partnership for Change* (Oakland Department of Human Resources, 1967).

62. Kirp, "Race, Schooling, and Interest Politics," 357–58; May, "Struggle for Authority," 87.

63. See May, "Struggle for Authority"; Murch, *Living for the City*, 59–60.

64. On spatial rifts between the "Flatlands" and the "Hills," see Brown, "Class Aspects"; and Tate, "New Black Urban Elites."

65. See Self, *American Babylon*, 198–210. For more contemporary discussions of Oakland's Model Cities Program, see Jeffrey L. Pressman, *Federal Programs and City Politics: The Dynamics of the Aid Process in Oakland* (University of California Press, 1975); Ralph Kramer, *Participation of the Poor: Comparative Community Case Studies in the War on Poverty* (Prentice-Hall, 1969); Martin David Lowenthal, "The Politics of Planning in the Model Cities Program: A Case Study" (PhD diss., University of California Berkeley, 1970); and May, "Struggle for Authority."

66. Pressman, *Federal Programs*, 60–65.

67. For the assertion that "Black professionals . . . assumed a tutelary role," see Judith V. May, "Two Model Cities: Negotiations in Oakland," *Politics and Society* 2, no. 1 (December 1971): 64.

68. For discussion of the police review board, see Lowenthal, "The Politics of Planning," 75–76; Kramer, *Participation of the Poor*, 136–39; Rhomberg, *No There There*, 151.

69. Reading quoted in Rhomberg, *No There There*, 157.

70. May ("Struggle for Authority") notes that there were two other participants in this power struggle. One was a coalition of groups centered on the Peter Maurin Neighborhood House. This group was poorer and more isolated than the WOAC, and were more likely to have white reformist leadership (68–69). The second group was the Oak Center Neighborhood Association. See also Rhomberg, *No There There*, 159.

71. See May, "Two Model Cities," 64.

72. Hayes, *Power Structure*, 123.

73. May, "Two Model Cities," 72.

74. Black Panther Party for Self Defense, "Black Panther Party Platform and Program," October 18, 1966, https://archive.org/details/Blackpntrs10Pnt.66.

75. These programs are published in David Hilliard, ed., *The Black Panther Party: Service to the People Programs* (University of New Mexico Press, 2008).

76. See Hilliard, *The Black Panther Party*, 43–44. Daniel Willis noted that despite its inclusion in the survival program, the idea was "never implemented [as] the necessary money could not be raised to buy into the real estate market." See Willis, "A Critical Analysis of Mass Political Education and Community Organization as Utilized by the Black Panther Party as a Means for Effecting Social Change" (EdD diss., University of Massachusetts Amherst, 1976), 83.

77. See Hilliard, *The Black Panther Party*, 69–70, 71–73.

78. See "Tenant Terror," *The Flatlands*, September 24 to October 8, 1966, 2–3, https://revolution.berkeley.edu/assets/Tenant.Terror.pdf.

79. See "Tenant Terror."

80. See "Tenant Terror."

81. Between 1962 and 1967, the city built five conventional public housing projects: Chestnut (1962), Westwood (1962), San Antonio (1962), Palo Vista (1963), and Tassaforonga (1966). See "Celebrating 80 Years of Progress," Oakland Housing Authority, accessed April 10, 2025, https://www.oakha.org/AboutUs/Pages/History.aspx.

82. On the postwar creation of the "second ghetto," see Amanda I. Seligman, "What Is the Second Ghetto?," *Journal of Urban History* 29, no. 3 (2003): 272–80, https://doi.org/10.1177/0096144202250377; Arnold R. Hirsch, *Making the Second Ghetto*, 2nd ed. (University of Chicago Press, 1998).

83. The response to this crisis was partially resolved with the introduction of the Lanham Act in 1940, which provided localities with funds to build temporary housing for war industry workers. Dozens of housing projects ranging from trailers and dormitories to apartment buildings were built in the East Bay to satisfy the demand. In keeping with

rising racial tensions that had occurred during the war, the OHA as the administrator of the units created "distinct zones of migration" that reinforced existing patterns of segregation and created new segregated areas if deemed necessary. Housing units also became segregated. Before the war the OHA used a "'checkerboard pattern' (Blacks and whites living side by side)" as well as a "'patchwork pattern' (segregation by areas or buildings)" in administering their buildings; by the end of the war the OHA had adopted "outright segregation by housing project." See Johnson, *Second Gold Rush*, 97–109.

84. An insight into this attitude can be seen in an article published in the community newspaper *The Flatlands*. The article, titled "Big Daddy O.H.A.," argued that the "fear of losing housing keeps many tenants from demanding their rights." *The Flatlands*, March 26, 1966.

85. The "beautification" controversy is briefly covered in Christopher Russell, "A Tale of Two Cities: How the Government Caused and Maintained Racial Inequality in Oakland, California, 1945–1970" (undergraduate thesis, University of Massachusetts Amherst, 2010), 33–35, http://scua.library.umass.edu/wp-content/uploads/2011/04/flura_russell.pdf.

86. Mayor Reading quoted in Russell, "A Tale of Two Cities," 22.

87. See Jill Griffin, *View from the Inside: An Assessment of the New Turnkey Program in Oakland as Seen by Turnkey Residents* (Oakland City Planning Department, 1969).

88. On the environmental hazards of these sites, see Griffin, *View from the Inside*, 4–5.

89. Barnes quoted in Russell, "Tale of Two Cities," 21.

90. See Barnes quotation in Russell, "Tale of Two Cities," 21.

91. HOPE (Housing Opportunities for People Everywhere) VI was enacted in 1992. See Andrew Cuomo, *HOPE VI: Building Communities Transforming Lives* (U.S. Department of Housing and Urban Development, December 1999), https://www.huduser.gov/portal//publications/pdf/hope.pdf. See also Lawrence J. Vale, *Purging the Poorest: Public Housing and the Design Politics of Twice-Cleared Communities* (University of Chicago Press, 2013). For discussion of the program's implementation in Oakland, see "Celebrating 80 Years."

92. For discussion of the role of members of the Men of Tomorrow such as Sam Odell, as well as the role of the Beneficial Development Group in Acorn's development, see McGrew, "The History of Residential Segregation," 1029–38. See Beneficial Development Group, "The Acorn Proposal," December 1, 1964.

93. Two of the architects were Edmund Burger and Patricia Coplans. Burgers's work on Acorn was "considered impossible at the time" and "earned him recognition in the Encyclopedia Britannica." See "Edmund Burger Obituary," *San Francisco Chronicle*, December 27, 2015. For a brief discussion of Kawamoto's career, see Mary Brown, *San Francisco Modern Architecture and Landscape Design, 1935–1970: Historic Context Statement* (San Francisco City and County Planning Department, January 12, 2011), 86, 282, http://sfplanninggis.org/docs/Historical_Context_Statements/Modern%20Architecture%20Context%20adopted%20Jan%202011.pdf.

94. Members of the Beneficial Group planned on routing the project's financing through a Black-controlled financial institution, Trans-Bay Federal Savings and Loan. This plan would fail with the bank's collapse. See "How Two 'Janitors' Bought White Bank in Texas," *Ebony Magazine*, June 1965, 119–26; "Collapse of Bank Leads to Lawsuit," *New York Times*, April 8, 1964, 57.

95. See Beneficial Development Group, "The Acorn Proposal," 3.

96. See Beneficial Development Group, "The Acorn Proposal," 3.

97. Moriah Ulinskas, "Imagining a Past Future: Photographs from the Oakland Redevelopment Agency," *Places*, January 2019, https://placesjournal.org/article/imagining-a-past-future/.

98. See Rhomberg, *No There There*, 156. McGrew argues that the requirement to pre-pay deferred property maintenance made smaller community-based developers unable to compete. Legislation introduced by Senator Edward Brooke removed that exclusion. See McGrew, "The History of Residential Segregation."

99. On Oakland city government's obstructionism and the "complexity of joint action," see Jeffrey L. Pressman and Aaron Wildavsky, *Implementation: How Great Expectations in Washington Are Dashed in Oakland* (University of California Press, 1980), 94–102.

100. Ulinskas, "Imagining a Past Future." See also Jim Wood, "Acorn: Acres of Vacancy," *Oakland Tribune*, July 10, 1967.

101. Rhomberg, *No There There*, 164. On the reluctance of the building trades to hire Black and non-white workers, see, Thomas J. Sugrue, "Affirmative Action from Below: Civil Rights, the Building Trades, and the Politics of Racial Equality in the Urban North, 1945–1969," *Journal of American History* 91, no. 1 (2004): 145–73.

102. "Changes in Urban Life," *Oakland Tribune*, January 28, 1968; "Oakland's Redevelopment Project Ready for Public," *San Francisco Examiner*, September 16, 1968.

103. Jim Wood, "Acorn Project Aims to Attract Whites," *Oakland Tribune*, May 26, 1968.

104. Jim Wood, "Here's A New Way to Live," *Oakland Tribune*, June 19, 1968.

105. "Award for Acorn," *Oakland Tribune*, June 7, 1970.

106. "Acorn Project Is Blasted on Upkeep, Racial Balance," *Oakland Tribune*, April 6, 1972.

107. See Beneficial Development Group, "The Acorn Proposal," 23.

108. Gutman, *A City for Children*, 327–29.

109. See "Building Begins on Acorn Project," *Oakland Tribune*, December 30, 1971.

110. Kennard and Silvers would design the Marcus Foster Middle School in 1978 in addition to other projects. See Buffy Gorrilla, "Long Ignored, Black Modernist Architects Get Recognition," All Things Considered, National Public Radio, February 28, 2025, https://www.npr.org/2025/02/28/nx-s1-5288915/black-modernist-architects-recognized-kennard-livingston-gantt; and Ummi Green, "Yesss, There Is Black Architecture in West Oakland!" *Medium*, August 27, 2021, https://medium.com/@ummingreen/yess-there-is-black-architecture-in-west-oakland-56aa84c17b05.

111. For discussion of GSCA, see John J. Rosen "'Work for Me Also Means Work for the Community I Come From': Black Contractors, Black Capitalism, and Affirmative Action in the Bay Area," in *Black Power at Work: Community Control, Affirmative Action, and the Construction Industry*, ed. David Goldberg and Trevor Griffey (Cornell University Press, 2010).

112. See "Council Stalls on City Center Housing," *The Black Panther* 10, no. 20 (September 29, 1973), 1.

113. "Building Begins."

114. Rhomberg, *No There There*, 164.

115. See Rosen, "'Work for Me'"; and Rhomberg, *No There There*, 164–65.

116. "People's Victory: City Center Replacement Housing Won," *The Black Panther* 11, no. 13 (March 23, 1974), 1–3. See also Hilliard, *The Black Panther Party*, 54–55.

117. The units had "an approximate cost of twenty-two thousand dollars per unit to be financed through a tax increment plan of six hundred thousand dollars annually." Also, rents would "not exceed 25 percent of the monthly income of the tenants." See Hilliard, *The Black Panther Party*, 55.

118. Hilliard, *Black Panther Party*, 55.

119. Rosen, "'Work for Me,'" 80; and Rhomberg, *No There There*, 164.

120. See Rosen, "'Work for Me,'" 79.

121. Rhomberg, *No There There*, 165.

122. Rosen, "Work for Me," 84.

123. Gutman, *City for Children*, 328.

124. "Huey Newton Killed; Was a Co-Founder of Black Panthers," *New York Times*, August 23, 1989.

125. Gutman called the Acorn project that took the place of the Fannie Wall facility a "very expensive, colossal catastrophe" and a "purpose-built construction dependent on erasure [that] had resoundingly failed" (*City for Children*, 328).

126. Black women tenant leaders like Janet Paterson and Mattie Witfield began to press for tenant self-management and ultimately ownership. Rick DelVecchio, "HUD May Raze or Redo Oakland's Acorn Complex," *San Francisco Chronicle*, February 17, 1995.

127. DelVecchio, "HUD May Raze."

128. Gerald D. Adams, "Housing Projects Get Whole New Look in Bay Area," *San Francisco Examiner*, May 10, 1998.

129. Adams, "Housing Projects."

130. "Acorn Town Center," Bridge Housing, accessed April 11, 2025, https://bridge-housing.com/properties/acorn/.

131. In addition to Kirp, "Race, Schooling, and Interest Politics," for a history of the Oakland public schools, see Kitty Kelly Epstein, *A Different View of Urban Schools: Civil Rights, Critical Race Theory, and Unexplored Realities* (Peter Lang, 2012); Jesse J. McCorry, *Marcus Foster and the Oakland Public Schools: Leadership in an Urban Bureaucracy* (University of California Press, 1978); and John P. Spencer, *In the Crossfire: Marcus Foster and the Troubled History of American School Reform* (University of Pennsylvania Press, 2012).

132. "Hill Area School Border Protested," *Oakland Tribune*, January 11, 1961; "School Boundaries Get Board Study," *Oakland Tribune*, January 25, 1961.

133. See Epstein, *A Different View*, 28.

134. Statistics are presented in Ira Michael Heyman, *Civil Rights U.S.A.: Public Schools in the North and West 1963; Oakland* (United States Commission on Civil Rights, 1963); see also Kirp, "Race, Schooling, and Interest Politics," 360.

135. Heyman, *Civil Rights U.S.A.*, 20–21.

136. Until Barney Hilburn was appointed to the board in 1961, it was all white and six out of seven of the board members resided in the Oakland Hills. Hilburn, a Black Republican, resided in North Oakland. Even with the addition of Hilburn, the members reflected a fairly limited socioeconomic class. Board members included "three lawyers, [a] doctor, [a] business executive, [an] auto dealer, [and a] housewife active in PTA affairs." See Kirp, "Race, Schooling, and Interest Politics," 365.

137. See Heyman, *Civil Rights U.S.A.*, 4–5; Kirp, "Race, Schooling, and Interest Politics," 359; McCorry, *Marcus Foster*, 27–33.

138. Kirp, "Race, Schooling, and Interest Politics," 376.

139. Demands—in Oakland and elsewhere—for the decentralization of large urban educational systems into smaller and more locally controlled subdistricts and even schools had emerged well before New York City's Ocean Hill-Brownsville struggle in 1968. See Heather Lewis, *New York City Public Schools from Brownsville to Bloomberg: Community Control and Its Legacy* (Teachers College Press, 2013); and Jerald Podair, *The Strike That Changed New York: Blacks, Whites, and the Ocean Hill-Brownsville Crisis* (Yale University Press, 2002); Preston R. Wilcox, "The Community Centered School," in *The Schoolhouse in the City*, ed. Alvin Toffler (Praeger, 1968); and Whitney M. Young Jr., "Minorities and Community Control of the Schools," *Journal of Negro Education* 38, no. 3 (1969): 285–90.

140. Kirp "Race, Schooling, and Interest Politics," 373.

141. See Epstein, *A Different View*, 30–31.

142. For discussion of the Ad Hoc Committee on Equality group, see Kirp, "Race, Schooling, and Interest Politics," 361–80.

143. Kirp, "Race, Schooling, and Interest Politics," 374.

144. Kirp, "Race, Schooling, and Interest Politics," 394.

145. Not surprisingly given this conflict, Mason turned down Oakland's offer. See McCorry, *Marcus Foster*, 22–26.

146. See David L. Kirp, *Just Schools: The Idea of Racial Equality in American Education* (University of California Press, 2024), 238–39; also Spencer, *In the Crossfire*, 186.

147. A state audit revealed that the district was "not targeting $5 million in Title I funds to needy schools" but rather was "dispersing funds throughout the districts." This meant that schools in affluent (and majority-white) areas could use the funds to support normal operations, thus allowing schools with active PTAs to use their parent-derived extra funding to buy more AV equipment, better playground equipment, or more field trips. Again, these extras stood in stark contrast to the poor schools, which had terrible, overcrowded classrooms and a lack of resources like working AV equipment or safe playgrounds. See Kirp, *Just Schools*, 238–39.

148. See Kirp, "Race, Schooling, and Interest Politics," 378–79; and Epstein, *A Different View*, 29.

149. Kirp, "Race, Schooling, and Interest Politics," 380.

150. McCorry notes that Foster's selection initially caused some controversy as "many of the black activists represented by the Oakland Black Caucus [believed that] Foster was a black pawn foisted on the community by a board who could not be trusted" (McCorry, *Marcus Foster*, 33–41.

151. For discussion of Foster's decentralization plan, see McCorry, *Marcus Foster*, 95–115; and Spencer, *In the Crossfire*, 204–7.

152. See McCorry, *Marcus Foster*, 57–62.

153. McCorry, *Marcus Foster*, 58.

154. See Kirp, "Race, Schooling, and Interest Politics," 382.

155. Spencer, *In the Crossfire*, 185.

156. Kirp, "Race, Schooling, and Interest Politics," 384.

157. Kirp, "Race, Schooling, and Interest Politics," 385.

158. The "Ebonics" proposal was very controversial and generated a lot of media attention. See, for example, Elaine Woo and Mary Curtius, "Oakland School District Recognizes Black English," *Los Angeles Times*, December 20, 1996; "Black English Plan Baffles Some Students in Oakland," *New York Times*, December 21, 1996; "Oakland District Says Policy on Ebonics Misunderstood," *Los Angeles Times*, December 31, 1996. For the Oakland proposal, see "Full Text of 'Ebonics' Resolution Adopted by Oakland Board," *Education Week*, January 15, 1997, https://www.edweek.org/leadership/full-text-of-ebonics-resolution-adopted-by-oakland-board/1997/01.

159. Mary Rhodes Hoover, a linguist, East Palo Alto activist, and administrator at Nairobi College (in East Palo Alto) was an early pioneer in this field; see Mary Rhodes Hoover, "Community Attitudes Toward Black English," *Language in Society* 7, no. 1 (1978): 65–87.

160. Richard Lee Colvin," Oakland District Says Policy on Ebonics Misunderstood," *Los Angeles Times*, December 31, 1996.

161. For Honig's quote, see Epstein, *A Different View*, 43.

162. Edwin Rios, "How Black Oaklanders Finally Expelled the School Police: 'A' is for Abolition," *Mother Jones*, November/December 2020, https://www.motherjones.com/crime-justice/2020/10/how-black-oaklanders-finally-expelled-the-school-police/; Shanthi Gonzales and Roseann Torres, "Memo to Board of Education: Elimination of Oakland Schools Police Department," June 10, 2020, https://blackorganizingproject.org/wp-content/uploads/2021/07/The-George-Floyd-Resolution.pdf.

163. Gonzales and Torres, "Memo."

164. Rios, "Black Oaklanders."

165. See Rhomberg, *No There There*, 57–62

166. Karl E. Johnson, "Police-Black Community Relations in Postwar Philadelphia: Race and Criminalization in Urban Social Spaces, 1945–1960," *Journal of African American History* 89, no. 2 (Spring 2004): 119.

167. Johnson, *Second Gold Rush*, 164–71.

168. See Self, *American Babylon*, 78; and East Bay Civil Rights Congress, "Report on Police Brutality," June 18, 1949, https://howthebaywasbuilt.com/wp-content/uploads/2019/01/1949-east-bay-civil-rights-congress_police-brutality-report.pdf.

169. See also Sean L. Malloy, *Out of Oakland: Black Panther Party Internationalism During the Cold War* (Cornell University Press, 2017), 63; See also Amory Bradford, *Oakland's Not for Burning* (D. McKay, 1968), 131–37.

170. Murch, *Living for the City*, 58–61.

171. Hayes, *Power Structure*, 38–39, citing Jerome Skolnick, *Justice Without Trial: Law Enforcement in Democratic Society* (Quid Pro, 2011); See also Kramer, *Participation of the Poor*, 136–42.

172. Rhomberg, *No There There*, 151.

173. Hayes, *Power Structure*, 38–39.

174. Tyner, "'Defend the Ghetto.'"

175. Murch, *Living for the City*, 131–37.

176. Murch, *Living for the City*, 38–40.

177. "Why was Denzil Dowell Killed," *The Black Panther* 1, no. 1, April 25, 1967, https://www.marxists.org/history/usa/pubs/black-panther/01n01-Apr%2025%201967.pdf.

178. "Panthers Demand Independence for N. Richmond Area," *The Black Panther* 1, no. 3, June 20, 1967, 2, https://www.marxists.org/history/usa/pubs/black-panther/01n03-Jun%2020%201967.pdf.

179. Lowenthal, "The Politics of Planning," 98.

180. Lowenthal, "The Politics of Planning," 98; May, "Two Model Cities," 65.

181. Lowenthal, "The Politics of Planning," 82.

182. De Baca "was a 23 year old Chicano Mexican American Fruitvale district resident who was shot and killed by an Oakland Police officer on February 5, 1968. On February 5, 1968 Oakland Police Officer Walter Gibbons noticed a man in a car on 35th Ave near Galindo St in the Fruitvale district. Officer Gibbons confronted the man and a foot pursuit happened. The man ran up Galindo St and Officer Gibbons ordered him to stop. Then he fired 6 rounds. One of the rounds hit the man in the heart, killing him." "Charles Pinky De Baca," Oakland Wiki, accessed April 12, 2025, https://localwiki.org/oakland/Charles_Pinky_De_Baca.

183. "Many older Chicanos in Oakland will agree that Mr. De Baca's death was a focal point in the radical Chicano mobilization in Oakland. Some say it was the start of the radical elements of the Chicano movement in Oakland." "Charles Pinky De Baca."

184. Quotation from Rios, "Black Oaklanders." See also Murch's *Living for the City* and Self's *American Babylon*. Both give very similar accounts.

185. Toni Cervantes, "Their Legacy Lives On: The Spirit of the Black Panthers' Free Food Programs Is Alive at Laney Today," *Medium*, February 16, 2018, https://medium.com/laney-tower/their-legacy-lives-on-c7eb6765469f.

186. Self, *American Babylon*, 244.

187. Victoria Sung, "Berkeley Artist David Huffman's New Show Pays Tribute to His Activist Mother," Berkeleyside, August 13, 2021, https://www.berkeleyside.org/2021/08/13/david-huffman-berkeley-art-center.

188. "How 12 Cars of Fuzz Busted Two Black Oakland Housewives," *Berkeley Barb*, June 14–20, 1968, 5.

189. "Small Businessmen in a Squeeze: Life Behind Picket Line at Housewives Market," *Oakland Tribune*, May 17, 1968, 17.

190. "Newspapers: Bill v. the Boycott," *Time Magazine*, Friday, June 14, 1968, http://content.time.com/time/subscriber/article/0,33009,900153,00.html.

191. "Citizens Pledged Against Coercion," *Oakland Tribune*, May 23, 1968, 9.

192. "Newspapers."

193. "William Knowland's 'Tribune' Holds a Gun to the Heads of the People," *The Black Panther*, October 4, 1971, https://washingtonspark.files.wordpress.com/2020/06/1971-10-04-black-panther-vol-7-no-5.pdf.

194. Rios, "Black Oaklanders."

195. Rios, "Black Oaklanders."

196. See Elizabeth Hinton, *From the War on Poverty to the War on Crime: The Making of Mass Incarceration in America* (Harvard University Press, 2016), 238.

197. "Oakland, Cal. Mayoral Candidate Bobby Seale: 'You Can't Drop Out of the System,'" *Ann Arbor Sun*, April 23, 1973.

198. "Oakland, Cal. Mayoral Candidate."

199. David Fenton, ed., "Bobby Seale: As Radical as the People," *Ann Arbor Sun*, November 30, 1973, https://aadl.org/node/196149.

200. "Petition Statement for Community Control of Police," in *Off the Pigs! The History and Literature of the Black Panther Party*, ed G. Louis Heath (Scarecrow Press, 1976), 327–28.

201. "Community Control of the Police: Black Panther Party Map of Oakland," courtesy of Swann Auction Galleries.

202. "Voters in Oakland, Cal., secured repeal of a civil service board rule requiring residence of all applicants for city jobs (Oakland, Cal., Civ. Serv. Bd. Rule 4, § 4.03 (1971)), in a public referendum on Nov. 5, 1974." See "Municipal Employee Residency Requirements and Equal Protection," *Yale Law Journal* 84, no. 8 (July 1975): 1685n8, https://doi.org/10.2307/795471.

203. See Dan Siegel, "Justice for Tyrone Guyton," *Crime and Social Justice*, no. 2 (Fall–Winter 1974): 61–63, http://www.jstor.org/stable/29765913.

204. Siegel, "Justice for Tyrone Guyton," 62.

205. Dan Siegel was a participant-observer of the protests. In addition to "Justice for Tyrone Guyton," see Dan Siegel, "What Defunding the Police Can Look Like," *Scheerpost*, July 1, 2020, https://scheerpost.com/2020/07/01/what-defunding-the-police-can-look-like/.

206. Rob Arias, "E'ville Archive: The 1973 Emeryville Police Killing of 14-Year-Old Tyrone Guyton," *The E'ville Eye Community News*, August 2, 2020, https://evilleeye.com/history/eville-archive-the-1973-emeryville-police-killing-of-14-year-old-tyrone-guyton/.

207. Hans Toch et al., eds., *Agents of Change: A Study in Police Reform* (Wiley, 1974). Two examples of OPD reformist public relations include the 1974 documentary film *The People and the Police* (KRON-TV, 5 min. 32 sec., January 31, 1974, https://archive.org/details/People-And-Police-Oakland-Film) and a film for local television (*Montage: The Making of An Oakland Cop* [KTVU, 26 min. 50 sec., 1980, Bay Area Television Archive, Leonard Library, San Francisco State University, https://diva.sfsu.edu/collections/sfbatv/bundles/229259]).

208. See the summary at "Documentary Film: *The People and the Police*," 1974, https://archive.org/details/People-And-Police-Oakland-Film; and *Montage: The Making of An Oakland Cop*, January 1, 1980, KTVU Collection, Bay Area TV Archive, San Francisco State University, https://batv.quartexcollections.com/Documents/Detail/montage-the-making-of-an-oakland-cop/634.

209. See Frédérick Douzet, "Race, Crime, and Justice," in *The Color of Power*, 209–49.

210. See "Police Department," Oakland Housing Authority, accessed April 12, 2025, https://www.oakha.org/OHA-PD/Pages/default.aspx.

211. Brenda Payton, "Police Use of Deadly Force in Oakland," *The Black Scholar* 12, no. 1 (January–February 1981): 62–64, http://www.jstor.org/stable/41067967. See also Brenda Payton, "White Cops, Black Youths," *San Francisco Examiner*, April 4, 1979; and Brenda Payton, "Cops' Judgment Questioned in Youth's Death," *San Francisco Examiner*, September 15, 1979, 2.

212. See Rufus P. Browning et al., *Protest Is Not Enough: The Struggle of Blacks and Hispanics for Equality in Urban Politics* (University of California Press, 1986); and Sandra Bass, "Policing Space, Policing Race: Social Control Imperatives and Police Discretionary Decisions," *Social Justice* 28, no. 1 (Spring 2001): 156–76.

213. See Payton, "Police Use of Deadly Force."

214. Payton, "Police Use of Deadly Force."

215. Bass found that the "lack of confidence in the board's ability to 'police' the police is reflected in the steep decline in cases filed with the board. Even as the filing of excessive force complaints to the city's internal investigative body went up, complaints filed with the civilian review board went down." See Sandra Bass, "Negotiating Change: Community Organizations and the Politics of Policing," *Urban Affairs Review* 36, no. 2 (November 2000): 148–77.

216. Scott C. Johnson, "How a Dirty Police Force Gets Clean," *Politico Magazine*, March–April 2015, https://www.politico.com/magazine/story/2015/03/oakland-police-reform-115552/; David Ehrlich, "Stream of the Day: 'The Force' Makes a Powerful Case for Why Police Reform Doesn't Work," *IndieWire*, June 5, 2020, https://www.indiewire.com/2020/06/watch-the-force-documentary-netflix-1202235456/; Abené Clayton, "This City Was Working to Cut Its Police Budget in Half—Then Violent Crime Started to Rise," *The Guardian*, March 19, 2021, https://www.theguardian.com/global-development/2021/mar/19/defund-the-police-gun-violence-surge-oakland.

217. Michael Hanchard, "A Theory of Quotidian Politics," in *Party/Politics: Horizons in Black Political Thought* (Oxford University Press, 2006), https://doi.org/10.1093/acprof:oso/9780195176247.003.0002.

218. "Oakland, Cal. Mayoral Candidate."

6. EAST PALO ALTO

1. This chapter pieces together the history of East Palo Alto (EPA) from a variety of sources including personal interviews, oral histories, and newspaper articles. Scholarship on EPA is limited and fragmentary. See Lily Batchelder, "The Incorporation Movement of East Palo Alto: Renegotiating the Boundaries of Community Organizing Theory" (undergraduate thesis, Stanford University, 1994); Michael J. Berman, "Race, Ethnicity and Inter-Minority Suburban Politics: East Palo Alto, 1950–2002" (master's thesis, Stanford University, 2002), https://catalog.epacommunityarchive.org/document/vt150j424; Daniel Lars Berumen, "The Push and Pull Factors of Development in East Palo Alto, CA" (master's thesis, University of Oregon, 2012); Bayinaah R. Jones, "The Tinsley Case Decision" (PhD diss., University of North Carolina–Chapel Hill, 2006); Michael Kahan, "Reading Whiskey Gulch: The Meanings of Space and Urban Redevelopment in East Palo Alto," *Arcade: A Digital Salon*, 2023, https://shc.stanford.edu/arcade/publications/occasion/race-space-scale/reading-whiskey-gulch-meanings-space-and-urban; Robert Eric Lowe, "Ravenswood High School and the Struggle for Racial Justice in the Sequoia Union High School District" (PhD diss., Stanford University, 1989); Alison Post, "The Great Society and Its Discontents: The Story and Impact of 'Community Action' in East Palo Alto, CA" (undergraduate honors thesis, Stanford University, 1997); Rhonda Rigenhagen, *A History*

of East Palo Alto (Romic Environmental Technologies Corp., 1993); David Skidmore, "The Nexus Between Rent Control and Incorporation in East Palo Alto: A Case Study in Community Organizing," unpublished manuscript, 2021. Michael Levin, dir. and prod., *Dreams of a City: Creating East Palo Alto* (first aired KTEH San Jose, April 14, 1997, 55 min.) is an invaluable documentary of the city's history.

2. Sue Dremann, "Sand Hill Property Company Buys 'Four Corners' Property in East Palo Alto," *Palo Alto Online*, November 20, 2019, https://paloaltoonline.com/news/2019/11/19/sand-hill-property-company-buys-four-corners-property-in-east-palo-alto.

3. For discussion of the Black Power spatial imaginary, see Kimberley S. Johnson, "We Are From Nairobi (#panthershit): Black Power Spatial Imaginaries in Silicon Valley," *Metropolitics*, October 17, 2023, https://metropolitics.org/We-Are-From-Nairobi-panthershit-Black-Power-Spatial-Imaginaries-in-Silicon.html.

4. Angela Swartz, "Since 2000, Enrollment Has Fallen 76% in Ravenswood Schools, Report Shows," *Palo Alto Online*, February 6, 2023, https://paloaltoonline.com/news/2023/02/06/since-2000-enrollment-has-fallen-76-in-ravenswood-schools-report-shows.

5. On the aesthetics of Blackness and gentrification, see Brandi Summers, *Black in Place: The Spatial Aesthetics of Race in a Post-Chocolate City* (University of North Carolina Press, 2019).

6. The Nairobi campaign was reported in a number of places. See "Coast Area to Vote on an African Name," *New York Times*, April 4, 1968; "New Name Defeated for East Palo Alto," *New York Times*, November 6, 1968; Earl Caldwell, "Renaming of Town Divides Negroes on Coast," *New York Times*, December 26, 1968; Jeannette Bradley, "Nairobi, Calif: East P. A. Name Changing . . . Gradually," *Palo Alto Times*, August 18, 1969; Dickens Olewe, "American City Was Almost Renamed Nairobi," *The Star*, July 29, 2015, https://allafrica.com/stories/201507290600.html.

7. For quote and discussion of Black Panthers in EPA, see Russell Rickford, *We Are an African People: Independent Education, Black Power, and the Radical Imagination* (Oxford University Press, 2016), 102.

8. See Caldwell, "Renaming of Town"; Bradley, "Nairobi."

9. For contemporary formulations of "African" peoplehood, see Rickford, *We Are an African People*; also Komozi Woodard, *A Nation Within a Nation: Amiri Baraka (LeRoi Jones) and Black Power Politics* (University of North Carolina Press, 1999).

10. In addition to small businesses and cultural organizations, residents would "sign it as a mailing address on personal checks, business, cards, and letters." See Lowe, "Ravenswood High School," 121.

11. Caldwell, "Renaming of Town."

12. EPA was named "murder capital of the nation" in a number of publications. See, for example, Bill Workman, "First '93 Slayings in East Palo Alto: State, County Helping Patrol Last Year's 'Murder Capital,'" *San Francisco Chronicle*, March 31, 1993.

13. Ruth Wilson Gilmore, *Golden Gulag: Prisons, Surplus, Crisis, and Opposition in Globalizing California* (University of California Press, 2007).

14. See "Japanese-American Internment: Palo Alto's Deported Patriots," Palo Alto History.Org, accessed April 15, 2025, https://www.paloaltohistory.org/japanese-american-internment.php.

15. On blue-collar suburbs, see Becky Nicolaides, *My Blue Heaven: Life and Politics in the Working-Class Suburbs of Los Angeles, 1920–1965* (University of Chicago Press, 2002). On the early history of Black residents in Silicon Valley, see Herbert G. Ruffin, *Uninvited Neighbors: African Americans in Silicon Valley, 1769–1990* (University of Oklahoma Press, 2014). On EPA housing developments, see Post, "The Great Society," 12; and Lowe, "Ravenswood High School," 22–42. The first development was the 281-home Palo Alto Gardens built in 1947.

16. By 1952, East Palo Alto would have six thousand residents and by 1953 that number would double to twelve thousand. See Lowe, "Ravenswood High School," 27.

17. The homeowners' association made a variety of attempts, including vandalism, to force out the first Black family to move in. See Alan Michelson and Katherine Solomonson, *City of East Palo Alto Historic Resources Inventory Report* (San Mateo County Historical Association and San Mateo County Historic Resources Advisory Board, February 1994), 70–71, https://www.cityofepa.org/planning/page/historic-preservation.

18. For a discussion of the resettlement of Japanese Americans, see Lowe, "Ravenswood High School," 43, 52. On the "Fair Play" program, see Ruffin, *Uninvited Neighbors*, 43.

19. See Berumen, "Push and Pull Factors," 17–18.

20. See Richard Rothstein, *The Color of Law: A Forgotten History of How Our Government Segregated America* (Liveright Publishing, 2018), 27; Berman, "Race, Ethnicity," 4; Lowe, "Ravenswood High School," 37–38.

21. For discussion of the GM plant's relocation, see Robert Self, *American Babylon: Race and the Struggle for Postwar Oakland* (Princeton University Press, 2003), 125–27; and on the attempt to build integrated housing in Milpitas, see Rothstein, *Color of Law*, 27, 95.

22. See Berumen, "Push and Pull Factors," 19.

23. On Black suburbs, see Mary Patillo-McCoy, *Black Picket Fences: Privilege and Peril Among the Black Middle Class* (University of Chicago Press, 1999); on Black middle-class suburbanization in the Bay Area, see Eric S. Brown, *The Black Professional Middle Class: Race, Class, and Community in the Post-Civil Rights Era* (Taylor and Francis, 2013).

24. See Kahan, "Reading Whiskey Gulch."

25. The reconstruction of the Bayshore Highway followed the pattern of other urban highway plans: Out of the fifty-eight businesses located in the area that was slated for highway construction, only five businesses would survive, with fifty-three businesses "displaced." See Berman, "Race, Ethnicity," 9; and Rigenhagen, *History of East Palo Alto*, 10–14.

26. The issue over integration and school boundaries was covered in the NAACP's *Crisis* magazine. See Rachelle Marshall, "Concrete Curtain—the East Palo Alto Story," *The Crisis* 64, no. 9 (November 1957): 543–48; and Lowe, "Ravenswood High School," 427–62.

27. See Lowe, "Ravenswood High School," 50.

28. On tolerance for racial integration in schools outside of the South, see June Shagaloff, "A Review of Public School Desegregation in the North and West," *Journal of Educational Sociology* 36, no. 6 (1963): 292–96; and "Public School Desegregation—North and West," *The Crisis*, February 1963, 92–95. See also Zoë Burkholder, *An African American Dilemma: A History of School Integration and Civil Rights in the North* (Oxford University Press, 2021).

29. The NAACP also petitioned the county to establish a human relations commission (Post, "The Great Society," 24).

30. Lowe, "Ravenswood High School," 52.

31. For example, Menlo Park High School went from 90 percent to 100 percent white under the new attendance boundaries. Prior to the new high school's construction, Black students had attended Menlo-Atherton High School, also a predominately white school. The new boundaries not only contained residents who lived east of the highway, but also scooped up the now majority-Black enclave of Belle Haven that had been annexed by Menlo Park in 1940. See Lowe, "Ravenswood High School," 51–55.

32. Marshall, "Concrete Curtain," 544. See also Matthew F. Delmont, *Why Busing Failed: Race, Media, and the National Resistance to School Desegregation* (University of California Press, 2016).

33. Marshall, "Concrete Curtain," 545.

34. Marshall, "Concrete Curtain," 545–46.

35. Lowe, "Ravenswood High School," 57.

36. Wilks quoted in Caldwell, "Renaming of Town."

37. Marshall, "Concrete Curtain," 547.

38. EPA's white residents had led earlier incorporation drives up through 1953. See Lowe, "Ravenswood High School," 62–66.

39. Lowe, "Ravenswood High School," 65.

40. Post, "The Great Society," 15. On "places of their own" and postwar suburbanization in places similar to EPA, see Andrew Weise, *Places of Their Own: African American Suburbanization in the Twentieth Century* (University of Chicago Press, 2004), 215–17.

41. The largest private landowner was the Kavanaugh family, which voted against incorporation, thus freeing their land to be annexed by the wealthier Menlo Park. See Post, "The Great Society," 15.

42. On emergence of a "suburban ghetto," see Ruffin, *Uninvited Neighbors*, 97; and Harold Rose, *The Black Ghetto: A Spatial Behavioral Perspective* (McGraw-Hill, 1971), 82–83.

43. Post notes that the Alto Park Council was created by the county in the wake of the failed 1958 incorporation campaign (Post, "Great Society," 170). See also San Mateo County, *A General Plan for East Palo Alto* (The Commission, 1963).

44. San Mateo County, *A General Plan*, 5.

45. Discussion of local meetings of this group and other insights on Black political mobilization and organizing in East Palo Alto are drawn from the transcript of an interview with Bob Hoover (1983), Institute for Diversity in the Arts, records SC1179, Department of Special Collections and University Archives, Stanford University Libraries, Stanford, California.

46. Post, "The Great Society," 45.

47. See Greg Gavin et al., *Ravenswood: An Impressionistic Tribute to Ravenswood, a School, a Community of Diverse Individuals, an Object of Bitter Debate* (Pressed for Time Press, 1976), 38.

48. Post, "The Great Society," 47.

49. Discussion drawn from Phyllis Barusch and Harriet Nathan, "The East Palo Alto Municipal Council: A Black Community's Experiment in Local Self-Government," in *Emerging Issues in Public Policy: Research Reports and Essays* (Institute of Governmental Studies, University of California, Berkeley, 1973), 185–91, 187. See also Max F. Rolih, *East Palo Alto Annexation Study* (San Mateo County Local Agency Formation Commission, January 1967), https://purl.stanford.edu/gz378cw6105.https://purl.stanford.edu/gz378cw6105.

50. See *East Palo Alto, Municipal Council, 1968–1973: A Five Year Report to the Community* (The Council, 1973), https://purl.stanford.edu/ft396yy2636; *Demonstration Cities Grant Application for East Palo Alto* (County of San Mateo, May 1967), https://purl.stanford.edu/wy874vc9359; and *Model Cities Grant Application Submitted for East Palo Alto–East Menlo Park by San Mateo County and the City of Menlo Park, California* (East Palo Alto Municipal Council, April 1968), https://purl.stanford.edu/hy249dy5442.

51. "The East Palo Alto Municipal Council: A Voice Out of the Future" (Board of Supervisors, County of San Mateo, 1968), 1.

52. Herbert Rhodes, "The East Palo Alto Municipal Council: Grass Roots Democracy in Action," speech to Western Governmental Research Association Annual Conference, August 1969, https://purl.stanford.edu/tx731gv5260.

53. Rhodes, "East Palo Alto,"

54. See Rhodes, "East Palo Alto."

55. See San Mateo County Department of Environmental Management, Planning and Development Division, "East Palo Alto Community Plan: Preliminary Draft" (1980).

56. Patty Fisher, "Fisher: Mortgage Mess Snares Savior of East Palo Alto Community," *The Mercury News*, July 15, 2007.

57. See Scott Wilson, "In East Palo Alto, Residents Say Tech Companies Have Created 'a Semi-Feudal Society,'" *Washington Post*, November 4, 2018, https://www.washingtonpost.com/national/a-semi-feudal-society-in-east-palo-alto-the-influx-of-tech-companies-pushes-residents-to-a-breaking-point-over-gentrification/2018/11/02/03e1004c-d17c-11e8-b2d2-f397227b43f0_story.html.

58. Article XXXIV Public Housing Law, §§ 1–4, California Legislative Information, accessed April 18, 2025, https://leginfo.legislature.ca.gov/faces/codes_displayText.xhtml?lawCode=CONS&division=&title=&part=&chapter=&article=XXXIV; Times Staff, "Why It's Been So Hard to Kill Article 34, California's 'Racist' Barrier to Affordable Housing," *Los Angeles Times*, March 14, 2022, https://www.latimes.com/california/story/2022-03-14/why-killing-article-34-on-affordable-housing-has-been-hard.

59. "Why It's Been So Hard to Kill Article 34."

60. Aaron Cavin, "A Right to Housing in the Suburbs: James v. Valtierra and the Campaign Against Economic Discrimination," *Journal of Urban History* 45, no. 3 (June 2017): 427–51, https://doi.org/10.1177/0096144217712928.

61. See Chris Bonastia, "Hedging His Bets: Why Nixon Killed HUD's Desegregation Efforts," *Social Science History* 28, no. 1 (2004): 19–52, 26.

62. For discussion of the 235 program, see Bonastia, "Hedging"; and also Kevin Fox Gotham, "Separate and Unequal: The Housing Act of 1968 and the Section 235 Program," *Sociological Forum* 15 (2000): 13–37; for discussion of Section 235 and predatory inclusion, see Keeanga-Yamahtta Taylor, *Race for Profit: How Banks and the Real Estate Industry Undermined Black Homeownership* (University of North Carolina Press, 2019).

63. See Kevin Fox Gotham, "Beyond Invasion and Succession: School Segregation, Real Estate Blockbusting, and the Political Economy of Neighborhood Racial Transition," *City & Community* 1, no. 1 (March 2002): 83–111.

64. See Taylor, *Race for Profit*; also United States Commission on Civil Rights, *Home Ownership for Lower Income Families: A Report on the Racial and Ethnic Impact of the Section 235 Program* (United States Commission on Civil Rights, June 1971).

65. Davis's testimony is included in United States Senate, *Abandonment Disaster Demonstration Relief Act of 1975 : Hearings Before the Subcommittee on Housing and Urban Affairs of the Committee on Banking, Housing and Urban Affairs*, Ninety-Fourth Congress, First Session on S. 1988 (US Government Printing Office, 1975), 141–44.

66. US Senate, *Abandonment Disaster*, 142. See also US Commission on Civil Rights, *Home Ownership*, vii–x; and Taylor, *Race for Profit*, 217–23.

67. Juliet Saltman, "Housing Discrimination: Policy Research, Methods and Results," *Annals of the American Academy of Political and Social Science* 441, no. 1 (January 1979): 186–96.

68. See Rosalind Greenstein and Yesim Sungu-Eryilmaz, "Community Land Trusts: Leasing Land for Affordable Housing," Lincoln Institute of Land Policy, April 1, 2005, https://www.lincolninst.edu/publications/articles/community-land-trusts/.

69. David Harvey defines the "right to the city" as "more than the individual liberty to access urban resources: it is a right to change ourselves by changing the city," 23. See David Harvey, "The Right to the City," *New Left Review* 53 (September 2008): 23–40.

70. For discussion on the battle for incorporation, see Batchchelder, "The Incorporation Movement"; Berman, "Race, Ethnicity"; and Berumen, "Push and Pull Factors."

71. On the intertwining of incorporation and rent control, see Skidmore, "The Nexus Between Rent Control."

72. For discussion of the conflict between African Americans and Latinos over the distribution of affordable housing, see Berman, "Race, Ethnicity," 18–19.

73. See Karla Kane, "Market Rising from the Ashes: Economic Climate, Mortgage Crisis Hit East Palo Alto Hard," *Palo Alto Online*, October 14, 2010, https://www.paloal-toonline.com/news/2010/10/14/market-rising-from-the-ashes. On the impact of the fore-closure crime on communities of color, see Joe T. Darden and Elvin Wyly, "Cartographic Editorial—Mapping the Racial/Ethnic Topography of Subprime Inequality in Urban America," *Urban Geography* 31, no. 4 (2010): 425–33.

74. See Rob Fladeboe, "Growing Number of People Living in RVs on Palo Alto City Streets," *kron4.com*, October 2, 2018, https://www.kron4.com/news/growing-number-of-people-living-in-rvs-on-palo-alto-city-streets.

75. Jack Slater, "Learning Is an All-Black Thing: California Community Creates Its Own School System," *Ebony*, September 1971, 88–92.

76. Slater, "Learning Is an All-Black Thing," 89.

77. Slater, "Learning Is an All-Black Thing," 92.

78. Slater, "Learning Is an All-Black Thing," 90.

79. See Rickford, *We Are an African People*, 106–10.

80. For discussion of the Day School, see Mary Eleanor Rhodes Hoover, "The Nairobi Day School: An African American Independent School, 1966–1984," *Journal of Negro Education* 61, no. 2 (1992): 201–10.

81. Nairobi College was established in 1969 with only twenty-five students enrolled in its first year. See Rickford, *We Are an African People*, 199–211; and Martha Biondi, *The Black Revolution on Campus* (University of California Press, 2012), 220–26. See also Orde Coombs, "Nairobi College: A Unique Experiment; A Black Community-Conscious Insti-tution," *Education Digest* 39, no. 2 (1973): 39–42; John Egerton, "Success Comes to Nairobi College," *Change: The Magazine of Higher Learning* 4, no. 4 (1972): 25–27; and Valerie Jane Miner, "Nairobi College: Education for Relevance; One Interpretation of the Community Service Function," unpublished paper, December 1969, https://files.eric.ed.gov/fulltext/ED038131.pdf.

82. See Biondi, *The Black Revolution*, 221.

83. R. W. Apple Jr., "School for Blacks Offers Money-Back Guarantee," *New York Times*, June 4, 1975, https:// www.nytimes.com/1975/06/04/archives/school-for-Blacks-offers-moneyback-guarantee.html.

84. Biondi, *The Black Revolution*, 222.

85. See Apple, "School for Blacks."

86. Apple, "School for Blacks."

87. "Families that can afford it pay $1,000 a year in tuition. This fee covers all the chil-dren in any one family for a full year. Of the 35 families now in the Nairobi school system, 28 are given financial assistance. Some families pay nothing, some pay $200, some pay $500, and a few can afford the $1,000" (See Apple, "School for Blacks").

88. For Nairobi College there were two sources of support during the 1970s, "a white heiress and the federal government." The "white heiress" was a member of the Colgate family who had previously supported Hoover's work at San Mateo Junior College. The donor gave $150,000 the first year and then $120,000 every year over the next decade. See Biondi, *The Black Revolution*, 223–24.

89. Biondi, *The Black Revolution*, 224.

90. Despite efforts to retain white and middle-class Black and other minority stu-dents, Ravenswood's demographics continued to change by 1970. With declining overall enrollments (to 781 students), the school's Black student population reached 64 percent of the total student body. See Lowe, "Ravenswood High School," 190n96.

91. For a discussion of Black Power activism among students, see Gavin, *Ravenswood*; and Robert Lowe, "Benign Intentions: The Magnet School at Ravenswood High," paper

presented at the annual meeting of the American Educational Research Association, San Francisco, April 1992. Mitchell's quote is in Gavin, *Ravenswood*, 32.

92. See Lowe, "Ravenswood High School," 154–64.

93. For discussion of Black Power pedagogical demands, in addition to Gavin, *Ravenswood*; see Lowe, "Benign Intentions," 3–7, 165.

94. Robertson was one of the pro-integration board members; his account is found in an online self-published book: Jack Robertson, ed., *The Conscience of a Community: Integrating Mid-Peninsula Schools, 1969–1986* (pub. by editor, 2002), https://holtz.org/Library/Social%20Science/History/Atomic%20Age/EastPaloAlto/2002%20The%20Conscience%20of%20a%20Community.pdf. See Marion Softky, "Jack Robertson Led Fight to Desegregate Schools," *The Almanac*, August 21, 2002, https://www.almanac-news.com/morgue/2002/2002_08_21.robertson.html.

95. For discussion of federal involvement, see Robertson, *Conscience of a Community*, 23–70. For discussion of the report and case, see Stanton v. Sequoia Union High School Dist., 408 F. Supp. 502 (N.D. Cal. 1976).

96. The reality of segregation starkly overwhelmed the open enrollment plan. Over two hundred students applied to leave Ravenswood (of these students, 170 were Black), while only one student (race unknown) applied to transfer to Ravenswood. See Jones, "The Tinsley Case Decision," 22.

97. See Jones, "The Tinsley Case Decision," 22; and Lowe, "Ravenswood High School," 166–68.

98. Under a proposed racial balance plan, the minority population of each high school would "not be permitted to exceed 25% of the school's total population" with "minority students" defined as "Negro (Black) and Spanish surnamed students." The board also considered a mandatory desegregation plan in which students were sent to schools outside of their "home" attendance zone in order to achieve racial balance, if voluntary transfers did not meet the goals of the racial balancing plan. Jones, "The Tinsley Case Decision," 27.

99. Caldwell, "Renaming of Town."

100. Lowe, "Ravenswood High School," 326–27.

101. Lowe, "Ravenswood High School," 199.

102. Gavin, *Ravenswood*, 38.

103. Gavin, *Ravenswood*, 38.

104. Gavin, *Ravenswood*, 44–51.

105. Lowe, "Ravenswood High School," 339.

106. See Elizabeth Hinton, *From the War on Poverty to the War on Crime: The Making of Mass Incarceration in America* (Harvard University Press, 2016), 23. See also Edwin Garcia, "Sheriff Plan New Station in East P.A.," *San Jose Mercury News*, November 21, 1994.

107. See "East Palo Alto Future: It's Getting Brighter with Plans for New Shopping Center," *San Jose Mercury News*, June 20, 1995.

108. This discussion is based on interview with Bob Hoover, 1983.

109. Prior to his appointment, Hayman was the first Black principal of Belle Haven Elementary School and was subsequently promoted to assistant superintendent. Hayman also served as board chair of Nairobi College. See interview with Bob Hoover; and "Hayman Appointed Chief of Ravenswood Schools," *Palo Alto Times*, July 12, 1973, https://catalog.epacommunityarchive.org/downloads/1n79h439x?locale=en.

110. See interview with Bob Hoover.

111. See Robertson, *Conscience of a Community*, 11.

112. Robertson, *Conscience of a Community*, 11.

113. Fischel defines home-voters as homeowners who are voters that act to protect their home values. See William A. Fischel, *The Homevoter Hypothesis: How Home Values*

Influence Local Government Taxation, School Finance, and Land-Use Policies (Harvard University Press, 2001).

114. Robertson, *Conscience of a Community*, 11, 116.

115. See Faiza Hasan, "'Opening the Door': East Palo Alto Mother Margaret Tinsley Blazes a Path for Public Education," *Palo Alto Online*, September 4, 2002, https://www.paloaltoonline.com/weekly/morgue/2002/2002_09_04.tinsley04.html.

116. See Hasan, "'Opening the Door.'"

117. Ravenswood's next-door neighbor, Palo Alto Unified School District (which was located in Santa Clara County), was also named in the suit. The other eight districts were located in Ravenswood's home county of San Mateo: Menlo Park, Redwood City, Los Lomitas, Portola Valley, Woodside, San Carlos, Belmont, and Sequoia Union High School District. Robertson, *Conscience of a Community*, 117.

118. See Robertson, *Conscience of a Community*, 118.

119. Robertson, *Conscience of a Community*, 120.

120. According to Jones, there were three main objectives in the settlement: "a Voluntary Transfer Plan, a Model Schools Study, and a Ravenswood Improvement Program. The respondents in the Order are: the nine elementary school districts (Belmont, Las Lomitas, Menlo Park, Palo Alto, Portola Valley, Redwood City, San Carlos, Woodside, Ravenswood—in the 1991–1992 school-year, Redwood City was no longer required to admit non-district minority students, as the Redwood City District's natural/informal demographic changes had exceeded a 60% minority cap used by the Court to determine integration) that feed into the Sequoia Union High School District, the County Superintendents of Schools of Santa Clara and San Mateo Counties, and the California Department of Education." Jones, "The Tinsley Case Decision," 2.

121. The settlement imposed a strict cap on the number of students who would be able to voluntarily transfer (about 166 students at any one time). Second, it limited the eligibility for transfer out of the Ravenswood district to second graders and below, as it was argued that it would be too difficult for older students to make the transition given the poor quality of the district's schools. Jones, "The Tinsley Case Decision," 2.

122. On the LGBTQ+ history of Silicon Valley, see Michael Flanagan, "BARchive: Between the Cities; an LGBTQ History of the Mid-Peninsula," *Edge Media Network*, November 3, 2022, https://www.edgemedianetwork.com/story.php?320145.

123. See Flanagan, "BARchive."

124. See interview with Hoover; and transcript of an interview with Ed Becks, Institute for Diversity in the Arts, records SC1179, Department of Special Collections and University Archives, Stanford University Libraries, Stanford, California.

125. On police reform in Menlo Park, see Stuart Schrader, "More Than Cosmetic Changes: The Challenges of Experiments with Police Demilitarization in the 1960s and 1970s," *Journal of Urban History* 46, no. 5 (2020): 1002–25, https://doi.org/10.1177/0096144217705523.

126. See Terry Ann Knopf, "Youth Patrols: An Experiment in Community Participation," *Civil Rights Digest* 3, no. 2 (Spring 1970): 1–7.

127. Knopf, "Youth Patrols," 3. In addition to East Palo Alto, there were youth patrols in Tampa, FL; Dayton, OH; Atlanta, GA; Des Moines, IA; Grand Rapids, MI; New Rochelle, NY; Saginaw, MI; Providence, RI; Pittsburgh, PA; Boston, MA; and Newark, NJ.

128. Shrader, "More Than Cosmetic Changes," 1012–17.

129. See Barusch and Nathan, "East Palo Alto," 188.

130. Barusch and Nathan, "East Palo Alto," 188.

131. Barusch and Nathan, "East Palo Alto," 189.

132. On the role of the California Youth Authority and the rise of the carceral state, see Donna Murch, *Living for the City: Migration, Education, and the Rise of the Black Panther*

Party in Oakland, California (University of North Carolina Press, 2010), 40–42; and for the post-Keynesian extension, see Gilmore, *Golden Gulag*, 107–13.

133. See Rhodes, "East Palo Alto," 12.

134. See "Murder in Your Own Back Yard: 15-Year Old Brother Slain by Pigs in Neighbor's Yard," *The Black Panther*, March 18, 1972, 4, 15. See also Shrader, "More Than Cosmetic Changes," 1013–14.

135. "S. M. Deputy Is Cleared in Death of a Boy," *The Times* (San Mateo), May 3, 1972; "E. P. A. Leader Raps Grand Jury Report," *The Times* (San Mateo), May 4, 1972.

136. See "E. P. A Leader."

137. On penal populism, see Michael Javen Fortner, *The Black Silent Majority: The Rockefeller Drug Laws and the Politics of Punishment* (Harvard University Press, 2015); and James Forman Jr., *Locking Up Our Own: Crime and Punishment in Black America* (Farrar, Straus and Giroux, 2017).

138. "Ghetto's Own War on Crime," *San Francisco Examiner*, September 17, 1971.

139. See "Citizens in California Town Launch War to Halt Crime Wave," *Baltimore Afro-American*, December 4, 1971.

140. See "Police Needs of the Poor," *Sun Reporter* (San Francisco), September 18, 1971.

141. See "Police Needs."

142. See "Police Needs."

143. "Citizens in California Town," *Baltimore Afro-American*, December 4, 1971.

144. "Profile of Community Youth Responsibility Program Honored as the State's 'Most Significant Program for the Prevention of Juvenile Delinquency,'" *San Francisco Examiner*, March 18, 1973.

145. Indeed, this same critic argued that middle-class nationalists, including the founders of Nairobi College, viewed the world from "ghettoist conceptions" that started from an "acceptance of the basic conditions of the ghetto." See Barry Zverkov, "Nationalists Join Hysteria Against Crime," *Bulletin: Weekly Organ of the Worker's League* 8, no. 18, January 10, 1972.

146. Gertrude Wilks, "Bus the Teachers, Not the Children," *San Francisco Examiner*, December 7, 1977.

147. On the local "war on drugs," see Bill Workman, "New Police Dept. to Start Tough Job in East Palo Alto," *San Francisco Chronicle*, June 29, 1985; Workman, "East Palo Alto Wants Citizen Drug Fighters," *San Francisco Chronicle*, November 11, 1987; Workman, "Peninsula Drug War Pledged," *San Francisco Chronicle*, July 8, 1988.

148. Perry Lang, "Fleeing Gunman Kills East Palo Alto Cop," *San Francisco Chronicle*, June 23, 1988. See also Workman, "Peninsula Drug War"; and Jane Gross, "2 California Cities Share Grief over Slain Officer," *New York Times*, July 3, 1988.

149. Allyn Stone, "Vicious Dope Den Will Be Bulldozed," *San Francisco Chronicle*, December 21, 1988.

150. Don Kazak, "RED Team Showed It Can Be Done," *Palo Alto Online*, March 17, 1999, https://www.paloaltoonline.com/weekly/morgue/cover/1999_Mar_17.SIDE171.html.

151. Kazak, "RED Team."

152. Kazak, "RED Team."

153. Richard C. Paddock, "Affluent Cities Help Neighbor Turn Back Crime," *Los Angeles Times*, January 8, 1994.

154. See Rebecca Morales and Manuel Pastor, "Can't We All Just Get Along? Interethnic Organization for Economic Development," in *The Collaborative City: Opportunities and Struggles for Blacks and Latinos in U.S. Cities*, edited by John J. Betancur and Douglas C. Gills (Garland, 2000), 157–75.

155. The program was also extensively covered in *Black Enterprise* magazine. See "The MESBICS Are Coming—But Slowly," *Black Enterprise*, September 1970, 26–31.

On Nixon's Black capitalism, see Laura Warren Hill and Julia Rabig, eds., *The Business of Black Power: Community Development, Capitalism, and Corporate Responsibility in Postwar America* (Boydell & Brewer, 2012); David Goldberg and Trevor Griffey, eds., *Black Power at Work: Community Control, Affirmative Action, and the Construction Industry* (Cornell University Press, 2010); Mehrsa Baradaran, *The Color of Money: Black Banks and the Racial Wealth Gap* (Harvard University Press, 2019); and Dean J. Kotlowski, *Nixon's Civil Rights: Politics, Principle, and Policy* (Harvard University Press, 2002).

156. Quotations from Lawrence E. Davies, "Negroes Building West Coast Mall; 'Black Business Coalition' Backs Economic Power," *New York Times*, February 16, 1969.

157. Davies, "Negroes Building."

158. Rev. Varner was "instrumental in forming the Black Business Coalition" through his church's "Action Coalition" (Davies, "Negroes Building").

159. See Randolph E. Weems, "The Ideological Origins of Richard M. Nixon's 'Black Capitalism' Initiative," *Review of Black Political Economy* 29 (2001): 49–61.

160. See Wallace Stegner, "East Palo Alto: Changes in the Black Ghetto," *Saturday Review* 53, August 1, 1970, 12.

161. Stegner, "East Palo Alto," 12.

162. Blake Clark, "An Enterprising Minority," *National Civic Review*, October 1970, 477–81.

163. Funding also cited in "From the President's Desk" in *Measure: For the Men and Women of Hewlett-Packard* (July 1971), 14.

164. "From the President's Desk," 15.

165. See Stegner, "East Palo Alto," 15. A *New York Times* article notes that "several projects [have turned] sour" including the "nonprofit cooperative supermarket" and "several Black owned businesses in the center." See "Coast Towns Get Interracial Help," *New York Times*, September 6, 1972.

166. See "Coast Towns."

167. See "Black Aid Agency Bold in Approach," *New York Times*, June 29, 1970.

168. See "Black Aid Agency.

169. Quoted in Rickford, *We Are an African People*, 103.

170. See Black Panther Party, "A Structure for Survival: East Palo Alto Branch Black Panther Party Opens with Community Survival Day," *The Black Panther*, vol. 8, no. 27, September 23, 1972.

171. See "Black Aid Agency."

172. See "MESBICs: Comforted by Legislative Bandages, the Program May Yet Recover," *Black Enterprise*, January 1973, 19–22; and Paul Delaney, "Minority-Aid Model is Failure on Coast," *New York Times*, April 17, 1971.

173. See "East Palo Alto's Nairobi Center Bulldozed," *San Francisco Chronicle*, February 28, 1989; and "Raze the Shopping Center at Last: East Palo Alto Declared Nairobi Shopping Center a Nuisance," *San Jose Mercury News*, December 22, 1988.

174. See "Raze the Shopping Center"; and "'East P. A.'s Unattractive Nuisance': City Tackles Dilapidated Shopping Center," *San Jose Mercury News*, August 17, 1988.

175. "East Palo Alto's Nairobi Center Bulldozed."

176. This insight as well as the quote is from Post, "The Great Society," 65–66.

177. See Batchelder, "The Incorporation Movement," 120.

178. Batchelder citing a personal interview with Gertrude Wilks (Batchelder, "The Incorporation Movement," 121).

179. See Janet Wells, "East Palo Alto's Fiscal Crisis: Despite a Flood of Bills, Revenues Only Trickle In," *San Jose Mercury News*, September 6, 1987; and on Califonia cities, see Landon Curry Jr., *The Politics of Fiscal Stress: Organizational Management of Budget Cutbacks* (IGS Press, University of California Berkeley, 1990).

180. Kahan, "Reading Whiskey Gulch," offers a detailed history of EPA's post-incorporation redevelopment era; see slso Berumen, "Push and Pull Factor," 24–28; and Berman, "Race, Ethnicity," 18–22. See "Gateway/101 Project Area," City of East Palo Alto, California, accessed April 19, 2025, https://www.ci.east-palo-alto.ca.us/econdev/page/gateway-101-project-area; and "University Circle Project Area," City of East Palo Alto, California, accessed April 19, 2025, https://www.ci.east-palo-alto.ca.us/econdev/page/university-circle-project-area.

181. For details on displacement, see Berman, "Race, Ethnicity," 44. See also "East Palo Alto's Future: It's Getting Brighter with Plans for a New Shopping Center, *San Jose Mercury News*, June 20, 1995; and for project summary, see "Gateway/101 Project Area."

182. "Gateway/101 Project Area."

183. Sue Dremann, "Jones Mortuary Could Be Uprooted for Office Building," *Palo Alto Online*, June 24, 2019, https://www.paloaltoonline.com/news/2019/06/24/jones-mortuary-could-be-uprooted-for-office-building/.

184. For visual documentation of this process of displacement and (sub)urban renewal, in addition to Kahan, "Reading Whiskey Gulch," see Levin, *Dreams of a City*.

185. While all of the nonprofits were rehoused in EPA, the city noted that "15–20% of the households relocated purchased homes elsewhere in the Bay Area." See "University Circle Project Area."

186. See Kahan, "Reading Whiskey Gulch," 1, 10.

187. "University Circle Project Area."

188. Kahan, "Reading Whiskey Gulch," 3; quoting Henri Lefebvre, *The Production of Space*, trans. Donald Nicholson-Smith (Blackwell, 1991), 53.

189. For use of the Black Power spatial imaginary by both community members and developers, see Johnson, "We Are from Nairobi."

CONCLUSION

1. Louie Robinson, "Oakland: That Other Great City by the Bay," *Ebony*, October 1980, 52–69.

2. Malik Edwards, *A Chicken In Every Bag*, illustration, *The Black Panther*, vol. 8, no. 2, April 1, 1972.

3. Donna Murch, *Living for the City: Migration, Education, and the Rise of the Black Panther Party in Oakland, California* (University of North Carolina Press, 2010), 198.

4. Murch, *Living for the City*, 200.

5. "Showdown in Oakland: Bobby Seale and Otho Green Battle to Become Mayor," *Jet*, April 12, 1973.

6. See Murch, *Living for the City*, 208; also Chris Rhomberg, *No There There: Race, Class, and Political Community in Oakland* (University of California Press, 2004), 169–70; and J. Phillip Thompson III, *Double Trouble: Black Mayors, Black Communities, and the Call for a Deep Democracy* (Oxford University Press, 2005), 147–50.

7. "Oakland Mayoral Runoff Election Result," KPIX-TV News, May 14, 1973, Digital Archive System (DIVA), San Francisco State University, https://diva.sfsu.edu/collections/sfbatv/bundles/238254.

8. "Oakland Mayoral Runoff Election Result II," KPIX-TV News, May 14, 1973, Digital Archive System (DIVA), San Francisco State University, https://diva.sfsu.edu/collections/sfbatv/bundles/238255.

9. Rhomberg, *No There There*, 79.

10. "KDIA Radio Station," Oakland Wiki, accessed April 15, 2025, https://localwiki.org/oakland/KDIA_Radio_Station.

11. On the co-optation of the Black Power movement, see Devin Fergus, *Liberalism, Black Power, and the Making of American Politics, 1965–1980* (University of Georgia

Press, 2009); Tom Adam Davies, *Mainstreaming Black Power* (University of California Press, 2017); and Keeanga-Yamahtta Taylor, *From #BlackLivesMatter to Black Liberation* (Haymarket Books, 2016).

12. Joshua Bloom and Waldo E. Martin Jr., *Black Against Empire: The History and Politics of the Black Panther Party* (University of California Press, 2016), 170–79.

13. See Russell Rickford, *We Are an African People: Independent Education, Black Power, and the Radical Imagination* (Oxford University Press, 2016).

14. Payton quoted in Robinson, "Oakland," 60.

15. Payton quoted in Robinson, "Oakland," 60.

16. Cobb quoted in Robinson, "Oakland," 61.

17. On the roots of white support for Proposition 13, see Daniel HoSang, *Racial Propositions: Ballot Initiatives and the Making of Postwar California* (University of California Press, 2010), 2–23.

18. Arthur L. Tolson, "Reaganomics and Black Americans," *The Black Scholar* 16, no. 5 (1985): 37–49.

19. N. D. B. Connolly, "A Black Power Method," *Public Books*, June 15, 2016, https://www.publicbooks.org/a-black-power-method/.

20. Eve Ewing, *Ghosts in the Schoolyard: Racism and School Closings on Chicago's South Side* (University of Chicago Press, 2018), 155–56.

21. Kwame Ture and Charles V. Hamilton, *Black Power: The Politics of Liberation in America* (Vintage, 1992), 132–37.

22. Black Panther Party, "The Ten-Point Program" (October 1966), in *The Black Panther Party: Service to the People Programs*, ed. David Hilliard (University of New Mexico Press, 2008), appendix A.

23. Chuck Stone, "Black Politics, Third Force, Third Party or Third-Class Influence?," *The Black Scholar* 1, no. 2 (December 1969), 8–13.

24. Neil Kraus and Todd Swanstrom, "Minority Mayors and the Hollow-Prize Problem," *PS* 34, no. 1 (2001): 99–105.

25. See Clarissa Rile Hayward, *How Americans Make Race: Stories, Institutions, Spaces* (Cambridge University Press, 2013), 80, who quotes Nathan Glazer, *Cities in Trouble* (Quadrangle Books, 1970), 24.

26. On the civil rights state, see Hanes Walton Jr., *When the Marching Stopped: The Politics of Civil Rights Regulatory Agencies* (State University of New York Press, 1988); also Desmond King and Robert C. Lieberman, "The Civil Rights State: How the American State Develops Itself," in *The Many Hands of the State: Theorizing Political Authority and Social Control*, ed. Kimberly J. Morgan and Ann Shola Orloff (Cambridge University Press, 2017), 178–202.

27. These cities included Atlanta (1973), Birmingham (1979), Cincinnati (1972), Dayton (1970), Detroit (1974), Los Angeles (1973), New Orleans (1978), Oakland (1978), and Washington, DC (1975). See Daniel J. Hopkins and Katherine T. McCabe, "After It's Too Late: Estimating the Policy Impacts of Black Mayoralties in U.S. Cities," *American Politics Research* 40, no. 4 (2012): 665–700.

28. Gibson's image is on the cover page of *Newsweek*, vol. 76, no. 5, August 3, 1970.

29. Surprisingly, there are few in-depth studies of the NCBM. This section relies heavily on a thesis by Jonathan Zamuna, "The National Conference of Black Mayors, Inc. (NCBM) in an Environment of Increasing Conservatism" (master's thesis, Atlanta University, July 1982).

30. As one newspaper article covering the US Conference of Mayors 1982 would later note, the vast difference between the cities of Beverly Hills and East Orange called into question the utility of such a broad-based organization for the unique needs of Black

communities. See Lynn Darling, "The Tales of Two Cities: Pursuing Dreams in Beverly Hills, Struggling to Survive in East Orange," *Washington Post*, January 29, 1982.

31. Paul Delaney, "Mayors Head Off a Divisive Battle Over Watergate," *New York Times*, June 24, 1974.

32. Paul Delaney, "Gibson Chairman of Mayors' Board," *New York Times*, June 27, 1974.

33. Gibson was accused of blunting criticism of Watergate and acceding to a dilution of the resolution meant to strengthen revenue-sharing models in favor of lower-income and majority-minority cities. See Delaney, "Mayors Head Off a Divisive Battle."

34. Delaney, "Gibson Chairman of Mayors' Board."

35. Chuck Stone, "Black Politics."

36. For "archaeology of failure," see Taylor's work which builds on Peniel Joseph's insight. James Lance Taylor, "The Politics of the Black Power Movement," *Annual Review of Political Science* 24 (2021): 443–70, 457.

37. See Chuck Stone, "Black Political Power in the Carter Era," *The Black Scholar* 8, no. 4 (January–February 1977): 6–15.

38. Christopher Lydon, "Carter Defends All-White Areas," *New York Times*, April 7, 1976; Lydon, "Carter Issues an Apology On 'Ethnic Purity' Phrase," *New York Times*, April 9, 1976.

39. Stone, "Black Political Power," 6.

40. James E. Carter, "A Message to the Black Community: The Present Administration and Its Domestic Achievements and Goals," *The Black Scholar* 9, no. 2 (October 1977): 10–14.

41. See Carter, "A Message," 11.

42. See Zamuna, "The National Conference."

43. G. Thomas Kingsley and Karina Fortuny, *Urban Policy in the Carter Administration* (Urban Institute/What Works Collaborative, May 2010), 2.

44. James E. Anderson, "The Carter Administration and Regulatory Reform: Searching for the Right Way," *Congress & the Presidency* 18, no. 2 (1991): 121–46.

45. Lou Cannon, "Reagan Campaigning from County Fair to Urban League," *Washington Post*, August 3, 1980.

46. Francis X. Clines, "Reagan Goes on Attack by Quoting Democrats," *New York Times*, October 16, 1984.

47. Demetrios Caraley, "Washington Abandons the Cities," *Political Science Quarterly* 107, no. 1 (1992): 1–30.

48. Caraley, "Washington Abandons the Cities," 8.

49. The following cases sharply limit the civil rights state. All are found on Oyez, accessed February 25, 2024: Shelby County v. Holder (2013), https://www.oyez.org/cases/2012/12-96; Students for Fair Admissions v. President and Fellows of Harvard College (2023), https://www.oyez.org/cases/2022/20-1199; City of Richmond v. J. A. Croson Company (1988), https://www.oyez.org/cases/1988/87-998. For "civil rights state," see Desmond King and Robert C. Lieberman, "The Civil Rights State: How the American State Develops Itself," in *The Many Hands of the State: Theorizing Political Authority and Social Control*, ed. Kimberly J. Morgan and Ann Shola Orloff (Cambridge University Press, 2017); and Rogers M. Smith and Desmond King, "White Protectionism in America," *Perspectives on Politics* 19, no. 2 (2021): 460–78.

50. Associated Press, "Cabinet Aide Greeted by Reagan as 'Mayor,'" *New York Times*, June 19, 1981; and Philip Shenon, "Samuel R. Pierce Jr., Ex-Housing Secretary, Dies at 78," *New York Times*, November 2, 2000.

51. David Johnston, "Pierce Helped His Old Law Firm on H.U.D. Requests, Files Show," *New York Times*, August 6, 1989.

52. Irving Kristol, "Common Sense About the 'Urban Crisis,'" *Fortune*, October 1967.

53. Kerner Commission, *Report of the National Advisory Commission on Civil Disorders* (US Government Printing Office, 1968).

54. Ta-Nehisi Coates, "The Case for Reparations," *The Atlantic*, June 15, 2014.

55. See Christopher Jencks and Paul E. Peterson, eds., *The Urban Underclass* (Brookings Institution Press, 1991).

56. Public Enemy, *Fear of a Black Planet*, Def Jam Recordings, April 10, 1990.

57. James Boggs, "Blacks in the Cities: Agenda for the 1970s," *The Black Scholar* 4, no. 3 (1972): 50–61.

58. William E. Nelson, "Black Mayors as Urban Managers," *Annals of the American Academy of Political and Social Science* 439, no. 1 (1978): 53–67.

59. See Stone, "Black Political Power," 13.

60. See Stone, "Black Political Power," 13.

61. See Megan Ming Francis and Michael C. Dawson, "Black Politics and the Neoliberal Racial Order," *Public Culture* 28, no. 1 (2016): 23–62; Lester K. Spence, *Knocking the Hustle: Against the Neoliberal Turn in Black Politics* (Punctum Books, 2015); Timothy Weaver, *Blazing the Neoliberal Trail: Urban Political Development in the United States and the United Kingdom* (University of Pennsylvania Press, 2016); and Jason Hackworth, *The Neoliberal City: Governance, Ideology, and Development in American Urbanism* (Cornell University Press, 2007).

62. On the clearance of "New Deal relics," see Edward G. Goetz, *New Deal Ruins: Race, Economic Justice, and Public Housing Policy* (Cornell University Press, 2013); and Lawrence J. Vale, *Purging the Poorest: Public Housing and the Design Politics of Twice-Cleared Communities* (University of Chicago Press, 2013).

63. See Elizabeth Hinton, *From the War on Poverty to the War on Crime: The Making of Mass Incarceration in America* (Harvard University Press, 2016); Ruth Wilson Gilmore, *Golden Gulag: Prisons, Surplus, Crisis, and Opposition in Globalizing California* (University of California Press, 2007); and Michelle Alexander, *The New Jim Crow: Mass Incarceration in the Age of Colorblindness* (The New Press, 2012).

64. On "predatory inclusion," see Keeanga-Yamahtta Taylor, *Race for Profit: How Banks and the Real Estate Industry Undermined Black Homeownership* (University of North Carolina Press, 2019).

65. For discussion of the damaging effect of the Section 235 program, see Taylor, *Race for Profit*; Brian D. Boyer, *Cities Destroyed for Cash: The FHA Scandal at HUD* (Follett, 1973); and Jeff Crump et al., "Cities Destroyed (Again) For Cash: Forum on the U.S. Foreclosure Crisis," *Urban Geography* 29, no. 8 (2008): 745–84.

66. Kimberley S. Johnson, "We Are From Nairobi (*#panthershit*): Black Power Spatial Imaginaries in Silicon Valley," *Metropolitics*, October 17, 2023, https://metropolitics.org/We-Are-From-Nairobi-panthershit-Black-Power-Spatial-Imaginaries-in-Silicon.html.

67. Darren Tobia, "East Orange Residents Forced Out of Home by Code Violations Still Have Nowhere to Go Tomorrow," The Four Oranges, October 10, 2023, https://thefouroranges.com/east-orange-residents-forced-out-of-home-by-code-violations-still-have-nowhere-to-go-tomorrow/.

68. See Fox Butterfield, "Experimental Class in Newark School Is Indoctrinated in Black Subjects," *New York Times*, April 10, 1971; and David W. Chen, "After More Than 20 Years, Newark to Regain Control of Its Schools," *New York Times*, September 12, 2017.

Index